Also by John Cheever

THE JOURNALS
OF JOHN CHEEVER

THE JOURNALS OF JOHN CHEEVER

ALFRED A. KNOPF   NEW YORK   1991

THIS IS A BORZOI BOOK
PUBLISHED BY ALFRED A. KNOPF, INC.

Portions of this work were originally published in *The New Yorker*.

ISBN 0-394-57274-2
LC 91-52728

Manufactured in the United States of America
First Edition

CONTENTS

INTRODUCTION

WHEN JOHN CHEEVER died on June 18, 1982, he left—in his journals—a vast, unedited, unpublished body of work. It is from these
twenty-nine looseleaf notebooks that Robert Gottlieb has fashioned the
book that follows.

Most of the people I know reacted with enthusiasm when portions
of the text ran in *The New Yorker*, but a few were hurt and bewildered
by what they found. Those who broached the subject with me had two
questions: Did John Cheever really want this material published? And
if so, why?

I sympathize with this distress. I found reading some parts of this
work to be exquisitely painful. But my father wanted his journals published. I know because he told me. I also think I know why.

The journals were not initiated with publication in mind. They were
the workbooks for his fiction. They were also the workbooks for his life.
He'd buy a miniature looseleaf, fill it up, then buy another. The notebook
in use would sit on or near his desk. The lined sheets of filler were
easy to distinguish from the standard, yellow foolscap he used for his
stories and novels.

These pages—feverishly typed, with floating caps, misspellings, and
cross outs—were nevertheless readable, and so they presented an extreme temptation. We were not supposed to read them. I don't recall
his exact instructions, but they were sufficiently explicit, and expressed
with an edge of menace.

Therefore I was surprised when he first began to hint about their
possible publication. This was in December of 1979. I had left my first
wife and come to stay with my parents. I thought of my return as joyous,
something approaching the triumphal. In his journals I later learned
that my father's feelings were not unmixed. He wrote: "On Saturday

morning our son Ben, after a week in a spiritual retreat where he got fucked, has left his wife and returned home, for it seems only a few hours."

A couple of days later he was resigned to the prospects of a long visit. "My son is here. I think that we do not know one another; I think it is our destiny that we never will. I observe, in a comical way, that he does not flush the toilet. He observes that I snore. Another son returns tomorrow. I feel that I know him better, but wait and see." And then, a little ruefully: "Some part of loving one's children is to part with them."

I stayed for months. And he seemed to enjoy my company. (In the journals I begin to appear again as a "beloved son.") We talked a lot. He wanted to talk about the journals. He had sent the notebooks out by twos to various distinguished libraries. I was surprised by this, and envious. He wanted to know if the librarians would be scandalized. I don't know if they were scandalized, but their response was disappointing to him in some way, because after a certain amount of time had passed, he'd retrieve the books.

He wondered aloud to me if his journals had any value as a document. He asked me repeatedly what I thought. I said I didn't know. I said I assumed that there would be interest in anything he had written. I said I couldn't judge, because I'd never read them.

Then one night in January, he presented me with one of the notebooks. He asked if I would mind looking at it.

We were in the dining room. I sat in a chair and read from the journal he had given me. He sat in another chair and watched. He asked what I thought. I said I thought that the journal was interesting; I thought it beautifully written. He asked me to read some more. I did read some more. At one point I looked up, and I could see that he was crying. He was not sobbing, but tears were running down his cheeks. I didn't say anything. I went back to reading. When I looked up again, he seemed composed.

I told him I liked it.

He said he thought that the journals could not be published until after his death.

I agreed.

Then he said that their publication might be difficult for the rest of the family.

I said that I thought that we could take it.

He wanted to know if I really thought there would be interest.

I said that young writers would certainly be interested. Then I asked if he wanted them published, and he smiled. He seemed almost gleeful about the prospects.

The subject came up quite a few more times in the weeks that followed. He kept asking me if I really thought there would be interest. I kept saying there would be.

After that, I was allowed to read the journals. And I did. But it wasn't fun. This was not the witty, charming man in whose guest bedroom I had been sleeping. The material was downbeat and often mean-spirited. There was a lot about homosexuality. I didn't quite get it, or maybe I didn't want to get it. I was also surprised at how little I appeared in the text. I was surprised at how little any of us appeared, except perhaps my mother, who was not getting the sort of treatment that leads one to crave the limelight.

THIS BRINGS US to the second question: Why would anyone want this material published?

By 1979 John Cheever had become a literary elder statesman. "I'm a brand name," he used to say, "like corn flakes, or shredded wheat." He seemed to enjoy this status. He must have suspected that the publication of the journals would alter it. His public image was that of a courtly English gentleman who lived in an antique farmhouse and raised bird dogs. His later books had expressed a candid interest in other facets of life, but it was certainly conceivable that this interest was purely intellectual. Few people knew of his bisexuality. Very few people knew the extent of his infidelities. And almost nobody could have anticipated the apparent desperation of his inner life, or the caustic nature of his vision. But I don't think he cared terribly about being corn flakes. He was a writer before he was a breakfast food. He was a writer almost before he was a man.

In notes and letters many writers of astonishing talent will let down their guard, and one can see them blundering along like the rest of us, searching clumsily for the cliché. This didn't happen to my father. "I know there are some people who are afraid to write a business letter because they will encounter and reveal themselves," he used to say with disdain. I can see now that the person he was disdaining was himself.

He couldn't write a postcard without encountering himself. But he'd write the postcard anyway. He'd encounter himself, transform himself, and you'd have a hell of a postcard.

He saw the role of the serious writer as both lofty and practical in the same instant. He used to say that literature was one of the first indications of civilization. He used to say that a fine piece of prose could not only cure a depression, it could clear up a sinus headache. Like many great healers, he meant to heal himself.

For much of his life he suffered from a loneliness so acute as to be practically indistinguishable from a physical illness. "Loneliness I taste," he wrote in early 1979. "The chair I sit in, the room, the house, none of this has substance. I think of Hemingway, what we remember of his work is not so much the color of the sky as it is the absolute taste of loneliness. Loneliness is not, I think, an absolute, but its taste is more powerful than any other. I think that endeavoring to be a serious writer is quite a dangerous career."

He meant by his writing to escape this loneliness, to shatter the isolation of others.

I recall him telling me he had received a thankful letter from a man who had read the novel in which Coverly Wapshot dreams that he has had sex with a horse. The passage had relieved this admirer of some burden of anxiety; it had lessened his loneliness. This pleased my father immensely. So he meant with the journals to continue this process: he meant to show others that their thoughts were not unthinkable. He meant to do good works, but there was also an element of pleasure in his anticipation of the publication of such an inflammatory body of work.

By the time we talked in 1979, he was a lot less hard on himself. The remorse he felt about his bisexuality had been almost unendurable when he was a young man. By 1980, he could write: "In the thirties and forties men seemed to fear homosexuality as the early mariners feared sailing off the end of the ocean in a world supported on a turtle's back."

A simpleton might think that bisexuality was the essence of his problem, but of course it was not. Nor was alcoholism. He came to terms with his bisexuality. He quit drinking. But life was still a problem. The way he dealt with that problem was to articulate it. He made it into a story, and then he published the story. When he discovered that he had written the story of his life, he wanted that published, too. And

I think the prospects of publication somehow lessened the fear of death. Suddenly death was an opportunity.

MY MOTHER IS the literary executor of my father's estate, but she has always been guided by the desire to please her children and to honor the memory of her husband. We were all involved in the decision to publish the journals. The project is therefore our responsibility. It is not, however, our book. First and foremost it is John Cheever's book, but after that it belongs to its editor. Robert Gottlieb was my father's editor at Knopf. It was he who convinced my somewhat skeptical father that there was indeed a need for the collected "Stories" that appeared in 1978, and he who made the selection. The book was a best-seller and won the Pulitzer Prize. But, more than that, it was almost proof of the validity of my father's life and art.

Robert Gottlieb gave this book its shape, its continuity, and somehow he did it without distorting the nature of the life portrayed. My family watched this process with awe, acting primarily as a back-up team. We suggested the inclusions which expanded the six excerpts from *The New Yorker* into this book. We also provided assistance in establishing chronology. But most of our work has been as an exercise in restraint. We did not interfere. We did nothing to protect our father. We did nothing to protect ourselves. We stood aside. My sister, Susan, my brother, Fred, and I did most of the backing up; my mother did most of the standing aside. Our job took time, hers courage.

BENJAMIN H. CHEEVER

THE LATE FORTIES
AND THE FIFTIES

In middle age there is mystery, there is mystification. The most I can make out of this hour is a kind of loneliness. Even the beauty of the visible world seems to crumble, yes even love. I feel that there has been some miscarriage, some wrong turning, but I do not know when it took place and I have no hope of finding it.

Thinking for a week about Leander, Betsey, and Eben without writing a word, without making any progress. And so I see all my plans—the voyage to Genoa, etc.—collapse. Is there something intrinsically wrong with these three, that I can't grasp them? Thinking this morning to discard the opera.

Yesterday was rainy and deeply overcast. At four B. and I walked up Holbrook Road to the K.s'. The clearing wind had begun to blow. As the overcast was displaced with brilliance and color, as more and more light poured into the valley, the hour seemed tumultuous and exalting. Backgammon and gin.

Skating one afternoon at the Newberrys'. The end of a very cold winter day. The ice, contracting in the cold, made a noise like thunder. Walking up the frozen field to the house we could hear it thundering. We went back that night. There was no one else on the pond. The G.s' dog was barking. There was no moon and the ice was black. It seemed, skating out into the center of the pond, that the number of stars I could see was multiplied. They seemed as thickly sown as a rush of snowflakes. As I skated back to the end of the pond, the number seemed to diminish. I was confounded. It could have been the whiskey and the wine. It could have been my utter ignorance of cosmology.

•

To church; the second Sunday in Lent. From the bank president's wife behind me drifted the smell of camphor from her furs, and the stales of her breath, as she sang, "Glory be to the Father, and to the Son, and to the Holy Ghost; As it was in the beginning, is now, and ever shall be, world without end." The Old Testament dealt with should the Father eat bitter grapes; the New with an eye for an eye and a tooth for a tooth. The sermon with the doctrine of Incarnation. The rector has a plain mind. If it has any charms, they are the charms of plainness. Through inheritance and cultivation he has reached an impermeable homeliness. His mind and his face are one. He spoke of the impressive historical documentation of Christ's birth, miracles, and death. The church is meant to evoke rural England. The summoning bells, the late-winter sunlight, the lancet windows, the hand-cut stone. But these are real fragments of a real past. World without end, I murmur, shutting my eyes, Amen. But I seem to stand outside the realm of God's mercy.

I would like not to be vindictive or narrow. I would like to avoid phony compassion. Thinking of the midsummer night, "*Parlons français*," the drunkard said. I see that this is small. I see in the five-and-ten-cent store yesterday that my descriptions of Betsey's pleasure are small. It stinks of peanuts and cheap candy. A love song drifts over from the phonograph-record department. The salesgirl is elaborately painted. You buy what you want; and you leave. The street is sunny. The blind Negress on the bus says, "I'm by myself. I'm by myself at home now. I'm by myself on the street. I'm by myself. I'm by myself so much I'm like a statue. I'm by myself like a statue all the time." She shakes her portable radio. "She ain't working. I've had her on since Ninety-sixth Street and she ain't made a sound. I guess I'll have to get her fixed again. She wears out quick." The man on the train. "*Well*, I guess I look cheerful enough, but I'm on my way to the hospital. They just called me from the office to tell me that C. fell out of an apple tree and broke her leg in two places. They called me at the office a few minutes ago and I rushed over here and took the train. . . ."

•

These Westchester Sunday nights. There has usually been a party on Saturday night so you wake up with a faint hangover and a mouth burned by a green cigar. The clothes you have left in a heap on the floor smell of stale perfume. You take a shower. You put on old clothes. You drive your wife to church and your children to Sunday school. You rake the leaves off the flower bed. They are too wet to burn. You put a chemical fertilizer on the lawn and examine the bulbs. The Rock-inhams, on their way to a Sunday-lunch party at the Armstrongs', shout their good mornings from the sidewalk. "Isn't it a glorious day; glorious, glorious." Your wife and children return from church, still in their stiff clothes. You have a drink before lunch. Sometimes there are guests. You take a walk; you rake more leaves. The children scatter to play with other children. The southbound local, the train that aunts, uncles, and cousins who have gone into the suburbs for lunch take home; the train that cooks, maids, butlers, and other menservants take into town for their half holiday. Sunday is almost over.

•

Awake before dawn, feeling tired and full of resolutions. Do not drink. Do not et cetera, et cetera. The noise of birdsong swelling: flickers, chickadees, cardinals. Then in the midst of this loud noise I thought I heard a parrot. "Prolly want a crackeer," he said. "Prolly want a crackeer." Woke tired and took the 7:44. The river blanketed with a mist. The voices overheard. "Well, then she boiled it and then she *broiled* it." He raised his face and drew over it a beatific look as if he were tasting last night's dinner again. "Well, we've got one of those electric rotisseries." "Oh, New York's nothing like Chicago; nothing like it." On Twenty-third Street I read a sign: "DON'T LOSE YOUR LOVED ONE BECAUSE OF UGLY FAT." There was a window full of crucifixes made out of plastic. The surface of the city is paradoxical. For a mind cast in paradox it is reassuring to find this surface. Thinking again, in the dentist's chair, that I am like a prisoner who is trying to escape from jail by the wrong route. For all one knows, that door may stand open, although I continue to dig a tunnel with a teaspoon. Oh, I think, if I could only taste a little success. But don't I approach it by deepening the pit in which I stand? Mary in the morning, asleep, looking like the girl I fell in love with. Her round arms lie outside the covers. Her brown hair is loose. The abiding quality of seriousness and pureness.

•

In the dark hour you cannot call on goods and chattels to save you, or old ski trails or the paths to streams. You must find something greater. And the mind in which the forces of contumely and destruction seem greater than the forces of creativity. Creativity is there, but it seems, in relation to the forces of destruction, like the nipple on a balloon. So, made up of so much destruction and with such a slender knowledge of love he appears poorly as a husband, son, and lover—masked in a rag of a smile and a striped tie and a few faint observations. Oh so deeply rooted in this mind are the needs and the habits of prayer. Having triumphantly separated himself from the foolishness of religion, he goes by the church—he hears the bells in the morning—in the churlish and unhappy frame of mind of a man who has been excommunicated. He feels the lash of expulsion. And oh this poor mind, casting desperately around a room for some detail that will give it form and meaning, seizes always on an ashtray heaped with butts or a crooked stocking, a tear in the rug. And then he sees the sky! the poignant blue, the line of darkness rising like a lid; the perfect clearness of line and color that means that a northwest wind has scoured the overcast and blown it out to sea. So his mind wanders between the ashtray and the twilight while most of the known world lies somewhere in between. He worries, he worries about his mustache, his old navy raincoat, his weight, his hair, his teeth, the stiffness in his left knee, and if his anxiety ever transcends this it is to worry about a nation of paltry men, conceived in his image and likeness—or, if he is a world federalist, to worry about a world. Why has the sweetness gone? It would all come back with a new car or a bonus or a little of the recognition that he deserves for his hard work. A convertible; a trip to Spain.

•

The stubborn dreariness of this rainy Sunday. Down at the station there are only a few travellers for the southbound local. A cook with a paper bag full of leftovers and a hand-me-down coat is going to Yonkers to visit her relations. A maiden aunt out for Sunday lunch is returning. The last is a figure of mystery, a man in a worn polo coat beneath which show the striped pants and boiled shirt of a tuxedo. These are the only passengers and they seem to have come here unwilling to catch a train and make a hopeless journey. In the waiting room and the cabstand, both of them unattended, a telephone rings and rings and rings. Fishnets for shad and bass are strung out into the water, and the rain, like a much finer net, encircles the county with a stir of reassuring and dreary noise. Racks of string hang above the railroad track like the old-fashioned fly nets worn by livery horses. It is a stubborn and an infinite dreariness, rooted in the stupor, the discomfort, or the downright misery of a heavy churchgoer's lunch. The ballgame has been rained out but not the "Emperor" Concerto or the "Jupiter" Symphony. More than half the world is in an unrefreshing sleep.

But between the waiting room and the freight house there is a view of water and mountains. The eye goes up for miles and miles, for while the little rain makes the shore dim, nothing is obscured. Here there is more power and space than you had expected. The smudge from a distant tugboat, discouraged and scattered by the little rain, drifts toward the water. There is a mountain as round as a plump knee and a mountain cut like a cock's crest and even a faint smell of the wilderness—dead bloodworms and wet corduroy—for three fishermen are strung along the narrow bank between the railroad tracks and the water. Oh it is so dreary that one's teeth seem literally to ache. The smell of boiled beef lingers in the upstairs hall.

•

As I approach my fortieth birthday without having accomplished any one of the things I intended to accomplish—without ever having achieved the deep creativity that I have worked toward for all this time—I feel that I take a minor, an obscure, a dim position that is not my destiny but that is my fault, as if I had lacked, somewhere along the line, the wit and courage to contain myself competently within the shapes at hand. I think of Leander and all the others. It is not that these are stories of failure; that is not what is frightening. It is that they are dull annals; that they are of no import; that Leander, walking in the garden at dusk in the throes of a violent passion, is of no importance to anyone. It does not matter. It does not matter. . . .

•

In town for lunch. The air-conditioning, the smell of perfume and gin, the attentions of the headwaiter, the real and unreal sense of haste, importance, and freedom that clings to the theatre. It was a beautiful day in town, windy, clear, and fresh. The girls on the street are a joy. A girl with bare arms by the St. Regis; a girl with bare shoulders on Fifty-seventh Street; dark eyes and light eyes and red hair and above all the wonderful sense of dignity and purpose in their clear features. But there is the imperfect joining of the carnal world and the world of courage and other spiritual matters. I seem, after half a lifetime, to have made no progress, unless resignation is progress. There is the erotic hour of waking, which is like birth. There is the light or the rainfall, some ingenuous symbol by which one returns to the visible, perhaps the mature world. There is the euphoria, the sense that life is no more than it appears to be, light and water and trees and pleasant people that can be brought crashing down by a neck, a hand, an obscenity written on a toilet door. There is always, somewhere, this hint of aberrant carnality. The worst of it is that it seems labyrinthine; I come back again and again to the image of a naked prisoner in an unlocked cell, and to tell the truth I don't know how he will escape. Death figures here, the unwillingness to live. Many of these shapes seem like the shapes of death; one approaches them with the same amorousness, the same sense of terrible dread. I say to myself that the body can be washed clean of any indulgence; the only sin is despair, but I speak meaninglessly in my own case. Chasteness is real; the morning adjures one to be chaste. Chasteness is waking. I could not wash the obscenity off myself. But in all this thinking there is a lack of space, of latitude, of light and humor. Thinking back to "The Reasonable Music," it seems to me, for this reason, to be a bad, a febrile, story. Play a little baseball and the Gordian knot crumbles into dust.

•

Is there anything more wonderful than the Monday morning train: the 8:22? The weekend—say a long summer weekend like the Fourth—has left you rested. There have been picnics, fireworks, excursions to the beach—all the pleasant things we do together. On Sunday we had cocktails late and a pickup supper in the garden. We see the darkness end the weekend without any regret—it has all been so pleasant. In the garden we can hear, from the west, the noise of traffic on the parkway rise to a high pitch that it will hold until nearly midnight, as other families drive back to the city from the mountains or the shore; and the sleeping children, the clothing hung in the backseat, the infinity of headlights—the sense we take from these overcrowded Sunday roads of a gigantic evacuation, a gigantic pilgrimage—is all a part of this hour. You water the grass, tell the children a story, take a bath, and get into bed. The morning is brilliant and fresh. Your wife drives you to the train in the convertible. The children and the dog come along. From

the minute you wake up you seem to be on the verge of an irrepressible
joy. The drive down Alewives Lane to the station seems triumphal, and
when you see the station below you and the trees and the few people
who have already gathered there, waiting in the morning sun, and when
you kiss your wife and your children goodbye and give the dog's ears a
scratch and say good morning all around the platform and unfold the
Tribune and hear the train, the 8:22, coming down the tracks, it seems
to me a wonderful thing.

•

Concerned over my brother. A man who conveys a feeling of deep
perplexity. Things have not turned out the way he meant them to. The
way he speaks and looks, the mind that strikes almost always idly or in
self-defense, the way he pares his fingernails and wipes his mouth on
his sleeve, the bullish hang of his head—everything about him expresses
deep perplexity and suspicion. He pares his nails because he suspects
refinement and delicacy, or is reacting against some unrewarded delicacy
in himself. Sullen, contradictory, and laconic. I am troubled because
he is my brother and because he has for years been the man of the
family. Now all these transformations have left him incompetent.

•

She is Mrs. Fuzzy-Wig; she is the nonconformist. She lives in a
little house on a back street and paints lampshades. Her five children
are married and scattered, and she does not want to visit them at all.
They dread the time when she will become so infirm—she is in her
eighties—that she will be forced to live with them. But they do not
dread it nearly as much as she does. I will not go to live with them—
she thinks, of her children; I will die before I go to live with them. I
will die. Now she is obsessed with impressing onto every surface that
she touches the image of a rose. The hall carpet—all the carpets—
represent roses. The hall is papered with a galaxy of bloodred roses
that are all as big as lettuce heads. The effect is confusing. But you are
not through with roses in the hall. Every chair and stool and sofa in
the living room is covered with cloth that is stamped with roses. Here
they are bigger—they are as big as cabbages, and those on the chair
seats are repeated in the wallpaper, just as big but of a slightly fainter
shade of red. Step into the dining room, and the situation is the same.

There are roses on the bedroom carpet, roses on the bedspread, roses on the wall, and roses have been painted on the pin tray, the lampshades, the wastebasket, and the matchbox. It is with things like these last that she is now occupied; there are still plenty of surfaces in the house that lack a rose. She has covered all of the lampshades and many of the chair backs, but there are still plenty of cannisters, boxes, etc. that present bare surfaces. She is very happy.

Below the surface I see the nonconformist. In a sense this is admirable. Here is independence, and yet all her children, looking to her for the graceful discharge of affection, have been rudely discouraged. She has arbitrarily, now and then, laid claim to their affections. She taught poor Eben to bake, sew, and generally conduct himself like a young girl, and in a small town today you can see their kind; the boy of twelve, the effeminate youth, clutching his mother's arm as they cross the street from the corset store to the millinery store. All of this is past for them and yet, because she did not conform at all, they will all, for the rest of their lives, laugh uproariously when they see a woman of her kind slip on a banana peel—with that unhealthy mixture of tenderness and loathing that she has implanted in them.

After I had driven all day through a tiring light, there was the restless night in Quincy, the smell of smoke. Then a breakfast with the umbilical cord seeming to have been cut but to lie, ragged and bleeding, on the table between us.

Driving down the road yesterday, I saw a long snake. I stopped the car, and J. and I got out. Incidentally, I behaved like a fool, but enough of this. The snake was marked with brown saddles. Instead of taking off into the woods, it coiled to strike, and raised and vibrated its tail like a rattler, although it had no rattle. I mangled its head with a rock. J., picking up another rock, finished it. I am not, like poor D., afraid of snakes, but I am interested in the hold they have on the imagination. This green shire is supposed to be free of snakes. A few things depend upon a snake. The cook, I think, would leave. There are the children, P.'s cow, etc.

•

Back down into the country, the valley of the commuters. Train smoke, bells, women driving over to Harmon to meet the 6:00; eat your

supper and water the grass. The empty house did not disturb me, but
this is a usable premonition of death. The evening clothes in the closet,
the pile of toys upstairs, the shelves of glass and china; the warmth of
ownership, of life, has gone off all these things; these are all ghostly
things now.

The usual fracas in trying to go to sleep; but some of this violence
has been overcome by age. I can remember walking around the streets
of New York on a summer night some years ago. I cannot say that it
was like the pain of living death; it never had that clear a meaning. But
it was torment, crushing torment and frustration. I was caught under
the weight of some great door. The feeling always was that if I could
express myself erotically I would come alive. Then I stopped in a bar
where a pleasant and foolish man engaged me in conversation and told
me that his father had, for years, been superintendent of the hospital
on Welfare Island. Then the crushing weight was lifted; it was merely
a summer night in the city. I put this down because I think it all belongs
to the past. Most of the aberrations seem to belong to the past.

•

The cook goes into town on Thursday, but on Friday morning, when
you come down for breakfast, there is no sign of life in the kitchen.
When you knock on her door no one answers, and when you open the
door you examine the room with a practiced eye.

The photograph of her brother is gone. You throw open the closet
door. The hangers are all empty. They are stirred by the draft from the
open door, and they ring like tin bells. You see a pair of her shoes in
the corner, but you can see the floor through the worn soles. She has
gone. An empty sherry bottle lies on its side.

•

We drove to the Vineyard on a day when the light was hazy and
brilliant, a tiring light to drive in. It was after Labor Day but there
were still many people travelling, still many people with their clothes
hung in the back of the car. Late in the day the sun was warm; then,
approaching the canal, we ran into a sea turn. A salt fog obscured
everything. We missed the five-o'clock boat and walked around the
streets, the foggy streets. Piano music from a bar. "I'll get by as long

as I have you. . . ." Boat whistles, sirens, delays. It was dark when we
boarded the boat. Susie was timid. But as soon as we got into the harbor
a wind scattered the fog and we saw the moon, the lights of West Chop.
Over the dark roads to the house: talk; I went swimming in the sea. I
met J.H. walking on the beach. His engagement was broken and he
had received his induction notice. To bed, the noise of the sea.

I walked up the beach before breakfast. To write about my response
to this landscape with the greatest honesty. The hills, the scrub growth,
as yellow now as it was green, the black roofs of the bathhouse—all
these lines remind one of Japanese drawings. The hills seem barely to
have risen from the sea; although this is not the case. This is a falling
coastline. The old man who died the year before last claimed to remember a meadow where there is deep water now. Across the Sound
the cliffs of Naushon are ragged where they have fallen, bit by bit, into
the sea. The stones where you walk are strangely colored. The multitude
of forms confounds you and makes you happy. A hundred yards inland
there is a spiral shell with a spiderweb spun over the mouth. The rocks
offshore—the tide is ebbing—are half covered with beards of gold-green
weed. Here is a shell like a smashed ball with a pink core. The line,
the crooked and the changing line, marked by sea grass and grocery
crates, ships' booms and a broken tiller, this endless line is the one of
death's countless images that seems to hold no terror, or very little, for
here is change, here is recrudescence and decay—the air stinks of it,
the noise of it sounds most of the time. And then on the other hand
you sit by the side of the sea and drink gin, you smoke, you gossip, you
talk too much and to no purpose, you take off your shoes and walk up
and down the floor of the world, thinking about bad debts, tuition bills,
and overdrafts.

•

Last night to see the Tennessee Williams play, "A Streetcar Named
Desire." As decadent, I think, as anything I've ever seen on the stage,
with gin-mill or whorehouse jazz in the dark between the scenes, a
cellist playing during the play, a rhinestone, a torn evening dress, a
crown, a homosexual, a beast, insanity, crimes, dim lights, tinsel flowers, and the cellist playing a lewd ballad. At the same time, Williams
gives the theme some universality, and, having taken a daughter of joy,
he makes her seem, without irony, to possess a pure heart. There is
much else; the wonderful sense of captivity in a squalid apartment and

of the beauty of the evening, although most of the chords struck seem to lie close to insanity. Anxiety, that is—confinement, and so forth. Also, he avoids not only the common clichés but the uncommon cliché, over which I so often trip, and also works in a form that has few inhibitions and has written its own laws.

Hearing yesterday from Marion Shaw that Irwin is writing seventeen pages a day troubled me, and I will refrain from writing here this morning the things I've written in this notebook for fifteen years about writing a novel. Maybe I can finish the Sutton Place story tomorrow.

To write well, to write passionately, to be less inhibited, to be warmer, to be more self-critical, to recognize the power of as well as the force of lust, to write, to love.

•

May 4th, my son Benjamin was born. My splendid, my forgiving, my gentle wife. Both of us caught up on a tide of stronger circumstance. In the hospital the lamps blooming in the linoleum floor. The delicate lights of the distant amusement park; the city; the highway. The sense that one's heart and watch are nearly stopped. And Mary's talk of the universal subconscious, the illusions of gas and ether, the parched taste, the coronas and ridges of fire. The uprush of human greatness that answers to charity and pain. Holiness. The remote neighborhoods of the city—the hospitals, graveyards, and wharves—that we forget. The day that you were born I broke a bottle of bay rum on the bathroom floor. The night before I'd taken your mother to hear Maggie Teyte.

•

Very pleased and excited by Mailer's book "The Naked and the Dead." Impressed particularly with its size. Despaired, while reading it, of my own confined talents. I seem, with my autumn roses and my winter twilights, not to be in the big league. Particularly impressed with his description of one man, an Italian, watching Red, an old soldier, and thinking first, This man is comical; then, This man is brave and knowing; then that this man is stupid, reflecting perfectly, clearly a responsive and immature spirit.

Knowing at last that the smell of birch in a Franklin stove is not everything. The morning returns to me my self-confidence and all my limitations. Eccentric I must be, gentle, soft in some ways, brooding, subjective, forced to consider my prose by the ignobility of some of my material.

•

The park on a Sunday night. The light withdrawing from the sky and the life on the walks darkening and intensifying. The unrelieved sexuality of the experience. Small breasts in the streetlight; breasts held in a black dress so the crease shows. Young men travelling in pairs, in threes, whooping, wrestling in the grass. The round lights blooming, the shapes of the trees, the shapes and lights of venery itself. And the music, the much-used, the ill-used music, music that had been played through rainsqualls and thunderstorms, music to which people had eaten in restaurants and on park benches, music used to swell a climax in a radio play or to bring to their resolution the terrible problems of a movie; music played in high-school auditoriums with that smell of radiators, played from memorial bandstands in India, Italy, New Hampshire . . . At a turning of the path, the fragrance of a garden. The strong sense of youth, although many here are old; the innocent lusts.

•

We are as poor as we ever have been. The rent is not paid, we have very little to eat, relatively little to eat: canned tongue and eggs. We have many bills. I can write a story a week, perhaps more. I've tried this before and never succeeded, and I will try again.

•

New York–Quincy–New Haven–New York. I took a plane late Thursday morning. This casual sense of travel, of writing about it easily, garrulously. The taxi, the delayed plane, a Martini and a roast-beef sandwich in the Commodore or Longchamps, the dark half-empty news-reel theatre, the gray-and-white refugees that have for so long been marching across its screen, the bus to the airport and the plane itself, hot and decorated for some reason like a bedroom, the place names on its window curtains. The revved motors, the instantaneous charm slums achieve when they have fallen a thousand feet beneath your wings, the sense that the small plane remained earthbound and overburdened and remained a few thousand feet above Long Island only because of the greatest exertion of its motors. A storm at the edge of the afternoon, like a fire in heaven, the smoke of which was blown down from the clouds and spread over the earth, the dimness of smoke. That Boston from the air seemed to have an Irish complexion . . .

How small and ingenuous Boston seems. Out to Quincy. Mother, still restive, still willful. In the morning the train to New Haven, the cast of characters there. And also Quincy, this bleak town on a Christmas Eve. The people waiting in the glow from the drugstore window for the trolley car to the shipyards, the ironworks. The Christmas plumage of the women and the men. And all through the day, all through the night, from hidden and from unhidden amplifiers carollers singing "God Rest You Merry, Gentlemen" and bells playing "Silent Night, Holy Night." The beauty of a piece of tail.

•

The New Yorker has turned down "Vega," "Sisyphus," "The Reasonable Music" and probably will turn down "George." The fact that they have paid me no bonus this year and less than a living wage sets me off, frequently, on an unreasonable tangent of petulance. This is a patriarchal relationship, and I certainly respond to the slings of regret, real or imaginary.

•

I have a slight cold, nothing serious, but it acts as a depressant, and fever and a hacking cough have always affected my stability. Also the fact that I infrequently cough up a little blood fills me with premonitions of death that seem to be pure petulance. Last night, for reasons that I understand, my wife suggested that I leave her for a little while, a suggestion that I can't take reasonably. The kind of pride that can articulate itself only in something perverse, like a long separation or a divorce, has been excited. A long separation would be dangerous since neither of us is very communicative or forgiving. There is some part of her that is not gregarious or affectionate, that has never been yielded to me or to anyone else without pain. She was alone much when she was a young girl and the habits of solitude sometimes return to her. Now and then, by a complete absence of privacy, she feels suffocated. She is entitled to this—I recognized it when I met her and married her. There is also the fact that my life, recently, has had all the characteristics of a failure.

•

Last night, folding the bath towel so the monogram would be in the
right place (and after reading a piece on Rimbaud by Zabel), I wondered
what I was doing here. This concern for outward order—the flowers,
the shining cigarette box—is not only symptomatic of our consciousness
of the cruel social disorders with which we are surrounded but also
enables us to delay our realization of these social disorders, to overlook
the fact that our bread is poisoned. I was born into no true class, and
it was my decision, early in life, to insinuate myself into the middle
class, like a spy, so that I would have an advantageous position of attack,
but I seem now and then to have forgotten my mission and to have taken
my disguises too seriously.

•

Love, love on a spring night. The cotton lace of her nightgown, the
fresh perfume of some lotion or cologne she has used in getting ready
for bed, her dark hair and her pale and hardly visible face and the lace
of broken and reflected streetlights, scored by the window frames and
the folds of the curtains, that lie across both our bodies. The perfect
unburdenment of tenderness and disappointment, the perfect response
of one body to another, of one answering the other, and the slow journey
toward that captivation of our faculties, into that country whose violence
remains alien and overwhelming; and then a sweet sleep.

The pyramid, the gods.

Read the Italian grammar, read whatever French you happen to
read with a dictionary. How we will eat this month is a real
question.

I have recounted my unsuccessful stories over again and again,
planned to revise them and felt that this was aiming below the mark,
and so have waited for something better, but nothing better has come
and I must look on these stories as a business venture and finish them
off, as second-rate as they seem. I will have "The Reasonable Music."
This should be revised again and sent off.
There is "Vega," this lacks some intrinsic drama. I want to dramatize
the irresponsible interference of the intellectual. I can't seem to breathe

fire into Atcheson. I will read that over again, at once, and see what I
have.

There is "Christmas Is a Sad Season for the Poor." This can be a
reasonably funny story.

There is "Emma Boynton." This is slight, but it might sell.

•

Back from two days fishing at Cranberry with G. and J. (the eleventh
of May). Very little to report; less than from most trips. There seemed
to be nothing—no color, no sound—that I had to name. We took the
train to North White Plains, where J. met us. We got worms at Armonk,
fish poles in Chappaqua, and then started north, up the Taconic Parkway. An unseasonably hot, late afternoon in the early spring and at four
or five turnings in the road the green valley country, below us, opened
like a vision of the peaceable kingdom. We stopped at an inn in Rhine-
beck for supper, ten minutes before dark. Green light. A woman taking
down the flag in front of the post office. A summer evening in a river
village that, even on the eve of war, would lose none of this repose,
this fat tranquillity. Then up through the dark, through Albany and
Saratoga, to Glens Falls. A hotel room, a hotel bar, a window looking
out onto an empty, green park with a white bandstand, a self-contained
city with trees everywhere, settled comings and goings, continuity, custom. A sinking moon. Sitting naked in the rock-maple armchair, drinking straight Scotch, unable to sleep, thinking of my wife's face in its
frame of brown hair; unable to sleep; watching the moon set. In the
morning a stubborn rain was falling through the elms, the graceful
elms in the park. The settled comings and goings of this city in a May
rain.

Then up through Lake George and Warrensburg; reminded by Lake
George of that particular life; sunburn and swimming, Peg and gin.
Then up into the mountains through a light so powerful and colorless
that it seemed, as it does in New Hampshire at dawn, as if you were
looking through a lens. To Cranberry and up the lake by Warren's boat
to the camp. Here, briefly, a peculiar, a nearly indescribable disorder.
Old *Saturday Evening Post* and *Woman's Home Companion* covers nailed
with rusted tacks to the walls, the Grecian Arts calendar of 1909, wall
after wall curtained with old clothes, old union suits and Norfolk jackets,
old flannels with moth grit in their folds, and from a crisscross of wires

on the ceiling, hung by their laces, holey saddle shoes and sneakers, moccasins, pack boots, leather-and-rubber high boots, none of them useful but all of them saved for some use in the future. This collection of useless clothing embodies something for her, perhaps for both of them.

The ugliness and wildness of this country. Like derelict masts, dead pines stand in all the shallow water. New poplar and yellow birch cover the hills. Beaver dams. Ducks and geese. We fished off a dock on Saturday and caught ten trout, throwing your baited hook into the dark body of the lake to connect with a pugnacious trout. We fished off the dock Saturday, Saturday night I couldn't sleep again, and on Sunday G. and I packed the rubber boat and walked through the woods to Darning Needle Pond. The striking bleakness the dead trees give to the pond, as if they were the relics of some human failure. White light reflected on the black water. Cold. Misery. Frying eggs. Fished all day and took nineteen trout. Back through the woods just before dark and across the lake in an outboard. Saw a deer. Slept soundly.

•

These two people, or these three, counting myself. He never smiled at her, or gave her a kind word, and whenever she began to express an opinion he sighed and left the room. His impatience and neglect is expressed in her long face. She seems pleasant sometimes and sometimes convinced—by his impatience—that she is a fool. Did her brothers, her father do this, too? A lonely woman. A lonely and foolish woman, doing what is expected of her. Making the beds. Having the fires lighted when we return. Cooking our dinner. And then, long after we have finished, making herself something to eat, drinking six cups of coffee, forgetting her lighted cigarette, reduced to a mean position and reconciled to it, almost as if she were an alcoholic or sustained some similar, hopeless weakness—foolishness perhaps—a weakness that was not discovered until after the marriage contract, after the children were born, and, talking once all night, they have agreed to include this vice, whatever it is, in their marriage and to live with it until they die. Now that I think of them sitting by the fire, I think of them as a man and a woman, not speaking, who are bound together by the knowledge they share of some tragedy, some hideous miscarriage of their efforts, but who will remain together because of their love of their children and their regard for law. I know that this is not true, that none of their children drowned, that they have not poisoned a relative for his money, that this unspeakable crime that lies between them is only the consequence of their ordinary comings and goings, of an unkind word here, a disappointment there, but it lies on them as heavily as any vice, as murder. He has an exalted regard for social law, a puritanical regard for this, and is so diffident that it was hard for him to point the privy out to me, and when I took off my pants to dry them I think he disapproved. He looks with disapproval on all nakedness, as my father used to. I like him; sometimes I feel for him the profound delight of friendship but when I feel this, it seems like misery speaking to misery. What an exchange. How despairing. He is not a guilty one, but he seems to move, ahead of me, down the trail to the lake, like one who has become involved by chance in a hideous crime.

After drinking two bottles of beer in the diner, I decided that man is not physical, man is bestial. I am troubled, however, by the sexual interpretation I put on everything—that the mountains should look to me like knees and clavicles—but this seems to be one of the burdens of men without grace. Within ten minutes a trainman at Tupper Lake, a porter, two waiters, and a salesman told me that they could use a good eight inches of it; they could give a good eight inches of it. Money and lust are prevalent in the talk you overhear.

I am tired, but this will pass. I love my wife's body and my children's innocence. Nothing more.

•

Yesterday. A hot, midsummer day, past haying weather. Hot. In the back rooms the smell of burning paper from the heat. Then how subtly the air becomes fresh at dark and how a perfectly round, pale moon comes out of the woods. There is the excitement of autumn in the cool damp air and the light of the moon, coming back across the field through the orchard, the rich smell of windfalls, the beautiful flavor of an apple—and the next day will be still, hot, the next moonlight night will seem like fall; this variety, this continuous and stimulating play on your senses and your memory. How subtly the autumn arrives on the northwest wind and the full moon. There is really no summer at all; the summer is an illusion. The flowers are formed on the goldenrod by the Fourth of July, the green of the maples has begun to fade. The calendar of flowers, gin bottles, steak bones.

•

I keep telling myself that this cannot go on, no, no, no, that this is all wrong. Lunch at the Algonquin, the Shaws coming back from Cap d'Antibes. Eleanor from Rome, the Perelmans from Siam, Capa giving Irwin a party in someone else's apartment, the feeling when I hear the mail slap the floor of the hall that among the letters there may be a message of love, friendship, an honor or a check. That sitting at the breakfast table I must be saved. Waking after a deep sleep, so invigorated with sexual energy there is no room in my world for doubt. But why then are my evenings so different: gin, the smell of cooking, the sound of children's slippers on a staircase, the feeling that one is incarcerated by beautiful and hideous things. Wondering, should this be fatal, whether I have the brains to extricate myself.

•

Nov. 27th. Snowing.

•

Dec. 5th. Partly at my wife's suggestion I've given the Saul Bellow novel a thorough reading. Here is the blend of French and Russian that I like, the cockroach and the peeling wallpaper described with precision and loathing. The principal force of the work I think is poetic. Some of it ("I stand upon bones," etc.) is bad poetry. I think some of it is very good. I have always been pleased with light and I am always pleased with descriptions of it. Through the desperate choices of my own un-happy mind I have developed, and struggled to discard, a detailed method, but I find Bellow's detail impressive. It comes back to trying to find justification for the sentiment, carnality, and melodrama in my own work.

Yesterday I took Susie to a party on Fifth Avenue given for their daughter by a French-Swiss couple. The pretty parlormaid, the melo-dious French voices, the pink rooms, the smell of candy and perfume like an expensive confectioner's on a late-winter afternoon; and my own awkward shyness. I asked the elevator man to wait for me and left her at the door, although I can at least do this much better. Then walking down Fifth Avenue; the crowds pouring out of the Metropolitan, the people walking north from the Frick gallery, where the Stradivarius had been playing a Beethoven quartet. The light in the sky is sombre, there is a brume in the air. The dead city trees of Central Park are massed like a thicket in the sombre light. In the brume the long double track of street lamps seems yellow. This appears to be a city of the Enlightenment—like Paris or London at the turn of the century; the irreducible evidence of man's inventiveness; progress.

My style seems ruminative and soft; my descriptive powers are not what I would like them to be. I want to let some air and light into this room; waking up this morning I thought that I could use a brisk fistfight. I would like to write a story but not the New Jersey night, not the man in Columbus Circle, nothing overbalanced with morbidity, something with bulk and power. Not the heat wave. The news that it was snowing in Berlin.

A guest at the Shaws', like P., who should, by the way, have come from the West. She came from the West. The delicate coloring of a young woman, a slight cast in one eye, a purple scarf printed with green triangles tied around her neck. "You know that this is the Feast of the Immaculate Conception?" she asked. Then she went on to say that she had been brought up as a Catholic, that her parents had objected to her marrying a Jew, that they still referred to her by her maiden name. "And that's nothing," she said. "On the day we were married, they tried to stop it physically." What I mean is that she is more simple than we. We were sitting around drinking cocktails and eating hors d'oeuvres. She said, "I want a truthful answer: What is a Jew?"

•

Christmas in Boston, Quincy, New Haven, etc. It is a tonic for my self-respect to leave the basement room. The plane to Boston was delayed. The flight was through clouds, and rough. My taxi in Boston got locked in a traffic jam in Charlestown and I walked into the city. Dark and rainy. I go out to Quincy, by trolley car, subway, and bus. In inlets, bays, and tidal rivers along the north-Atlantic coast there are many one-room yacht clubs, ramshackle boat liveries, shacks where bait is sold, oars and dinghies are rented that look as if they had been built, and may have been built, from rubbish salvaged from the sea bottom or left by the tides on the clay banks. The tin chimneys are wired together out of scrap. The crackers and cheese are hung in a basket from the ceiling to protect them from water rats. The signs—Bait for Sale, Boats for Rent—might have been printed by a child in the first grade. In looking at these enterprises, these shacks and piers, it is impossible to draw a line between human endeavor and the sea. Salvaged out of sea waste again. Along the sinking coastline the temporalness of these bait shacks and boat liveries seems to spread into the towns and cities. The biggest houses—the bank—could be demolished by a wave. The sea is omnipresent. At high tide a lake of brine appears in the parking lot of the paint factory. There is a foot of water in the used-car lot. Etc.

My family, etc. My mother, a woman of eighty, told me that my father had left on his desk, for her to read after his death, a letter excoriating her. She tried then to repair the story. Sitting with her, I feel that I do not have the eyes to see her. To Boston in the morning again by bus and subway; then to New Haven on the train. Innes Young's cook had dropped dead the previous day. Freddy took me into the library and showed me two antique watchcases. When you remove the velvet backs there is a pornographic painting of a woman with a large and funny-looking penis, etc. P. seemed to me, some of the time, mischievous. I seemed to myself oversensitive. Mary cried before lunch. But taking a walk with Susie on a rainy morning, the day after Christmas, I felt like myself—free—strong—loosed from the sense of inferiority that has given me so much pain and trouble. This is the consequence of having taken a train, of having left the basement room for a day or two. It is the only frame of mind in which it is tenable to live—or write—and I only seem to enjoy it when I leave the room where I work. The contemptible smallness, the mediocrity of my work, the disorder of my days, these are the things that make it, to say the least, difficult for me to get up in the morning. When I talk with people, when I ride on trains, life seems to have some apparent, surface goodness that does not need questioning. When I spend six or seven hours a day at my typewriter, when I try to sleep off a hangover in a broken armchair, I end by questioning everything, beginning with myself. I reach insupportably morbid conclusions, I wish half the time to die. I must achieve some equilibrium between writing and living. It must not continue to be self-destructive. When I wake in the morning I say to myself I must hit harder, I must do better, I must at least leave a respectable and enlightening record for my children, but an hour later when I sit at my typewriter I lose myself in a haze of regrets and write a page or two about Aaron sitting alone in a room, feeling the walls of his soul collapse. I must bring to my work, and it must give to me, the legitimate sense of well-being that I enjoy when the weather is good and I have had plenty of sleep. Good health is instinctive with me and it can be with literature.

•

When the beginnings of self-destruction enter the heart it seems no bigger than a grain of sand. It is a headache, a slight case of indigestion, an infected finger; but you miss the 8:20 and arrive late at the meeting on credit extensions. The old friend that you meet for lunch suddenly exhausts your patience and in an effort to be pleasant you drink three cocktails, but by now the day has lost its form, its sense and meaning. To try and restore some purpose and beauty to it you drink too much at cocktails you talk too much you make a pass at somebody's wife and you end with doing something foolish and obscene and wish in the morning that you were dead. But when you try to trace back the way you came into this abyss all you find is a grain of sand.

•

Halloween afternoon; a small town; most of the store windows decorated with gravestones, witches, devils, and ghosts. Childish drawing. A little girl dressed as a rabbit being led across the street by her mother. A little boy in his mother's skirts and shoes, his face smeared with her lipstick, leaning against a lamppost. The excitement of a holiday. Over the river a beatific sunset. Waiting for the train, for Mary or a cook. The elderly man in a raincoat and tuxedo pants; an unemployed waiter. The secretary; the naked excitement of travel. After dark, children approaching lighted doors. A trick or treat. At ten or eleven a cold rain established itself firmly. I think that I learned to listen to the rain in the lapses of a quarrel. It meant that the quarrel would end. It meant infinity. It fell on the quick and the dead and on the unborn. What a profound pleasure I took in hearing it fall. How clearly I saw the complexity of the ground where it fell; dry leaves, curved leaves, hair moss and partridgeberry.

•

I heard the wind come around on Tuesday night. A cold rain began before dawn and the season changed. The gloom and the cold and the rain continued until late Saturday afternoon, when the wind came directly out of the north and the sky cleared. I walked down to the post office. The leaves, yellow and green, lay thickly everywhere, like bank notes. I looked up the river into the mountains. They were covered with snow.

To a party Saturday night; here is the visible grain of sand, here is the instability that conquers me, here is the question put and evaded as, in another connection, my mind shies and wanders when it is confronted with a sequence of hard facts. Interest rates, bank balances, batting averages, political statistics seem to induce in my mind a kind of shyness. I turn to the theatrical section. I remember that I am uneducated.

•

Last night to see some old newsreels of Charles and Anne Lindbergh. A young man, whose nerve seems to be that of a young man; of one who looks on the natural world as an easily met challenge. Like B.M., bold and stupid. The transcendent flight, the feeling that this puts him into a nearly supernatural position. His reception at Le Bourget. The adulation of the city of Paris. Pictures of him on the balcony of the Embassy. Self-possessed, direct. Pictures of him on the cruiser that brought him home. Coming into New York Harbor and the celebration here that was greater than the celebration that signified the end of the war. The impulsive storms of paper that were never seen again.

He falls in love with Elisabeth Morrow. Her death. Her death. But well before that, Anne; he falls in love with her. She must have been shy. Their marriage.

Their flying trips. Their first child. The German pervert. Almost a perversion of the times. An insanity. He steals their child and murders it senselessly and cruelly. Then the moving pictures shown of the child for identification. A beautiful child. The trial. L.'s impassive testimony, his determination to kill the pervert. The curious division of sympathy in the press. Anne's misery. The death of Hauptmann. The birth of another child.

Their sequestration. Their unhappiness together. Their inability ever to divorce. The deepening of this misery. The man preserves the nerve and directness of youth, although he has grown old. His sympathies lie with Fascism, with an élite. How differently she feels; how little she dares to say. Talking with her today: her pleasant eyes, her crooked mouth. Her face ravished with strain. The sense of talking with Antigone. To make it an obscene tragedy, the situation could be one where she fell in love with a man who resembled the man who had murdered her firstborn son.

The story would be cruel and indiscreet; in some ways impossible, since it is difficult to find something, anything, to compare with his flight of the Atlantic. But, to speak to no great purpose, it seems that here we part company with Flaubert, for unlike the France of his time we have a hierarchy of demigods and heroes; they are a vital part of our lives and they should be a vital part of our literature. If I could only align the fields with some newspaper tragedy. These are public people. This is public tragedy. They are known. They view publicity and privacy with the values of a reigning king and queen. When they close the doors of the house in Englewood, it is like the closing of the doors in "Oedipus" and "Medea." We are shut out.

As a part of moving I have had to go through some old manuscripts and I have been disheartened to see that my style, fifteen years ago, was competent and clear and that the improvements on it are superficial. I fail to see any signs of maturity, of increased penetration; I fail to see any deepening of my grasp. I was always in love. I was always happy to scythe a field and swim in a cold lake and put on clean clothes. I was more exuberant and naïve about both this and love than I am now, but this is not a change for the better. There are thousands of notes, thousands of pages of description, thousands of striking conversations, and because they all lack an inner logic, because they lack passion, they are of no import.

•

Maine, New Hampshire, and Vermont remind me of three apples: a russet, a McIntosh, and a pippin. New Hampshire, my favorite, is the russet; a golden winter apple, with a coarse flesh and a strong flavor. I can't say why this country seems to me incomparable. I have seen many hills that are just as green, and bigger trees and mountains. The Helderbergs seem as high as the mountains near Franconia. But it is the highest land on the eastern seaboard, these are the oldest escarpments on the earth's crust, and the winds that blow across it are mountain winds. The quality of the air is omniscient. In the morning the air is cold and dark and as clear as glass. The darkness in the clear air seems nearly visible, as if it were made up of fine particles of silt, and yet you can see for fifty miles. At this hour the air is too cold to have a distinctive fragrance. You smell mostly coffee, sausage, the salt pork for the chowder at lunch. By eleven o'clock the sun has warmed the air. It smells now of the garden, the pines, the weeds and wildflowers in the pasture behind the barn. The air is warm, but it is still light and changeable. It will not be heavy until after lunch. Then the air smells like sugar and spice, but as it grows heavier and warmer the weeds in the pasture dominate. Their smell is stronger than spice, they smell like drugs. During all this time the air on the mountain has remained cold and changeable, and at five or six when the children come in to get their supper the cold air mushrooms down through the woods like a cloud (feel the mountain air). The smell of spice and drugs is lost, but the cold air spreads unevenly, and on the terrace or walking out to the woodshed you can feel the eddies of coolness and warmth, clearness and fragrance as distinctly as the currents in the lake. After supper the air on the terrace is cool and dark again and too light to hold many smells (unless it should rain), but sitting on the terrace or in the house you are still conscious of the changeable air. The window curtains move. The smell of cold stone from the massive pieces of granite on the open chimney is flattened against the wall and falls to where we are. Then this is gone again and we smell the heavy odor of cut flowers. It rains somewhere in the neighborhood—in Hebron or Alexandria—and for ten minutes the air smells of the pungency released by a rainfall. Then the permanent smells of the room, panelling and ashes and flowers, are still. It is this continuous play of light and air and water that makes my response to that country so keen. It is also the sense of summer and youth. Driving down the parkway, through Ossining and along River Road, I felt the proximity of the city, I felt that I was driving into an increase of ugliness.

•

Into Ossining to buy a loaf of bread, a can of Spam, and the Salinger book. I felt the way I used to feel when I was a soldier. The sky was gray. It was muggy. Ossining looked like an Army town. I felt sad, but it was a useless sadness. I miss Mary and the children. I hear their voices upstairs. I come back here every year to work hard and establish my independence from them, but I never really leave them, and away from them I feel maimed and foolish. I call up everyone I know. They are away. I leave messages with maids. I drink a Martini. I wait for the phone to ring. When I'm unlucky I get drunk and go to the movies and return to Bristol. The idea is to get away from one place, but I never get away, I never reach another place. I try to struggle with the things that bind me, but I forget the nature of the bonds. I go to the movies. I get up at four and read until dawn. I do everything but the work that I came here to do.

Tense last night. We had been talking earlier about the presence of the dead in this place. I do not believe in the supernatural. I despise it. There is a sense of unrequitedness here, or rather the evidence of unrequitedness: the run-down buildings, the overgrown garden. Read some Turgenev, took a bath, got into bed. As I was going to fall asleep that nervous reflex that is usually the last thing I remember before sleep seemed to rebound—I heard some noise from the children's room—and I was wakeful and frightened. Then suddenly my daughter spoke hoarsely in her sleep, eight or ten times, a name. The voice was guttural and unlike her waking voice. I went into the room and stood by her bed until she had stopped talking. Then there were many voices and noises hour after hour. There was the illusion of a man's voice, a little more than a sigh. I think I have never been so frightened before. My flesh crawled. I was subjected to the beating of my heart. Who would the spirit be if there were a spirit? A sickly banker, troubled because he had never been given credit for organizing the Federal Reserve Board? The advertising executive who offered to hang the traitor with his own hands? The impostor?

•

To bring out a collection of short stories this fall: "Torch Song," "O City of Broken Dreams," "Emma Boynton," "The Day the Pig Fell into the Well," "The Enormous Radio," "The Season of Divorce," "The Sutton Place Story," "The Pot of Gold," perhaps "The Radio Man," I mean "The Elevator Man," and to write a couple of stories to complement the collection, a couple of long pieces with no dying fall. Read at the office yesterday most of the stories I've written in the last five years and was, quite incidentally, exhilarated and happy to leave the office for the open streets at five. The stories didn't seem too good. The war stories are spoiled with chauvinism, a legitimate weakness. I also found pitiful evidences of poorly informed snobbism, an exaggerated wish to impress my knowledge of Army prose upon the reader, and associated with this a tendency to use verbatim conversation rather than the remarks that should be made by my characters. Some of the best of it seems to be the set of descriptions of character: Emma Boulanger had the soul of a housemaid; etc. This I picked up from Flaubert and it is showing signs of turning into a bad characteristic of generalization. I can use these set pieces if they are integrated into a crisis. My interim narrative style needs a lot of work. Love of sorts is reasonably well described. There are too many scornful and fine phrases.

•

On Christmas Eve, a little before dark, I took my son over to see the skating rink in Central Park. Young and made timid by the strangeness of the place and hour, he held my hand firmly and was a model of docile obedience and agreement. In the dark I seized him and kissed him with forlorn love. I can remember when my daughter was younger and could be made by darkness and strangeness to be as docile. He looked to me for everything. What I did, he did. When I exclaimed about the lighted rink and the music he repeated my words. When, waiting for a bus, I crossed my legs, he crossed his legs. I have never seen the city before on Christmas Eve, I think. There were jocular groups on street corners, people going off to parties in evening dress, a young man with a package and a dozen roses hailed a cab—but, perhaps because of my own mood, whole neighborhoods seemed desolate and forsaken and I felt myself sad and alone.

•

The sense of fear—or at least the sense of lacking courage—associated with retracing courses of thought and action is probably linked to the fear that one will destroy one's usefulness as an artist. But the usefulness of the artist varies from time to time, and since these are hours and days out of one's life, can there be any other course but to look back into them, even though at times they seem like waste? You have been lost in a wood. You know how the mind works. When you realize that you are lost, the mind is instantly animated with a kind of stoic cheerfulness. How much worse it could be, you think. You have warm clothes, dry matches, and half a cup of water left in the canteen. If you have to spend two or three days out you will surely survive. You must avoid panic. You must keep your eyes and your mind in the most accommodating and relaxed condition. Within an hour your calmness is rewarded. There is the trail! A new kind of blood seems suddenly to be let into your heart. Your strength and your wind are refreshed and off you go. There has been a delay, of course, but if you keep to a decent pace you will be back to the shore where the boat is by dark. You hold to the pace. You keep your eye sharply on the thread of trail. You do not stop to drink or smoke or rest at all. You hike until the end of the afternoon and, seeing that the light has begun to go, you stop to see if you can pick out the noise of the waves that you should, by now, be able to hear. The place where you stop seems to be familiar. You have seen that dead oak before; that wall of rock, that stump. Then you look around. There is the heavy creel that you discarded at noon. You are back at the point where you discovered that you were lost. The lightness of your heart, your refreshed strength, the illusion of walking toward water that has heartened you all afternoon was illusory. You are lost; and it is getting dark. This is a situation in which I find too many of my characters. Presently one makes camp for the night, thinking that things could be much worse. But I never seem able to bring them out of the woods, on the one hand, or to transform the world into a forest. My children are indeed lost, but they are lost in a world in which almost everyone else seems to know the way. They rebel passionately at being set apart as the lost. They seem to have been victimized by an imbalance of courage and wisdom. The specious cheerfulness of the lost, their fetid compassion, their devotion to deep chords of laughter, to kindly faces in lighted rooms, seem not to be a competent moral or aesthetic resolution.

•

The strain of debt; the difficulty of trying to write one's way out of it. There are seven more days, six more days, etc. Once in New Hampshire for three months I tried unsuccessfully to rip a story out of my brain or to patch together a series of incisive notes with no success at all. I have at times been able to sweat out a story, at times I've failed.

It helps to be relaxed.

The lonesome road. You drive for twenty-five or thirty miles on a spring night along a strange road without meeting another car. A few houses are lighted, but most of them are dark. You hear peepers as you drive—the spring night sound swells in your ears and then fades—as you pass a marsh or a pond. There seems to be a lot of water in the neighborhood—ponds and brooks. The road turns, drops, and you see a sign, "7 Tons Max. Load," and then a little bridge. Most of the houses must be summer cottages; that would account for their being dark. But it's a lonesome road. You see the headlights of another car—the first in an hour—coming toward you. It is a big, high-bodied interstate bus and as it passes you can see that most of the passengers are sleeping. Then it is gone and you are alone again on the dark road. The noise the peepers make sounds sad.

Yesterday a beautiful day. You sweat in the sun; shiver in the shade. Walked to the station, thinking of the story. The sense of light pouring into the mind. The noise of an outboard motor and its multitude of associations. The sense of the day as if it were reflected in a piece of bull's-eye glass. Spherical, as round as an apple. To the movies last night; the bizarreness of the village. The façades bent into the street-light like masks on a stage, grotesque, lighted fronts. The twilight, the afterglow standing behind them, a clear and stormy light. The lobby stinks of peanuts and stales. The old woman who sells you a ticket wears a dress that glitters with brilliants. She wears a necklace of brilliants; her fingers are loaded with rings. You look from her to the twilight, the paper buildings. The picture was "Come Back, Little Sheba." I thought it was very good. The library at Beechwood was lighted when I drove home. I seem to hold the mirror up to a lot of foolishness. There should be nothing to worry about if you tell the truth.

•

These green, these fragrant, these carven cavernous and not cold days of spring. The smell of fish skin and bloodworms; the chill water.

•

One of the children had a toothache in the middle of the night. Mary got water and aspirin. Her patient, sleepy voice. The sense, then, that one was face-to-face with transcendent patience. Many of the promises have been broken, etc., but here, like the ability to rise to love, like the strength summoned in the throes of childbirth, there is a patience, there is a calmness of spirit and mind that seems womanly and transcendent. It is two in the morning. She gets an aspirin and draws a glass of water. Everything is unhappy, broken, insubstantial, but for an hour it doesn't matter at all. And for Eben the rain falls on the roofs of the houses where his enemies are asleep. Under the roofs on which he hears the rain fall strangers and enemies are sleeping. In the noise of the rain he hears the slippers coming downstairs and the boots mounting. For Eben the rain, even the rain, falls into the grass of a hostile and foreign country.

New York on a summer night. How many lights are burning? A man sits on the front steps of the public library wearing no coat and no shoes and a dark felt hat. His shoes are beside him on the marble step.

•

Now I resent the tiredness of my mind, from having drunk too much; I resent the craving for some erotic tenderness that is the only end, the only beauty for these days. Seeing an elderly man and woman having breakfast with their son—who may be taking summer courses at N.Y.U.—I yearned to discharge with competence and strength the responsibilities of a family man, to carve for my children something that has moral splendor—I glimpsed the lacks I show in turning my daughter s loneliness into a poor anecdote—in asking advice everywhere. And with my mouth tasting of old wine, and with this gray sky, I find it so hard not to be incredulous in recalling the wonderful hours and days in the mountains, the cleanliness, P. coming back to the house with her flowers, the breadth of the view, swimming in cold water, making love under a thin roof; and I think now of the months that I have longed to write a story that will be fine, that will be singing, that will have in it all kinds of lights and pleasures.

As for failure and despair, they seem aggravated by the climate of

New York and the suburbs. Both New York and Scarborough seem in some cases to produce an egotism that needs the health and vigor of youth and an imitation of these energies when they are gone themselves. In both places there are portents of the abyss, and now and then you hear the voices and glimpse the faces of the fallen. Waiting to get your fried egg in a dirty cafeteria, you see, through the window between the counter and the kitchen, an old man bent over a stove. He is dressed in a loose white shift—prisoner's garb—and his face is sullen and bitter. "It is quite cool out," the baby-sitter says, handing you her seamy furs, and you recognize at once in the grayness of her face and the elegance of her voice that she has come to you from the abyss. The house that the A.s rented at the corner of Alewives Lane is empty again. They struggled for a year and left in the middle of the night, leaving unpaid bills everywhere. But in New Hampshire there are no portents, no manifestations of the abyss, no obligations to imitate the energies of youth, no dread of falling, of loneliness and disgrace, and the smell of wood smoke and the noise of the wind have a direct bearing on our lives. There we understand calmly how we live and how we change. Think of the autumn twilights; think of the old woman cutting her flowers, think of the roar of the purple sea on the island beaches.

A Sunday afternoon; a little rain in the village. A man practicing a violin. On the heels of the rain, dense humidity. Walking over to the C.s' for dinner. A young man with a suitcase, hurrying down Fifth Avenue. A dressy Englishwoman imperiously hurrying her husband across the street. Cocktails and supper. Farther east a Puerto Rican carrying a suitcase up the steps of a rooming house. Past the Lafayette, now half demolished. Light pours from the sky through the collapsed ceilings of the dining room, the lobby, and the bar. It is easy to remember these rooms on a spring night when the big windows were open, when the room was full of light, friends, the smell of chicken and wine, and that these rooms where we used to come to celebrate arrivals and departures are half demolished and flooded with the light of the sky makes a cheerful memory a poignant one. On Third Avenue a man carrying a suitcase. In a dirty window a Cuban girl in a white skirt that must be new since she seems so delighted with it that her pleasure can be seen as you walk past this rooming house. Later thunder; then a flood, a gorging rain.

•

Driving for seven hours, straight into the sun, tired my eyes. "How lush and green it is here," my wife said, and I saw how the lawns were shining but I was not particularly happy to be back. It was coming back to offices, back to Grand Central Station, back to the evening train home, back to the discomfort of a full suit on a hot day, back to tiredness, back to parochialism, back to a small part of the world, back to a lack of excitement. That there are no heroes here does not mean that there are no heroes anywhere. I would like to keep the sense of being away from New York, away from the noise and excitement there. I would like to keep the sense of what a small part of the world this is; to master it, not to take it too seriously.

•

Labor Day; storm warning up; a hurricane. The end of the season on the islands and the mountains; the tentative sunlight. The end of the year. Dark and humid here; a little rain. The kind of dim hangover that I haven't experienced all summer. I am homesick for the islands or the mountains, for something other than this valley, this suburb. It seems to have the subtle power over my spirit of a baneful light—the return, in spite of myself, of passiveness. I still have not satisfied myself as far as discipline and concentration go.

•

Every time I read a review of Saul Bellow I get the heaves. Oh this big, wild, rowdy country, full of whores and prizefighters, and here I am stuck with an old river in the twilight and the deterioration of the middle-aged businessman.

Into New York—frowzy—the men working to form a concept of race—their hair cut so short that it fits over their scalp like a cap of felt—a woman, and through her veils, her feathers, her furs, her pearls and brilliants, there shines a smile of perfect plainness and sweetness. Over to *The New Yorker*, where there are mixed opinions about the suburbs. Walked up Fifth Avenue. A fine procession; it is a procession. At the Fifty-seventh Street crossing the crowds seemed to group themselves for a second to form the features of a matriarchy. It was an ugly thought and it passed. A lot of homosexuals drifting around in midmorning. Up along the edge of the Park to the museum. The Assyrian kings. Some early Aegean grave figures—the sense of early time—lions. The exclamatory Etruscan warrior; Mars; a sad athlete with a fillet. All the things found in rivers. The treasure of Constantinople, found in the Rhône, plates and belt buckles found in the Loire, swords found in the Danube, Venus in the Tiber. Aphrodite, fair and still. Some of Constantine's jewelry, some of the Albanian treasure, Morgan's thing. My feeling for sumptuousness has changed. At one time these things seemed precious, idle, adolescent, foolish. Now sumptuousness seems to be a legitimate need. Some sallets, visors, basinets, long snouts, idiot grins, old gods. Some swords of great weight and beauty, swords of meaning chivalrous, his heralds of glory, lethal symbols or worship. Waiting for a bus; the general lack of humor with which we regard one another. The tense atmosphere of an economic and a sexual content. Barring the admiration that follows pretty women, there is a good deal of tension—true ignorance—in the scrutiny New Yorkers give one another. There is not much geniality or trust in the looks on Madison Avenue. In the morning the river looked cold; it had an inhospitable gleam. Of the families that have been strung along the banks all summer—the mamas and papas and grandpapas and children—sitting in their underwear on folding chairs, swimming and eating and basking in the heat of the sun—there are now left only a few men, most of them old, with scarves around their necks, their hats pulled down to keep their ears warm.

•

Yesterday, cold and rainy. A dark day, a black house, the exacerbating worries of indebtedness. Today the burnished light makes your eyes smart. Polished blue and burnished gold, brimming with brilliance. The north wind, the air smells of water, purple here, green there. The wind came around before dawn. The leaves are piling down. A tumultuous, a harmless wind.

This house, with its long living room looking north and south so that there are only a few days in the year when the sun enters it, with its pretentious and inefficient equipment, with its jumbled memories, dark and often cold, depresses me and seems to challenge the health I have enjoyed. It is perhaps the closeness of our life here and the dullness we run into when we try to vary it. These habits, these days, like old

clothes. Yesterday a day of brilliant light, acoustical brilliance—the
ringing of wheels on rails from distant trains sounded clearly. Sinus
pains. Drove Ben up the hill to see the sunset, the clear darkness, the
hills, the distant lights, the dyed clouds, the lavender-and-lemon-colored
sky.

•

Some brief reassessment might be in order. This role was always
volatile; but it's difficult to recall. There was the accumulation of things
over two years, self-protests, bad book reviews, a feeling of having grown
away from the lamentable influence of my mother, a decrease in the
fear of loneliness, and a conviction that most of the conflicts in my
disposition are guises of emotional ignorance that I inherited from my
parents. I was made so happy that there seemed, in my thinking, to be
a trace of hysteria. In the middle of this, the Saul Bellow book had on
my mind the power of shock. My identification with it was so deep that
I could not judge it sensibly, and there is a grain of legitimate identification here. Then there was sickness, weakness, and the exhaustion
I felt when I finished Mrs. Wapshot. There was a sick, rainy day in
New York when Lexington Avenue seemed like a catacomb. There are
my very legitimate troubles with *The New Yorker*. What it adds up to
is that I have never felt so strong and so happy and feared hysteria so
deeply. I think that a few days in the mountains would solve all these
problems, but I cannot go. And what it adds up to also is that in making
such a profound change in the attitudes of my mind, the body may be
laggard. I do not have the sweetness of some of the people in question
and it is an insupportable strain to aim for it; but I have my own
sweetness and I see no reason why coming on this in the forty-first year
of my life should undermine my health.

•

Waiting at the R.s' for Susie to finish her French lesson, with Ben.
A northwest wind and a winter twilight, a moon already bright before
dusk and a cold night on the way. This hour when we seem caught in
the bluff death of the year. The light loses its breadth, but not its clarity
or its power. These subtle blues and lemony lights are like the lights
of anesthesia, lust, repose. The stars come out and the play of light
continues. It is not that the light goes; a dimness falls from the sky over

everything, obscuring the light. The dimness falls over everything. The
cold air makes the dog seem to bark into a barrel. Bright stars, house
lights, rubbish fires.

•

Waking and dreaming I seem caught in this ridiculous cycle of
petulance, suspicions, and hostility. Working, and at the hour of waking, I see clearly what it is that I want: love, poetry, inestimable powers
of understanding or forgiveness if that is needed, humor that is not
rueful. But I seem to see much too clearly the deterioration of my high
spirits. I seem to see much too clearly the working of an idle and a
morbid imagination, I see myself succumbing to all kinds of imaginary
meanness and, what's more, how can I take pride in my skin when my
skin seems lacerated? But I also see that we perform our passions in
the large scene of what we have done and left undone in the past and
that now and then the curve of feeling—hostility—seems to intersect
the structure of my disposition, for this painful feeling of laceration was
felt years and years ago. Reason cannot enjoin the carcass to be cheerful
and lusty—and when my powers of desire are maimed, so are my powers
of wisdom—but I can persist at least in my hopefulness—in my knowledge that a simple cure—a trip, some skiing, the heat of the sun—will
set the mind free.

•

Not working well: how deeply buried in this community are the
dramas of hardship and lust. Or so it seems to me. Traces of midwinter
angst. Asking myself each minute: This is not the maximum of my
happiness. Why am I not as happy as I was in the golden days of autumn?
To read the hardy text of this bright day: all bold things. Hill the bright
colors of smoke, in the winter sun's heat the fragrance of last year's
leaves, the bewilderments of childhood; also fishing trips in the north.
Now love. Skunk cabbages pushing through the dead leaves. And still
the brook runs. Sweet and hardy, life seems like the faintest perfume,
coming and going. Why, I wonder. I am poor and I am bored. But this
day should shatter all these things. Looking up from the sawhorse in
the woodpile, he saw the winter twilight. Pruning the apple tree that
was planted on their tenth wedding anniversary. Drinking gin before

an open fire; in one another's arms: these passionate, strong, and capricious things.

I do not seem able to call up, at will, the sweet flavor of compassion, but I think I can conclude that life, as it passes before our eyes, is a creative force —that one thing is put usefully upon another—that what we lose in one exchange is more than replenished by the next, that it is only us, only our pitiful misunderstandings that make for crookedness, darkness, and anger. There are times when I seem to see nothing but that world that lies in the corner of the eye: the leering stranger, the flick of a mouse in the hammered-brass woodbox, the prostitute in the drugstore. And there are times when the juices of understanding and love seem to flow freely through my arms and legs and all my parts. That she would never quite lose the appealing look of an American girl in a foreign boarding school. Her dark yellow hair; her white blouse There is some special bad luck that seems to strike at the end of their journeys, holidays, and excursions. The curl mysteriously slips out of their hair, dust seems to settle on their hats and the shoulders of their coats, their lipstick smears, their eyeglasses steam, and the gay smile with which they meant to face the world lapses into the scowl of loneliness which is their habitual expression. Their white gloves get dirty, their ribbons come undone, and although they have attacked the problems of homeliness with spirit—even with gallantry—they are finally discouraged.

•

What a beautiful day; what a fair day. "It's the kind of weather," the maid says, "that makes you glad to be alive." The early-morning air is moist, and mingling with the sweet fragrance of the earth is the smell of smoke, frying fish, and the slack river water. It is no wonder that we are stirred by this show of light and color; it is the plain difference between sanity and horror. I am lifted so high that I think of stopping my conversations with B.G., or at least telling him that I only want reassurance; that I want only to be told that the smell of laurel is not an aberration; to be encouraged in this belated discovery of personal strength. Some of what he said seemed to throw light on a part of the mind that has never been lighted before and there I found a kind of man-made cobweb—a complicated contraption of string, bits of glass,

small bells, old Christmas-tree ornaments, and other rubbish so tied
and woven that to touch the web at any place would make every last
ornament bob and jingle. I may not be able to destroy this contraption
with one blow but at least some clear light has been turned onto it.
And to describe the feeling of mystery we experience on stepping out
of the house on a morning like this. The April dusk that smells unac-
countably of mushrooms, the west wind smells of lemon trees.

•

When Huxley speaks of the rut of connubial bliss, I wonder if this
is where I am, for walking after dinner with the children and the dog
I am very, very happy. My son and I wait at a turn for Mary and Susan
to appear. The woods where we stand are dark but it is light beyond
the bend. Mary comes into view. Her shoulders are bare; her dress is
cut low. She carries an armful of lilies, trailing this way and that their
truly mournful perfume. She seems content and so am I and when she
takes my arm and we continue to walk under the trees in the last light,
under the beeches that spray like shrapnel, arm in arm, after so many
years and with so much sexual ardor I think that we are like two
sheltered by the atmosphere of some campus; that we are like a couple
engraved on a playing card. There is a lack of space and motion and
money, to be sure, but I can't feel that sexual depravity would enlarge
our horizons, although the advice seeps in, at times. We are happy, we
are lucky, and if we steer clear of sugary dependence it can be let go
at this. Venus and Eros are capricious and we may be fighting tomorrow,
but we do not lose sight of the fact that with some patience and wisdom
the resumption of good feeling is inevitable.

•

Overcast, unseasonably cold day for the last of June. Depressing
cocktail party. Worked at Moses and Clear Haven. Read "The Confi-
dential Clerk" and some of "The Victim." The set pieces about the city
in the heat are fine. Nothing is in jeopardy. It is encouraging to see
good work in this direction, and this direction is a record of the phenomenon of light; that we have always found heart in seeing a piece of
wet paving; the trees whitened; the thrill of watching the 7:46 roll down
the tracks this morning. Here are water lights and water smells; pristine
economic and sexual energies. I think, Make some money to travel.

Made some cherry jam last night. Four pots boiling on the stove. The fragrance of cherries boiling in sugar spread all through the house. Pleasant things.

Cocktails on Teatown Road; the tag end of the holiday. Mary worried about my gin-drinking distempers, but stayed too long. So we drink too much and become cross. Then to Fred's, where everything seemed garbled. "Now lissen," he said, "Langer is juss like McCarthy, and the reason for this is it's a big goddam country, and the East is nothing buda patch." Played some badminton; played some at dusk with the old lady. "He is very affable, now that he has sold the house," she said. "Of course, we've always been very good friends, and my husband loved him." Magnificent evening, with a changing wind; putting the rackets into the frame: a magnificent twilight. Then, not a collapse of propriety but of consecutiveness. Everyone wandering around with a glass of gin. "Stigaround, stigaround," he says. "I'll toss some gurry in a frying pan and we'll have a bite. Stigaround." I don't want to eat gurry, I think, and rebuke myself for fastidiousness. Pissed on the driveway, and got my pants wet. Rose plaintively to every taunt. Bored and cross with Mary. Troublemaker. Wanted to get away. Pack my bag and take the midnight. Find some dark-skinned lady who would love me, or some old man. These interminable cocktail hours leave me with a sprained sense of charity and love; leave me spiteful and mean. But there is room for some spite in the picture. It will pass. Equilibrium in good shape, but still some romantic fantasies about us. If I should love my enemy, surely I should love my brother.

•

Back here with mixed feelings. I have known much happiness and much misery under this roof. The house is charming, the elm is splendid, there is water at the foot of the lawn and yet I would like to go somewhere else; I would like to move along. This may be some fundamental irresponsibility; some unwillingness to shoulder the legitimate burdens of a father and a householder. It seems, whenever I return, small in measure, dense in its provincialism. It is partly the provincialism in the air that makes me want to kick over the applecart. I long for a richer community, and who doesn't. Woke up at dawn. Wandered around the lawn in my birthday suit. Enjoyed the pale sky and the monumental elm but I kept thinking, It is better in the mountains; it is better everywhere. I have been here too long.

•

There are pleasant things here, pleasant and unpleasant memories. The slum yards blazing with roses and hydrangea and later with dahlias. The people waiting, corner after corner, for the seven-o'clock bus to the station. The pretty girl with the kind of shawl that is fashionable today; the young executive in his uniform; the old woman dressed as a nurse, her cheeks painted a faded pink. There are all kinds of good things, but I might look into my resistance. I feel that this house, tree-shaded and standing at an east-west angle, has some depressing powers. I dread losing my equilibrium here, as I have done before. I see the charm in the valley and its houses—a sense of place—but I feel the force of provincialism within this charming front. This is friendly and clement, etc., but there is some conformism in the climate. There is perhaps the dread promise of permanence. I may be speaking of provincialism; I may be speaking of a deep strain of irresponsibility in myself; I may be speaking of that which in my marriage overwhelms me from time to time. Driving into the village I go along roads where I have been needlessly miserable and depressed. I like to think of a world much bigger than Shady Hill. I suppose every man does. I am not sure how it lies—Venice, New Hampshire, Martha's Vineyard. I would like to settle and to preserve at the same time some breadth. The flaw in all this may be under my nose and yet I do not see it. We can live here through another winter, but I wish my anticipations were more cheerful. Perhaps I can make them so.

The midsummer night. Undressed, and walked in a towel down to the pool. The air was still and humid; the fountain and the pool lights were turned off. A single pattern of light came from the street through the leaves of the trees; in the distance, the lights of my own house. Waited, in a libidinous humor, for Mary. In the humid stillness, the throbbing of a ship's motor sounded clearly from the river. It was some big craft—a tanker or a freighter, riding high. The sound of the screw deepened as she passed Clear Haven and then slacked off as she went upriver. Overhead, a plane crossed with all her gaudy landing lights still burning; her cabin windows lighted where thirty-four men and women, and a baby perhaps, sat in the febrile heat reading *The Ladies'*

Home Journal and *Time.* Upholstered, curtained, well-stocked with coffee, Dramamine, and Danish pastry—an image of ennui and meaningless suspense—she seemed to proceed very slowly below the large stars. The tree frogs sang loudly; so on will come the winter cold. It was the hottest night of the year. At my back, I heard some rats in the cistern. In the little skin of light on the water I saw a bat hunting. For a second everything that was familiar and pleasant seemed ugly. In the woods a cat began to howl like a demented child. The water smelled stagnant. I went in, swam, climbed out, and walked back over the grass. Religious things, superstitious things, what Veblen calls the devoutness of the delinquent—whatever it was, I seem to step into a pleasant atmosphere of goodness, a turning in the path that seemed to state clearly, Joy to the world, lasting joy. Awoke at two, smoked on the stones; still the loud noises of tree frogs. The cat drifted home. Many stars.

•

When I think of Mother, I think of the streets of Quincy, where she spent most of her life. It appears to be a small place, dark, a sphere among larger and more swiftly turning spheres; and to go from one to the other meant the severance of many moral and emotional ties. It was the common situation of having to break with one's origins or live in despair. She is a woman of many excellent qualities. I think that she has not been secure in many of her immediate relationships. She seldom spoke of her numerous friendships without hinting at the power of loneliness. It was a powerfully sensual world; the smell of fires and flowers and baking bread and peaches cooking for jam and autumn woods and spring woods and the hallways of old houses and the noises of the rain and the sea, of thunderstorms and the west wind. This is a red-blooded and a splendid inheritance.

•

Quincy Journal. On the train downriver from Scarborough, much speculation. The feeling that Mother, with her natural impetuousness accelerated by some desperation or pain, has worked out her problems within such a narrow or egocentric sphere that the application of her principles to any broader field would result in the utter desolation of sexual anxiety. The sky and the water were overcast. At Tarrytown I

saw a boat that had been sunk by the autumn rains. Boarded the one
o'clock for Boston. Drank some whiskey in the diner with a cheerful
businessman. The diner smelled of spoiled food. The linen was sordid;
the waiters sullen. In the washroom the toilet was broken, and looking
into the pot one saw the ties stream by. Outside, the autumn countryside; the brooks risen over their banks, and the sea, which seems, along
the coast, to relate a sad, sad tale. I have made this journey thousands
of times, and I suppose it is only natural, considering the past, that I
should feel anxious; that I should revert to childish things; that I should
be afraid not of any image but of shades, of that creation that lies in
the corner of my eye. Back to the diner at the end of the trip for some
more whiskey. The same smell of spoiled food. The waiters were changing their shoes—when the last woman had left the diner, their trousers.
Outside, a fine blue in the west and a shower of rain. Only after drinking
a little whiskey do I feel the simple pleasures of travelling through the
tag end of this rainy day. Oh, where are all my claims of wholeness?
Where are all my gifts of judicious self-admiration?

To Quincy on the local; the flat industrial coast. This poignant,
debauched countryside; street lights, mud puddles, and the evening
star, and these sodden people—all but the pretty girls and the wild boys.
Mother in bed with a stroke. Her speech thick, but her mulishness,
her hearing, her appetite, and her intellect unimpaired. Josephine—a
plain-minded woman—who has been engaged for twelve years to a sailor
who has never brought his ship into a U.S. port. Some bad feelings,
some good. The energy and the vigor of anxiety may fill a life with
activity and invention, but it is an egocentric performance. Some supper;
some whiskey; and Fred called. My failure at this relationship is one
of the things I dread. My tendency is to call him a clumsy sorehead.
Perhaps if I wrote about him as a sorehead it might help; it might take
off some of the steam. I would like to call him a blundering, irresponsible
fool, but I feel that one of my first responsibilities is to love him. A bad
television show, and to bed. A room in which the ceiling is enamelled
bright red and in which, I think, a dossal drape once hung. I can see
a weak-minded pansy trying to redress this dreariness. Woke at four
and wondered if such a neighborhood wouldn't be full of voyeurs. But
the crickets sing here, and the smell of the sea is fine. Concluded, half
asleep, that all delight is an illusion; love is a shipyard tart, etc. The
sweet ringing of iron bells; an ugly nightmare. Walked through the

morning under the painful charge of anxiety; this utter desolateness. Thought of Mother's ethical card house and the multitude of escape signs in this dreary place. A Viennese waltz plays in the supermarket; on the wall of the laundromat there is an English hunting scene; in the bowling alley there is a mural of some Indians, canoeing over the crystal waters of a mountain lake.

•

To church on Sunday; a fine autumn day although the foliage is not so bright this year. Raked and burned leaves with Ben. Much pleasure in this. The leaves a little damp, the fire moving in waves, each leaf taking shape in flame. As much smoke as a small battle. As it grows dark, the fire lights our faces; the trunks of the trees, gray ashes, flat, like a stain. The little boy, running barefoot over ash heaps, the warm ash heaps in the cool evening, as we used to do. Thought of last year's passionate autumns where love obscured the crack in the ceiling and the dust under the bed and how this terminated in spitefulness and bewilderment. But these are not the things that will kill us. It is like the man who, suffering the agonies of vertigo, gets run over by a taxi. I have no time to waste and yet I waste my days. There is "The Journal," "The Housebreaker," and notes to be kept up, and "The Wapshots." I ought to finish the journal today.

•

What we take for grief or sorrow seems, often, to be our inability to put ourselves into a viable relationship to the world; to this nearly lost paradise. Sometimes we see the reasons for this and sometimes we do not. Sometimes we wake up to find the lens that magnifies the excellence of the world and its people broken. Saturday was such a day. Planted some bulbs, drank some gin before lunch. But jumpy. Later to play some football, and here seems to be a step in the right direction; here is a means of putting ourselves into a relationship to the blue sky, the trees, the color of the river, and to one another. A dull dinner party among friends and neighbors. To early church. An unobstructed and splendid day. The S.s for drinks. I gave them "The Country Husband" to read. I can see where, in a social crisis, they might fail, and that this story may repel them. However, I love them. Late in the day, took a walk with the dog through the ruined garden. Found a dead cardinal bird on the stones under the big arbor. A few scrubby chrysanthemums growing among the stones, and the bird's bright blood color. The porous marble of the ornaments is still dark with last week's rain. Took a look in the greenhouse. The fig trees are loaded with fruit but some of the leaves are blighted. This, like the dead, brightly colored bird—a bird I always associate with love and cheer—seemed vaguely portentous—foolishly so—but a part of the clearness, the coldness, and the beauty of the afternoon. But everything, the lights burning in the big house, the fine gold of the trees, seems to affirm our natural good health. This is beautiful, then, I think, the branches of the sycamore alley gleam like picked bones. This is beautiful then, I think, but is my good cheer rigged on a rich man's park? There is unavoidable ugliness in the world—in its streets and faces—and would the text be the same if I were looking at a miserable tenement? I think it would be.

•

Anxious about being depressed on the way to Quincy and presently depressed. Down along the river here, and down along the Sound on the noon train, two Martinis and the charcoal-broiled, etc., and the interior dialogue with peculiar vehemence and in a space the size of a pinhead. Thinking of Coverly seeking for that precise moment where the visible and the invisible worlds bisect one another. Walked off the train at Back Bay, carrying my beaten suitcase. A lonely business, and I was deeply depressed by this time. How energetically the mind casts around for some escape from this conception of oneself as an ugly and useless obscenity; how stubbornly I refuse to pray. Walked across Copley Square; the sky was dark, my left foot hurt. Down Boylston Street past the stores that are all now cheap. Down to Washington Street—an eighteenth-century street, shining cheerfully with red neon light. Up a dark side street and then down around Scollay Square. Old and crooked places, melancholy lights, flophouses with armorial names, rat-toothed whores and old men. Up Joy Street and in a window I saw an old man and an old woman in a room lined with books. The room could never have had any sun, and it seemed to be where they ate, slept, etc. A depressing picture. Past chambers of old gentlemen and down Mount Vernon Street. Here are the traces of a city that, in the immediate past, had a well-regulated society, an opera season, débutante and fund-raising balls, shops, social contests, palaces, and dinner parties, but this core is broken and uninhabited now and the strength of the city has been drawn out into the suburbs, a kind of spawning ground that spreads out for thirty miles in every direction excepting due east, where the sea is. A provincial city. At nine o'clock the lights begin to go out. In a bar where I stopped for a drink, three soldiers picked up a whore, dated her, quarrelled among themselves about the bar check, and left the poor woman alone once more. People praising McCarthy in the bar. "Communists," they say, "Communists, the world is full of Communists." To the theatre, a provincial theatre. A play has stopped here on its way into New York. The old ticket-taker courteously asked me to put out my cigarette or suggested that I smoke it in the lobby; there was time. A hall of dusty mirrors, old red carpeting, much dark gilt, and everything supported by cupids in flight, by ropes of oak and laurel. They support the mirrors, they seem to hold the boxes in midair, even the balcony is suspended by this winged host of dingy gilt spirits. Pillars of chalcedony and an old curtain that sheds so much dust as it rises that it can be smelled. A bad play; applause. A pretty young woman with a date, taking off her coat and spreading it over the back of her seat, smiling up at the dark-gold host and the dim light that falls squarely into her face. How pure her pleasure is.

But that night, and I am reluctant to say so, there was no health in me, nothing better than patience. I see a world of monsters and beasts; my grasp on creative and wholesome things is gone. To justify this I think of the violence of the past: an ugly house and exacerbating loneliness. How far I have come, I think, but I do not seem to have come far at all. I am haunted by some morbid conception of beauty cum death for which I am prepared to destroy myself. And so I think that life is a contest, that the forces of good and evil are strenuous and apparent, and that while my self-doubt is profound, nearly absolute, the only thing I have to proceed on is an invisible thread. So I proceed on this. Quincy only deepens my depression. Why should I, a grown man, be thrown back so wildly into the unhappiness of the past? Where are those eruptive and clear springs of feeling that I claim to be able to count on? So back once more on the train, abjectly miserable. The sweet water of inlets, salt inlets and fresh brooks, coming down to the sea. An Italian family waiting on a platform for a passenger who does not seem to have arrived. Wild high-school children travelling between Providence and Mystic. Thick speech, animal noises. Seeing the lights of the city, my heart begins to rise. I seem to have over-scrutinized my dilemma. And as I am about to give it its seventy-first formulation (violence in my formative years cum uxoriousness cum anxiety) I stop. So this morning, zipping up my fly, I am cocky and happy. But I resent it that there should be parts of the world that have the power to do me so much harm.

•

To town with Susie for the annual Christmas journey. A very cold day, a pleasant girl of eleven with many damn-fool questions. The bows and rigging of ships, going upriver against the wind, white with ice. Many gulls, some ducks and geese. In the city a bitter cold and gale winds kept us from walking much. The tinkle of Salvation Army bells; the imitation leather of the Santas' boots, their ill-fitting beards. To St. Patrick's to see the windows; the smell of tallow and incense around the altar; my ideas on the papacy are only vaguely formed, but the cathedral does not seem to me a scene of depravity. To a bad Chinese restaurant for lunch, a place decorated with big stars made of mirrors and with red table tops scarred with cigarette burns. Spoiled meat. Then to Radio City Music Hall. I've written about this before and have nothing much to add. A cheerful folk rite without much depth of any kind. A medley of semiclassical music; some underplayed operatic selections; two first-rate acrobats and a patriotic finale—flags, and the whole cast singing "God Bless America." The movie drenched in tears, and performed by men and women whose eyes are as big as skating ponds. You could drive a jeep down the shadowy division of the ladies' breasts. Some clichés, but why put them down? My senses mightily offended by the bony charms of a dancer, her skinny legs, her tiny breasts, and her smile animated by the purest ambition. Rosemary Clooney—a young woman with an unusually deep front and a very heavy and unquiet mantle of yellow hair. Her features are far from fine. Her mouth is large and generous, so is her nose; her brow is wide. It is the kind of beauty that promises intractableness and deep and uncomplicated emotions, and that suggests a background—I don't mean any place—I mean that mystical power of suggesting a horizon that most beautiful women possess. As for the skinny dancer, what affected me most were her shoulder bones. How these women with their toothy smiles, their manes of artfully dyed hair, seem betrayed, as they turn away from the camera, by the thinness of their shoulders—the bones of a hungry child.

•

I dreamed that Mrs. V. was excited about a game that consisted of stringing puns together to make multisyllabic words and that I was at the big house and under some pressure to play it. The dream was discolored by spilled things—there was food on the pages of a book, and dirt on the floor. Her son sat on a terrace talking about the scandalous marital mix-ups of a Roman noblewoman. I dreamed that the ending of a play that opened last night was changed and that someone explained this to me in detail. I dreamed that I returned to Quincy and found my father there and thought how unhappy it would make my mother to have him return from the dead. He looked fine, but refused a drink. The kitchen where he stood was full of mice. I dreamed that in making love I was continually interrupted by doorbells and telephone bells. I dreamed that T. played the pun game expertly and that I excited Mrs. V.'s impatience.

•

The winter fires of New York burn everywhere like the ghats in Benares. On the valueless land north of the ship canal some children, dressed like aviators, are burning a Christmas tree. An ashcan is blazing on the banks of the river. Rubbish fires glow in the backyards of Harlem. Farther south, where a slum is being cleared, there is a large conflagration of old lathes. Another rubbish barrel and another Christmas tree are burning on Ninety-sixth Street. On the curb at Eighty-third Street an old wicker table is being consumed with fire. In a vacant lot in the fifties some children are burning a mattress. South of the United Nations there is a big fire of cardboard cartons behind a grocery store. Many fires burn in the gutters and backyards of the slums; there are bonfires of wooden crates in front of the fish market and on Battery Park, untended, an iron basket, full of waste, lights the gloom as all these other fires do on a winter dusk when the dark begins to fall before the lights go on. So think about "The Housebreaker." You're damned near broke once more.

To church this morning. I think I will be confirmed. The idea that I take this morning is that there is some love in our conception; that we were not made by a ruttish pair in a commercial hotel. I can reproach myself for being plainly neurotic and for dissembling my inadequacies with worship, but this leads me nowhere.

•

S. says, "I never have a drink before dinner, because if I did I'd be too sleepy to watch TV. Sometimes my hubby has a Martini and the funniest things happen. When he has a second Martini he always tells me that I speak beautiful French. We were in the same French class in high school, and I always got A's, and he never could understand French at all. He always remembers this when he has a second Martini. Then when he has a third Martini he begins to chase me around the house."

R. asks, "Does he often drink three Martinis?"

S. says, "Oh, goodness, no. Just on the Christmas holidays."

R. asks, "What does he do when he drinks three Martinis and you're not around?"

S. says, "Oh, I trust my hubby. Why, I'd trust him alone on a desert island with two hundred women. He's a one-woman man. His father was like that, too, and so were all his brothers. It runs in the family."

R. says, "Don't trust him with me."

•

There is a time to write and a time to walk and a time to reflect and a time to act and I come unwillingly to this journal today, wanting to do something less reflective and feeling that I sometimes strip myself of my most reasonable attributes, bent over this machine. However, any feeling of good health ought to be able to withstand a little looking into. Firstly Ash Wednesday on 125th Street. The spring sunlight spreads along the uptown streets. This is a poignant and unsettling light and Gawd, was I ever depressed. Then in the morning up into the mountains, taking a valley road up through the Berkshire hills and mountains; milk country, I guess. Thinking how unportentous is this journey to the north; how all your premonitions of death are no more than that, than premonitions; how all your journeys to Samarkand are for old ladies with empty heads. Patches of snow here and there; the hills like the winter coats of animals that we see; hock-deep in mud at the door to the barn; then the fume-colored mountains seem to strike us between the eyes and we raise our heads, our shoulders we brace. The air is finer to breathe and late in the day we follow a pass along the banks of a river which has written its black course crookedly in the ice. From farmhouses here and there we smell the wood burning in the cookstove.

In the villages we see old ladies, two by two, helping one another over the ice. The farm is lighted when we get there and as in all ski places the heat in the rooms is so intense that we sweat and feel short-winded. And then we ski and I like to ski.

•

You meet a classmate, someone like that, on the street, and accept an invitation to dinner. As soon as you step into the apartment you know that something is wrong. Your hostess has been crying and your old classmate seems to be drunk. It isn't that he staggers, but he seems to have hit the recognizable nastiness of some drunks. If you refuse the peanuts, he gets sardonic. Before you get to the dinner table he has begun to abuse, vilify, and ridicule his wife, and in the middle of the soup he tells you that she is a dirty slut. She seems to be a plain, sweet-tempered woman. She is crying and he is accusing her of all kinds of improbable filth when you get your hat and coat and leave in the middle of dinner. Ten or fifteen years pass and, leaving the theatre one evening, you are hailed by your old classmate again. He has the same wife with him and looking curiously into her face you see that she seems to be contented. Their apartment turns out to be near where you're living and you share a taxi and stop in for a drink. Everything is pleasant for ten minutes and then your old classmate asks his wife why she doesn't make some sandwiches; why doesn't she get off her fat arse and do something useful. She begins to weep and goes into the kitchen and when you get your hat and coat he begins to shout after her that she's a bitch, a dirty slut, a whore.

•

And what does it matter if, on our entering the poorly heated stone church on Sunday, the priest with his candles and bells reminds us of some rite or initiation in our childhood—some hayloft or woodshed ceremony when we were inducted into the mysterious order of the Green Hornet—what does it matter? What does it matter if our minds wander to subjects unsuitable for prayer, or if we study the burst cushions or sniff the perfume of the woman ahead of us or review our sex life or dream of hot coffee or say the responses in a voice louder than the voice of the man across the aisle, what does it matter?

•

Easter; the altar blazing with candles and white flowers; a baseball game in which, for some fishy reasons, I do not play; and yet baseball is like a sacrament and if you take one you should take the other. However, there is no sense in going into a tailspin over this. It is not that we pray for continence; it is that we seek it.

•

A dance in Hastings; cocktails, wisteria, etc. "I'm just going to introduce myself," a haggard woman with straw-colored hair said. "I'm here and I'm just going to introduce myself to everybody and enjoy myself. C. won't introduce me to anybody, but she's never neglected to ask me to these dances. I've never been able to get to one before, but she always writes and asks me. For three years she's been asking me to these dances. The children tell me the only reason she asks me is because she expects me to clean up the mess, but I'm not afraid of a little work and while I'm here I'm going to enjoy myself."

•

Jim Agee died yesterday in a taxicab. He was very generous to me and I think perhaps it would be hypocritical and dishonest of me to go to any services for him. We were not good friends. He had many gifts of friendship, much vitality. Our pace was different, but beyond that I don't know why we weren't sympathetic. Today is largely dappled— masses of darkness and brilliance, all of it moving. It is a landscape and a time of year when it is impossible to harbor any bad feelings.

I think, niggardly perhaps, that there may have been some imbalance between the relationship of Agee's work to the people who appreciated it and the relationship of this work to everybody else's work. I am sad to think that he is dead.

•

Thunderstorms in the night and at half past three a settled rain. At half past five, the gray skies dourly lighted and rabbits on the church lawn. Coffee with A. and then up to the West Branch, a nearly empty world. A heavy succulence in the woods after the smashing rains. Grass root and flower root and the leathery-smelling stream taking a sensual hold on the mind. The water smoking after the rain and turbulent, here and there. Humid and still in the pools. Water dropping off the pines. A trout rising in the deep pool under the maple. Below the surface of the brook a still world, Avernus, of round stones. All the dead men in Parson's pond and the slender margin between the dry world and the watery. The chill through my waders and hug of the water. Nereids I think of, and the hairy river gods. There is a mingling here, at day-break—the air heady with laurel and water on which the heart-shaped dogwood petals sail—of sweetness and lewdness, too. Maidens and satyrs both. At the crossing below Harcourts, the little bridge made of maple saplings is sprouting leaves. Against the bridge a thick cuff of white scum. At my back the brook speaks with the tongues of "Parthians, and Medes, and Elamites, and the dwellers in Mesopotamia, and in Judea, and Cappadocia, in Pontus, and Asia, Phrygia, and Pamphylia, in Egypt, and in the parts of Libya about Cyrene, and strangers of Rome, Jews and proselytes, Cretes and Arabians"; we do hear the brook speak in all these tongues. And thinking of fleshly things: of that which can illuminate and darken the conscience; of that which tempts us to peer under window shades and all other kinds of lewd follies; and that also which furnished us with tenderness and patience. This gentle larceny of feathers that we commit. Then the light of the sun fell into the valley; humid and golden. And then upstream the trout strikes with the noise of breaking dishes: a clatter, and we have him. The rod bends, and through the clear water we see him sound, this way and that, silver and rose, our sunken treasure.

•

Sitting in a chair on the stones before the house drinking Scotch and reading Aeschylus, I think then of how we are gifted. Of how we have requited our appetites, of how we have kept our skin clean and warm and satisfied our various appetites and lusts. I would not want anything finer than these dark trees and this golden light. I read Greek and I think that the advertising man across the street may do the same; that given some respite from war and need the mind, even the mind of the ad salesman, inclines to good things. Mary is upstairs and I will have my way here, very soon. This is the sharp thrill of our mortality, the link between the rain-wet stones and the hair that grows from our bodies. But it is while we kiss and whisper that the children climb onto a stool and eat some sugary sodium arsenite that is meant to kill ants.

There is no true connection between the love and the poison and yet they seem to be points on the same map.

The child is vomiting. Into town on a Sunday night to get an antidote. For this corner drugstore, a Sunday night is its finest hour. All its prosperous competitors have shut. It is the only lighted store on the street. The jumble of displays in the window—a picture of Pythagoras, Venus in a truss, douche bags and perfumes—is continued in the store itself. It is like a pharmaceutical curiosity shop, a fun house, a storeroom for cardboard women anointing themselves with suntan lotion, card-board forests advertising pine-scented soap, bookshelves and bins filled with card-table covers and plastic water pistols, and a little like a house-hold, too, for the druggist's wife is at the soda fountain, a neat, anxious-looking woman with photographs of her three sons in uniform arranged on the shelf at her back.

When we leave the drugstore it is a summer twilight and the street is nearly empty. Then down the street swagger the hoods, two by two, stinking of marijuana and baying like she-wolves at the new moon. They are strange to us, for how to fit them into the picture? Greece, and a poisoned child and the whispering in bed—they are strange and pred-atory and truly dangerous, car thieves and muggers—they seem to jeop-ardize all our cherished concepts, even our self-esteem, our property rights, our powers of love, our laws and pleasures. The only relationship we seem to have with them is scorn or bewilderment, but they belong somewhere on the dark prairies of a country that is in the throes of self-discovery.

Back through a summer night, noticing for the first time the smell of honeysuckle. The child is sick but we continue our whispering; put out the lights. Then I dreamed that I seduced L.E. and believe me it took some doing and I do not understand the capricious lewdness of the sleeping mind.

•

This house, charming and medicinal. The accrual of many summers. The kind of books that guests bring—orphans now. Glass saucers and clamshells, painted, on rainy days, with anchors and leaves. All the walls matchboard; some of it a silky yellow, or lighter, almost white, and in the western rooms where the storms blow and the roofs leak the wood is the dark color of tobacco. Creaking wicker chairs, in which to watch the sunset. The staircase, like a companionway, scarred at the turning by many heavy trunks; and the whole house like a frail sounding board, creaking in the night winds with a glassy sound—a sounding board for the rain.

•

Walked up the beach with Mary for a picnic. Gin in the thermos. Swam ballocksy. Tried to do the tender act but was gently dissuaded. Thinking of the vividness of need, of the sea, of fire, and of sexual desire. How readily, in a manly state, the beauty of the world appears to us. How blue and fine the sky, and how loud the thunder of the sea. Up to the sea pond to get many clams and scallops. Back here to make love at six and seven—the children downstairs playing chopsticks on the piano. The sun was low but not setting, and from the bed we could see, out the long narrow windows, the bay and the sandbar and the ocean beyond it and the nineteenth-century flavor that clings to this old coast, for the Coffins' dreams of Spanish esplanades and Japanese lanterns and band concerts are as much a part of the past as the whaling relics. And the joy of lying together in our skin under these pleasant lights. The children go out to play kick-the-can.

Later, to the inn for dinner. While we were drinking our coffee some college kids came in and ordered beer and began to dance to the recorded music. At the first notes of a German waltz, I grabbed Mary by the waist, and we began to dance. Then, one by one, the young kids left the floor and drifted off into the lobby. We were spoiling everything with our middle-aged ardor. When we gave up dancing and went back to our table I heard one of the kids in the lobby say, "It's all right now; they've quit." Then they all came back and danced. Walking out the front door of the inn, we saw some waiters playing tag with children. Back here to sit in chairs on the porch and admire the distant lights of Nantucket and the evening wind.

•

Slept all day after the departure of houseguests. Drove many children to Sankaty Head at dusk. The impact of a lighthouse, its circular staircase traced by narrow and staggered windows, the doors to the balcony open, and the beacon covered with a cloth; this machine that saves the lives of strangers far at sea, and one of the oldest things on the island. The light went on when we were there—or the lights—there are two, each of them masked on one face. From the Head the land drops eighty-five feet to the beach, and we can see down beyond the rain-dark tower of Chadwick's Folly toward Great Point. This high above the surf, we see it fan out like lace. The waves are colored with sea grass and seaweed. Then the children climb down the Head to the beach, getting smaller and smaller. They are very small when they get to the sand, where they collect seaweed and spell out their names. Susie Cheever, Nellie Thompson, Tommv Gleed Thompson, Nora Boynton, Benj C. Nellie does Ben's name for him, since he can't spell. Then suddenly they scramble up the escarpment—it is getting dark, and they don't want to be caught on the beach at dark—and one of the lighthouse keepers joins us and says that he has to keep an eye on the beach. People often write obscenities there with the seaweed. It is nearly dark then, and we can see how strong the beam of the light is. In Sconset we buy the children double-scoop coffee ice cream. Says Susie, "I hope ice cream is good for the complexion." Says Nellie, "Well, of course it isn't. I mean eating it isn't good for you; it gives you pimples. I get a little sore on the end of my tongue when I eat too much candy. Right on the tip of my tongue. I was watching television once and eating candy, and I ate practically a whole box and got this sore right on the tip of my tongue. I think Walt Disney's lost his touch."

•

Lunch with L., my melancholy friend. "I don't want to move to California until I'm sure that I've failed here," he says, but he's been here for twenty years and has not done much. I think he is what we mean by a melancholic—full of ambitions that he does not have the vitality to requite, a sensualist, but an inhibited one and a man who came to his wife with such a deep feeling of his own imperfections that he was uxorious and dependent. And here is a man without a defense against loneliness, without the vitality to seek friends or girls in a strange city; a man who, finding himself alone in Rome or Paris, would sit in his hotel room, writing letters to his wife and children. He must have been terribly lonely and so decided to surprise his family by returning home on Christmas Eve. His wife met him at the airport with the news that she had fallen in love with another man and had been living with

him for three months. She went on and on, and he said, O.K., he had
the basic facts, all she had to do was to leave him off at some hotel.

And then she says, "How could you be so inconsiderate? The tree
is lighted and we've bought presents for you, and Mummy and Daddy
and the children are waiting for you."

Then he says, "Look, you've just told me that my life with you and
the kids is just over. You've just told me that I'm through and out. Now
you want me to go back and play Santa Claus. I never liked your parents
anyhow."

Then she says, "Oh, I never knew you could be so cruel. It wasn't
my fault that I fell in love with Henry. I didn't have any choice in the
matter. You're behaving as if I did it deliberately. And how can I explain
the whole thing to Mummy and Daddy? They don't know. We've spent
all evening decorating the tree, just for you. They're all waiting; they
all have on their best clothes."

And so he, wanting to see the children, wanting to see his own four
walls, goes back. It seems to be his luck to find life a sad, sad tale. And
I wonder how he could do better. And like many melancholics his sexual
arrangements are extremely important and yet never very vivid. Speaking
of homosexuality in Europe, we both mantle and lower our eyes as if
we were virgins, as indeed we are; but I don't suppose it would do him
any good to spend a honeymoon in Verona with a Negro bootblack. I
wish he were happier and I don't see why he isn't.

•

Feeling very lousy with a sore tail, and off to Barnard saying I am
tired of this thread of love and whiskey, of courage and memory that is
the only thing to hold my world together; I am tired of threads and all
other frail things. And the lewd man, half asleep and weary of his
mind's sportiveness, thinks then of bridges and how bridges leap and
multiply in his head; suspension bridges in thunderstorms and marble
bridges in Venice; railroad bridges over the Susquehanna and the Del-
aware and wooden bridges over mountain streams, Seine bridges and
Loire bridges, Hudson River and Bay bridges, and that lewdness is the
energy, the touchstone, for all of this cannot matter.

Feeling sick and not knowing if I should go to the hospital. These
things are hard to decide. Using whiskey as a painkiller much of the

day. Happier elsewhere than here and yet not knowing where to go. Yaddo seems like such a position of retreat. The rubbish of pain, a sense of closeness, a small attic of the emotions, unlighted, unventilated, some closet perhaps in which as a child, playing hide-and-seek, one was locked. I am, I say, a lambent flame with piles. And then I think, In the morning it will be better, it is getting better. I should learn to be less intense, a message I seem to read while raking leaves. I rake them in a frenzy. So then we hear the wind change its quarter suddenly and flow freshly out of the west and we are delighted, because this reminds us of our own recuperative powers.

Our stores of humor and goodwill seem depleted by illness, and the misery we feel when we are separated from our amiability does not seem to do anything to restore it to us. And then, when we seem about to repose on the gravel bed, the mind springs up, strikes and rebels, and we see flags, red and gold, and other signs of cheerfulness and vitality. I can understand that I should be sick, but I cannot understand why this feebleness should spread into my emotional life—why a kid, slipping on a sky-blue sweater, should bear down Pine Street like the very angel of destruction, armed to the teeth; why I should have no taste for light, why should I be left with nothing but my misty ambitions for the good weal. But at least I have these; at least, at three in the morning, I can feel all warm and pleased with the thought of some clear relationship.

All day in bed; a beautiful day; but I won't take the beauty of the world as a reproach.

•

Sunday, an overcast day, snow in the dark clouds, it seemed, but the air warm. Played a little football, and how much I like to do this. Drank a beer and to bed early. Very jumpy on Monday morning; also a sore tail and dyspepsia. Took a pill, telling myself that my only trouble is intensity. Lunch with Mr. K. and H.T. Ready to jump out of my skin at any moment. The usual atmosphere of crucifixion in the classroom. Downtown in a bus. Now I am most miserable. Drank two Martinis in a dirty saloon. Then over to the Shaws'. A two-room suite, the roses three days old, two private telephone lines, three television executives. I admire and perhaps love Irwin but he is so rich and has dined so often with the Duke of Argyll and I am so poor that these

differences come between us. The TV executives tried to place me and
failed. I may have behaved drunkenly or clumsily, but I will not reproach
myself. I read the Sunday paper while Irwin talked large sums of money
with Hollywood. And I remember a character in one of his novels—an
expatriate musician—whose struggle with art ended in suicide and I
think that perhaps Irwin judges my own struggle with pity and con-
descension. Then I leave, perhaps drunk, and oh Lord I am miserable.
But where will I turn? My only friends in the city seem to be very
gloomy people and I don't want them to dress my wounds. And I do not
want to chafe my wife's ears with my long tale of bitterness and woe.
And I am so sensitive that I seem to be insane; even the stars in heaven
discountenance me. And I think, tearfully, of my lonely life. Alas, alas.
Even the voice of the conductor, calling out the place names, seems to
heap scorn on my wretchedness. And then I wake in despair at 3 A.M.
and try to think of good things—sailing and skiing and the high spirits
of children—I fail.

•

In town and theatre with the B.s, me high-spirited after, Mary
squinchy, as she is so often on these trips; and I think that while a
marriage is like a boat there is a point where we can dive from the bow.
And then the city seems beautiful, hustling, full of purpose and life
and vitality, and I would like only to be happy and enjoy myself. We
meet the B.s at one of the inner parlors of the Harvard Club and Mary,
or so I think, is at once animated and flirtatious. Now I may be insane,
neurotic, queer, impotent, and worthless, and I may imagine all of this,
but my pleasant evening begins to come to pieces. It is not significant,
I think, but on the way to the checkroom I am accosted by old Walker
Evans, whose face looks very puffy. Mary chats gaily with B. and I am
consumed with jealousy and hopelessness. She turns to me once during
the intermission to express a flat contradiction and whether or not this
is imaginary I feel disembowelled. After this there is no civility left in
me; my toys have been broken. Coming home I throw a beer bottle
against the wall of the garage. I will curl up on the sofa and weep bitter
tears; and then it seems that I have wept too many tears, gin tears,
whiskey tears, tears of plain salt, but too many; I have walked around
these paths too often, hump-shouldered, trying to spin a happy ending
for this capriciousness. And now today I have no will, no guts, no

stomach for inventing hopes. I dream of some gentle wife and lover, blond or dark-haired, who has some clearness in her disposition. And how will I ever find her, bent over this typewriter in a room with a shut door? I should go away and yet I postpone my goings away interminably. I could take a plane to France; all I lack is guts. I may be completely mistaken in all my feelings; but they are mine at the moment.

•

So I wonder if it is my legitimate business to probe into these matters—if perhaps I don't make trouble by holding every word, every change rung in the emotional climate, up to the light and examining it carefully. That if I were an account executive or had the charge of a television program, left here in the dark of morning and returned in the dark of night, things might go along a little easier. I dream of Mary, I seem to pursue her through the many courtyards of what are called garden apartments, but she escapes me, she closes the door in my face. And then I see a reconciliation, a regular valentine in which she lies on a bed of those light-pink roses. Very libidinous. And it seems to me that I try to repair a web that is everywhere broken; that with every reparation I find that a new part has been broken or kicked loose. I think perhaps that Mary is in love with X or Y or Z but I will never be told and I will never know, although it's a subject that I can't think about without getting weak in the belly. I bring in my jokes, my presents, my scraps of news, and all I harvest are sidelong glances and bitter contradictions and I take long, sad walks. And I wonder sometimes if I am not face-to-face with a destructive force; something with which I am unable to cope. If there was a quarrel a sad tale might be told me; I have been impossible, ill, nagging, mean, and cruel, but there are limits to my self-reproach and I don't have the stomach for a Donnybrook. I do not want to spend my Christmas alone in a rotten hotel nor with gentle friends (my God). I would like to smell the green tree and give my children their presents and go to church and carve my turkey and sit on the sofa drinking whiskey and brooding on the richness of life; but I do not know what to expect. It could be a season of the most exacerbating distempers, tears, slammed doors, hysteria and dark looks and silences lasting for a week. Today I wake up in the morning feeling lewd and high-spirited, but my only harvest is haggard looks and bitter contradictions. I can blame myself. This seems to be the only direction in which hope lies; and I trust that everything will work out; work itself out. My jealousy is a laughable aberration. Who cares, who cares?

•

For Coverly she was his notchke, his hunchke, his everything that the dry vocabulary of St. Botolphs gave him no help in expressing—she was his mouse and his turtledove, and how gently and like a turtledove she seemed to flutter and tremble when he mounted her, but more than this she was the key to that simple, or perhaps crude, poetry that made up the bulk of his life, such as the sound of changing winds, and snow in the embers of the hearth, and the bloom of winter afterglows, and stealing roses past midnight in the rain, so that her distempers, whether or not he was to blame for them, took from him nearly everything that seemed alive.

•

A fine winter day, and I think I make some progress with Coverly. That point where men extricate themselves from what is in theory a hopeless situation; that moment where, in theory, all should be silence, a healthy and impertinent question is asked. Banked the roses with dead leaves. A little dry snow blew crosswise on the north wind although there was much blue sky. How fine it feels. The sun going down takes many forms; gold, brass cauldrons, streaks of lemon yellow and then, unexpectedly, a field of rose. I drive Susie into town and think what a joy my life is, for I feel healthy, passionate, and useful and all in all the pitfalls of my life are not as hazardous and deep as I make them out to be. It seems that we must do some penance for our sins and the sins of our fathers. And so we do our penance and it is done. And so we watch the winter twilight and drink too much gin and help the children address their Christmas cards. And go to a party for the choir with the S.s, A. angry at the poor director with his haunted eyes and his thin lips and his ailing wife and his sweet daughter. You could pick him up with one hand and if you shook him he would rattle.

And so we wake at dawn on Monday morning (up on the hill there is one other light burning in someone else's bathroom) and shaving we seem to be overtaken by a subtle and pervasive grief. We have most of what we want and need and yet our feelings are saturated with this disenchantment, like a filament filled with light. It is perhaps no more than that we glimpse the possibility of failure or that we drank too much on Saturday night. What we seem to see is our incurable tenderness. But on Tuesday morning we seem to have woken from a splendid dream of the Mediterranean and some of its civilizations and we are bushy-tailed and full of high hopes.

•

Drank a good deal of whiskey, trying to relax so that I could read the Wapshots. I don't know what to make of it. The whole picture of Leander has got to be refreshed. I can't say that I know what the novel is about. I don't know the moral within Leander's tragedy. He breaks with tradition or is made to break with it and suffers. He is growing old, and suffers. But he is like a figure in a minor poem. Colorful, erratic, and not filled out. But the tragedy of Clarissa ties up with the tragedy of the Topaze. It is the time after this that I don't understand. He is nothing but an old man waiting for a grandson, and that is not enough. And I have to do much work on Sarah and insert Lulu. One of the things I have to worry about most is haste: haste and money. And I want it to have some moral value. Since it is not Leander's fault that the Topaze is wrecked, how can he redeem himself? It is the complexity of life that wrecks the ship and I would like to show his triumph over this complexity. And I don't, so far.

•

Pain in the chest. Rowed with Mary about lingering glances; very depressed; practically insane. A call from Quincy to say that Mother is very sick. Emotional hurly-burly; some tears. Got a room on the Owl for Boston. The atmosphere of all such places seems to me to be the atmosphere of erotic misdemeanor. This may be a subjective projection. Rainy dawn in Boston; rainy Sunday morning. The unregenerate slums of Boston on a dark day. How lasting they seem; unassailable. Found mother very withered now, weary (she says of life). Her wits and her hearing are sharp. "I shout at Mrs. Bacon and she doesn't mind. Other people don't like to have me shout at them. She was talking on the telephone—she was telling someone about her cardiograms. I shouted at her, 'Nobody wants to hear about your cardiograms.' She didn't seem to mind." Old and feeble and alone and helpless as she is, I still seem to lay at her feet the sense of a tragic misunderstanding. "He's a *regular* boy," she says of someone and I still flinch. Home on the 1:00 and up the banks of the Hudson after dark to this warm and comfortable house. I have my troubles, but they do not seem to be insupportable. I would not like to be the kind of writer through whose work one sees the leakage of some noisome semisecret.

•

Mother died on the 22nd, and I do not note this any more than I note the walls of the chalice full of wine. The A.s' antic house. This strong emotion as we follow a path to the grave. Norwell covered with old snow.

•

The train yards at Harmon on an overcast day. I wonder, Has my life become so ingrown that I cannot travel—but I can. A reproduction of a Cézanne on the train coach. A couple returning from a visit to New York: "On Wednesday afternoon we saw 'Bus Stop.' On Thursday morning we went to Radio City. Then we had lunch on the top of the Empire State Building. Thursday night we saw 'Tiger at the Gates.' We saw CinemaScope Friday afternoon," etc. Farther north, snow on the ground. It lies sparsely and like powdered sugar on a winter-killed landscape, bitter as gall—and I think I do not want to make such notes, to write for the sake of writing. I want to celebrate, praise the Lord, discover and restate man's freedom, although my vision is far from clear. I think of love's two aspects: all that is gold and splendid, even the dust under the bed, and that other creation of soiled underwear and sidelong glances; both being a part of my nature. Met by a gentlewoman and an old friend, and off to the baths. White matchboard cubicles, a stained tub. Reading the *Herald Tribune* in a hot room. An old man with a towel around his middle massages my bum with sandsoap. The last days of Rome. But what, then, is this body that can be enflamed with fruitless desire when a stranger rubs witch hazel between my toes? The most I can do is to make a joke, and not a sad joke. Whiskey and talk and, later, thunder, lightning, the end of the skiing here. When I was younger I was delighted to lie on this bed, dreaming of what I would have—a good wife and lively children but now the mind seems stained with desire, and I travel through some erotic purgatory wondering, Is this a lack of character, of will, a misunderstanding of the meaning of discipline, infantilism, sickness? These are no more than the trials of a lewd and a gentle nature. There are worse. Oh, how I long for what I have known; that healthy sense of self—aging, composed, industrious and unbeautiful. Where are my dear children? Where is Marcie?

•

On our knees in church (even in the cathedral) we are face-to-face with the bare facts of our humanity. We praise Him, we bless Him, we adore Him, we glorify Him, and we wonder who is that baritone across the aisle and that pretty woman on our right who smells of apple blossoms. Our bowels stir and our cod itches and we amend our prayers for the spiritual life with the hope that it will not be too spiritual. The door at our back creaks open and we wonder, Who has just come in? Arthur? Charlie? Henry Penrose? Who is the boy in the plaid shirt? When was he confirmed? Why is the lady in the first pew crying? And even as the service rises to the great poetry of Bread and Wine we continue our observations. We see that the acolytes' red plush cushion is nailed to the oak floor of the chancel and that the altar cloth is embroidered with tulips. And then for a moment a knowledge of His magnificence and man's giftedness draws together, in at least a promise of ecstasy, all these bare and disparate facts.

•

Up to the West Branch with A.S. Very cold, the ground frozen. Some ice in the brook. The saplings very red, like a cardinal's wing, but not much cheer or color. No fish, not even a strike. But the pleasure of wading this stream, although I dream of a stream with more fish in it. And the great pleasure I take in A.'s company. I have always felt that this would someday be revealed to me as a union of mysteriously broken hearts, like so many of my friendships, but there has never been a grain of evidence. It is as light, as solid, and pleasant and clear as any friendship I have ever known. And for all my wool-gathering and troublemaking I cannot find a hint of darkness or sordidness in it.

•

Thinking, while fishing, and remembering the night, that love produces its own restraints and governments and that a man whose passions are powerful and requited is usually clean-mouthed. And it may be only the emotionally frigid who can be called lecherous. Whatever we may intend, the act of love is not friendly. We may laugh and joke and talk familiarly about what is going on, but before we are done we will have a blinding vision. Today, a good one, when I feel my age, my gifts and limitations. I feel contented and strong.

•

Scarborough–Portsmouth–Friendship. The preposterousness of the congratulatory letters I write myself. Feeling sleepy, dreary maybe; going into a liquor store for a pint of whiskey for the trip, I meet the image that represents the point of breakdown. A greasy, amorous, or so I think, clerk. The proneness to see the morbid potential in every situation. The bridge will plunge its passengers into the river and the youth under the street lamp will murder me.

The limited point of view of a driver who seems to mine, not swoop, through the parkways at seventy m.p.h., unable to see the country, garlanded and spread with such an open hand, and sees only that they have passed through the country of red clay into the country of black dirt, counts the bridges and smells the sea.

Proceeding two by two through what seems to be a run-down or even whory neighborhood—Mother, Father, Son, Daughter, and a brace of expensive dogs, we seem preposterous.

The evening light on this coast is the most beautiful that I have ever seen. The light is raked as it is in the mountains, and twilight is like the exciting gloom before a thunderstorm. The greens are bright and deep—we say "an unearthly light," meaning, I guess, a light that isn't solar. This crumbling and lovely coast.

•

I continue to write myself congratulatory letters, choose the Wapshots for a book-club selection, beam and bow as I accept prizes, ribbons, and awards of all kinds, and refuse to contemplate any weaknesses that I know the book to have, such as Leander's financial arrangement with Honora.

•

And coming here this morning, out of idleness and habit, I am face-to-face with the fact that this is, at times, a kind of retirement from the excellence of life. Any search for truth or beauty is perilous and this is a common peril. There is a world of difference between taking out a sailboat and filling in the pages of a journal and I would like to bring these worlds together. Wisdom we know is the knowledge of good and evil—not the strength to choose between the two—and sometimes it seems that we inadvertently do as much to corrupt our readers as to cheer them. Writing is allied with many splendid things—faith, inquisitiveness, and ecstasy—and with many bad things—diddling, drawing dirty pictures on the walls of public toilets, retiring from the ballgame to pick your nose in solitude. But it is, like most gifts, a paradox, and I will play my cards close to my vest and trust in the Lord.

Took a secret slug of whiskey at eleven on Independence Day. Two straightforward Martinis at noon. Took Mary out to Sand Island in the outboard. Drank gin-and-tonic, ate crabmeat sandwiches, made love in a cove above the sea, the grass very scratchy and me not wanting to be implicated in pagan matters and thinking that these are our gifts as surely as the gifts of piety. We struck a bargain. I could have my way if I would take her around Long Island, everything lying in this thunderstorm light, the island fields a blazing green, etc. Found our way through Friendship Gut and delighted to see the village unfold on the hills as we came through the rocks. Drank Martinis on the grass and very much at peace with the world. Birds singing, the raked sunlight, the noble clouds in the sky.

•

Brilliant, overcast weather, not warm, the light past the low clouds gleaming like a sword, steel, unkind, anyhow. Studied Italian, thinking now and then of that country as the seat of moral depravity. *Che cose desidera?* Ah ha. Took Ben for a ride after supper, but he didn't want to go. He didn't want to run the boat. He only wanted to play with his friends. Ate too much dinner, perhaps, and had a tic or quaver in my gut which I basted with whiskey. Drove Susie to church and so didn't go myself. A gray sky, the air fresh, cold, and salt-smelling. Standing on the porch I pray to understand the transports and infirmities of my flesh; not to be spared the pain of sickness and hurt but to understand it; and to be spared the pain of what I think of as moral uncleanliness. And if my prayers mean so much, I think, Why don't I go to the Methodist church? I do not and wonder if I am irresolute. I think of those whose lives are a compromise with their burden of wild dreams, lewd fancies and discontents; of D., his eyes bugged out as if he sat on a tent peg and with his uncommonly stupid and pretentious wife; and I think of A., who has followed his capricious cod over hill and dale and looks, as a result, very weathered and sometimes silly. D. might be admirable. The whole thing breaks down to the fact that I don't have enough substance myself, much of the time, to make collected judgments.

•

The city seems strange or unattractive and I am depressed. It is quite possible that my equilibrium is such a touchy piece of machinery that I only waste time in trying to control it. But this slip of a youth, I wonder, carrying groceries across Park Avenue, is he taking them home to his wife or is he an international whore. In short, I do not have that which I so often have—a strength of heart and bowel, a pleasant sense of self-esteem which is the point of view from which I certainly reach the most practical, happy, and charitable judgments on strangers. I go to see "Moby Dick," which has some wonderful stuff in it and many clichés. Dissolve from a dramatic scene to waves breaking over the bow. I think of poor Jim Agee, who would have done better. I eat a sandwich at Reuben's and think I see an old schoolmate in the next booth. A party of middle-aged couples comes in—all of them sun-black—all of the ladies wearing jewels and furs, their hair and their dresses cut with much thought, but there seems to be some discrepancy between this outlay and their appeal, at least to my senses. I may be depressed. In front of the hotel I see a slender woman with bare shoulders and bare heels, but she does not please me. I think she is not as pretty as the girl in the Waldeboro laundromat. I go to bed with a bottle of beer, but I cannot sleep and I don't know why. I cannot blame it all on Mrs. Loins' spectres and so I make a tedious review of my sexual autobiography. It all adds up to the fact that I have received most generously a force of life that gives proportion to all this trivia. I read the abridgment of a bad novel and turn on the TV at 2 A.M. and am bid good night by a minister. I read the abridgment of another bad novel—my bones, my eyes, and my head are tired and I cannot sleep. I read the abridgment of another novel and go to sleep. It must be four o'clock. In the morning the air is stale. I say my prayers at St. Thomas, eat breakfast at Longchamps, and come back here.

•

Since I seem to weigh, on the streets, step by step, minute by minute, some idea of beauty, I might try to state or restate this here. By beauty I never mean anything that is not close to sensual. In these beauties, I recognize clearly forces that appear triumphant and forces that seem destructive. The sea is fair and blue but if my boat should capsize I will drown. The stranger's cheek is fair and round, but if I caress it I will end up in the police station. But these anxieties seem to stand in a realm where the light is dim; they do not seem to rise from our deepest nature. On the other hand, the sea is fair and blue and a pleasure to sail upon and my love's cheek is round and soft, and if I caress it I will be rewarded with inestimable riches. It is this contest that I do not understand; that conflicts with an instinctive feeling that life flows or should flow like the waters in a stream.

•

O fall. This summer's places—Friendship, where the bedsheets smelled of kerosene; the Hotel Madison, the lovely house at Tree Tops, the Hotel Dauphin; I am most comfortable here, feel most productive, most enjoy waking at night and hearing the wind change its quarter and seeing the dark sky through a hole in the trees. And going into town yesterday, the fishermen along the banks of the river. Their seasonal appearance. In the early spring, the early birds with scarves and hats and then as the summer comes on they seem to bloom; they are joined by their girls, their wives and children; they undress, they drink beer, they spread out on the banks of the river like the flowers in an unweeded garden and they scatter, all but the most hardy, when the first cold winds begin to blow. And then the last of them—hats, scarves, their noses cherry-red. And also the relationship between these fishermen and swimmers, the overdressed and the undressed, the sober and the beer drinkers.

•

Up to Saratoga. Very hot here. Smell of burning rubber in the valley. Some French Canadians on the train. A not young woman with brilliants in her hair. I smoke in the toilet and look out at the Hudson River, which seems broad, handsome, and sad, and with the leaves falling I think that I will not see my country for another year. I buy some coffee and drink whiskey out of the empty paper cup. I go up to the diner and lunch with a pleasant Swiss who is travelling in this country for the first time. Outside the window we see hardscrabble fields, abandoned garages, a gas station, its unused tanks wrapped in burlap. I point out to him the monumental ruin of an old mill along the banks of the river, but he seems perplexed; unimpressed. I go from the station to the spa and take a Turkish bath, which seems a good idea since my anxieties about the masseur seem unfounded and in general if you pursue these things the truth turns out to be cheering. As I waited on the porch for a taxi, a thunderstorm broke. The smell of rain as it is blown in on a porch where you sit. I am taken by P. through the house, which looks very pleasant to me, to a large room with a view of the lawn, fountain, and Vermont mountains. I wander around in fact, memory, and purpose. It is not in me to settle down in a businesslike way with some galleys. I talk with Harvey Swados and leaving the house run into Saul B. I drink cocktails at E.'s with Dick Eberhart, whose plain, healthy, and unshadowed mind amazes me, and with M., who is a first-class gossip. At dinner I am conscious of being in the same room with Saul. We speak after dinner and I am delighted by his presence. He is about my size, I guess, his hair quite gray, and I think I feel here that sometime tragic fineness of skin, that tragic vitality. His nose is a little long, his eyes have (I think) the cheerful glint of lewdness, and I notice his hands and that his voice is light. It has no deep notes. So we take a walk and I have nothing to say but I remember my other passionate friendships on this road—R. and F.—but I have no way of judging my feelings. I cast around for some precedent of two writers with similar aims who are strongly drawn to one another. I do not have it in me to wish him bad luck: I do not have it in me to be his acolyte. Today all this seems foolish.

•

I go to town; I go to the Italian Consulate and wait and wait. It is my first brush with this classical red tape. The vestibule is full of people waiting for some scrap or particle of their identity to be certified or returned to them. We are all loaded down with photographs of ourselves and we wait and wait. The bureaucrat has patent-leather hair, patent-leather shoes, and a suit as black as death's advocate's. It is his pleasure to keep us waiting. We—this cheerful generation—notice the variety and the patience in the faces.

I walk and walk. I say a prayer on Fifty-third Street. I have lunch and see the ballgame. I come home on the train, drink some gin, and study Italian. I wake at three in the morning, paralyzed at the thought of what I have left undone, such as my teeth. And then I think I see clearly that passage in human relationships where the line between creativity and light, and darkness and disaster, is a hair. And I think this is an inherited burden, one that Mother carried much, and that, as in everything else, light will triumph. But I think I see the seductive face of wisdom, articulateness, and poetry; that it can be cultivated and made to bloom like a perverse lure, a chain of false and gentle promises, an artificial land of milk and honey. So I say there is a worm in the rose, but it is not fatal. But I would like to be spared this vision of disaster and pray for this, or for a fuller and more relaxed understanding of the fact that the force of life is contested.

•

Observe then this man, woken by his bladder at 3 A.M., and who, returning to bed, finds himself wakeful; more so, much more so than he will be at seven, when the alarm rings. There seems to be some excitement in the darkness. There is a little sweat in his armpits. Something is happening, he thinks, and he thinks he hears a footstep in the gravel outside. It is the footstep of a dope addict, armed with an icepick, who has come to murder his children, but listening for the opening of the front door and the footstep on the stairs and hearing nothing his mind wanders to a voyage he is about to take. The ship sinks and he is in a lifeboat with his wife and children—one of a convoy led by a navigator—but the wind and the tides separate them from the convoy and he realizes that he knows so little about navigation that even if he were only five miles from the Azores he would not be able to sail his beloved family to safety. He rolls onto his back and at this point his male member, bristling with usefulness and self-importance, takes the center of the stage, but since the night offers no promise of requition this seems a foolish performance. Then thoughts of such lewdness cross his mind that he rolls onto his side and sends up toward Heaven an earnest prayer for some better understanding of cleanliness. He is back in the lifeboat once more. Now he lies on his stomach and prays once more, this time for the simple gift of sleep, and he seems to be enfolded, but enfolded in the wings of some rented angel's costume with an unclean smell. He rolls onto his back and suddenly it is Christmas. It is Christmas Eve and he is a boy again, beloved, naked and cuddly in the clean sheets. Up goes his cod again, followed by his prayers, and so forth and so forth, ad nauseam.

•

On my first night in Rome I walk to the Spanish steps. I am a little disappointed. But I find the people very handsome and not covert as is the case at home. The girls lovely and the men good-looking, gallant When I see an American he does not seem as well integrated or as well dressed. We are not a nation of voyeurs but we seem introspective. I have not been happy here, and waking at three in the morning I worry about everything. But there is no point in writing a story about poor Bierstubbe, the TV writer who came to Rome to write a great play about sex; who was shortchanged everywhere, whose money flowed like water, who was depressed by the dash of the Roman men and reminded of his own contested sexual identity, who wondered why he had ever left his cozy home, who drank gin before lunch, etc. So I will not write any such story.

•

Poor Bierstubbe, very homesick, watching people on the Via Veneto boarding the airplane bus for the U.S.A. Never in his life, not even as an infantry private under a sergeant who was court-martialled for cruelty and drunkenness, had Bierstubbe been so homesick. And, having dreamed half his life of sailing away, he dreamed away his days and nights of sailing home.

The hassle with the real-estate agents which seems to come to nothing, although there was no legal or emotional difficulty that I did not imagine. Leaving the Palazzo Doria at five or six—the tumult of a great city at nightfall—much worried and sorely wanting a drink.

•

It is four o'clock and I am in Rome and want a drink. Out of my window I see an orange house which is being turned into apartments and a man walking out of an alleyway in little steps as he buttons up his fly. Mary and Susie have gone out to meet Ben, home from his first day in school. I went to the American Express this morning and found my money waiting. I had been sure that this would not happen. Then I went to the Società Romana di Elettricità with La Signora Muni, where I saw some people of considerable beauty. Through my head run such scraps as this: my life is in the nature of a bargain and a very fair one; I believe in the miraculousness of life but my belief has never been so strained; this painful sense of not having a well-integrated body or mind is all the fault of my poor dead mother, whose life was so ridden with anxiety; look at the pretty girl; pray; of the two— the duchess in a mink coat and the wide-eyed child with a little hump to her shoulders—I prefer the child; perhaps this journey from one country to another puts too searching a light on the jerry-built structure of my life; a searching light is being brought to bear; people speak of Rome as we used to speak of Scout camp—you will hate it for two weeks and then you will not want to leave. So the intelligent thing is to ride out these storms of strangeness and see where you are in two weeks or a month. And so we leave the Società Romana di Elettricità.

•

After lunch I walk in the streets and observe how the facial traits of the people differ from the massive and weary countenances of the emperors and their wives. It may be no accident that much of the Roman portrait statuary we see in America reminds us of Americans. I don't know. And the ease and grace with which they embrace one another, call after the pretty girls, kiss in doorways or sit on the wall up by the Gianicolo with a girl held cozily between their legs is very different from our idea of things. This is not a difference of language, race, climate, or custom; it is a vastly different approach to the wellsprings of humanity.

•

This is the kitchen of the Palazzo Doria, where I hope we will pass an affectionate and a useful year. The gas stove leaks. The drains are clogged. It is a dark day in Rome with a heavy rain. This is not classical weather. Ben and Mary are both coughing. Susie went off to school in tears. This is the first time in nearly a month that I have sat down and tried to make sense, and now my thoughts, gathered at rainy street crossings and high windows, in damp churches and strange beds at 3 A.M., and gathered often about the full limbs of comely strangers, seem about to leave me.

First there was the voyage, and this was ruled by my fear that the ship would sink. I don't think a day passed without my being made uncomfortable by this foolishness. And when I woke, at 3 A.M., to the noise of smashing flower vases and medicine bottles, my parts would shrink and my heart would flutter like a lark. This is a deck, I would tell myself, walking back and forth; these are stanchions, these are lifeboats and that is an empty swimming pool, and these momentary things are the usable truths, but then seeing darkness off the bow, and in the west a prophetic and baneful light, and noticing that the speed of the ship had slacked off until she hardly seemed to move, I would feel sure that we were done for. Off the starboard bow I saw the snow-covered mountains of Corsica and thought that this would be a dangerous coast to land our boats on.

•

As for ruins, the American printing salesman who has flown in for an eight hour conference says, in the bar of his run-down hotel, "Jesus, you can see where we all come from: I mean the sense of the past is so *terrific*." But it is not always easy to come by. The guidebooks, the guides, our friends and acquaintances, and even strangers urge us to succumb to the sense of the past, but what about the present? Standing in the Pantheon I am impressed with the dome, but the children are pulling at my coat and asking me to buy them pastry or take home one of the splendid cats loafing under the portico. Going to meet E. at the Baths of Caracalla in a rainy dusk, I look in briefly at the colossal heaps of brick and then watch some kids practicing soccer shots on a little field. I am much more interested in thém. Ben and I walk by the Forum, which, with the green grass still growing among the stones, seems to be a double ruin: a ruin of antiquity and a monument to the tender sentiments of eighteenth- and nineteenth-century travellers, for we see not only the ghosts of Romans here but the shades of ladies with parasols and men with beards and little children rolling hoops. In the Colosseum I tell Ben that Christians were devoured by lions, although I think this is untrue. I am impressed with the massive outer archways—and yet I am not taken as directly by a sense of the past as I was in a Portsmouth countinghouse. We strive to feel the presence of Romans and then we pet a stray cat.

Homesickness here is not a string of specific images, evoking the pathos and sweetness of American life; it is mostly purse sickness, war sickness, the unease of not understanding the simplest remarks that are made and the chagrin of being swindled. I don't long for the rivers or for the place-names or the mill-town parks. Not honestly.

"This is your past," we say to the Romans and the Americans from small towns. I have a past—houses and people and traits and an old name. The Mediterranean is not a part of it. And yet I have dreamed of the Mediterranean for ten years; it is in some way a part of our dreams.

The rain lets up at noon and either the moods of this city or my own are mercurial. The sun bursts into the streets. Life is exciting and beautiful, and the sound of so many fountains is relaxing. I look with scorn at the Americans in the Piazza di Spagna, ripping open their letters from home and stopping in the middle of the sidewalk to read the news from Pelham, but receiving a letter myself I do the same. Smiling and chuckling, I walk down the street bumping into Romans, with a scrap of paper that seems to refresh my identity.

Mary and I lunch at a trattoria near the Pantheon. The fountain sparkles in the sun. We walk under the great porch and through the giant doors. It is impossible to mark the proprietorship of pagan and Christian, but the dome with its circle of blue seems triumphantly clear and free. As Americans we observe the ruined paint and the filth. The candlesticks and tombs of the Lombards are black with dirt. Even the wax of the candles is dark and the flowers on Raphael's tomb are straw.

Some other Americans come in. They are followed by a guide. "I just want to look at the place; I don't want to hear about it," one lady

says to the guide. "And anyhow I can't understand what you're saying."
Back here I snooze on the sofa, then go to meet Susie, climbing up the
Campidoglio. Flooded with light it seems very rich, but the heads of
the Dioscuri seem large and only intensify my affection for Marcus
Aurelius and his shadow of gold. I walk up through the gardens, thinking
that I will push a baby carriage here in the spring. The wind is northerly
and the sky is full of that moving darkness and brilliance that we see
through the fine dark leaves of many painted trees in many landscapes
in many museums. Susie buys a doughnut in a *pasticceria* and we meet
Ben. There is a gas strike. Dinner is delayed and I fill up with gin.
Susie tells me that a boarder at school has stolen a pot of jam and the
mother superior has put the school into Coventry. Prayers are said each
morning for the thief. If this were at home we would rebel. We have
a fine dinner, but after dinner I find Susie in bed, crying bitterly and
asking to be taken home. This for Bierstubbe when I get around to him:
the crying of his children.

•

We go to the Museo del Palazzo di Venezia. So cold it would chill
your marrow. Shabby and unclean and the paintings so ill lit that half
of them can't be seen. The glare of light on the varnish is so harsh that
we can't make out what is going on. A painted ceiling where much is
going on. Sea monsters abducting naked women. A roomful of bronzes,
copies of which I think I've seen. Some lewd, some satyrs, a firm figure
of a man. An armory and much early painting but not easy to see or
admire. The gold gleams, but the faces seem dim and strange. It is, I
think, this jumble of arsehole jokes and golden piety that I admire; it
adds up to an honest measure of our nature. In one of the rooms we
find all the guards smoking cigarettes and shooting live-lire coins down
a long table.

We sit in the sun and climb to the Campidoglio. It is autumn, but
it is best for me not to say, "It Is Autumn In Rome" but just "it is
autumn." The grass on the slope is that crabgrass which takes hold at
the end of summer. A few marigolds bloom in the plots. Tourists are
as scarce as flowers and a guide trails us around the statue of Marcus
Aurelius, complaining about the autumn and the bad business. A crowd
of Americans comes up from the Forum but they do not say a word.
The only sound is the whirr of moving-picture cameras and the click

of shutters. Going down the Campidoglio we pass a party of Germans. The yellow snapdragons that grow out of the cornice of the Church of Jesus, the tufts of grass and mullein that grow, like hair from a man's nostril, from every orifice in Aurelian's wall, the bluets that grow in the chinks of the Porta Pinciana, and the thick stand of grass around the bell tower of Santa Maria have all begun to fade.

•

What I am determined to get away from are set pieces, closed things, shut paragraphs.

The doorways of Europe, varnished and polished and waxed, even if the houses they secure are crumbling, in this vast city that is painted the color of spoiled lemons. The high doorways of Portugal with their stained-glass transoms built to accommodate a thin and a melancholy man on stilts. And the *portoni* here, built to withstand armed men on horseback and battering rams. You turn the key in the lock and the cumbersome door swings open. This is your place. You, among the many people on the street, have the key. When you close the door behind you it is dark and cold and the noise of the fountain sounds very loud. You unlock the elevator gate, part the frosted-glass doors . . .

•

I take the children riding in the Borghese Gardens. The old baron trots along beside the moth-eaten pony that Ben rides. Susie rides with an instructor. A man rides a white horse strenuously, bringing it again and again to a jump where it balks. "*Che brutto,*" say the grooms. When he is finished the horse is in a lather and the rider, when he dismounts, is breathing heavily and seems drawn and tired. He is a small man. I wait and watch the children and for a moment—not much longer—the place, the gardens seem to enter my head and I think, I hope, of possessing an earlier and happier view of Rome. I wonder what it is that I lack. I wonder if I have ever seen any place without the excitement of falling in love; at least of making friends. I make no friends here, and Mary's fine condition cuts down on my sport. And I wonder if what I long for—shoot at—is not the pleasures of a young man in love. I see the details. San Pietro in Vincoli, Vittorio Emanuele, and the two charioteers on the monument, all moving off toward the same compass point—St. Peter's. And I travel, admittedly, with a good deal of useless emotional baggage: hunger, thirst, anxiety, and cold feet—all things that plainly cloud my vision. My ambition is to familiarize myself with the city—to include it—and not at a literary level. Mary drinks tea with a divorcée on the Via Veneto. "Oh, the light was so beautiful," she says, "and we didn't see an American." She seems to see the thing more clearly than I.

A reception in a palazzo; the quintessence of Roman dreariness. Rooms that were meant to be lit by candles or maybe torches do not seem to lend themselves happily to the kind of indirect lighting that latter-day Romans go in for. The upshot is a dimness or dinginess that has an appreciable effect on my spirits. My feet ache from standing, but if I sit down I may get trapped. Butlers pass trays of bad brandy and bonbons. Ciardi complains about Rome. "If I'd known it was going to be like this," he says, "I wouldn't have come." It is dreary; it is dreary; it is like the bus to the Termine Flaminio at rush hour on a rainy night; it is like pouring bad wine for dull guests.

It seems to me that in the United States the contest between youth and age or between youth and un-youth, between those men whose hash has been settled and those who are still in the throes of a gruelling search, is exacerbated to the point of sexuality and sometimes brutality. The hood under the streetlight, with his tight pants and his snap knife, and the well-dressed businessman, walking his wife's poodle in the park, exchange a look of naked detestation—murder. The natural fact of a difference in age has made them enemies. I do not seem to find this in Europe. These may be difficulties of my own, but we will see.

•

I am uneasy, beset by emotional chills and drafts. Back here I see the fine sky from the windows and at five o'clock I read *The New Yorker* and drink a Martini.

And I think of the rooms you go into—that one, quite small, the home of an unmarried and practically unknown English novelist; the large abstract painting, done by a friend; the few Roman art objects, the black window curtains that may have been left over from the war, and the gas heater that gives off a dry heat and consumes the oxygen in the room at an alarming rate. And the people. First we have the two

American homosexuals who have every reason to be pleased at finding themselves in Rome. Here they are not the talk of their landlady; rough boys do not whistle at them as they go down the street, nor do respectable householders look on them with loathing and scorn. Then there is the Negro and his girlfriend. The trouble in the South is not on his conscience here. Nine-tenths of the city is not shut to him and he will never be embarrassed in restaurants and trolley cars. No one here thinks twice about the fact that the girl on his arm is white. And he seems to hate his own country; speaks of it always critically. Next we have the American novelist and his newspaperwoman wife. He is the son of an interfering and troublesome woman—such a thing is possible—and she is the daughter of an alcoholic, and they both speak frankly of getting away from this pair. He wrote one novel twelve years ago, and has not yet settled his plans for a second, but whereas in New York this would be spoken behind his back—where his delayed career would be the subject of anxiety or even ridicule—no one in Rome cares. She must have spent her youth in a very small and squalid place, for just the bare fact of being in Rome pleases her as if this city still had for her all the connotations of flight and breath that it must have had for her as a child. Next is the American divorcée. She had a love affair with a neighbor, and her husband divorced her, not on these grounds but for these reasons. Her parents, her brother, and the community where she lived censured her cruelly for her unfaithfulness, and knowing—or suspecting—that what she did was not so uncommon, she feels that she has been exposed to a shocking amount of hypocrisy and is happy to be in the Mediterranean, where the life of the flesh is not a source of so much anxiety. Her favorite subject of conversation is morality in the United States, and they all—the homosexuals, the Negro, the couple with difficult parents—like to talk about what they have escaped. Next we have the maverick of an American family—one of those families so famous for its wealth and power that the name is known to everyone. But she does not want to be the daughter of this household, to make the kind of marriage expected of her, to appear in public and have her picture in the paper. She has done what she wants, and what she wants seems to have been calculated to offend her family deeply. She is married to a hysterical ballet dancer and has written a novel in which her father, undisguised, appears to be a moral ogre. And there are many more—the Grub Street artists, the forgotten playwright, the sad rich man, etc.

When we go around the room, what we criticize is that in these people the force of escape seems to overpower the force of a search. We say goodbye—the drinks are terrible, and I don't like cakes at six-thirty in the evening—and it seems that we are as deeply implicated as anyone else in the room.

•

What I escape is the alcoholic life of a minor literary celebrity in Westchester; also the trying company of people I dislike; also perhaps a degree of sexual anxiety, based on some unhappiness in my youth and refreshed by the same scenes and types—scenery and people I don't see here. And I escape the languor of wanting to escape.

•

And walking back from the river I remember the galling loneliness of my adolescence, from which I do not seem to have completely escaped. It is the sense of the voyeur, the lonely, lonely boy with no role in life but to peer in at the lighted windows of other people's contentment and vitality. It seems comical—farcical—that, having been treated so generously, I should be stuck with this image of a kid in the rain walking along the road shoulders of East Milton.

•

To Naples for a day. I felt so heavyhearted and sad here at parting, as if I might never return. Also premonitions of illness sweep my frame and of being found murdered and naked in a back street. Leaving Rome, the sense of leaving an immense physical and intellectual explosion; the ruins of. South, all the fruit trees are in bloom and all the gardens green; but he looks out of the window, appalled at this reflection of his life, a creation of physical comfort and the ability to attract affection. I walk in Naples, up past the Rotunda and the Palace to the Galleria and drink a vermouth. I have my shoes shined by a man who says he will pray for my wife and my family, and I say we will need these prayers. Dinner with the Warrens, much loud music, and I take another walk and go to bed. In the dining room, an American ham with scrambled eggs and make it snappy. I start for the museum, in two minds about the Pompeian frescoes. It is morning in a strange city, even as in Glens Falls. The sun bright, people hurrying through the smell of coffee to work. In the museum much to see and many relics of a licentious civilization and I wonder where the frescoes are. Then I am taken in hand by a guard who does not want to show me shady frescoes but fine paintings, and I think then, Ah, this, this is life. But then I enter another room where the poor guard tries to do no more than is done on the walls and I escape, my teeth chattering with the cold. I wool-gather about this, walking back in the sunlight—smell of burned coffee, church bells, and then at a turn in the street I step into the smell of the sea, strong and fresh, and my woolgathering is ended. The smell is persuasive, and this persuasion is: to have faith in men. There in that dark gallery for a minute or two we stumble on midnight, on the borders of the conscience, where we doubt the promise in the faces of strangers, we doubt that life has any spiritual value. Then I lunch with the Warrens and board a first-class local, a little compartment lined with red plush like a box at the opera, and so we speed north again toward Rome, me in the company of an old man, a young student, and a soldier. I see the fruit trees again and the trees hung with vines and the famous sea, and rising from the shacks of a disreputable summer resort a round tower and, with it, memories of heroes, purple cloth, its splendor and its disappearance. And then I can only exclaim, watching the country in the dusk, how incomprehensible life is: there is the son my wife carries, the guard caressing the marble limbs of Achilles, the smell of the sea, the love I bear my children, the fruit trees that seem to make their own light in the dusk, the conversation among the three passengers, which I cannot understand, the sparse farmhouse lights, the carts and bicycles on the roads leading into every village.

•

A copy of the book arrives, and also a generous letter from S.B., and I am intoxicated or at least upset—mostly because I may commit the sin of pride; find humility difficult to arrive at. But if the book is any good it is plain luck and there is no point in my assuming that it is a product of industry, passionate application, etc. But dizzy with excitement I went out to buy cigarettes, and the pretty girl at the café, quite a flirt, gave me a look of pure uninterestedness and so I am crushed and feel like myself again. But perhaps by seeing the book in print I may be able to put it behind me. It has been a kind of keyhole, a very restricted point of view, and I would like to see it turn into cold pudding

so that I can go to something better. I felt that way with the "Goodbye,
My Brother" story. For nearly a year it seemed to me an adequate piece
of self-expression and then when I reread it one day it was cold pudding
and so we proceed.

•

Still with a cold, I walk in Rome after lunch. A nice day, the sun
very hot, the last of Carnival. My nose is running and I feel a little
strange, all of which, in some way, seems to endear the city to me. I
see blue sky through the windows of a ruin. By accident, I approach
the tomb of Augustus, with its trimmed greenery, and turn back. I
approach the Pantheon and go right down the Navona. The fountains
are turned off and the man with the *brutto muso* and the fish between
his legs seems to be compensating. The sunny tables of the café I like
are full of Americans. They are not pretty, and a skinful of wine and
the glare of the sun make them less so. The clock at Sant' Agnese strikes
three, and every single one of them—six in all—shoots his cuffs and
checks his wristwatch. I turn left and go up a dark street that I do not
know. The street rises, a hillock of brick, and out of a narrow alley
comes a hunchback or dwarf holding by the hand a child dressed as a
fairy princess—a blue gown sparkling with brilliants and pointed silk
hat with a long veil. Then I hear drums and see through the dark alley
into a little piazza made by the junction of several alleys. There are
more stairs and little hillocks of paving, and the squash-colored buildings
are more random than usual. I see a woman with a mop of dyed-yellow
hair leaning from a window into the sun beside a younger woman with
black hair. But it is the drumming that fills the air, it is the drumming
that is compelling. Compelling, harsh, as unmusical as the grating beat
of a strained heart and so bare that it seems to state the facts of life:
lust, hunger, or, if you will, the demands of a full bladder—something
inescapable. The company is quite large as these things go. There are
two drummers dressed as sailors, two men with tambourines, dressed
as sailors, and two dancers, all the costumes shabby and stitched together
out of Christmas leftovers in some cold hill kitchen and the whole thing
dictated by a tradition that is probably no better known to the Romans
than it is to me. So the dancers move around one another to the music
of the gallows drum. They are both men, one dressed like a prince or
grandee and the other like I don't know what. He has a shawl over his

head, a mask over his eyes, his back is humped way up above his head, and tied to his groin is an ugly doll with the face of a witch. He wears over his trousers a skirt and an apron. The dance is stamped out on the paving: primitive, simple, full of sexual movement performed with perfect weariness and indifference, and when it is done the whole company marches on—the drumming has never stopped and I can still hear it as I head for the Corso. Here I see, in a traffic jam, a boy in a *carrozza*, dressed as an Indian prince, his face all powder and rouge, scattering confetti. I go into Gesù to say my prayers. All the front pews are taken by men from the German college in their red robes. To my left is a man who is either drunk or asleep and who changes his position with a thump, while I pray, but who goes on sleeping. Back here the children throw confetti from the balcony and I take my temperature, which is normal. Then we go to hear four Beethoven sonatas—violoncello and piano. Very good. Such music seems to me, more than anything else, proof of peaceable intent.

I hope to go without strong drink before lunch, but if Mary has our baby today I think I will ask an indulgence. And sitting at the breakfast table today I think about the anarchic possibilities of human conduct, which seem, without light, to be inestimable.

•

On the day after my son is born, I wake up filled with good wishes for him: courage, love, virility, a healthy sense of self, and workable arrangements with God. I will climb Mount Chocorua with him. I tell the maid and then the children how fine he is. I am very excited and, still having a cold, find my eyes sore and watery. I do not go to church, feeling that this observance is not necessary. I take the bus with Ben and Susie to the hospital. Walking from the bus stop to the gates, we pass through a dark turn in the streets—I mean emotional darkness. K. has told me that a murder was committed here and I think I detect an atmosphere of sexual roughhouse, the smell of piss, a cat sleeping in an ashcan, and some very dirty drawings on the walls, which I examine. In the hospital there is Mary and my fine son and all the things I plan to do for him. I don't ever remember loving a child so much. So then we go home in a bus that is crowded and smelly. I have a drink and feel very odd—the cold, I guess—and looking down from my balcony into the street I covet the freedom of young bucks in open cars going down to Ostia to raise hell, and observe how a man can be given nearly everything the world has to offer and go on yearning. We go to the Palatine after lunch and now I think the world seems very strange, perhaps through the caul of my cold. The sky is lovely, the light brilliant and spotty, but a chilly wind is blowing from some quarter and the leaves turn and move in this, and the uneasy sound reminds me of autumn. I sit here and there in the sun but I cannot get warm and chemical storms or distempers seem to be raging in my veins. Back here and coming down the stairs, for some reason I think what a struggle it is to admit the existence of evil in the world and in ourselves, how difficult it is to strike that balance between our self-expression—our extension—and that which we know to be right.

Back to the hospital again—I am very tired—and then to bed. I wish I could lose this cold.

·

The reviews come, but this is a nothing.

·

Walking Ben to school, I see a man struck by a car. The noise rings up and down the street—that surprising loudness of our bones when they are given a mortal blow. The driver of the car slips out of his seat and runs through the courtyard of the Palazzo Venezia, knowing that if he is caught he will be jailed without bail until his case comes to court sometime next year. The victim lies in a heap on the paving—a shabbily dressed man but with a lot of oil in his black, wavy hair, which must have been his pride. A crowd gathers—not solemn at all, although a few women cross themselves—and everyone begins to talk excitedly, but nobody lifts a finger to help the victim, whose lifeblood is spreading over the cobblestones. Here is the dangerous Rome. It is not a question of precautions—traffic lights and police at intersections—but of an entirely different point of view about continuity and the valuableness of life. It seems, to an American, to be an inability to concentrate, an inability to grasp the weight of consequences. The dying man is put on a stretcher and carted off while the crowd goes on regaling one another with opinions and reminiscences. The murderous stream of traffic is resumed, and Romans dart in and out among the cars like crazy hens.

Yesterday I saw two limousines, full of diplomats coming back from a Vatican audience, going about one hundred miles an hour up the wrong end of a one-way street.

Federico is registered at the Embassy, and the next thing I must do along these lines is to buy a car. Federico is up much of the night. I feel sleepy.

•

To tell the truth, I bemuse myself at three in the morning with the day I win the Pulitzer Prize. I see the story in the Ossining paper, the *Rome-American, Il Messaggero*, etc. I also imagine the cable that tells me it has been bought for a hundred and fifty thousand dollars, I see an editorial in *Life* with a photograph of me here in the Galleria or coming down the Spanish steps.

Communion breakfast with Susie; frozen orange juice, Nescafé, all things from the PX. A heavy nap after lunch, from which I wake for once refreshed and not depressed—but it is a gray day, the worst kind of day in Rome. Mary takes the children to the zoo and I memorize *"avere"* and take care of Federico, who is fretful and has a cold.

•

Mary says that if the book is a success I will get swellheaded, and I think about the nature of success. One does not want to be a failure, a kind of wood violet, and yet perhaps the responsibilities of success are what I dread. I seem to yearn to live behind the scenes. But it is true that when I cannot sleep—when I am unhappy or lonely—I bemuse myself with imagining fourth and fifth printings and the ascent of my name on the best-seller list in the same way that whenever I am unhappy I console myself with imagining pieces of good news.

•

To church for Palm Sunday and my eyes fill with tears. My tears are lewd, I think. I cry at horse races and dirty jokes as readily as I do at the Passion. And I am afraid of sentimentality here—of what someone has called the deliquescent aspects of religion. And at the altar rail, feeling a very deep emotion and challenging it, I say, How else can we express our deepest feelings of aspiration, our determination, in spite of considerable odds, to lead a useful and an inspired life? One can express these things, a rationalist would say, by developing those gifts we have for continence, industry, fairness, love, etc., and yet as I see it there is something else.

•

At seven the sky is all pink and gold; but just as we plan to leave for the Rocca a dark sky moves in over the Campidoglio: thunder, lightning, and torrential rains. I have the wind up—am worried about the driving, everything—and take a pull at the Scotch bottle, which makes me feel considerably better. What I want, I think, walking back from the cigarette store, is the laughter in life, and I think of the old prayer—"Prepare us for adventure, but do not spare us the hazards," etc. The air is dark with swallows, there is more thunder and lightning as we leave. I get the B.s at the Gianicolo and we start down the coast road in unsettled weather. The landscape, or what I see of it from the driver's seat, is lovely, but I say this: that the role of a writer is not to seek out the most beautiful places in the world and describe them—at least not my role. The Campagna is so green that it will seem at dusk to shine. There are thunderclouds over the mountains, streams and spouts of rain, and a clearing over the sea that is the fine blue of clear, saline water—but a richer blue than the Pacific. The whole countryside is a carpet of flowers. I have never seen anything like it, but somehow we are still travellers. We are in a hurry. We look for nothing here that is precious to us. The great Campagna with its cover of flowers is, in a sense, a locked sight. We go through Civitavecchia and under the walls of Tarquinia. The darkness and noise of the storm is still on the mountains. The light over the sea is brilliant. The Rocca is beautiful today. Lupine and snapdragons hang in long garlands from the walls. The air smells of salt. There is a mountain—a dead volcano, I guess, from the looks of the rocks on the beach—and in the distance a hill with a tower or castle, like a few broken teeth. And I miss again the fact that I am not young and in love, for these are the landscapes and places for young lovers. The whole thing seems to unfold as that. So much of the world seems to me to be a place where a young man leads a young girl.

•

I dream about the White House. It is after supper in a bedroom
that I have seen on postcards. Ike and Mamie are alone. Mamie is
reading the Washington *Star*. Ike is reading "The Wapshot Chronicle."

•

Driving over the Ponte Flaminio to see Susie graduate, we seem
very middle-aged. The nuns have worked over the ceremony and it seems
sympathetic and comprehensible to me. The last high-school affair I
attended, I nearly got into a fight with two hoods who were feeling a
little girl in the auditorium. But here there is no conflict between youth
and age, chaos and substance. The boys are no less vigorous, but they
are polite. And oh, the girls. The chinless one, and N., whose beauty
is like an ache and it will be gone, as sure as winter comes, within
three years. The girl from Boston with a boy's face, a child's hair ribbon
and yellow hair as fine as silk way down her back. The nervous girl,
the girl with spit curls, the plain girl at the end who nearly fell down.
A string trio plays "Pomp and Circumstance" at an excruciatingly slow
pace and the girls come down the center aisle like brides, holding flowers,
their eyes on the carpet, or peek to the left and right to find their parents
or, more often, their friends, since this is an International School and
many of their parents are away. Women cry. Men smile foolishly. Everyone is immensely moved at this spectacle of female youth and its wealth
of opportunity. Next comes His Excellency all dressed in red, including
his complexion. His face is as vast and meaty as a six-rib roast and
pursy, too, if you can imagine a pursy roast. Then the Ambassador of
Panama compares the girls to a flock of birds, flying hither and yon. He
also quotes from Cardinal Newman. His Excellency quotes from Pius
XII. Diplomas and prizes are given out. Then the string trio strikes up
a capriccio and His Excellency leads the procession into the vestibule.
It is so much like a wedding that now the girls beam and smile at
everyone. We are presented to His Excellency, the Romans kneeling to
kiss his ring and the Protestants manfully shaking his hand. There is
punch and sandwiches in the garden. The girls say goodbye and promise
to write. I do not fail to get an eyeful of the Princess Barbarini, who
looks as she should, only very Madison Avenue. The Prince is nothing.
The school stands on a little hill, just outside the boundaries of Rome.
Vigna Clara, a new housing development, expensive and unsightly,

stands on the next hill. But the valley between the two is still a piece of the Campagna—yellow wheat and red poppies—and the famous shadows are beginning to fall. So we drive back through the traffic jams, the dusty parks, the apartment-house neighborhoods, fashionable and unfashionable—the outskirts of any big city.

A poor day and I wonder how I spoil it. Swimming with a mask, I see my son, swimming with his. It is strange and touching to see him underwater, the little sand he touches rising slowly, like smoke. Sitting on a rock in the sun, I wonder about that emotional debility that strikes me. And it seems that we cannot reform our sexual natures. And there is a point where denial is sheer hypocrisy, with its train of gruelling and foolish anxieties. One must act with a free heart—there can be nothing covert—and seek the best ways of expressing ourselves within the conditions under which we live. And waking I think how narrow and anxious my life is. Where are the mountains and green fields, the broad landscapes?

•

This in the bedroom in Scarborough, and I must find a place to work. After much foolish—senseless—anxiety I pried the nameplate off the door in Rome, loaded the car, and left Rome for Naples, followed by the best wishes of the porter and his wife. We stopped in some place like Terracina for coffee and reached Naples in time for lunch. The hotel was comfortable and seemed elegant, although I think there were bugs in the bed. The next afternoon I took the children up Vesuvius, suffering from vertigo. Coming back on the bus I sat with a pretty Danish actress. I meant to ask her for this and that, to at least send her a copy of the novel, but everything was put off and she left the bus suddenly at the railroad station without my finding out her name. Back at the hotel I had a hooker of whiskey, and standing on the balcony with my glass, looking at a vacant lot, an unfinished building, and the cranes and machines of the port, I yearned, I longed, I seemed to be in love, and so much for this capriciousness. In the morning we hired a car and driver to take us to Pompeii. Our driver was overwrought and spoke English with difficulty. We were joined by two young Americans who seemed so much to be their mother's best, so weary and effeminate, that life seemed completely withheld from them. In the morning, after much sweat and nervousness, we board the ship, and go on deck, after lunch, to make our farewells. After having wondered for so many months about the depth and reality of my love of Italy, after having imagined this scene so many times, I stand at the stern deck, staring at the cliffs along the coast; it all slips and falls away as insignificantly and swiftly as a card house.

"You got some rope?" an American asks me. "I want to tie on a hat. Ha-ha-ha."

"I'm never going back," an old lady says in the dining room. She sounds petulant; her feelings have been hurt. "I'm accustomed to conveniences," she says, "and now I want them. I lived in a little shack until I was married."

"My daughter keeps buying old houses and doing them over," says another, reminding me of American decorative arts and their curious place in our lives. By dusk there is no land to be seen.

•

Lunch at the Century with M. "The book," he said, "made quite a ripple." Really very condescending. It is, after all, my first novel. The atmosphere in the streets of a financial and sexual contest is very vivid: I am richer than you, poorer than you, more virile than you, less virile than you, the graduate of a better, more exclusive college than you, and you can tell by the cut of my coat and my hair that my social orientation is better than yours; I work for a smaller but more potent advertising agency than you, my clubs are better than yours, my tailor, my shoemaker, yea, even my lights and my vitals are better than yours. Or lesser. In the public urinal I am solicited by the man on my right but I do not dare turn my head. But I wonder what he looks like. No better or no worse, I guess, than the rest of us in such throes. Whichever way we can most swiftly dismiss these matters seems best. It would matter less (I think) in Rome.

•

What the travel books don't mention is the sense of danger experienced by the visitor to Rome. Driving back into the city after a long weekend you see at the gates of the Campo Verano a long line of hearses. Nearly every hearse and mourner's coach in Rome is there, and while you watch, two more roll up and join the end of the line. There must be twenty-five. You ask one of the drivers what the occasion is and he says it is the epidemic. He has been carrying the dead out of Rome for three days now without time to eat or drink or sleep. He makes the sign of the cross and moves slowly forward to the gates. In the city, in the Piazza Venezia, it is a winter's night with the especial, cheerless dampness of that part of the world. The floodlights aimed at the monument, the yellow clouds of a big-city fog. You park your car and lock the ignition switch, the steering wheel, and all the doors, since car thefts go on every night in this quarter. You go into a bar to buy a package of cigarettes and the place is so damp and cold that the poor girl who waits on you—she wears three sweaters and fur-lined boots—is shivering. You buy an evening paper. In the bar and in the streets everyone is coughing. You ask the porter at our house what he knows of the epidemic and he says that there is one, a *peste*, but through the infinite grace of God his family and his house have been spared. His sister has taken her children out of the city to Capranica to escape the poisonous air but he has no place to send his children. He can only pray. Upstairs in your flat you pour a drink of whiskey for medicinal reasons and step out onto your balcony to examine this dangerous and mysterious city. You telephone a friend and someone answers the phone to say that your friend has left suddenly for Switzerland. You call another friend who has gone to Majorca. Then you call your doctor. He is short-tempered because he has been called from the dinner table to answer the phone. You ask him if the city is dangerous. He shouts his reply. "Yes, the city is dangerous. Rome has always been dangerous. Life is dangerous. Do you expect to live forever?" He ends the conversation with a bang. You look in the newspaper for some account of the plague. There are the usual government crises, new oil fields have been discovered in Sicily, and there was a murder on the Via Cassia, but the only news of the epidemic is that Masses will be sung in six churches for the health of the city of Rome. You might fly, like your friends, to Switzerland or Majorca, but how can you flee until you know what it is you are fleeing?

•

   The mystery of a gratifying sense of identity that I don't recall experiencing in Europe. In an upper-class gathering I suddenly think of myself as a pariah—a small and dirty fraud, a deserved outcast, a spiritual and sexual impostor, a loathsome thing. Then I take a deep breath, stand up straight, and the loathsome image falls away. I am no better and no worse than the other members of the gathering. Indeed, I am myself. It is like a pleasant taste on the tongue.

Perhaps I had less time for self-consciousness abroad.

I dream that I travel through the mountains in an express train and make love to a woman I have never seen. And the body is a fool, this flesh and bone is a fool; philandering, complaining, demanding, the gullible dupe of con men and subversive agencies, capricious, cowardly, the essence of inconstancy.

•

Skating on the K.s' pond last night after eating too much ham. Eight-thirty. Many stars. No moon. Orion's sword and girdle brilliant and all the other constellations whose names I have forgotten or never knew. I am reminded of my youth and its skating ponds, of the ardor for strength, courage, and purpose excited in me then by the starlight. It is nearly the same. My feelings may be less ardent, the stars seem to burn more tenderly these days, but my openmouthed delight in finding them hung above the dark ice is no less.

•

Parties on Friday and Saturday, and on Sunday we take a walk. The wind off the river is very cold, but in sheltered places where the sun shines we can smell the earth and leaves and oh, I am very happy with all of this, the valley, my wife, my children, and the sky. And then I think of secrets and mysteries, those forms that lie way below our commonest worries. What is the sexual longing I feel when I step out of a railroad station onto the streets of a city where I am unknown? What sort of tenderness is it that I seem to need so passionately that my common sense is damaged? What is this mysterious need? In a crowded Roman trolley car at closing time on a winter night, someone touches me by chance on the shoulder. I do not turn to see who it is and I will never know if it was a man or a woman, a tart or a priest, but the gentle touch excites in me such longing for a sort of helpful tenderness that I sigh; my knees are weak. This is not a violet-flavored sigh or a Chopinesque longing; it is as coarse and real as the hair on my belly.

•

By lewdness I mean just that: raised petticoats in kitchens and back stairs and long afternoons in bed when the sheets smell like the lagoons of Venice; but if my hands tremble with desire they tremble likewise when I reach for the chalice on Sunday, and if lust makes me run and caper it is no stronger a force than that which brings me to my knees to say thanksgivings and litanies. What can this capricious skin be but a blessing?

In the morning I am tired and go into town. The sky is dark. It is raining. I walk around the streets near Times Square and look at the photographs on display of some ballroom hostesses. The first is not young, forty I should say or more, a motherly sort for a lonely sailor. A few loose strands of hair lie along her neck. She wears draperies to display the promise of her voluminous, soft, warm, and un-young front and gives to the camera the smile of a good-natured drudge. Another has marked Italian features, her front tightly corseted—two gleaming globes. Another reminds me of a childhood friend: adventurous, a horse-woman, much married, presently an alcoholic. Here are the same heavy brows, the light hair, the same look of freshness and desperateness. One wears a little gauze, her shoulders bare, and holds her breasts in her hands and she is the most touching of all, for she is bewildered. Since this seems to be what is expected of her, this is what she will do, and the face seems so immature that she cannot be credited with conscious regrets, but bewilderment, yes. She had, in her bones, expected something very different. "Which one you like best?" a man asks me. He carries a piece of pastry and a paper container of coffee.

I answer him cheerfully, but I think the romantic image of the prostitute today, in this country, this rainy morning, is indecent.

•

Feeling poorly. The beating of my heart seems strained. I cough blood. My reflexes are slow. We go unwilling to a P.E.N. party. Driving into New York through a rainy dusk, the clouds in the west colored orange from the discharge of industrial waste; and I think of Rome, the tragedy of her incompetence at coping with the problems of a modern city—smoke and traffic—for who could ever explain to Luigi that he should not burn waste in his stove? At the party I meet M., a young admirer who seems to be his mother's boy, and I think of how creative such a relationship between us might be, but then I think that in this country it is colored with suspicion and anxiety, beginning with my own.

•

And who are all these friends who seem so strange to us? The gamine. The man who puts on smoked glasses to walk through the rain and the dusk. The stiff man aboard ship with the phony English accent and the checked coat. The woman who complains of her husband's impotence at a cocktail party. The man who drinks to refresh his bitterness. The pig. Forget them.

The most wonderful thing about life seems to be that we hardly tap our potential for self-destruction. We may desire it, it may be what we dream of, but we are dissuaded by a beam of light, a change in the wind.

•

Housework seems trivial, but for what it means. One of my greatest difficulties with women has turned on this. It begins with my grandmother. When she, through some breakdown in service or finance, was obliged to wash the dishes, the men of my family suffered. It was our fault that she, a distinguished, wellborn, and intelligent woman, was bent over a dishpan. If we offered to help, she would wave us away; but we had failed her, not only as providers but as men. The same was true of my mother. When she was obliged to do housework and wash dishes, the sense was always that she had been martyred by the inadequacy, the stupidity of the male sex. Why was this distinguished and intelligent woman suffered to wield a carpet sweeper? It was because her sons and her husband were next to worthless. I used to take the carpet sweeper away from her; I used to wash the dishes; but it never quite repaired the damage. The sense of guilt was always there.

•

We recognize the force of the mystery that keeps us from wrongdoing, but what do we do when this force collapses: when the scale is tipped for evil? The scale is weighted, we know, with blue sky, common sense, and the breathing of our children while they sleep, but why, while we sleep, should it plunge downward?

•

Sitting on the platform of the Institute, I see the famous movie actress in the audience. I give her a big eye and think I may get something in return but perhaps I kid myself. She wears a black dress, her front can be seen, a small gold cross. The feeling, whatever it may be worth, is of devastation. I am smitten. Here, I think, is the face that launched a thousand ships. For this pale hair, boys and grown men with families will run away from home. The crowing of a sweet child, the pleas of a lovely woman, the comforts of the hearth, the endearments of our grown children; nothing will matter. But this is no sloe-eyed, sinuous beauty. I am captivated by what seems to be the perfect sweetness in her face, and this through the long and tiresome citations, the heat, does not change at all. Later I see her on the stairs in a stronger light. The paleness of her hair is a dye and her face is painted. And in the still stronger light of day a little more is lost. But she still seems wonderful: a truly pretty woman.

•

Read "The Deer Park" and tossed it into the fire. Much better than most of what I've been reading, although I think he imitates Saul or I imitate Saul or he imitates me. I have written first-person slang long before "Augie March" appeared and I'm not sure who began it but there has been enough of this carefree fellow. Of the principal character Elena, I know only that she is sloppy and depraved. This is not enough. I don't necessarily hold with my kind of old-fashioned fiction, but if you throw it out you have to pick up something else. The candor does not concern me, but I sometimes wonder where he stands—as a participant or as a voyeur. There is this danger. The climactic writing seems to me not eloquent enough. But he seems to me an estimable man.

•

A hassle. For four or five days such tenderness as I have to offer has been refused. Mary especially *maldisposta* on Saturday. While we are dressing P.B. enters and begins to strum the piano. "Doesn't it sound nice?" Mary says sweetly. It does not. He is the kind of pianist who, should you hear him from the next room, you would swear was playing with his feet. She seems pleased to see him, or perhaps her displeasure with me is lessened. On Sunday I am all love and tenderness

but no soap. On Monday I quit this sullen task at three and, having a
bellyache, take a Martini, and then my son for a stroll. He seems fair
and strong to me: what we mean by life. At dinner I reproach Susie for
eating butter with a fork.

"Shut up," says she.

"Leave the table," say I.

She does. Presently I suggest that if she would like to apologize she
may come in and eat her strawberries.

"Let's you and I go to the movies," says Mary when she returns.
Susie does not deserve to go to the movies because of her incivility to
the master. I take my son for another walk. It has cleared at last. It is
a summer evening, one of the few we've had this year. The light lies
golden on the grass and warm. We walk. He picks weeds and eats them.
I speak to him dolefully, as I used to speak to the dog. It seems that I
have walked on these paths, this grass, under these trees too often,
looking to the color of the sky, a chance star, or a flower for some
understanding of my wife's distempers. I have done this so often that
it seems now I am tired—my considered choice of word with all its
connotations of collapsed vitality. It seems that I must contest, not with
the facts of our marriage, our relationship, but with the facts of some
incident in her childhood that was enacted years before we met. I think
of the rainy afternoon when her father lacerated her with a belt. I think
of her early years' having been lived near to his irascibility, his gifts for
cruelty, and that she will never be requited with a tranquil life. She
needs love, yes, but it seems that she also needs its opposite to feel
alive: that her equilibrium depends upon an unusual degree of nastiness.
It seems that in all these years of marriage I have been the merest
visitor, stopping in after lunch on some rainy day in her childhood, but
Mother and Father are expected at five and I will go away. I get angry.
I speak passionately to my son, who does not understand a word and
only makes sweet sounds of pleasure at the sight of the evening.

I stay away until they have gone to the movie and then, meanly,
think of them eating popcorn in the gray light and watching the romantic
misfortunes of Marjorie Morningstar. I grow angrier and angrier, and
why should my emotions take such a violent turn? Nothing important
has happened. I have mustered a sense of humor for much more trying
situations. But I cannot control my ill temper, it mounts like a fire.
The boy goes to bed and I follow him, but my mind still spins around

her intractableness, her obtuseness, and my lack of patience. Her approach to the children—I think—is often more wayward and perverse than loving. She showers them with presents, but the kind of loving and intelligent discipline I think they need is, I think, beyond her. I grow so excited that I take a sleeping pill, but as soon as I fall asleep the baby begins to cry. Walking him in the bedroom I think, how meanly, of Mary weeping childish tears over the disappointments of Marjorie Morningstar. I think I will write a rebuttal to the California poets: something in defense of the genteel tradition, something about sitting in a broken rocking chair in a remodelled toolshed where I make my living writing stories about the country-club set. But it seems that I have neither the wit nor the substance to write such a piece, and the idea does not afford me the escape from anger that I sincerely want. When the baby has fallen asleep I take another sleeping pill and just as I am about to fall asleep Mary comes up the stairs. "My God, here she comes!" I exclaim angrily. Then when she says that she enjoyed the movie I say, with shocking nastiness, that she is like the heroine, she is like Marjorie Morningstar. Now my heart is pounding so that I take a third sleeping pill and I am so angry that hateful, physical violence is in my plans. I will strangle her. So I compose myself and go to sleep.

Sitting on the toilet in the morning I am unforgiving: I have had it, I repeat to myself, and get into the garbage pail of a contemplated divorce. I don't want a divorce; I want things to be exactly as they were, there having been much more good than bad in the relationship; I don't want to part with my children and I suspect that I don't want to part with the comforts of my home, a place where I can count on warm meals and company. I am afraid of living in hotel rooms and eating in cafeterias, and this seems to reflect on my courage. I am much too attached to cut flowers, to holding a seashell to my son's ear to see the intent look on his face, to the smell of peonies (oh how brief) in the stairwell. But is it wrong for a man to make a house, a place where he can return in the evening? Is it wrong to avoid the venereal ghosts in cheap hotel rooms and the odd sticks who share your table at the Automat? I don't want to make a life with my bachelor friends or be a dog in the households of the married people I know, bringing a bottle of wine for dinner or a present for the child. I don't want my taste for domestic comforts to involve meanness or fear of the world, although I doubt that I can cope, with the equanimity and calm I cherish, with an empty hotel room.

This may all come to nothing. I would like it that way. Angry, I think: I will not drive her to New Hampshire. And at the bottom of this, I suppose, is some mean petulance, some wish to punish her. This is followed by an extensive digression on the subject of her car. I don't want to drive her to New Hampshire if she is in a bad humor is what I seem to mean. But I expect that, for the trip, she will put herself into a charming frame of mind. In any case, I should not think in terms of nasty punishments. I hesitate to justify myself by saying that I have been forced into such a frame of mind, but if I am that susceptible, that easily moved in the wrong direction, that fault is mine.

•

I am a solitary drunkard. I take a little painkiller before lunch but I don't really get to work until late afternoon. At four or half past four or sometimes five I stir up a Martini, thinking that a great many men who can't write as well as I can will already have set themselves down at bar stools. After half a glass of gin I decide that I must get a divorce— and, to tell the truth, Mary is depressed, although my addiction to gin may have something to do with her low spirits. The gin flows freely until supper and so do my memories of the most difficult passages in our marriage; and I think of all the letters I have received from literary ladies implying that my experience with the sex must have been un-naturally difficult and that I deserve better. How right they are, I think. I am deserving of much better. I am sweet and good-humored and I deserve a lovely and an intelligent wife. The fact that my marriage is subject to excessive scrutiny does not occur to me. The fact that other women I know have their intractable passages does not cross my mind. I am deserving. I should have something better. So the gin flows, and after supper the whiskey. I am even a little sly, keeping my glass on the floor where it might not be seen. Mary does not want to speak to me, to be sure. Her looks are dark and impatient. I rustle up a glossary of little jokes to prove the sweetness of my disposition, but she does not laugh. She does not even listen. She does not want to be in the same room with me. She would sooner stand out in the rain. I realize I have gone through this a hundred times before. Not my sources of patience, but my whole point of view seems to have undergone some change. I make another drink and try to read Italian but I am too drunk to make much progress; I doze on the sofa and then go to bed. In the morning

I am nauseated. My head aches. A rat has been in the house during the night and eaten the fruit on the table. It is humid and overcast as many of the days have been this year.

•

I drink whiskey before lunch; take Federico for a walk. There is a shower again but hardly enough to darken the walk. It is a terrible day, painful weather. Mary seems to make an effort to end the tension between us and I am very willing. But it comes to nothing over the issue of dishwashing. I am not to wash the dishes; I am to take care of the baby. I think it would be better if I washed the dishes and she took care of the baby. So I take care of the baby and the baby screams and she must leave the dishpan and I say, "We must talk; we must talk. This is unbearable. I have thought of writing you a letter."

"Write me a letter," she says, laughing, and the situation is hopeless. But there is no place where we can talk without being overheard by the children. But I decide then, and later at three in the morning, that I will make three points. (1) She must admit that she is the victim of capricious depressions and do something about this. (2) I will not drive her to New Hampshire. It will be good for her to make the trip alone and to spend some time with her father. (3) If she continues to complain about the house and long for other houses she should look for some modest rental where she can live alone with the children. But then at half past three there is a heavy shower of rain; the wind changes its quarter, one needs a blanket, and suddenly I am happy, well-disposed, cheerful. At perhaps the same moment the great rat, the monster, puts his head into the trap and his neck is broken in two. In the fresh light of morning all my resolves have gone like smoke. I will not mention the depressions; I will drive her to New Hampshire; we will look at a farmhouse this afternoon.

Sometimes, in my hankerings, I feel as if I had sold my parts to the devil. How can one imagine such indecencies without such a bargain having been made?

•

We start early on Tuesday for New Hampshire. Since my relations with Mary have not been good, I have thought of her parents with less and less friendliness, less and less love. We are on parkways most of the distance. I do not see much of this country I love. The car overheats and we must stop. I must seem rather tough to my son. The car overheats and we have to keep stopping. I have a muscular pain in my back but I interpret this as an infected kidney that will have to be removed before evening. It is foolish; and it is painful. We stop at the boathouse for a swim. The water is fresh and cold and limpid, but lifeless compared to the sea. There are the mountains, the pines, and I feel for a second the poignancy, the virile poignancy of this place. The wind sound in the pines; this endless noise of passing silk. There is some ease here in this fine air, some suspense of haste. At the stone house we are met by P. and W. He opens at once with a broad attack on *The New Yorker*. She has some gossip about Philadelphia. They talk loudly and at cross-purposes and when her back is turned he makes a face at her and says she is a stupid bitch. We have a drink and then go on to Ben's camp. I am too tired and have drunk too much to feel very strongly or to see very clearly the place where we are leaving him. I love him but he seems not quite ready to love me. Back at the house the loud, cross-purposes conversation continues. He does not answer her most civil questions. He leaves the room in the middle of her remarks; and so we go to bed in a fragrant, homely room where we have been very happy wrapped in the silky sound of the wind passing, streaming through the pines. But I discharge my conjugal responsibilities poorly, and meaning, at dawn, to make amends, I am rebuffed. I dress and go up the hill and make a pot of coffee. It is half past five. The air is very light and fragrant. It smells of flowers and hay. I have never known anywhere, especially not in the Italian hill towns, such a fine air. It is a summer place where a family has come of age. They are not, in my opinion, an especially fragrant family, but at this hour the fragrance of their lives seems to cling to the matchboard, which is fragrant with time. Here are the family photographs, the tastes, a detail from the Sistine Chapel; a picture of Mary and the other children, all of them but Mary bursting their best clothes. The sun has still not risen, and in this still and lovely hour I feel tenderly for all these people whose youth seems centered in these rooms.

•

My first feelings about the Kerouac book were: that it was not good; that most of its accents or effects were derived from some of the real explorers, like Saul; and that the apocalyptic imagery was not good enough—was never lighted by true talent, or deep feeling, vision. It pleased me to catch him at a disadvantage, to sum up the facts, which could reflect on my lack of innocence. Here is a man of thirty who lives with his hard-working mother, cooks supper for her when she gets home from the store, has a shabby affair with a poor Negress—who knows so little about herself that she is easy prey—wrestles, very suspiciously, with his pals, weeps in a train yard where his mother's image appears to him, discovers that he is deceived, and writes a book. The style has the advantages, to make a rough comparison, of abstract painting. When we give up lucidity we have, from time to time, the power of broader associations. Life is chaotic, and so we can state this in chaotic terms. In trying to catch him at a disadvantage, I find him vulgar, meaning perhaps unsophisticated—his sexual identity, his prowess, is not much. He is a writer and wants to be a famous writer, a rich writer, and a successful writer, but the question of excellence never seems to cross his mind. The question of the greatest depth of feeling, of speaking with the greatest urgency. My life is very different from what he describes. There is almost no point where our emotions and affairs correspond. I am most deeply and continuously involved in the love of my wife and my children. It is my passion to present to my children the opportunity of life. That this love, this passion, has not reformed my nature is well known. But there is some wonderful seriousness to the business of living, and one is not exempted by being a poet. You have to take some precautions with your health. You have to manage your money intelligently and respect your emotional obligations. There is another world—I see this—there is chaos, and we are suspended above it by a thread. But the thread holds. People who seek, who are driven to seek, love in urinals, do not deserve the best of our attention. They will be forgiven, and, anyhow, sometimes they are not seeking love; they are seeking a means to express their hatred and suspicion of the world. Sometimes.

•

If we do not imagine the future how can we believe it to exist? I think now that in a year or two the atmosphere will recuperate, the damage will be repaired, and we will walk in the clear light of day again. But I have never been so deeply conscious of chaos, as if we were in the act of falling from some atmospheric and moral orbit, as if the sweet seriousness of life were in great danger.

•

In town, and pleased to have this contest suspended for a day. At 11 A.M. on the corner of Park Avenue and Thirty-sixth Street a tart gives me the eye. I am alarmed, excited, astonished, etc., as we pass, but when we have passed my mind continues along at her side, climbs the stairs, waits while she turns the key in the lock and performs with copious and revolting detail the whole shabby encounter. This seems to me unclean, unmanly, and I protest, and there you have it, the mind climbing the stairs as the conscience calls it back and both of them powerless to change one another's ways. At the next corner I see a head of light-brown hair and that love of the future that is excited by my children leaps up in me like an illumination and I am refreshed by those sentiments that cool our blood. What fine things I will do for them. What tall things I will build. But the independence with which my imagination pursues the tart seems to reflect on the seriousness of my wish to lead a worthy and a cleanly life.

•

We climb Cardigan. I am short-winded. There are clouds, and from the summit we see their shadows—continents, with neighboring islands, moving over the hills. The air has a perfect lightness, perfect for carrying the smell of pine, moss, the delphinium that grows by the ranger's cabin. The granite down Firescrew still has the rush and flow of lava. I climb down slowly, relaxed from the trip up, sniffing the woods, admiring the moss with its second growth of red hair, microscopic flowers. The stone bed of the lowest stream is paved with moss. I remember coming down another mountain two years ago, my mind as lame as my legs, as lewd to boot, and hearing suddenly the noise of water pouring over stone and seeing it in my mind all green and golden in the pools, as it truly is in these streams; pouring, pouring, pouring, pouring, as sweet as the sounds of wine, oh, much sweeter, this pouring noise.

•

Waiting in the police station to pay a parking ticket, I hear on the radio that a middle-aged man, slight build, five feet seven, brown hair, is wanted for open lewdness. He unzipped his trousers at the corner of Elm Avenue and Chestnut Street and did the same thing twenty minutes later in front of the A. & P. He is driving a yellow convertible but the license number and the make of the car are unknown. A five-state alarm is out; and where can he be? Reading "Tommy Titmouse" to his children. Hiding in a garage, or a movie theatre. Drinking in a bar. I pray for him, among others, in church. It is a rainy Sunday and the smell of pew cushions is dense. One can hardly hear the priest, the noise of rainspouts is so loud. I seem to be back at the farm, a happy child, sitting on burlap cushions and hearing rainspouts. For a second the recollection is so vivid, so full, it is like the rush of memory brought on by a mouthful of hot pudding. I reproach myself. I reproach myself for reproaching myself. I contemplate the quality of introspection in church. I think that faced with the mystery and passion of life we are forced into a position of humility that is best expressed in the attitudes of prayer. I think of the mystery and passion of life. In front of me or behind me is a wayward youth and I brood on his problems. He seems, out of the corner of my eye, thoroughly depraved. I read the Sunday paper.

•

Walk with Federico at four. We see the sun setting when we come up by the rise above the river. A tawny light burns on the lower windows of the M.s' house, empty now for two years, a haunted house for children, a point of adventure for boys, a headache for the police department—and yet for a moment it seems that fires and lamps burn in the drawing room, the smell of cooking rises up the back stairs, order and love reign here; it seems for the moment that the sun lights the lower windows.

The grass is beginning to yellow; it has a yellowish look in the last of the light. The ground is still covered with cut-leaf maples. Federico sees the moon for the first time and is enchanted. He points at it, and I tell him the word in English. "Moona," he says, "moona, mia moona," and when we lose it behind a tree or at a turn in the path he says, "Ciao, moon, ciao," and is surprised and pleased to find at another turning that the light still hangs in the sky. Mary is covering roses in the garden, and he shows the light to her. In the house, he drags a chair to the window and stands on it to see the light.

•

How the world shines with light.

I dream of a better prose style, freed of expedients, more thought-ful, working closer to the emotions by both direction and indirec-tion, feeling and intelligence. A pleasant dream, and I feel like myself.

•

But my brother, now, what will become of him? There seems to be no way of appealing to him; he seems to be blundering impatiently toward his grave. And what about the children? S., whose beauty was refined and sweet, has dyed her hair an orangy yellow that makes her features seem sharp. But will he, in his blundering, be able to give her the support she needs?

We cannot cope alone with the devil; we cannot cleanse our hearts and minds by our own devices. When we sin, and I have sinned—I have indulged lewd fancies and read the writing on the public wall—it is not our own flesh and blood that we seem to disfigure or our chances at immortality that we seem to damage, but the whole picture of life, shining or dark as the case may be, seems to have been offended by our lapse.

Heaven may be no more than the tender memories of our friends and lovers; some ghostly reappearance that we make, touching on cour-age and humor.

My brother, when he got offensively drunk here and when I re-proached him later, used to say that he only wanted to educate his neighbors, but he did come into our comfortable house where our at-tachments are, as a rule, tranquil and affectionate, like a blast, a thun-derclap of obscene misery, a man utterly unable to cope with the problems of his life, deaf to every appeal, his mind, his sentiments, and his body ravaged with alcohol, a stupid and impenetrable smile on his face, and in his heart a determination to destroy himself. And I think of the pleasures of our life together when we were young: hockey games on the ice pond, Emerson's Pond, snowball fights, walks on beaches, rides on summer nights in the old roadster, high purpose, high spirits, clowning and love. Now he is so drunk that he cannot walk from the chair to the table and when he gets there he can't eat. He falls into a drunken sleep. He thinks the fault is hers. He wanted to leave at two and play touch football as we used to on Thanksgiving, but she delayed and delayed, she took two hours to dress, she denied him his touch-football game, this simple pleasure, and while he waited he got drunk. The fault is his, we all have to wait, but why in God's name does she lead him into destruction?

•

Lunch at the Plaza. Truman Capote is in the men's bar. His bangs are dyed yellow, his voice is girlish, his laughter is baritone, and he seems to be a conspicuous male cocotte. This must take some doing, but on the other hand it must be a very limited way of moving through life. He seems to excite more curiosity than intolerance. Almost everyone these days drinks a special brand of gin—Beefeater, House of Lords, Lamplighter—and vodka. I hear the orders come over the bar. The bartender calls to a handsome Italian waiter and they disappear into a broom closet, to straighten out their racetrack bets, I hope. But to someone familiar with a rigorous and a simple way of life these scenes might seem decadent and final, like those lavish and vulgar death throes of the Roman Empire that we see in the movies.

•

Waiting in a basement corridor of the Saratoga Hospital to have a chest X-ray I feel very tired and wonder when I will feel well again. It seems now that all my life is false—jerry-built—the structure is of the wrong design and set in the wrong place. What, I think, are the rewards of virtue? Respiratory infections, ulcers, and night sweats? Is it cant to turn from whiskey and debauchery and speak of the holiness, the dignity of life? But there it is, a most solemn and beautiful process. Here are our powers of foolish debasement. I deny myself to be myself.

Either because I am convalescent or hung over or because of the lights in this room, its remoteness and the heat from its radiators, I do not seem to find what I want. What I want is blue sky—some robustness, some escape from this perpetual half fever. Skiing on the lawn I seem to come close to it, some opening of the mind, some way of embracing the world—the lightness, vitality, and movement that the prose I've been writing lacks.

Finish "The Music Teacher" today. Walk into town. The grandiose architecture along Union Avenue. The spectacle of an American small town on a winter's day. Its stratified past, the rise of ground at the railroad crossing, the new bowling alley with a vestibule shaped like a tenpin, the faint flavor of England that hovers over the Episcopal church, dance music pouring out of the supermarket, the very fat dispatcher at the cabstand, her hair dyed and her face painted for some rendezvous, this plaintive, this complex and moving landscape of love and change. The high-school girls, their eyes mascaraed, their voices loud, their ways bold, followed by a pack of crotch-hitching boys.

•

"The Hill Town" finished and off and all right, I guess, although a little intense. On Saturday I feel fine; feel like myself at last. But Mary seems to me unhappy. Every surface and angle of life seems to frustrate and irritate her. She swears at the turkey and she swears at the mashed potatoes. I am in high spirits and contented with the children and the better I feel the more conscious am I of her unhappiness. After church I make a crude and foolish remark and there is a shower of tears. And I think that I cannot repair this again, there is nothing that I can do or say. I am not concerned any longer with my own happiness; I am concerned with protecting the children. After lunch we go skating at the B.s'. The ice is nearly a foot thick, black here and there, with stones and branches showing. The sky is a winter sky, a little overcast. The dogs are barking. I go up and down the pond, up and down, chasing a piece of wood with an old hockey stick, and I am very happy. This is my sanctuary, this is my pleasure. The ice rumbles and thunders. The wind sweeps off the little powder we have cut with our skates. It is cold. How I love this: the bare landscape, the color in the willows, the exertion, and the memories of a game. How far I am from the Borghese Gardens.

•

I dislike writing here about booze-fighting, but I must do something about it. A friend comes to call. In my anxiety to communicate, to feel

the most in warmth and intimacy, I drink too much, which can be two
drinks these days. In the morning I am deeply depressed, my insides
barely function, my kidney is painful, my hands shake, and walking
down Madison Avenue I am in fear of death. But evening comes or
even noon and some combination of nervous tensions obscures my memories of what whiskey costs me in the way of physical and intellectual
well-being. I could very easily destroy myself. It is ten o'clock now and
I am thinking of the noontime snort.

•

A dark day, the trees covered with ice and bent with the weight of
ice.
"Poor Susie had to walk to the train," says Mary.
"I am very sorry," say I, "I would have driven her had I known."
"*Ha*," says Mary.
"Please don't talk like that," I say. "It isn't necessary." But the
damage is done. Gloom is universal. There is, to be said against
myself, my fear of impotence; I may not be able to possess her. And
there is the chance that she might do or say something that would
make possession impossible. I have no taste for brutality. Love for me
is love. It seems to me that she is unhappy, that she seeks the
cause of this unhappiness in our marriage, and that it lies in some
much earlier time of life. But that she cannot, quite understandably,
face this.

•

Re my unpleasant remarks this morning, Mary absents herself at
lunch with the baby and the dog. There is no note, no explanation.
Although the valley is full of fog and the driving is bad, I am not terribly anxious. I drink whiskey and rail loudly to the kitchen walls.
The gist of my remarks seems to be petulant. But what is the most
reasonable and creative course to take? Things will fester if I don't
mention her absence. I will mention it calmly. I have no stomach for
a quarrel.
Re the above: I am far from calm. My voice quakes with anger.
"Where were you?" No answer. "Where were you and the baby?" She
had gone to visit an old dressmaker she once employed in the city who
has now married a lawyer and settled in the suburbs: a queer woman,

it always seemed to me, bony, shrill, and vulgar, with a Pekinese at her shins. At five I make a series of cocktails and wind an armature with Ben. He is not tremendously interested in electrical motors. What a nice father I am! How wise and patient. How many things I have constructed for him; how many more than most fathers. Mary goes off to sing, the baby goes to sleep in despair, and we three sit down contentedly to read; Ben reads "Tommy Titmouse," Susie reads "The Turn of the Screw," and I read Dante. When Mary returns I am very distant and cool. I read some more—wool-gather, to tell the truth—take a bath, make a curt good night, and sleep. The pump in the basement wakes me at half past three, my kidney aches, and my mouth is dry and sour. I go out to see if the cellar is flooded, but not yet. In the bathroom I smoke a cigarette and my anger at Mary's having lunched with a dressmaker seems trivial and childish. How could I have got myself into such a rage? I am deeply and painfully ashamed. But then I rally in self-defense. I am not vegetative. I am easily upset. Why, then, invent ways of damaging my equilibrium? The pump grinds on and on and by half past seven, when I shave for church (Ash Wednesday), I seem to have committed in the space of eight hours the sins of anger, pride (what a marvellous father!), carnal self-admiration (what a flat stomach!), lustful fancies, and drunken sloth. In church the Epistle is majestic but my mind wanders. Now a clearing wind has sprung out of the northwest. I will think about Hell and the family.

•

For the record: On Valentine's, I give Mary a string of pearls; she gives me a dish. I like china but I would have preferred a suit of underdrawers with hearts on it. I do not claim my pearls; I go to sleep before she comes to bed. I think tonight this fortress is not worth the assault, siege, ladder work, and sometimes broadsword fighting that might be involved. On Saturday we got to the K.s' for drinks before lunch and I was very happy to be out of my own house. I think I will have an affair. Whom will it harm? Everybody from the infant in the cradle to the old gentleman in retirement in Daytona. But my own house seems dark and darkened by distempers and I do not have the strength or will to overtake them. I feel, most painfully, the lack of tenderness. This involves two things: the lack, and my inability to dress it with humor and love. Susie returns late from town and I am pleased to talk with her. This was all I wanted. But I drink too much and in the morning my liver is painful. We go off to lunch at Z.'s, and sitting in this pleasant room with pleasant people I am at a hundred-percent loss. I can make the gestures, the noises, I can move from the chair where I drink to the chair at the table, but my mind and my spirit are in chaos. Randy at four, I go to bed alone at half past eight with a scalded liver. And lying in bed I lie in great fear of death: death as chaos; death as a force that exposes all the incompleteness in my work—stories half told or untold; journeys only begun; my sons not yet men.

•

And in my makeup there seems to be some kind of knot, some hard-shell and insoluble element that, as far as I can see, conforms to social usage and custom and contradicts the hankerings and declarations of my flesh. It has, I should say, functioned creatively; has made of my life a web of creative tensions. But today it matters less. Its threats, I know, are hollow. Since I am indebted to this mysterious persuasion, perhaps we can live as friends.

•

To Princeton on the three o'clock. The unrolling of this industrial landscape, powerful and ugly; but this is where they manufacture your vaginal jellies and your shoe trees, your inner tubes and your floor varnish, your girdles and your shingles, and if we demand so much how can we complain about industrial devastation? Princeton seems to me both tranquil and highly expensive. We seem much farther south. The ponds are stained with the streak of red dirt that runs south through Pennsylvania into Georgia. Distant chimes. Well-dressed youth. O'Hara comes to tea and I find him a fine gentleman but I run up against the old feeling that in the end I will turn out not to be varsity. In the final judgment it will be discovered that I eat my peas off a knife and that there is a hole in the seat of my pants. I speak to an audience of not much more than twelve. On the previous evening, three Beat Generation poets, one of them an advocate of buggery, drew a crowd of hundreds. But I am not very well known and may never be. Home again, pleased to see the landscape touched, oh so lightly, with the spring, and then once more the force and hideousness of the industrial stretches and the great marshes with their outcroppings of stone, their broken hoardings, their tall grasses, a last sanctuary for the criminal, the pursued, the last natural hiding place in this part of the world.

•

Easter Eve: dyeing eggs and stuffing the turkey, all pleasant. Easter morning sunny and cool. To church with Susie and Ben. The church for once is full. I am delighted to hear that Christ is risen. I think that it is not against God's will to have my generative powers refreshed by the face of a pretty woman in a forward pew or to wonder about the hairy and somehow limpid young man on my left. It is the combination of hairiness and wistful grace that seems to mark him. When I hear that Mary found at the tomb a man in white raiment I am incredulous. It is hard for me to believe that God expressed His will, His intent in such a specific image. But when I go to the altar I am deeply moved. The chancel is full of lilies and their fragrance seems as fresh as it is heavy; a sign of good cheer. And that this message should have been revealed to us and that we should cherish it seems to be our finest triumph. Here in the chancel we glimpse some vision of transcendent love, some willing triumph over death and all of its lewd guises. And if it is no more than willingness, how wonderful that is in itself. Walk with my youngest son in the sun. How my whole love of life seems to gather around his form; how he fills me with the finest ambitions. Birds sing. There is a little shimmer of heat. The moment of darkness is gone. He throws sticks into the water, which is a perfectly clear, shallow, and rippled scarf of light. He shuffles through the old leaves.

Later we go to the B.s' for the Easter-egg hunt; but I am smitten suddenly with shyness, my smile is strained, my sensibilities are in-flamed, I am round-shouldered and bent-necked and dreary and nothing but a pint of bourbon will straighten me out. I count on painkillers until ten, when I retire and, half asleep—courage, lustiness, cleanli-ness, love, charity, strength, industry, intelligence, vision—I recount to myself a dozen times those virtues I admire.

•

B. tells me Fred is suffering from something that happened to him before his adolescence and I think it may have been my birth. I have tried for years to uncover the turning point in his life but this had never occurred to me. This is a clinical or a quasi-scientific disclosure, but it seems to me as rich as any other revelation. I can readily imagine it all. He was happy, high-spirited, and adored, and when, at the age of seven, he was told that he would have to share his universe with a brother, his forebodings would, naturally, have been bitter and deep. They would have been deepened by the outrageous circumstances of my birth. I was conceived mistakenly, after a sales banquet. My mother carried me reluctantly and my father must have been heard to say that he had no love in his heart for another child. These violent scenes must have given great breadth and intensity to his own conflicts. His feeling for me was always violent and ambiguous—hatred and love—and beneath all of this must have been the feeling that I challenged him in some field where he excelled—in the affections of his parents. I have felt for a long time that, with perfect unconsciousness, his urge was to destroy me. I have felt that there was in his drunkenness some terrible cunning.

Here then are three worlds—night, day, and the night within the night. Here are the passions and aspirations of the dead, moving freely among us with malevolence and power. Here is a world of open graves. Here is a world where our imagery breaks down. We have no names, no shapes, no lights, no colors to fill out these powers, and yet they are as persuasive as the living. Out of his window he can see the city shining in the light of day and he adores it but he will be motivated less by this vision than by his remembrance of a scream heard in a dark stairwell fifty years ago. They seem to destroy him and to counsel him to destroy me. We seem to be at one another's throats. We hear the lashing of a dragon's tail in the dead leaves, the piteous screaming of a child whose eyes are plucked out by a witch, we smell the damps of the snake pit. This suggestion or disclosure seems very important to me and I pray it will be as helpful to Fred.

•

After dinner we hear "Tosca," which I think tremendous. I read "Oblomov" in this empty house. The big window stands open. The loud night sounds on the terrace outside make me uneasy. But what can I be doing that would trouble the unquiet dead? I sleep and wake at dawn—partly my bladder, partly the vigorous noise of nest-building going on among the birds. They can be heard dragging sticks over the tin gutters. They are all singing loudly. Then up springs my capricious muscle, all ready for fun. Downstairs I hear my friend coughing and flushing his toilet. I think about trout water but I resent this forced cheerfulness: I wade down the stream, pool after pool, catch a big trout, and use my hat as a landing net. My muscle keeps up its nagging and complaining and I do not want love or beauty or lewdness, I only want to get back to sleep. I fall asleep at last and have a sweet dream in which I crash a cocktail party at J. P. Marquand's. I am well liked and passed gracefully from guest to guest. Toward the end P. appears to be with me and when we speak Italian several guests speak Italian with us. At the end my brother appears, drunken, apologetic, and intractable. He comes to spoil the party, not because he wants to, but because he is driven by unreasoning forces. When he was a boy, and after my birth, there was a party in the neighborhood. He was not invited and he went to the house and threw a stone through the window. Now he is reliving this incident in our lives and in my dreams. I wake feeling rested and happy.

•

I must think of alcoholism as a progressive disease. It has been for a week or longer that I have, on almost every day, drunk too much. There is also the question of my being denied my desires. This has also been a matter of a week. Even before dinner is put onto the table, I am discouraged. "As soon as the dishes are washed," says Mary, "I am going upstairs and going to sleep." This may not be conscious but I think it is intentional. One thing or another. Last night such an array of metal rollers, curlers, and pins that it was discouraging. I awake with a thorn in my groin and think sentimentally of prostitution. Why should the whores be persecuted, arrested, and thrown into jail when all they mean to do is to lead us out of the dilemma, to let us live peacefully with ourselves? And I think of a man who has been denied for six weeks, who is in an agony of desire, who is driven. Where can he turn, where can he go?

•

I take Ben and his friends down to the river fishing. Spiders and bumblebees among the rocks on the embankment. The potency of this place, this milieu. Cinders, beer cans, the rusty siding, a freight train

pulling a hundred cars disappearing around the bend, an old man emp-
tying his bladder for the third time in an hour, boys throwing rocks,
tough angler in a rowboat—he picks on little kids and makes jokes during
catechism—the slow smiles of the Saturday passengers in a train as we
wave. A dead-end place but a very peaceful one. It is very peaceful to
sit here drinking beer, although I am afraid that the boys will fall off
the railroad bridge into the cove. What I am afraid of, it seems, is that
I will have to dive in after them. I am a coward.

•

Walk in the garden with Federico. He is full of beans. My love
muscle is restive. Federico admires the granite lion and the marble dog,
he stuffs the faucets with gravel and is not obedient. It will rain. I pick
him up in my arms and he falls into a deep sleep. "Oh, I love you," I
say as I carry him. "You are my best; you and the singing of the cardinal
birds dissuade me from lust and anger." I go with Ben to the doctor
and he slips his finger up his rump and knocks his b--ls together. What
a strange life this must be—this seascape of rumps. There is on his
face and in his manner the trace of a terrible loneliness. Mary watches
a flock of yellow finches in the garden. There must be fifty. I embrace
her and hope to declare my intentions for the evening but in the kitchen
there is some unpleasantness. I am oversensitive but what can be done?
Anyhow, my desires persist. I help Susie with her homework and go
upstairs early but it is already too late. The lights are off. Her eyes are
shut and there is so much hardware protruding from her brow that an
embrace might be dangerous. You could put out your eye.

All my kind feelings have been turned into bitterness and anger. I
sit on the edge of the bathtub smoking and I resent being forced into
this position but if I should earnestly try to explain it I might be answered
with peals of callous laughter. I am very angry and I think I have some
insight into the bewildering passions of a murderer. And I think that
a perverse woman can sometimes, as with my brother, destroy a man.
She denies with ridicule his deepest means of self-expression, his whole
power of love. He should take a mistress but where will he find one?
His secretary is too skinny and has bad breath. It would be indecent to
attack the maid. A is too fat and B is too short and C is too passionate
and D is not passionate enough and so forth and so on. Oh, she has
excellence and kindness, I know, but I do not feel like going on my

knees to ask her favors. This morning I feel sad and tired although I hope for the best. She is standing at the window watching the yellow finches in the garden. There are fifty—very shy—and at each movement or voice from the house they fly up into the trees, the hemlocks. Then when it is quiet they come down—yellow, and like a fall of leaves on a cold wind.

I go into town and decide to lunch with a pretty girl, but when I look up her number in the telephone book my eyes have grown too weak for me to read the pages. I must, to the amazement of a man behind me, strike a match and hold it close to the book to find the number. We will meet and so I walk on the streets for an hour, up past, by chance, the house—the windows—where Mary and I first became lovers. A fine day, and the weather has brought more beauties, more freaks, more everything out onto the sidewalk. It is a spectacle. It is spring and I am happy and will meet a pretty girl at a bar. The bar is dark and full of advertising men. They all seem to drink here regularly; they talk about what happened last night and the night before. R. comes in, very pretty, we lunch and I leave her at her door. I feel better, I am not depressed; there are plenty of pretty women in the world and I am not unattractive. I am cool to Mary. Why should I worry about her intractableness? We go to a concert—three quartets: Mozart, Debussy, and Beethoven—and it is the music that persuades me that I should try to understand Mary, that my emotional responsibilities lie here. This seems to be the purport of all the melodies. Later, when we are together in the bathroom, my desires seem maniacal. "I had lunch at the Nautilus," she said, "and it was expensive and awful. First I had a floury cup of clam chowder and some old salad, some leftover salad. Then mackerel, very greasy and not fresh. I can still taste it. And some awful broccoli. . . ." Oh please, please, I groan, please hurry. There is some difference of opinion here.

•

Wake at six to a day of such beauty that it seems as if this corner of the planet was all one bloom, all opening and burgeoning, and there is more here than we can say: prismatic lights, prismatic smells, something that sets one's teeth on edge with pleasure. The morning light is gold as money and pours in the eastern windows. But it is the shadow that is exciting, the light that cannot be defined, the maple tree, its leaves not yet formed, that is astounding in its beauty and its succulence and that is not itself but one of a million trees, a link in a long chain of experience beginning in childhood.

Rogation Sunday. There are two known worlds, the visible and the invisible, and this drop of wine and crust is the link between the two. I seem to see the chain of being, reaching from beneath the earth up into the sky. And I think of the prayers that rise up into the chancel: Shall I sell my beer stock? Shall I stay away from Mrs. Piggott? Shall I enter Ralph in Princeton? Shall I turn in the station wagon? But among them some of worth, some of the deepest yearning.

•

The lower school here burns down. A rambling frame building with turrets and amendments, saturated in creosote, it seems to explode in flame. Ten minutes after the old teacher smells smoke, it is a pillar of fire. The firemen can't approach it, the heat is so intense. All the surrounding trees can be seen to wither. Here is the savage power of fire, the smiting force, which, like so much else in life, evades precautions and is ruthless. Within half an hour everything is gone, the clothing, the children's toys, the souvenirs of travel and athletic prowess, the rich precipitate of their lives. At three o'clock they possessed an environment. At three-twenty they are naked and dependent upon charity. The bitter smoke.

•

Year after year I read in here that I am drinking too much, and there can be no doubt of the fact that this is progressive. I waste more days, I suffer deeper pangs of guilt, I wake up at three in the morning with the feelings of a temperance worker. Drink, its implements, environments, and effects all seem disgusting. And yet each noon I reach for the whiskey bottle. I don't seem able to drink temperately and yet I don't seem able to stop.

•

My forty-seventh birthday and I feel neither young nor old, sprightly in the middle, and pray that I will have done a decent book by the forty-eighth. Shaving, and trying to come to terms with myself, I think that I am a small man, small feet, small p---k, small hands, small waist, and that these are the facts. I must confine my attentions to little, little women, sit in tiny chairs, etc. And then I think of how I hate small men, those whose incurable youth is on them like a stain. How I hate small feet, small hands, small-waisted males who stand behind their small wives at cocktail parties in a realm of timid smallness.

•

I would like a more muscular vocabulary. And I must be careful about my cultivated accent. When this gets into my prose, my prose is at its worst.

•

A four-round booze fight, beginning when I take Susie into town and get a nervous stomachache in Ardsley. There is the usual psychological turmoil and I drink two Martinis before lunch and feel very playful. I seem entitled to these drinks. As the afternoon wanes the turmoil waxes, and when I get home I think I deserve a few cocktails. I know that in the morning I will have to take care of Federico—I can't work—and with this as an excuse I drink after dinner. In the morning I feel sick, disgusted with myself, despairing and obscene. I have a drink to pull myself together at half past eleven and begin my serious drinking at half past four, when I also begin the cooking. I have my excuses. My prudence has been destroyed and when I've finished with the dishes I take a tonic dose of nut-brown whiskey. On Saturday I feel even worse. I have a drink before lunch. This seems to leave me with a sick headache, nausea. After dinner we have to pay a call on La Tata; this is a mandatory courtesy, and S. keeps filling my glass with Scotch. On Sunday I feel the worst. I take Federico for a walk. At a quarter after eleven I write an attack on the evils of drink. Then I look up the telephone number of Alcoholics Anonymous. Then, my hands shaking, I open the bar and drink the leftover whiskey, gin, and vermouth, whatever I can lay my shaking hands on. Now the bout is over and I am myself again, but I wish I could be done with this.

At the station, Federico and I wave to the trains. The engineers wave to us, sometimes the conductors and the passengers raise their hands. Down the river in the morning light comes the train from Chicago. The windowsills of the coaches are lined with paper coffee cups. The first-class passengers sit alone in their roomettes, and how much

alone one can be in these places. The dining car is closed. The waiters
have stripped off the tablecloths and dressed in their street clothing.
Everything is in readiness, although it will be an hour before they reach
New York. The ladies have on their hats, they hold their gloves and
bags. And in this delay, this dogwatch, this point of readiness we wish
them, my son and I, Godspeed and a pleasant arrival. We hope that
they will be met at the station by their friends or their family or that
they will go to some place where they will be greeted with affection,
trust, and sometimes love. We hope they will not end up in a hotel
room.

·

I stopped smoking Saturday because it seemed to give me painful
indigestion. But at a party on Saturday night I must have smoked a
package of cigarettes. I smoked three cigarettes before noon on Sunday
and one in the afternoon. I smoked two or three on Monday. On Tuesday
I smoked one. Today, Wednesday, I have smoked none and it is a quarter
to ten. My chest promises to clear up and it is a pleasure not to have
a bronchial wheeze like a rusty gate. I cough in the morning but I cough
without a sense of guilt. However, the withdrawal from nicotine leaves
me quite dizzy, and we have to drive tonight to Sherman. It might be
dangerous. And yet having come this little way I hate to return to a
world where I am dependent upon cigarettes and, when travelling, upon
cigarettes made, it seems, of twine and dead leaves. We will come back
to this. My head is not where it belongs.
    I read "Where Angels Fear to Tread." When he writes of the love
of beauty and the love of truth he writes with purity and eloquence and
we seem to be in a place of some elevation; but in fact we are watching
two spinsters and one unfledged male steal a child and cause his death.
The death of this child seems to be idle and repulsive and I think that
in fiction, much as in life, we may not, without good reason, slaughter
the innocent, persecute the defenseless and the infirm, or speak with
idle malice. He has grace, sometimes elegance, and I think of the charge
of vulgarity made against my prose. If it is vulgar, and it may be, it is
an honest vulgarity, an incurable or congenital vulgarity, a vulgarity
that lies close to my heart. But when he speaks of the invincibility of
society I envy his lucidness; again, when he describes the vision, I can't
recall how, of the nature of our transactions here as a trial of what it

is men might accomplish. I catch him turning an epigram on the Sacraments, that is, that they are not the facts that they are not meant to
be.

I do not make much sense without tobacco.

•

July 8th. The twelfth day here. In the evening, the piece or reach
of sea between the dunes is as succinct as a shark's fin. This looking
northeast, the light at our backs. "Oh, how beautiful," I exclaim, "the
most beautiful peace." Said the same things at Port Ercole and Bristol,
New Hampshire. There is a place on the walk to Coskata where I get
spooked. But how legitimate, how primitive are our feelings about the
sea. This image of death. Brine thou wert and to brine returnest. The
sense of malevolence expresses perhaps nothing but my own morbidity,
but there it is. The sea is a claimant. Not even your finest will outlast
this simple wave. "Doesn't the Andrea Doria lie off there," Mary asks,
"the sea coursing through her lounges, iceboxes?" We walk to Coskata,
and I relate old and idle stories. At the pond, the incandescence of the
sea light. Wild roses and knife grass beautifully exposed. At the horizon,
always the incandescence of an afterglow.

Walk over to the bay shore to see the sunset, evening star, and new
moon. I wish devoutly that I were a better man. In the morning, Ben
and I go swordfishing. Our captain has a kindly, sunburned face, rucked
neck—deeply—a tonsure of gray hair, sound teeth. Driving past the
hayfields, he recollects the rigors of haying in his youth. This is the
image that stays with me. He is no longer youthful, but he has passed
most gracefully through the roles of his life—farm boy, high-school
student, husband, and father—and is their sum. As we go out to sea
he stands on the cabin roof wearing a heavy pullover, ravelled at the
elbows, and denims and sneakers. His feet are apart, one arm is looped
around an upright, the other arm hanging slack against his trouser leg,
but the fingers moving, nervous or ruminative. He seems to want to
find a tear in the smooth cloth. I find something in his figure that is
unusually fine and coherent, some fineness of penetration. You can see
in the cant of his shoulders what he was, what he may be. He scans
the sea for six hours, looking for a swordfish fin. His penetration, his
kindliness never varied.

We go out through the lethal shoals at Smith Point, where a big fishing boat, grounded there last week, is breaking up—her life rafts swinging from their tack, gulls plundering the wreck. I am intensely uncomfortable, but I think that if, at this time, life should prove to be so tonic and so bitter you have no choice but to take it—the galling elixir—or sink into the living death of a neurasthenic; a rainy-day boy, startled by the shadow of a falling leaf. I drink some gin and fall asleep; wake with a wonderful sense of refreshment. My under-consciousness is strengthened; my anxieties are gone.

•

Fred calls to say that he would like to discuss some business with me and I invite my brother to lunch. I have suspected that he was drinking again; but he was not today. Heavy-faced. A little alcoholic lameness. He gets up unreadily from his chair and flinches getting into his car. However, his constitution seems unusually strong and durable and I am happy to share this with him. After lunch I drive him to the station with my younger son and we park there waiting (1) for him to explain his visit; (2) for a train to pass, to the delight of my son. Finally a train passes and this much is accomplished. Fred talks on about his trip across the country in August and finally I ask him, as gently as possible, what is on his mind. "Nothing," he says, "nothing," but as I press him a little I find that he plans to open a men's-clothing store in either San Juan, Puerto Rico, or Palo Alto, California. He is going down to San Juan to look things over. He is also thinking of a little excursion to Nantucket. I ask if he would like some money. No, this will not be necessary; but we drive back to the house and I write him a check for five hundred dollars. He puts this in his pocket and leaves. I am not genuinely petulant—I have to work at the feeling—and Mary is not at all shrewish. The facts are only these: that to continue to make such contributions I must find ways of making more money. At least he does not suffer today from the illusion of being cunning. Mary points out that his wife will not work although she could very easily, and that he is unrealistic about looking for work; that he looks for nothing but the kind of job that will never come his way; but I sympathize with him here. I could not get a job as a haberdasher's clerk myself. I might get a job in the liquor store, and I could work as a gardener, but pride and status are nearly insuperable obstacles. "Neither of you will ever let a woman work,"

Mary says, and here we have a change of scenery, a change of atmosphere. This is a sore point. When my mother went to work she abdicated all of her responsibilities as a woman. Our house was cold. I was the cook, dishwasher, and cleaning woman. My father was wretched. I defend myself, confusedly, but I have no objections to a woman's working as long as she remains my wife, as long as there is no exchange of roles. And I come back to the bad feeling of a triangular relationship: that in my delight in erotic love I leave myself without a position of retreat.

I think the atmosphere has changed but the fault may be mine, there seems to be some canalization in my feeling, some inclination to seem grief-stricken, a lack of vigor. Mary talks with her sister on the phone for an hour and there is a change in her voice, her accent. She talks with her other sister for half an hour and there is still another change. We all, to some degree, continuously play out the roles of the long-since discontinued dramas of our childhood—and in myself I sometimes hear a change of accent in the company of my brother. Then she sends a cable to B. and here we have still another change. We talk about the administration of the summer place. "You don't have to worry about this," Mary says. The remark is simple enough but I think it is spoken meanly and I multiply the possibilities of bad feeling by asking sarcastically to be forgiven for my presumption. We kiss good night and sleep but I am angry and feel unclean, almost scabrous. The boy wakes and I take him into our bed and it is his power to remind me of the freshness and the cleanliness of love: to deliver me.

•

Coverly's return does not stand alone. I will try Honora's death. I think of a Saturday afternoon in childhood when our plans to play games misfired; the football was flat, and nobody could find a valve. It was autumn. We went over to the R.s' barn and had a penis-measuring contest, followed by an orgy, but when it was over I felt so guilty and ashamed of myself, so sorrowful and uneasy. All of life seemed to lie around us, but we could not escape into it, and how long, dear God, must we wait? I went home and ate a sandwich and was put by my mother into a bath so hot that it made my skin pucker and made the touch of everything unpleasant. My white shirt (too small and badly ironed by the old Finn) and my serge suit (also too small) felt like a punishment, and I couldn't find my dancing pumps. I connected this with my lewd behavior in the morning. I was being punished. I went into the closet, got to my knees, and said the Lord's Prayer three times, noticing, at the end of the third time, that my dancing pumps, in a serge bag, hung from a hook above me. At least this much of my prayer was answered, but I was filled with terrible longings, and I still felt, after the bath, parboiled and uncomfortable. I walked down to the Masonic Temple with Charlie and got there just as the grand march was beginning. I would have run away, except that my mother was a matron that afternoon, and anyhow where would I, in my blue serge, find a haven? They were building houses in the meadow; they were building houses in the woods. We spent the rest of the afternoon pushing little girls around the waxed floor and watching the light outside the windows get faint, and by the time dancing school was over so was that Saturday.

•

That was the year everybody in the United States was worried about homosexuality. They were worried about other things, too, but their other anxieties were published, discussed, and ventilated while their anxieties about homosexuality remained in the dark: remained unspoken. Is he? Was he? Did they? Am I? Could I? seemed to be at the back of everyone's mind. A great emphasis, by way of defense, was put upon manliness, athletics, hunting, fishing, and conservative clothing, but the lonely wife wondered, glancingly, about her husband at his hunting camp, and the husband himself wondered with whom he shared a rude bed of pines. Was he? Did he? Had he? Did he want to? Had he ever? But what I really mean to say is that this is laughable. Guilty man may be, but only an absurdly repressed people would behave this way.

•

I think very vaguely of The Death Of The Short Story; the year the squirrels came in; some projection of my feelings about returning to this country. I read two stories of mine and find them too breezy. They were deeply felt at the time but there seems to be a lack of deep notes; no bass clef; a lack of fundamentals. Why should some of these lines, drawn from the deepest pain and pleasure I have known, seem to be glossy and so little else? Haste, maybe. I think of Coverly as Apollo and Moses as Dionysus. And looking around for some general, some fundamental axe to grind, what do I come up with? The fundamental competitiveness of brothers. And of this society: it is not so astonishing that we should find violence here, but is it not nearly impossible to relate it to the niceness—the religion of niceness with its sacraments, its jealousies, and its demanding faithfulness that seems to be the religion of this province?

What is the meaning, though, of this sudden, this random tenderness that we feel for the woman in worsted stockings and the young banker from the Congo? What stirs in us? Is it the chance that we may be perfectly understood? Is it the thought of some peaceable kingdom where men and women love one another freely and without guilt? Or is it a promise of the conquest of death?

•

If I am writing narrative prose, and I sometimes am, I must content myself with these limitations. Every line cannot be a cry from the heart, cut in stone. But I do rebel against common speech, against the quality of filler I find in my work, and I try to escape in Leander's journal, the boy's story, the chambermaid and the latrine. But since I was not born with a strong accent I will have to get along on what I have.

•

Half asleep, I think or dream of fields that, when I was young, were fertile but that are neglected, forgotten now. How sad. And I think that we, who, when we were young, demanded brave and explicit counsel, find ourselves, in the middle of life, unable to answer any of the questions our children ask. I can't seem to get the drunk's voice off the page, to make him speak with color. You entered life with absolutely nothing and you'll go out with absolutely nothing. A bigoted and anesthetized world. But what I don't seem able to do is to pull up the vision: the feeling of what life can be without uncommon bigotry, censure, and repression. And I don't seem able to get the triangle, the balance between the niceties, the stress on the appearance of things, the natural violence that lies beneath all of this, and the vision of a world where the balance is more commodious; where the sense of tragedy is not lost in anesthesia.

•

The deadline seems to be an artificial one that I have set up myself to impress myself. It may be childish, but it's kept me occupied. I think

of Joyce, choosing here and there a word with such brilliance that it
floats through my mind all day and is hanging there when I wake. I
have my way in bed and seem returned, as I take her in my arms, to
some fine summer night. We cling to one another's lips as if we were
inhaling the warm dark, the warmest, darkest air. My son didn't dream
of the werewolf.

"Of course," Mary says, "it's only natural for a woman to be unfaithful to her husband." This re the man who delivers dry cleaning.
"Youse are very charming" is a sample of his style. Standing on the
threshold, he says, "I didn't pick up on Saturday because I've been
having this trouble. It seems I couldn't do nothing right. My wife went
off with this police lieutenant, the one who directs traffic at the corner
of Main and Broadway. Here's a picture of her. Pretty, isn't she? When
we got married, everybody said it was a perfect match. She run off
leaving me with the four little kids to take care of and the job and all.
Now she's come back but she don't sleep with me. She says she's saving
herself for him. She still thinks she's in love with him. But he, he don't
care about her anymore. He don't ever want to see her again. They told
me this at the police station. Next week we're going to see the monsignor
and talk it over with him and the Department of Welfare; they're going
to get a psychiatrist for her. She needs help and I'm going to help her.
I'm going to be very kind and strong. I'll bring the rugs back on
Saturday."

•

We run out of liquor as I had planned, at noon. At three I study
the bar with its empty bottles. At four I drink four cups of tea with
sugar. At five I stuff myself with bread and cheese and play backgammon.
At six, when Mary returns, I drink the last of the liquor in the house,
two fingers of cooking rum. This does not make much difference and I
begin to feel the symptoms of withdrawal. I shout at Federico. Drying
the dishes I think of my dead mother, lying in her grave; and death
appears to me to be a force of loneliness, only hinted at by the most
ravening loneliness we know in life; the soul does not leave the body
but lingers with it through every stage of decomposition and neglect,
through heat and cold and the long nights. Another symptom of withdrawal is anxiety. The oil burner will explode. Thieves will come in

and harm my children, etc. This morning (9 A.M.) I have also given up smoking. Walking down to the station I am pleased to fill my chest with the cold morning air. I seem to feel it refresh my blood. How much better this is for me than smoke. But in the last half hour I have begun to feel the absence of a habitual stimulus. I feel sleepy—horny in a disgusting way—my eyes are sore and my sense of things is faded and dim. Here is the letdown, the distortion.

Gino the barber looks out of the Saturday paper, gracefully brandishing his hairy forearms. In his middle twenties, I guess, and from south of Naples, he seems to be the archetypal Italian boy. His skin is a fine olive color, very fine, and drawn over a well-shaped, egg-shaped skull. His curls are black and well groomed. His eyes are large and full of appeal and he touches one on the shoulder, the knee, the arm and hand; his whole manner is of a continuous and fairly gay sexual flirtation, but if he were pressed I think he would claim to be innocent, and I think he is. His innocence is part of his democratization. In the New World one isn't rolled for three hundred lire; one is monogamous, one is innocent, one is pure. I think he is comical and charming but I also think that, having contented oneself with such an explanation, he might find that Gino was the destroyer of his way of life.

I dream of the photograph of a woman kneeling in a field and holding two yellow roses. The sense of the picture is that she is tributary to the roses; that the picture was taken for some rosarian who was proud of his yellow blooms. It seems to be in the past because her summer, cotton dress has long sleeves, a long skirt, and a high bodice, although this does nothing to conceal the fullness of her bosom. She is kneeling in a field of straw and holding the two roses over one knee. Her face is oval, very fresh in color, and her hair is the lightest brown. I don't mean blond; I mean a refinement of goldenness, of brownness that has no relation to a blonde or a towhead. Her hair is long. This and her skirts convince me that the picture is an old one. Her hair is drawn softly back from her face and fixed in a bun at the back of her neck.

Stew around and make a half-arsed attempt to stop smoking. Write some letters. Break down at ten past ten and cross the railroad bridge to the cig machine. Read some Mailer and decide that his prose has a better tone than mine. Acute discontent. Knock off at a quarter to four. A cold winter afternoon. Drive the cleaning woman home with Federico. Stop at the liquor store, where he gets a lollipop and I get gin and whiskey. Driving back home, past the prison and down by the river, the sky is gold, so gold that my cupidity is aroused. It is like the gold standard, the source of the legends of gold. An inscrutable wall of light. Back home I knock out some ice cubes, give the local paper a shake, and stand by the glass panes of the storm door thinking of the lover's sense of crises, the lover's fine sense of crises, the lover's sense of the hour of day, the lover's fine sense of hearing. Some part of the sentence seems to stand, and standing at the door I seem to find myself for five minutes: straight, spare, clearheaded, neither young nor old, and not much concerned with age, not concerned at all. What has been the matter: too much gin, too much smoke, too much crap of all kinds. So I make a drink and light a cigarette.

•

Touch and go with the booze, and I must have been disagreeable. At the table I accuse Mary of being negative. I do this freely and unfairly, since one by one the members of her family have taken me aside and asked if I didn't find her impossible. This is no way to behave. And I can't remember how the night ended. I read Nabokov, who is florid and who now and then makes a mistake and puts me at ease: brings me down from the ideal of "the lover's fine sense of crises," from my ideal of a prose that carries its vitality like a scraped wire. Something in between. But nearly every time I think of a story I see it set up in the magazine opposite a cartoon; and I must realize that the people who read my fiction have stopped reading *The New Yorker*, I must realize that the breach here is real and happy. I have spent the last three months trying to write three stories, wanting money, really: wanting to prove to myself that I can. I think I've wasted some time but I don't think all of it is wasted.

•

My sense of morality is that life is a creative process and that anything that chafes or impedes this forward thrust is evil and obscene. The simplest arrangements—trees, a line of bathhouses, a church steeple, a bench in a park—appear to have a moral significance, a continuity that is heartening and that corresponds to my whole sense of being. But there are speculations and desires that seem contrary to the admirable drift of the clouds in heaven, and perhaps the deepest sadness that I know is to be absorbed in these.

•

Mary sings at a Methodist church, a little, frame, brown-stained, self-respecting barn of a place that must have been a country church when it was raised but that is now crowded out by a firehouse, grocery store, apartment building, etc. We are early, and as we wait the old women of the neighborhood appear, some of them with sticks and crutches. Many of them wear Christmas-tree ornaments on their coats. They wear feathers and beads and are painted like savages. I notice the talismanic significance of mink. These are poor people and cannot afford pelts but every woman there sports a piece of mink as the women of Rome wear a talisman against the evil eye. One has a mink hat, another has mink buttons on her coat, another has a cloth coat woven to look like mink, another has a muskrat coat dyed like mink, even little children have mink cuffs, some scrap of the magical fur.

•

We drink champagne and have a fine supper. "Oh, I'm so happy," Mary says, stepping into my arms, and it seems to me that I can feel the happiness of other people in the houses around us. I think that everyone is happy tonight. Susie and I go to church and I am very happy at this, for, whatever my doubts are, this gospel of the Prince of Peace, born in a stable, expresses my deepest feelings about life. Two meddlesome vestrymen regulate Communion. Some strays, who have wandered in to hear the carols, are mystified by the liturgy. Across the aisle I see the face of a boy home from college: the son of a friend and neighbor. He has a sharp nose, his hair is a little long, and he reminds me of H., and it seems to me that in this relationship I may have been sinful, a force of corruption; but there is a great difference between these two faces. In this one there is authority, skepticism—the color is high and fresh—and he looks out at the world with a fitting tolerance and humor for this time of life. Another boy, home from college, comes into my pew and we share a hymnal and there is something so pleasant about this exchange, how well we get along with one another, how sometimes the meeting of strangers is like a bath in the finest brine. Home, we put the presents under the tree and fill the stockings; and I think back over the psychology of the hour: the authorities of goodness, Santa Claus and the heroic cowboy, in whose image and likeness we hope to be created. There is something like a nightmare in this excess of presents—crystal glasses, velvet robes, a shrimp dish, trucks and cars—but somehow, not soberly, I grope from some other, less bewildering, meaning in this nightmare and I think that with these foolish excesses we struggle, intuitively, to express our convictions about the abundance of life.

•

Skating at the B.s', first time out. Gray ice, a little rough. The wind swings around to the southwest and the day gets warmer as the ice melts. In the night, on the southwest wind, a torrential rain the sum of whose thousands of sounds is to raise in my mind the image of an English beauty in a colored advertisement for soap. Her hair is a subtle gold, and there is a blush on her cheeks. In the morning the dark curtain of rain is still falling and I am miserable with anxiety about the sump pump, the oil burner, and the laundry ceiling, a piece of which falls. To Holy Communion—with B.—where I think of how we obscure our self-knowledge with anxiety; that it is not what we desire but what we fear and dread we may desire that impedes us—a look at the poor quality of my devoutness and at the desirability of the posture of prayer, the attitude of solemn thanksgiving.

Two drinks before lunch, and then I take the boy for a walk. The rain has stopped, the air is fresh and soft, the wind has begun to move around to the northwest where it will settle. It is clearing. A beam of light, three yards wide and five miles long, falls through the mountains and across the river and into this moves a coal-burning freighter, the smoke from her funnel knocked forward by the wind over her bow decks, heightening the general impression of dishevelment. We watch a train come in and carry off a handful of passengers with bags. As I pass the B.s', Mr. B., who is not a friend, asks me if I think the rain is over. "I want to take the kiddies over to the skating rink at Bear Mountain," says he, looking suspiciously at the clouds, "but I wouldn't want to go if I thought it was going to rain." I assure him that the wind is moving to the northwest and we walk on. The brook is flooded with brown and noisy water. D. and his friends are building a dam. Past the mulberry trees, at the highest point of the road, the air is fragrant and warm, and here is a persuasive imitation of spring complete with bird-song, brilliant green grass, and a pleasant feeling of languor. The box-wood smells like a cat's lair. Later, we carry the tree and the wreaths across the lawn to burn them on the dump, and I remember my trip north at this time last year with the deceased trees, still wearing a little angel's hair, fired summarily into the ditch beside the tracks. The boys are playing football. And the wind is now out of the northwest, powerful, shaking the big trees with a percussive sound. It is all much more dramatic now. The wreath flares up. The smell of burning holly and hemlock is like a vital perfume of life: salt water and the breasts of a woman. Turning, we see that the sky to the north is lilac and sapphire and in the southwest an implacable wall of gold so pure, so brilliant, that it is my cupidity that is excited; and it is all thrown around, these colors and lights, in prodigious disorder.

•

I wander around the city. Here and there I see a face that reminds me of the sheer delight we take in one another's company, and I mean all kinds: friendship, horseplay, inventiveness, tenderness, and the darkest coupling. And here and there I see a face that reminds me with deep sadness of the fact that I am not young anymore, that I have suffered some losses and am not content, and that the sense of standing on a curb, looking out levelly at the world, as a young man does, is gone. I have my pleasures, God knows, and there is a thrust of life in me that time has not changed, but my eyes are no longer clear, my skin firm, or my hair bright. However, some girls still seem to like me, and you can't have everything. And here and there on the street an impression, a figure, seems inflicted on me; a figure in a belted trenchcoat hurrying up a side street. The figure seems to be one of supreme misdirection. There is some sexuality here, but of what sort? And the young men in cuffless trousers and Italian shoes mean to be attractive but attractive to whom? There is no doubt about the intentions of the men on the Corso, but these youths seem to me mostly to be flirting with the image in the mirror.

•

Susie comes home with news that she is on some sort of probation. Her negativism, her digressive negativism are thought to be bad attitudes in class. Our conversation begins in soft voices but then I begin to shout, she cries and throws herself onto her bed, I order her to get up and eat dinner and tell her if this were in Italy I would hit her over the head with a piece of wood, and Federico, catching the harsh or ugly notes in my voice, begins to cry. We sit down to a gloomy table. I read. At eight o'clock sharp the wind springs out of the north with gale force, an inundation of snow and rain. Susie goes for a walk in the storm. Later I speak with her. "I'm indifferent," she says. "I'm a mass of intelligence adrift. I don't care if I sleep in the street."

"Oh, you don't," say I, as the wind flings the rain against the windows. "Would you like to go out and sleep in the street this evening?" Here is sarcasm, fruitless and obscene. I apologize and plead with her for friendship, and lying in bed I ask myself, How can she be indifferent to the beaches of Nantucket, the city of Rome, the pleasures of skiing, the promise of love and friendship?

At four, Federico wakes with a scream. "Get the mother out of the way," he says, and goes back to sleep. What is going on in his mind? Ben is also awake and is afraid of the dark. Getting back to sleep I seem to enter the rich color and shade of a tapestry and lie under lemon trees in whose dark leaves there are many doves. Later, I fancy a very lewd orgy but without any sense of shock or revulsion. I seem to have come to terms with my bones and these courses of speculation and I hope it does not mean any loss of moral awareness.

•

Snow predicted. It begins at around nine in the morning, a dark sky but a hesitant and unimpressive fall. By ten o'clock the ground is covered. By eleven you hear the whining noise of a car stuck in a drift. By twelve all the back roads are closed and there is almost no traffic on the main highway. Schools close. Offices close. There is some primitive camaraderie in this convulsion of nature. I help to shovel the station platform. Mrs. M. suddenly turns on me a burst of confidence about Mrs. V. "My deah, she is ruthless and dishonest." She has the mind of a strong and ruthless man. By half past two there is ten inches or more of fine powder. My friend and I take a walk. Perhaps it is he, I think, who basks in my admiration. I think of animals in this weather, says he, cows and sheep, the doves in their cote. We walk through the Italian garden, all its form now somehow comical and absurd. Dunce caps of snow on the baroque pedestals. The boxwood hedge paved with snow. A peak on the heraldic lion. As we walk up the lawn the fall is so thick that we can't see the big house. I shovel a path and play with my sons. How pleased we are with this turn in the weather. A stray dog appears and disappears. Just before dark, before we draw the curtains, a blue light of great intensity fills the valley. In the dark, Ben and I take a walk. The snow is still falling, blowing. In the few lights, in the few streetlights, it shines with a hardness and a brilliance that is unlike its insubstantialness; it shines like cut steel. In the morning A. calls to cancel the trip and the speech. I stand by the bed with the telephone in my right hand and a stiff cock in my left and this is I.

•

Mary, showing me a piece of marble that I bought for her in Rome, says, "I must be kind and gentle, otherwise you would never have given me this." And I wonder, Is murder one of her considerations? I have wanted to wring her neck but I never thought of braining her with a rock. If she did brain me, I think it would be me as an image of someone else.

Federico's third birthday. I would like to write him a fine book and then another and then another, but I must take care of myself. Drank and smoked too much again last night, but coming toward the house— the sapphire lights of a winter day and cardinals whistling in the fir trees—I think that perhaps I can do it, perhaps I can make some sense of it.

Mary complains of fatigue at lunch and my response to this, both affectionate and bitter, is enlarged by a recollection of her mother's complaints. And I also, unfortunately, recall her father's—God rest him—preposterous performance in the kitchen. He mopped the floors when anyone came through, he guarded the stove as if it were a symbol of his honor, he raged and swore at the burdens that were put on him, but if anyone tried to help him by making a piece of toast or squeezing the juice out of a lemon he would go into an insane tantrum. Here are the unreasonable and insatiable hungers of our egotism. He was tired, he was overworked, he was misunderstood, his brilliant intelligence was wasted, and how he struggled, hour after hour, to put himself into this position, to transform himself, so to speak, into a cruel and an idle lash.

I ask if I shall cook breakfast in the morning but I am not allowed to cook bacon because I leave it too greasy, I may not poach eggs because the maid doesn't get the yolk off the plates, and I cannot heat milk because I will scald it and stain the pot. These endless obstructions.

•

A sixteen-year-old boy is arrested for selling pornography and sentenced to six months in the pen. His first offense was stealing hubcaps. The judge says that the sentence is the most sorrowful task of his fifteen years on the bench. He is a friend of the family. He admires the boy's parents. He compliments them on their intelligent efforts to cure a wayward son. He hopes that the boy's term in the pen will help to cure him of his lawlessness, will teach him to become, as he says, "a component of society"; and I hear in these words some contemptible prudery that seems to me worse, more of an impediment, than the boy's failing. I can imagine the scenes with the parents, their deep bewilderment and sorrow. Why, while other boys win national scholarships for scientific research, develop their athletic abilities, and lead cleanly and adventurous lives, should their son be destined to sell obscene pictures under street lamps to his schoolmates? I think of X, who posed for indecent photographs but was never apprehended, and R.'s friend in Naples who supported his four children in this way, most cheerfully. "The hours are good, signore, and the wages are fair, but it is difficult, one must always seem ardent, even when your head feels like a squash, and the girls are often not beautiful." In Naples it is nearly acceptable, it is almost comical; but not here. But there is something to be said for the boy. Perhaps he has no other way of impressing himself on his schoolmates; perhaps he has inherited his father's colorlessness, that he is driven to distinguish himself in this way. His interest in obscene pictures is natural enough, and through selling them he receives something like the admiration of his classmates and may make enough money to run away. This may be sentimental, but the prudish judgment from the bench seems to restate a false, a shabby vision of pureness that could be the beginning of the trouble.

•

Mary greets me at the door in utter confusion. She means to draw a look of composure over her feeling of revulsion but I step in too quickly for her to complete the maneuver and see how unwelcome I am. She cannot speak to me or look at me.

"Would you like to take a rest?" I ask, as kindly as possible.

"How can I?" she asks. "I have to put up my hair." It all seems comical, but it is a bitter comedy. What vast amounts of misery the spirit can absorb and still rebound, still refresh itself.

·

An unseasonably warm day: fevers in the blood. I walk with Federico. The sense of odors, exhalations, escaping from the earth is volcanic. The whole county stirs like a crater. The imperative impulse is to take off my clothes, scamper like a goat through the forest, swim in the pools. The struggle to sustain a romantic impulse through the confusions of supper, the disputes, the television, the baby's bath, the ringing of the telephone, the stales of the dishpan, but I have in the end what I want and I want this very much.

·

Tonight, dirty movies at the fire house. In the audience will be some of the police, perhaps not the ones who arrested and sent to the pen for six months last week a sixteen-year-old boy, but members of the same force. What is their reasoning? Is this all well and good for men of thirty, and criminal for boys? I can't see it; and for me the horror, the gruelling shame of watching, on a screen, a naked woman performing gross indecencies on a man with a long scar on his buttocks.

·

A philologist and his wife from Brown for dinner. One of the generation of Bazarovs. His ambition is to determine, by the use of electrical computation machines, the basic structure of language. Word values and evocations can be determined, he tells me, by machinery, and thus successful poetry can be written by machines. So we get back to the obsolescence of the sentiments. I think of my own sense of language, its intimacy, its mysteriousness, its power to evoke, in a catarrhal pronunciation, the sea winds that blow across Venice or in a hard "A" the massif beyond Kitzbühel. But this, he tells me, is all sentimentality. The importance of these machines, the drive to legislate, to calibrate words like "hope," "courage," all the terms we use for the spirit.

•

I think, walking with Federico on a spring day, that I will walk with X, find some cold lake or pool, swim in it ballocksy, and have my dirty way with his rotund arse. I let the reverie spend itself, and what does it matter? There is no X, and coming on a cold pool at this time of year I would not want to swim or do the other things I seem to want, but there does seem to be in my head some country, some infantile country of irresponsible sexual indulgence that has nothing to do with the facts of life as I know them. But what interests me is the contradictions in my nature, in anyone's nature, their grandioseness; that in the space of a few minutes I experience crushing shame and then swim into some pure source of self-esteem and confidence that wells up like a spring in a pond. And half asleep I wonder if I do not suffer from some uncured image of women, those creatures of morning, as predators, armed with sharp knives.

•

Mary says that my presence is repressive; she cannot express herself, she cannot speak the truth. I ask her what it is that she wants to say and she says, "Nothing," but what appears in some back recess of my mind is the fear that she will accuse me of being queer. I think this is ridiculous, the area of sensitivity that clings to an old wound. I know my skin, indiscreet and capricious, and can cope cheerfully with all of its ridiculous and romantic yearnings, but I wonder if any of this affects my son. He seems very ready to love me and we play catch on the lawn. At dinner Susie refers to my imminent death and I fly up like an old hen and must learn to have more reserve. I drink too much and have this morning an incoherent memory of what went on. My eyes are sore.

B. says, about our moving to the country, that the biggest difficulty may be Mary's melancholia. It is a strange thing to say, although he is the master of strange remarks, but I wonder again if something isn't going wrong. Her face seems so drawn, her lips set in pain or anger. I walk with Federico up to the ridge. The setting sun appears to be advancing toward the earth, its shape is so clearly incised in the atmosphere. Its color is a curdled red. Now the fruit trees are all in bloom. The Russian violets have bloomed and gone in the space of a week. Now there are periwinkles, primroses, other violets all in bloom. But

I am badly disposed and with no reason. We make love and yet I feel forlorn and feel forlorn this morning. A lovely summer day and the birthday of my son and wife. I am writing two pages a day. I should make it four or six.

•

I do a little work on the island, six or eight pages, and leave three days earlier than I had planned. Sit and talk with a pleasant, aging investment banker. Observe nothing of the land below. An overcast day in New York. The baneful green glass windows not really a submarine world, not the world in the light of a storm, not even a nightmare world; these travellers, some of them with orchids, moving in a poisonous green light. My homosexual anxieties seem allayed or cured by this change and motion, and I cheerfully watch the people come and go. I think I see a madam and two girls. The madam appears to be a substantial matron—extensively dyed dark-golden hair, a double rope of pearls, a nice tan, only a trace of calculation in the face. The first girl must be nearly fifty but her skin is still white and soft, her arms are round. She wears a hat nearly as big as a wastebasket and shaped like one, but made of the black lace and satin we associate with underwear. The second has green eyes, wears a huge mobcap, her hair dyed red and her lips a coral color along lines that do not conform to her mouth. She sits beside me, and from the heat of her body comes a nice perfume. I am delighted, tickled. Her manner is very genteel and prim, comically so, but at the bottom of her gentility there is some crudeness in speech, some mispronunciations. "My home was in Connecticut," she says, meaning to evoke swimming pools, golf links, but evoking instead the back streets of Bridgeport. I would like to buy her dinner and a drink and go back to her apartment for the night but I am sweaty and rumpled and have no fresh clothes and do not. Perhaps I should. As her taxi draws away she wriggles her gloved fingers at me. I take the train out, feeling contented and substantial. Mary seems happy to see me, and the baby, also the others. We have a pleasant dinner but when I go upstairs she is asleep.

The morning is very dark and the sense of the house is oppressive. I am served my breakfast with a scowl. I go into town, but when I return I feel that something has gone wrong. The fault may be mine. The faces on the street cut at my sense of self, my happiness. I am afraid of having an unsuitable erection. This is morbid, this is neurotic, but much that I see is morbid and neurotic. Very few of the faces I look into seem cheerful and self-contained. I read my stories and some of them seem to me good—"The Wrysons" very bad. Here is a contained, almost a complacent prose, and the substance of the story is nasty, nothing more. I wish my line were stronger, more vigorous, more involved, I wish I could strike a different level of seriousness. Lunch with B., home on the train, my cod sore. Mary cleaning the broom closet in the kitchen. She has repaired the toilet seat, which I should have done, painted the front door. I try to catch the roughness of my own nature, try to see how difficult I am, but there seems to be no bond between us, I seem to have no way of appealing to her. I feel that she does not love me, that she does not even imagine a time when she might. All the means of intercourse seem broken down. She seems crushed with unhappiness, with despair. I give the baby his bath, at the table I reproach Susie for grabbing a sugar doughnut and she cries. I ask why the table should seem so unpleasant and at the back of my mind is the knowledge that Mary's father's table was always a battlefield. I feel that I must speak and yet I do no good. I give the baby his bath, warm his clothes at the fire, and dress him. I read him stories, give him a bottle, and put him to sleep, virtuous I. Susie is out, so is Ben. The S.s come, the S.s go, I watch an old movie on TV.

The boat strike goes on and our plans are unsettled. Work in the garden, sweat, the S.s for drinks. Sickle the backyard, play badminton, go to a garden party. I see a woman I have been blaming for three years for her divorce, but now it occurs to me that perhaps her husband was a neurotic sorehead and that the fault was mostly his. Talk freely with Mary and tie a can on. A beautiful summer's day. Shifting winds.

THE SIXTIES

Memorial Day. A new notebook. A man wearing a powdered wig and a tricorne carries a bass drum past the liquor store. I do not take my younger son to the parade, as I would have done two years ago. I have grown this old, not to say jumpy. Taking Ben to see "The Bridge on the River Kwai" I think of X, who, suffering from melancholy, walked through the city looking for moving pictures that dealt with cruel and sudden death, torture, earthquakes, floods, and assassinations—with any human misery that would, briefly, make his own burdens seem lighter. And sitting in the movie I wonder if this *cafarde*, this immortal longing, this mysterious and stupendous melancholy from which I seem to suffer is no more than common alcoholism. So I look yearningly at the soft stars, but they will do me no good. I think of moral crises, but when have I known the taste of abstinence and self-discipline?

•

To describe human misery in all its vastness and intensity without creating an air of disqualification. To trim misery of petulance and morbidity, to give pain some nobility. But can one do this—can one handle tragedy—without some moral authority, some sense of good and evil?

•

Having drunk less than usual, having, as my father would say, gone light on the hooch, I find myself, for the first time in a long time, free of the *cafarde*. Quarter to nine. Eastern daylight saving time. It would be pleasant to consider this a simple matter of self-discipline. Thunder and rain in the middle of the afternoon; the first of the month. Our

primordial anxiety about drought and its effect on the crops, the crops
in this case being three acres of lawn and forty-two rosebushes.

•

In thinking of the book, I would like to avoid indecency, but to
overlook the fact that we have, after a long struggle, achieved a practical
degree of sexual candor would be like perching on a stool and writing
with a quill pen by candlelight. We have the freedom to describe erotic
experience, and it seems irresistible.

•

Since we lack a well-defined sense of good and evil, we find it
impossible to invent a villain, and villainy is essential to the dynamics
of narrative. The lecher is no longer villainous; in fact, his prowess is
a virtue. The usurious banker is admirable; the bugger belongs to a
minority that deserves our understanding; the murderer merely needs
psychiatric help. It seems to me that the young come at this with less
self-consciousness than we, and, feeling instinctively the need for villainy, conclude, perforce, that the adult world is at fault. Clean, decent,
lusty, youthful procreative men and women are the targets of their anger
and their scorn, while their only real fault is their inability to evoke a
figure of evil. Cancer is villainous, but the devil seen through a micro-
scope is lacking. In the end, we may put horns and a tail on death, that
most innocent fact.

The congress of church organists produces fewer odd sticks than I
expected. Several of the men would have passed in business; one of
them actually appears to be athletic. And one of them—a small man—
has a harried or demented look. The women have that look of widowhood
or bereftness that sometimes seems to follow a life dedicated to music.
Two of them are plump, florid, and dressed in pink. One of them has
a liverish face that is deeply and unremittingly incised with pain. She
appears to have been crying continuously. The national, cultural, and
economic differences in the houses of God are abysmal. The painted
memorial windows in the Polish church need repair. The church itself
has a vast and institutional bleakness. The Stations of the Cross are
bloody and vulgar. The floor is dusty. But, even so, there is something
here: the unequalled poetry of our faith, this vast reflection of human
nature, the need for prayer, love, the expressiveness of grief. Christ
Church in Greenwich is a triumph of wealth and Trinitarianism in this

leafy corner of the United States. In preparation for a wedding, florists are tying white stock to the ends of the pews. This scents the air, not with sweetness but with an exciting smell of earth. The stained-glass windows are explicit, gloomy, and dated, but they have, like everything else in this house, the authority of great wealth. There is no baroque foolishness about the organ, no liquid and nostalgic reach. It is straight-forward, wrathful, and thunderous, and has in its fainter ranges an echo like some sweetness of remorse. To be buried from this chancel would, it seems, assure one a place in Heaven.

•

The first land we see from the airport is France—Normandy, I guess. Gardens and rivers. Then the Alps rise up to the snowy massif—Mont Blanc; the massif makes a second horizon, and along the shore one sees Nice, Monte Carlo, Elba, and the house where we will stay. Like those people who, as the boat approaches Nantucket, point out loudly the houses of friends, we, approaching the coast of Tuscany, do the same. It is close to noon in Rome. Mary seems be-wildered and disappointed. Ah, yes, she says when she hears the coach horn on a bus. And it is the coach horns. The smell of coffee, the sound of bells. We go to the Eden and spend the afternoon shopping. I am drinking gin at a coffee bar when two Americans come in to discuss, in sign language, some hot dog sandwiches displayed in the window. I speak loud Italian and express in this way some of my divided feelings about my own country. We go to the villa for cocktails and see from the terrace the city like a painted backdrop; we hear the famous bells.

In all the fields, after the rain, men and women go out to gather snails. We climb the hill to San Filippo. The noise of traffic, sharp and loud, comes from the curved road below us. I see a house across the valley that reminds me of Pennsylvania—a particular measure of ver-dancy and tranquillity. The massive beauty of the Spanish fort. There is no festival, but just before dark the sounds from the village below us are the sounds of a country fair—bells, music, laughter, the hum of voices.

One sees here, in the space of an hour, the reversal of sexual roles. In the country the sky is black, there is thunder, and the farmers start coming in from the fields. The men ride comfortably astride their asses with bottles of good wine hung from their saddles. The women walk behind them, each carrying forty pounds of firewood on their heads and leading a fat sow by a rope. Along the Via Veneto some women stride along determinedly, each holding a guide book in one hand. Their husbands follow behind, sheepish, stooped, and depressed. Their clothes do not fit, and each carries in his breast pocket three cigars, two pens and a pencil. In a bar a man in shirtsleeves mumbles something to his wife, and she replies, in a voice that is light and tearful, "Well, it makes no difference to me."

So, we fly home. On the plane a heavy woman, a spinster, perhaps a schoolteacher, with flying gray hair, who takes from her pocketbook a dozen glass animals she bought in Venice and, unwrapping them one by one, holds them up to the light. Beside her a sexually uncommitted youth with large, well-cared-for hands, a pissy smile. In front of them a young man with a determinedly manly air, gruff voice, a manner that is both hearty and unfriendly. But halfway through the flight he finds an area of agreement with his companion, a soldier, and puts down his gruff and manly airs at the same time he puts down his paperback mystery. Now his face is clear, comely, pleasant to see; his smile is open; he seems as easy as a swimmer; and I think of the great energies we spend in imposture. As the plane approaches home again he is gruff and manly. And ahead of them an American, travelling with his wife and three children. His wife is brisk and attractive, but I think one could never find a Roman with so browbeaten an air as his. All the lines of his face are falling lines—formed, it seems, by worry, fatigue and disappointment. He looks—oh, so much more than his wife—like someone crushed by the cares of the household; he has the look of someone who has changed a diaper three times in half an hour. Now and then a little light comes into his face, and one sees that he must have been high-spirited and cheerful some years ago, but he seems to have lost his cheer in the dishpan.

And the expatriate—a woman, I think—returning. Speaking Italian in the grocery store, stripping the gears on the car, and in a sense using these accidents as a springboard to explain to friends that she has been living abroad. How romantic.

•

The dog days go on. I read the Hemingway book. This arouses those mixed feelings we endure when some intact part of adolescence clashes with the men we have become. When I was a young man, my absorption in his work was complete. I imitated his person and his style. He writes with the galvanic distortion that gives the illusion of a particular vision; that is, he breaks and re-forms the habitual rhythms of introspection. I think I think his remarks about Scott's cock are in bad taste, as may be the quarrel between Stein and her friend. I am for some reason embarrassed by his references to walking home on the dry snow and making love.

•

It was Sadie Hawkins Day at the country club. Women chose their golfing partners and paid for their drinks and their dinner. The double-entendres about balls kept them all laughing merrily from morning until night.

•

I read with great pleasure "Youth" and "The Secret Sharer"; but concerning the last I would like, at this time of life, to scour any hint of twilight from my work. There will be time enough for that. I would like to write something like Delacroix's "Sardanapalus."

•

In the men's room at Grand Central there is a scene not quite comprehended. Two men, I do not see their faces, are pretending to fasten their trousers but are in fact exposing themselves. Presently, the show ends, and they go away, but I am shaken and mystified. Later, while I am having my shoes shined, one of them returns. His whatsit as well as his backside is on display, and the opportunities that he represents seem to me dangerous and fascinating. Here is a means of upsetting the applecart in an intimacy, a word. One could, with a touch, break the laws of the city and the natural world, expose the useless burdens of guilt and remorse, and make some claim for man's wayward and cataclysmic nature. And for a moment the natural world seems a dark burden of expensive shoes, and garters that bind, tiresome parties and dull loves, commuting trains, coy advertisements, and hard liquor.

But I take Federico swimming and find myself happily a member of the lawful world. Decency, courage, resoluteness, all these terms have beauty and meaning. There is a line, but it seems in my case to be a very faint one. I seem to move only on a series of chance recognitions, and when there is nothing recognizable about the face, the clothing, or the conduct I seem threatened by an erotic abyss. The sensible thing is to stay out of such places.

•

I don't know how I will plan my three weeks alone here. I have no compelling work at hand. Loneliness is a kind of madness, but to take a room in town would expose me to questions and tensions for which I have no answers and no cures. My fatherlessness may be at the bottom of some of this, and if it is I would like to go on to something else, take another step, although I may resist maturity.

•

Either my age or some change in my humor makes the heaviness of the air in the valley these days depressing. At three there seems to be some intensification of this. The air appears to be smoky. There is a double note of thunder in the southwest. I observe that should the rain not come, should the storm not break, I would be bitterly disappointed. Then the storm moves around to the east and finally strikes the valley. The air is aromatic the instant the rain falls. Ben cuts a paper airplane for his little brother. The old dog will not leave my side.

•

There is a flight of black birds, starlings I guess, from the B.s' woods. They come in twos and threes, in dozens and larger numbers; they seem, like the leaves in autumn, to unwind from the dark woods. This is no season for migration. They cross the sky travelling from the B.s' woods to the S.s' in thousands; one had not known there were so many starlings around. My son bets me a penny that we have seen the last of them, and when we have made the bet another flight unwinds. Later, we see swallows in pairs, and, later, bats. The woods that stand all around the sky darken. It is beautiful, I think, more beautiful than the rest of the world, as if some curious competition went on between Tuscany and the Hudson Valley.

•

A bright, fine day and I accomplish nothing. Ben goes off with his effeminate friend at four. Federico and I walk over to the greenhouse to get some rosemary. We stop to watch a football game. The grass is green, its greenest; the trees are still full-leaved and beginning to color. Such a pure light shines on the cliffs of the river that the shadow, black, seems like a darkness deposited in the stone, on the stone, by the passage of night. It is a handsome scene—the well-dressed men and women, the brilliant red-and-maroon football uniforms against the green playing field. But my son, I notice, is not here—neither he nor his friend—and I wonder where they are. Are they cobbling each other as I sometimes did, in a damp toolshed, while the irrecapturable beauty of the autumn afternoon begins to fade? The beauty of the day seems to add some acuteness to my feeling. As we walk toward the temple of love, Mrs. V. speaks to us. Her face is clear in the autumn light, the features still striking, vigorous, and colorful. She wears a broad-brimmed straw hat, covered with autumn flowers and leaves, that she bought in Spain, she explains, many years ago. "What a beautiful scene," she says of the football game. "How beautiful motion is, isn't it? I love trains. I was born and brought up within sight of a railroad track. I like to see the sparks fall off the brake box, the lighted windows reflected in the cove. I can also remember the horsecars. I'm not quite sure whether they were drawn by horses or mules, but they were very light. By jumping up and down on the back you could nearly upset them." We say goodbye and go on, and she stands by the temple—an old lady, an autumn day, a garden close to ruin. Back at the house, Ben shows up and I ask him angrily to come in for a minute. I ask him why he didn't go to the football game, why he didn't have supper with his friends, where he has been. What I claim to feel is that he has turned his back on the beauty of the autumn day, the green playing field, and the decent people, but what I really fear is that he has been indulging in the vices of my own youth, smoking cigarettes and masturbating in the moldy-smelling woods. I ask him why he isn't out there playing, working as a linesman, bringing water to the players, and I do not seem to remember going to the meadow to play football one day and being overtaken by— what? shyness or cowardice?—and hurrying by so no one would invite me to play. So I seem to pour onto his broad and tender shoulders all my anxiety, my guilt. And yet, for all the depth and bitterness of my feeling—bitterness and tenderness—the scene lacks a degree of reality, the suburban sky seems to reflect a bland, an unserious light. Yes, there is some longing here, some real longing here, for a more tempestuous, more genuine atmosphere. What has gone wrong, that we should all seem to be made of paper and straw? What is the world I wish to achieve for myself and my sons? What would be a better scene for this discourse? God knows. A mountain pass, a long beach, the darkness just before a storm. Why does the man teaching his son to get out a fishing line, as I have done; the gallant old lady reminiscing about horsecars; me pouring onto the shoulders of my fair son the guilty vices of my adolescence— why should we seem to be no better than the characters in a vulgar situation comedy? By turning my head I can see the ancient cliffs of the river, still scored by the volcanic powers that shaped the planet, the days of creation, so why, as we quarrel, as his character is being made or unmade, should the air that my beloved son and I breathe seem so domesticated, so bland, so thin? Let us away to Italy or St. Botolphs.

·

Tired in the morning, and I tire myself mostly with drink and conviviality. I find the drive tiring, gruelling. I observe the works of man and nature—the fair pastures along the parkway and the grace of the elms. Farther north, some of the maples have colored—these incendiary colors that are so lambent they lie outside the spectrum. Up into the granite hills, the granite mountains, the fine, light air, carrying all the fragrance of the land so clearly, the deep blue of the shadows, rain-lights. I kiss Susie goodbye, and wish her good things in Italian. We have already been to church. Let us all make something decent and admirable of our lives. I dine on creamed chicken in a candlelit barn. In bed, my teeth ache, my heart is painful, my chest is sore, my back is lame. I dream that the atomic bomb is exploded somewhere off the Battery. Whose? Ours? I hear the hellish noise and see the mushroom cloud. Many men throw themselves into the harbor, shouting, "Let's get the hell out of this world." Mary wants to do this, but I say, "No, no, we will stay alive, we will do something with our lives." But my skin has begun to burn, and I realize it is too late. I am waked by a church bell that rings all the hours and has a pure and gentle note. I hear all the hours rung but five.

•

I spend the night with C., and what do I make of this? I seem unashamed, and yet I feel or apprehend the weight of social strictures, the threat of punishment. But I have acted only on my own instincts, tried, discreetly, to relieve my drunken loneliness, my troublesome hunger for sexual tenderness. Perhaps sin has to do with the incident, and I have had this sort of intercourse only three times in my adult life. I know my troubled nature and have tried to contain it along creative lines. It is not my choice that I am alone here and exposed to temptation, but I sincerely hope that this will not happen again. I trust that what I did was not wrong. I trust that I have harmed no one I love. The worst may be that I have put myself into a position where I may be forced to lie.

•

In town to the Institute. Dogged, it seems, by the need for some crude erotic imagery, I take a drink at half past ten and cure myself at least of this. The lunch is pleasant, and I enjoy my friends. Waiting for the 3:19 I think that now I will be at peace with myself at last. It seems so. The scouting, the defensive tactics, the forced forgetfulness all seem over. My war with the world is ended or suspended. As we come home on the train the conductor calls our attention to a swan in the river. I think the graceful white bird in the icy water is a good omen, talisman, portent.

But at three or later I am awake. I hear a boat on the river. There seems to be a ringing sound in the air. The tap in the bathroom drips. I think of C., think that I had from him signs and words of love, but that I cannot fit myself into such a relationship. My younger son speaks in his sleep, and I think that I will make something fine and decent for him. I invent a first-class-passenger list for a midwinter sailing. Fall asleep and wake feeling like myself.

To track again these emotional ups and downs with the hope of illumination. As I write letters on Saturday morning, the problem of C. asserts itself and finally dominates my thinking and my feeling and leaves me tense, excitable, and uneasy. Working it out in terms of fiction I think that I am the one who receives the letter and the twenty-dollar bill and that C. reappears, that there is a melodramatic speech in which I compare him to death. I drink to forget my troubles, but this only seems to deepen the abyss, and I think that if we met again it would be on the same terms, that it would mean an abdication of my personality, that there is nothing we could do together but drink gin and destroy each other. My flesh seems to yearn for C.; my mind takes a very different path, and I suffer despair and melancholy. I remember meeting a Danish actress on Vesuvius and thinking, after leaving her, that I was sick with love. I remember going into a movie theatre one morning, thinking that my life was nearly over, and helling over the roads of Fairfield that evening, thinking that I would live forever.

But I am melancholy because my sexual boisterousness is lost. I take a walk with A. The snow is deep; the footing is bad; I have blisters on both feet and do not see the countryside. The roar of the waterfall swells. I make a vain, an egotistical remark, and A., for the first time in this long and helpful friendship, turns on me the hard-bitten, implacable face of New England censure, of the laws of survival.

•

I suppose it is all tied up with my romantic agony. He leaves just before dark, and alone in the living room I feel sick—with what? Sick over a morbid and hopeless love, sick over my inability to resume the life I've chosen. We go out for dinner, and Mary, across the room, looks pretty and I remember the hundreds, the thousands of nights when I have sat cheerfully through the anecdotes, the arguments, the games, with the thought of a jolly hour in bed to keep me humorous and alert. But now my vitals seem sapped, I throw bad dice, I despair. But at home Mary takes me in her arms, kindly, tenderly, and I am myself. I have what I want, and waking in the morning, stiff and randy, I am as high as at dusk I was miserable. As I walk up from the station in the cold north wind some dream of love seems to spread out before me, golden ceilings and garlands of fruit, and gigantism and richness. We make love in the afternoon, and now the new house resumes its importance for the first time in months; we talk about painting the kitchen. So there are, I suppose, two faces to this: my fear of being caught in a world that bores me, and the sexual richness of my marriage. I think—foolishly but, nonetheless, with pleasure—of the house, of greeting guests, of pointing out the river view from the terrace. I am back in my own jolly country. Now the image of death is laid, it is insubstantial, and now that it is over, now that I am unafraid, I think that I will write C. a letter. But by doing this wouldn't I begin the whole cycle again, wouldn't I betray some incurable taste for melancholy?

·

The closing; and so I have at last bought a house. Coming home on the train, Mary speaks of the complexity of our lives—the red coat she wore to the hospital in Rome when Federico was born—and it does seem rich and vast, like the history of China. We move books. To Holy Communion, where I first express my gratitude for safe travels, luck with money, love, and children. I pray that our life in the new house will be peaceful and full. I pray to be absolved of my foolishness and to be returned to the liveliness, the acuteness of feeling, that seems to be my best approach to things. I remember walking in the autumn woods six or seven years ago when, in a powerful rush of feeling, I felt that my participation in life was a participation in something vivid and magnificent. It is a dark morning. The window above the altar shows only a few dark colors. Sleet, and, in the afternoon, snow. The driving is bad, we cannot move, and I find the suspense galling.

·

On Monday we pack. My feelings are mostly confused, painfully so, and are still confused today. On Tuesday the furniture is carted off, but I have no clear feelings about this house, now empty, where we have lived happily and unhappily for so many years. I remember coming to the place alone, with a box of books. I was ten years younger. In the dirty, cold, and empty room I had an enthusiastic vision of a dinner party—lights and pretty women—myself (yes, yes) in dinner clothes, and it all came true. "We gave a dinner party for cighty fivc," I told the young man, "the night before we sailed for Italy." We eat precooked frozen dinners off tinfoil plates, and I think of a family who customarily do this, and who speak to one another in advertising slogans. "Aren't these garden-fresh peas in fresh creamery butter delicious?" "And this tangy, zesty Swiss steak is served in such generous portions!" Even the littlest child has something to say along these lines. Even the babe in arms sings a commercial. Mary goes off to sing with A., and I am left alone in what seems to be a haunted house, but haunted by whom? The oil burner stinks and the fumes are so bad they make the baby ill. A.'s wife calls to ask where her husband is. "We've married wandering minstrels, haven't we," she says, "you and I?" I am sore but keep my temper. On Wednesday morning I wake asking for valor, courage, strength, largeness of spirit, all good things, and seem to have a few of them. We move. The new house is empty, and long after we have put down our rugs and arranged the furniture, long after the friends have come and gone with flowers and wine, after the pictures have been hung and the curtains drawn and the lamps lighted, the image of the empty house—cat smell in the upstairs hallway, and scuffed and faded paint—is much more vivid than all our arranging. The image of emptiness is for me a kind of horror. The lamps and flowers seem transparent. The arrangements go on through Thursday and Friday, and on Friday afternoon the snow begins to fall, and falls steadily for twelve hours. Old Mrs. L. once said that I should not be too sensitive, and I don't seem to be able to take her advice. My feelings about heating plants are conditioned by the fact that the heating plant in the old house frequently broke down and once blew up. There is a leak in the guest room. The oil burner seems erratic. I had a drink at half past eight.

•

More snow. Ben's school bus is late, and I bring him home. Shovel snow, blessed snow, until half past three, whereupon I drink too much and am unpleasant about the dressing room. Wake in the night to hear the domestic machinery making its own decisions. First the oil burner, then the icebox, the vacuum pump, the sump pump. I seem less anxious, more thick-skinned, I hope. I hope that inch by inch we will take possession of this house, this place. It does seem to be a struggle. Wake to a dark morning, heavy snow falling. I drive Ben to Scarborough, and there is that fine sense—adrenaline, I guess—my mouth dry but some new reserves seem called on. Mary is unforgiving, and I shovel snow for my good health, and I seem to move, through this simple exercise, from despair into hopefulness. I see the buds on the trees, I can imagine how it will look in the summer, I seem to hear my daughter's voice from the shore of the pond. I almost—but not quite—get into the beauty of the scene, away from the anxieties, an old man's rancorous feelings for winter.

•

To disguise nothing, to conceal nothing, to write about those things that are closest to our pain, our happiness; to write about my sexual

clumsiness, the agonies of Tantalus, the depth of my discouragement—
I seem to glimpse it in my dreams—my despair. To write about the
foolish agonies of anxiety, the refreshment of our strength when these
are ended; to write about our painful search for self, jeopardized by a
stranger in the post office, a half-seen face in a train window; to write
about the continents and populations of our dreams, about love and
death, good and evil, the end of the world.

•

He was one of those Americans who had suffered in the middle of
their lives a serious mental and spiritual breakdown. I have never observed it in any other country. The male menopause is, as we know,
an old wives' tale, a legend, and has nothing to do with the facts of the
case. I have seen this trouble overtake so many that we might point out
the symptoms. You can single out their faces at the railroad-station bars.
They were mostly handsome, but now their handsomeness is harried
with worry, and sometimes gin. Mostly, their hands shake. Their
friends, if they are left with any, say that X seems to be going through
some sort of psychological crisis. It usually begins with sharp discontents
about their business life. They have been treated shabbily and cheated
out of the promotions and raises they deserved, but their position at
this time of life, their security, is too precarious to allow them to express
any grievance. They are sick of ball bearings and bedsheets or whatever
else it is they sell. Sexually their wives have come to seem unattractive,
but they have not been able to find mistresses. Their friends bore them.
Their children seem, oftener than not, strange and ungrateful. The
financial burdens they have been forced to assume are backbreaking.
All of this is true, but none of this would account for the wanton
disappointment that engorges them. Something of more magnitude,
something much more mysterious than these bare facts would show,
has taken place. Valor, lustiness, hope—all these good things seem to
have been misplaced.

He finds the noise of his wife's voice insufferable, he strikes his
favorite son with a piece of firewood. He is lost, as lost as anyone on
the side of a mountain, and yet the way in which he reached this tragic
wilderness is hidden from him and from the rest of us. There is one
down near the service bar drinking a beer. Here comes another, in at
the door. That man in a silk shirt drinking a Martini is one of them,

and there is a fourth gazing at his wristwatch, although it makes no difference to him whether it is three, or four, or five in the afternoon.

•

I think unconcernedly of C.; I see the idiot grin, the uncut hair, the bohemian suit, the Desert boots, the ungainly shins, the lively body with its restlessness, its thrust—the pure waywardness. And I think of our cloudy feelings about the sexual commerce between men—that it is a legitimate but an unsatisfactory field of investigation, that it is undignified and sometimes comical.

•

I make no headway, and yet it seems best to come here every day and try. It is not easy. I have had winters before and will have them again, and do not seriously doubt that they will end—the winters—but it is not easy. I am reminded of the weeks and months in Rome when I saw nothing with the right eyes but a cobweb gleaming in the sunlight and an owl flying out of a ruin. Thinking of X, who was tyrannized by a fable of herculean sexual prowess but who was, like the rest of us, clay. The books and stories he read and the movies he saw stated or implied a lurid and nearly continuous eroticism, but when he seized his bony wife in his arms he was mostly frustrated. Why couldn't he get into the fun, the sport? Why weren't his days and nights, like every other man's, a paradise of wenching? Was he growing old? Was this the rumored falling off? Should he stand serenely and watch his leaves fall to the ground? Should he retire, and leave the field to younger men? But if there was some diminishment of prowess there was none of yearning. How he longed for that sensual paradise where he had so happily lived, where the noise of the brook and the sounds of the rain seemed to celebrate the skin.

•

Poor X. Anxiety kneed him in the groin, and he felt his lights and vitals succumb, one by one. He was afraid, among other things, of long bridges. He knew the symptoms. As he approached the bridge there would be an excruciating tightening of his scrotum, especially his left testicle, and a painful shrinking of his male member. As he began to ascend the curve of the bridge it would become difficult for him to

breathe. He could fill his lungs only by gasping. This struggle to breathe
was followed by a sensation of weakness in his legs, which would presently become so uncoördinated that he could legitimately worry about
being able to apply the brakes. The full force of the attack came at the
summit of the bridge when these various disturbances would seem to
affect his blood pressure and his vision would begin to darken. Once
he was over the summit there was some relaxation, but the seizure
would leave him so weak and shaken that—he had discovered—he could
not raise a cup or glass to his mouth for an hour or two. Once, at the
airport, he had ordered a cup of coffee and, trying to drink it, had
slopped it all over his clothes. You must have had quite a night, the
man beside him said, and what could he say? "No, no, I went to bed
early. It is only because I am afraid of bridges." He had not let his
anxieties halt his travels—he had never stopped the car—but once,
driving to Albany, he had hugged the west shore of the river until its
course narrowed at Troy, where there was a little bridge he could cross
without too much difficulty. He kept a flask of whiskey in the glove
case, and if he anticipated an unusually violent seizure he would stop
the car and strengthen himself with whiskey. That these were false
sufferings, he knew. And he knew that compared to the realities of pain
they were contemptible, and yet how could he cure them, how ever
could he admit them to his wife? As so often in the middle of life,
he seemed forced to play a role for which there was no demand.
Dressed, so to speak, in a doublet and tights, his well-memorized script
in his hands, he seemed condemned to wander forever backstage.
Onstage, the characters hurdled sofas and made declarations of erotic
love.

·

On Sunday afternoon my only brother comes to call. He is told that
if he drinks again he will die, and he is drunk—the bleary eyes, the
swollen face, the puffy hands, the drunkard's paunch. He wants to be
alone with me to tell me this story: "The funniest goddamned thing
happened to me. They gave me the Boston territory, you know. Well,
I was in a bar watching one of those TV debates, and I got so goddamned
stinking that I didn't know what I was doing. I decided that I wanted
to see Al Houston so I got into the car and started off and the next
thing I knew I was in jail and you know where? In our hometown. I

was in jail at home. Well, they took away my license and fined me a hundred bucks. It's the second time. So when they let me go I got a suspended sentence, and you know who was there? Mildred Cunningham. She married Al. You remember her. So I said, 'Hi, Mildred, I was going out to see Al a couple of nights ago.' And you know what she said? 'I buried him six months ago.' Funniest goddamned thing." What is involved seems almost beyond my comprehension. He is drunk. He has lost his job and will not be given another. And in his drunkenness he has tried to find a college roommate, an old friend of forty years ago, a homosexual friend for all I know—although this may be an ugly suspicion—and has ended up in the jail of the town where our prominent and respectable parents shaped a life for themselves and for us, and he refers to this whole series of events as an uproarious joke. I think this is insanity. I have been drinking and make my long complaints to Mary, who is most tender, but I do not make love to her, because I think I must carry this through alone.

•

Looking around me I seem to find an uncommon amount of misery and drunkenness. We are not cold, poor, hungry, lonely, or miserable in any other common way, so why should so many of us struggle to forget our happy lot? Is it the ineradicable strain of guilt and vengefulness in man's nature?

•

A warm day; we lunch on the outside steps and my old dick stirs in the sunlight like a hyacinth. Later, in the warmth, taking away wheelbarrow-loads of dead leaves, I am suddenly very tired. I move slowly and painfully, like an old man. Pain seems like a rivet put through my chest into my back. Then I think that I shall not live to see the spring; I shall soon die. "John is dead, he died quite suddenly. Do try to get to the church early. We are so afraid there won't be room." My muffled voice rises from the casket: "But I haven't finished my work. My seven novels, my two plays, and the libretto for an opera. It isn't done." The priest tells me to be still. Preparations are made for a crowd, but on the big day the telephone begins to ring: "It's Binxie's only chance to play golf. We're sure John would understand. He was always so carefree." "It's Mabel's only chance to go shopping." Etc. In the end no one comes. I see the disgusting morbidity of all this, I try to cleanse my mind. If we do not taste death, how will we know the winter from the spring? I paint shutters, cut a little wood, light a fire. The clear light of the fire is appealing; this, and the sound of water, is what I want. How far away from X's underwear, lying on the floor in a heap. I will have love tonight, I think, fire and water, and I drink to still my anxieties and misgivings, but I fail. I have been in this poor place before, and I shall find my way out.

●

I wake before daylight in an ecstasy of sereneness. I think that I will have it all back: the green seas of the North Atlantic, the wit and high spirits of a randy life, blue-sky courage, a natural grasp of things. I think that I will have it all back. I dream a pleasant dream with pleasant and unpleasant figures. The most unsavory drops his britches, but, dear God, why should I worry about this anymore? I meet old friends from my childhood. I see a quality of love like a length of cloth, tranquil and unanxious, a fine, sere shade. And I will go out of that dread country where I lie sweating in bed, waiting for the oil burner to engorge the house with fire, waiting to be crushed by my debts, my groin smarting like a wound. I will have it all back.

●

"The Bridge" off, and it may be less than nothing. I split some wood and talk with F.—a pleasant hour. Wake before dawn, thinking of several things, including the liverish-colored thigh of C. The book, the book.

●

Unable to work because of the dark, the cold, and the snow—a pitiable state of affairs—and so I lose a day. At the breakfast table I say, "I don't understand Susie at all," and I shiver with unhappiness or despair. "I've fed her, bathed her, taken her up in the night, plucked thorns and splinters out of her feet, loved her, taught her to swim, skate, walk on beaches, admire the world, but now when I speak to her she weeps and slams the door, hides in the woods on a fine Sunday morning, seems on the one hand merry and on the other to carry some unanswered question. Is this a glimpse of our inability to understand one another? I seem to know more about a stranger on a train than I know about my only daughter."

•

Let us pray for all of those killed or cruelly wounded on throughways, expressways, freeways, and turnpikes. Let us pray for all of those burned or otherwise extinguished in faulty plane landings, midair collisions, and mountainside crashes. Let us pray for all alcoholics measuring out the hours of the day that the Lord hath made in pints and fifths, and let us pray for the man who mistook a shirt button for a Miltown pill and choked to death in a hotel.

•

Hemingway shot himself yesterday morning. There was a great man. I remember walking down a street in Boston after reading a book of his, and finding the color of the sky, the faces of strangers, and the smells of the city heightened and dramatized. The most important thing he did for me was to legitimatize manly courage, a quality that I had heard, until I came on his work, extolled by Scoutmasters and others who made it seem a fraud. He put down an immense vision of love and friendship, swallows and the sound of rain. There was never, in my time, anyone to compare with him.

•

I get up at half past six to get breakfast—in a fair humor, I think, but while I am shaving, so to speak, Mary also rises, scowls, coughs, makes small noises of pain, and I speak meanly. "Can I do anything to help you, short of dropping dead?" I am offered no breakfast, so I have none—but that we, at this time of life and time of day, should reënact the bitter and ugly quarrels of our parents, circling angrily around the toaster and the orange-juice squeezer like bent and toothless gladiators exhaling venom, bile, detestation, and petulance in one another's direction! "Can I make a piece of toast?" "Would you mind waiting until I've made mine?" Mother finally grabbing her breakfast plate off the table and eating from the sideboard, her back to the room, tears streaming down her cheeks. Dad sitting at the table asking, "For Christ's sake, what have I done to deserve this?" "Leave me alone, just leave me alone is all I ask," says she. "All I want," he says, "is a boiled egg. Is that too much to ask?" "Well, boil yourself an egg then," she screams; and this is the full voice of tragedy, the goat cry. "Boil yourself an egg then, but leave me alone." "But how in hell can I boil an egg," he shouts, "if you won't let me use the pot?" "I'd let you use the pot," she screams, "but you leave it so filthy. I don't know what it is, but you leave everything you touch covered with filth." "I bought the pot," he roars, "the soap, the eggs. I pay the water and the gas bills, and here I sit in my own house unable to boil an egg. Starving." "Here," she screams, "eat my breakfast. I can't eat it. You've ruined my appetite. You've ruined my day." She thrusts her breakfast plate at him and drops it on the table. "But I don't want your breakfast," he says. "I don't like fried eggs. I detest fried eggs. Why should I be expected to eat your breakfast?" "Because I can't eat it," she screams. "I couldn't eat anything in an atmosphere like this. Eat my breakfast. Eat it, enjoy it, but shut up and leave me alone." He pushes the plate away from him, and buries his face in his hands. She takes the plate and throws the fried eggs into the garbage, sobbing horribly. She goes upstairs. The children, who have been waked by this calamitous and heroic dialogue, wonder why this good day that the Lord hath made should seem so calamitous.

•

Mrs. Vanderlip is having her bomb shelter, constructed for the First World War, made hydrogenproof. Inquiries on bomb shelters have increased two hundred percent. The general feeling is that they should be secret, that if their existence is known they will only be small battlefields. "I," says a woman in Cambridge, "wish to be part of that ten percent that will survive and reëstablish the world." "The sooner we are killed the better," says another. But this is it; this has never been seen before—the population of this mighty nation in utter confusion about the enduring nature of their sense of good and evil, about whether they should be prepared to live underground.

•

Susie due in at 2 A.M. I go to meet the train. This seems the end of the line: trains, bells, whistles, a shrill sound in the air like the trains of France and Italy, hammering somewhere, yellow headlights, showers of golden fire and modest lightnings. A pretty girl sits in the dark cabstand. One more train and her boy will take her home. I go into a bar. Two men play pool. One shoots a good and lucky game and has a most light and simple face and stance, as if life had been for him always a nourishing, uncomplicated, and easily digestible dish. "There's an extra *News* and *Mirror* here," one says, looking kindly through his spectacles at the others. "You want one?" "What did the daily double pay?" "Seven-fifty." "You had five, I had four." "We shoulda got together. I'll bring the chick over tomorrow night and we'll have some cherry." "I got two hanging right here," says the bartender, jiggling his balls. Drawn, thin, needing a shave, his apron soiled, does he feel the crippling need, mount his old woman, gasping, gasping, gasping? A nice, comfortable place.

•

A brilliant autumn day. Searching lights. Many vapor trails drawn high, due north. Are these warriors or businessmen eating butterfly shrimp off plastic trays? Is this the end of the earth or a bond to keep it from ending? Hot and cold, brilliance and darkness, the afterglow as fine as anything seen in the mountains; but X, studying the stars, would find in this wall of brilliance a reflection of his own emotional vacuity.

•

Hurricane watch, they say. Heavy rains after midnight. Gale winds. I wake at three. It is close. No sign of wind and rain. Then I think that I can do it, make sense of it, and recount my list of virtues: valor, saneness, decency, the ability to handle the natural hazards of life.

•

Ossining–Saratoga. September 22nd. Signs of autumn, going north. Goldenrod, asters, and what seems to be heather in the fields. The uplifting sight of the mountains and the sense of the agedness of the planet, the violence with which its crust was formed—now that Dr. Turnquist and other humble men who sometimes pick their teeth with matches can destroy this ancient carapace. We edge past a stern-faced woman in a red Volkswagen, a man and a girl side by side in a convertible, two gray-haired ladies, and an elderly couple. Truly objects in a stream. The gimcrack outskirts of Saratoga and this old and massive house, Yaddo; the shadow of a tower and battlements drawn on the grass.

•

Saul Bellow blows in at half past eleven. The fine, pale face, the uncommonly large eyes with their startling show of white—and for me, as often for a stranger on a train, a deep and sometimes troubling sense of kinship as if we had, somewhere between Montreal and Chicago, between Quincy and Rome, shared the burdens of a self-destructive uncle. This is not a friendship or an acquaintanceship; but when he comes across the hall to say goodbye my instinct is to hold him back, to plead with him to stay, although I never seem to have much to say to him. He has nearly finished another novel, and I have not.

The Yaddo board meeting as usual. I have the same trouble trying to make my presence in the gathering a reality. Now and then I catch the white of Saul's eye and think, He is my brother. But the exchange is startling. A., after wiring that he could not come, blows in late. A broad, Irish face, florid with drink. The large teeth, colored unevenly like maize. Long, dark lashes, and what must have been fine blue eyes, all their persuasiveness lost in rheum. He has the unmistakable grooming of the alcoholic, the foundering sport. Brass buttons on his jacket; the black hair, stained with gray, slicked down and secured by some preparation to his thick skull. In the end he may not make much sense, but you won't find a lock of hair out of place. With my long, long nose I smell the cutting stink of grain alcohol on his breath, but it is his style, what he has to say, that troubles me most and drives home the evils of drink. He speaks in the bemused soliloquy of someone with a bun on who, rising gracefully above his real troubles and worries, finds his life fascinating, his jokes funny, and the design and color of his digressions rich and splendid. And I think of some child, my own daughter, perhaps, listening to a drunkard's tales. During the meeting my own personality seems dispersed. I seem further demolished by the white of Saul's eye. I wonder foolishly about the supremacy of his creative energies. I gather myself together; I seem to move around the room stooping to pick up fragments of myself and binding my broken person together with a sense of humor.

•

Mary *maldisposta*, I think, and I think, after drinking, that in middle age we come into the big scenes; that I am perhaps no longer able to make a rueful joke of my disappointments; that I can no longer carry the burden of her eccentricity; that I must speak loudly; that I must say what I feel. It is not in the light of day that my disappointments are keenest, most painful. It is when staring into the dark, counting the figures on the wallpaper in the beam of light from the children's bathroom, that I feel my spirits collapse. I can't be sure that I don't imagine this, that the fault is not mine. When I see her, come near her, rage and hatred, a curdling sensation, rise up from my feet to the top of my head with the speed of light. I don't know what happened, and it is one of those situations where scrutiny is not rewarding. The turning point may have come when I asked her if she wasn't going out for the evening; it may have come when I poured a second drink. I was putting poison in the mole burrows, admiring the brilliance of the afternoon. "See how the cut grass, the last growth of the year, full of clover, takes the light? Isn't it beautiful?" I ask, but there is no reply. She hurries away from me. So the pleasures of the afternoon are over. I sit down to read. She slams a door. I quiz my son on his homework, heady with self-righteousness. But I cannot lie down beside her and sleep. So I retire to the spare room—the thousands of nights I have spent on sofas! My beloved son has a nightmare at three or four. The cat wakes me, going from room to room, meowing.

•

And thinking how our origins catch up with us I wonder what I will have to pay on this account. I have been a storyteller since the beginning of my life, rearranging facts in order to make them more interesting and sometimes more significant. I have turned my eccentric old mother into a woman of wealth and position, and made my father a captain at sea. I have improvised a background for myself—genteel, traditional—and it is generally accepted. But what are the bare facts, if I were to write them? The yellow house, the small north living room with a player piano and, on a card table, a small stage where I made scenery and manipulated puppets. The old mahogany gramophone with its crank, its pitiful power of reproduction. In the dining room, an overhead lamp made from the panels of a mandarin coat. Against the wall, the helm of my father's sailboat—long gone, inlaid with mother-of-pearl. Most of my characters are waited on by maids, but I was usually the one who brought the dishes to the table. My parents were not happy, and I was not happy with them. I was told that he meant to harm me, and I suppose I never forgave him. But my heart seems to have been open and I was innocently, totally in love with G. when I must have been ten or eleven. At twelve I was in love with J., at thirteen in love with F., etc. There was no possibility of requital for my feelings toward my father, and so I looked to other men for the force of censure, challenge, the encouragement that I needed, and was given this abundantly by W. But it seems, in retrospect, to have been almost entirely an improvisation. I have the characteristics of a bastard.

•

At the place where I go for coffee, three clerks from Stern's, their eyes as heavily painted as the queens of the Nile. "Last night," one says, "we had pork chops; I got them at the supermarket, a special, hickory-smoked pork chops. You know, an introductory offer. Very good. I mean they had this smoky flavor, and I opened a jar of applesauce. But you know what he says as soon as he tastes this extra goodness? 'Novelty meats,' he says. 'You're buying novelty meats. When will you ever get it through your thick head that I can't afford these novelty meats?' " "How are the birds?" one of them asks. "Oh they're so cute!" "We had chicken," says the second. "I bought two nice fryers on Thursday and there was enough left over for last night."

I feel hung over, relaxed, sensually wakeful and contented with things. I go for lunch to a hotel grill. At the next table a man says, "Well, when I get fed up I tell myself look, go somewheres and start over. You can do that, can't you? Just pick up and go somewheres else like down South or out West and start all over again." He picks the paper off four sugar lumps and drops it with great gentility onto the floor. When they have finished the vegetable soup, London broil, and apple pie, his companion, as he stands to leave, takes two crackers out of the bread basket, makes a sandwich with the leftover butter, and stuffs this into his mug.

"I'm Lila," says the waitress, a pleasant woman of forty. "Would you like something from the bar? And here," she says, "is your ice-cold dry Martini, lemon peel, just as you ordered. I'm putting it down with my right hand. That's quite an effort for me. I'm left-handed. It's an effort for me to do anything with my right hand. Now, I don't know whether you've been here before—you look familiar—but when you're ready to order I'd recommend the club steak, the London broil, or the chopped sirloin. With French fries and a tossed green salad. French dressing. Yes, dear." She is a friend to me, she is a friend to the world, and what I can see so clearly is the daughter or niece she is sending to college. She will major in modern languages and get a job at the U.N. But Lila seems to be a creation of a series of obvious needs. Some man has done her wrong, left her to bring up a fatherless child, but she has learned patience and compassion and—what's more—that the world is full of lonely, worried, and troubled men, and she makes, in my case, a very successful effort to turn this half-hour lunch into something easygoing and affectionate. And I think also of those people whose position in life seems immovable, of those who seem driven into their thankless pursuits like the nails in the floor. The clerk in the Turkish bath and the three masseurs; the elevator operator on Twenty-third Street; the old man who sells cigarettes on Second Avenue. You go around the world ten times, marry, divorce, raise your children and see them married, move from here to there, but when you return you find *them* where you left them, running the elevator, selling new brands of cigarettes. So I must work, and I think I can.

•

There is no point in my regaling myself with trifling injuries (you reflected on the quality of my mother's carpets, etc.), nor in my trying to determine what part the past plays in my so easily abraded feelings. What I must face is the small quantity of inferior work I have been turning out. Neither the novel nor the play possesses any form or shape or substance. It is not that I would mind going down in history as an inconsequential writer; it is that I would mind most bitterly going down as a writer who has wasted his gifts in drunkenness, sloth, anger, and petulance. I am no longer dealing with the common disadvantages of need, a poorly lighted room, a stomachache. I am dealing with time, with alcohol, and with death.

•

For what it may be worth: hung over on Saturday. Walk in the woods with Ben. Shoot at tin cans. On Sunday the dog wakes at six. She will have to have her breakfast, says Mary, and so I give the dog breakfast. It is not yet light. I try to get back to sleep again in the spare room, but the dog dumps a load on the floor, whines, chews the light cords, etc. I miss church. It is not a good way to begin the day. I drink some gin at half past eleven and Susie and I play recorder duets. I wash the lunch dishes and take care of the boy. I embrace him. My eyes fill with tears. But after playing a little touch football I feel much better. Susie and I cook supper, and I wash the dishes. The dog dumps another load on the floor, and I am enraged. I drive Susie to Mamaroneck and, driving back, regale the dog with my troubles. I plan this morning to go into town and look for apartments. But I do not. Now, I would not want to be the kind of sorehead who rages on about his disappointments but who is too slothful, lazy, drunken, and bilious to get off his arse; who claims to be indifferent to the play of firelight on the panelled walls, but who will endure every sort of humiliation rather than leave his cozy fireside; and yet it seems that some of my indecision is legitimate. I cannot afford an apartment in town, and I have put so much money and time into this house that I am entitled to at least a touch of reluctance about leaving it. So I shall today try to be hopeful and conduct myself like a loving and intelligent adult.

•

And so it is over as suddenly as it began; at four or five on an overcast afternoon, unseasonably warm for November, her step becomes light, she sings in the hall for the first time in six weeks, and I have my way.

•

I lay a fire, drink some gin, watching the last rosy light of this winter day pour in at the western windows. These wooden walls, old pictures, yellow silk chairs are what I wanted, so why does my admiration of the scene seem fatuous? In the pinewoods the last light glows like coals. We dine with the B.s, who seem unhappy but not unhappy about being unhappy. On a scrap of paper one reads: i am miserable and i wish my mummy and daddy would not fite. The first day of a new year. I pray to finish the novel by spring.

•

I have not repaired the shutter on the west window. I have not got sand for the driveway or mixed fuel for the chain saw. I have not taken my clothes to the dry cleaner's. Cutting into the roast and finding it underdone I have, without saying a word, been able to accomplish a devastating emanation of disgust and disapproval. Serving the flounder I have, by way of petulance, helped the family generously and given myself a boiled potato and a spoonful of grease. I have unjustly accused my wife of unfaithfulness, and called my only and beloved daughter plain and friendless to her face. I have been drunken, dirty, unkind, embittered, and lewd.

•

I spend the day, as do many others, in watching Glenn orbit on TV, and I torment myself for not working. Once the man is in orbit, the crowds leave the beach. It is always, for me, a moving sight, to see people pick up their sandwich baskets, their towels and folding furniture, and hurry back to the hotel, the motel, the cottage, the bar. Their haste, their intentness, is like the thoughtlessness of life itself; and something will always be forgotten—a pair of sunglasses, an inflatable rubber raft, an old man, a roll of film, a pimply youth with a volume of poetry. They will be remembered briefly as we remember the dead, but no one will go back after dark to look for the sunglasses, or cheer the old man. My heart gives a heave as they hurry off, as if I could see here the forces of life and death. The end of the ballgame, the last hour of the county fair.

•

Ossining–Tampa. P. and I leave in the fresh morning light. The quiet boy who wants to be a novelist; his little sister carrying a plastic horse; my friend. The heavy morning traffic, the overcrowded roads. The unreality of the massive city in the glancing light. The sense of travel as a sense of painful dislocation. The shabby building at the airport. Windowless. Artificial plants. Benches for waiting. Women in furs. The Florida-bound crowd whom I join so late in life. A man with a copy of *Variety*, three pretty children, a Scotch nursemaid with a head of long hair. A man with a beret. As soon as we are airborne, the woman on my left takes a plastic kit out of her handbag and begins to paint her nails. The man on my right introduces himself; "Pleased to meet you, John," he says. "I have a little present I'd like to give you." He gives me a gilt tie clip containing a thermometer. No, he doesn't manufacture them. "I just give them away because I like to. I travel a lot. I give away two, three thousand a year. It's a nice way to make friends, and

I like to make friends." We discuss the people we know who are dying
of cancer. He tells me the complete story of his life. Three anticlerical
jokes. The lion who says grace, the brigadier, and the cardinal. He
seems, telling his life story to a stranger, to be a large slice of my country,
my people. The white silk shirts the stewardesses wear have come
undone at the back. They keep tucking them in, but they come undone
again. A crew member wanders aft. He looks to have a terrible hangover,
and I think the stewardess gives him a drink. We rent a car in Tampa,
and drive south. Ugliness, but why bother to say so? Don't forget the
fellow with a lighthouse on his front lawn.

Walk along the beach. The sea slams its bulkheads, its doors, shakes
its chains. Drink gin in the hot sun and feel very happy. Waking in
the morning, I suffer an excruciating melancholy. I long for my wife,
I long for my sons. We swim before breakfast. Pelicans, willets. The
smell of wood smoke. Bitter. A warm, moonlit night. This, I guess, is
a tropical evening, and my love is far away. I wake at two or three.
Cats fight. A dog jogs under my window, jingling his rabies and his
license tags. Then suddenly I feel for my wife and my sons a great
power of love. I don't swim before breakfast, and, after, I feel lost,
melancholy, homesick. I don't know what it is. I am afraid that something may have happened to my family, although I know that my fears
bear no relationship to the truth. I chain-smoke.

•

We cross a bridge where many old people are fishing. There are so
many old. The main highway, the Tamiami Trail, is lined with super-
markets, diners, night clubs, seashell-and-driftwood shops, billboards
advertising developments; this is the misspelled, the -burger, the -rama
world—herburgers, Steerburgers, Smorgoramas. The pet cemetery and
crematorium—animals guaranteed to be buried above water level.
Trailer camps stretch for miles under the palm trees. There is a listless
air in the back and side streets of Sarasota. The light is bright. It is
hot. Old people snooze on bus-stop benches. Turn me around three
times and I couldn't say if I was in Los Angeles or Sarasota. The
atmosphere of domesticity seems dense. Mother, father, sister, and
brother walk past the little frame house where the Gypsy palmist recites
the past and the future. Next door is high colonic irrigation. This
atmosphere of domesticity seems to abrade my aloneness. What a faint-

hearted traveller! We go to a jungle gardens. Admission $1.50. The old
sit on benches watching flamingos, egrets. Here again are mother, father, sister, and brother. The warm air seems suffused with their kindliness. An old couple point out to strangers that a white peacock is asleep
under a bush. Mostly Southern and Midwestern accents. We drink in
one of those places where, on a platform, there is a set of music stands
and a trap drum covered with a waterproof. We eat in a Royal Pancake
Palace. The customers are mostly old. So back down the Trail, me with
a painful feeling of emotional suspense. At home, surrounded by my
family, I would say that this was the pain, the bite, of boredom. Now
I call it the pain of aloneness. Drink seems to be the only cure. So what
I am dealing with may be no more than crude alcoholism. And so I
drink to kill the pain, and so I wake again in the night to think of my
wife and my children. I seem to call out their names not in longing but
in contentment. In the fullness of the hopes I hold out for them. So
the day begins with the same pattern of longing, unease, thirst. There
are only two more to go. The strangeness of time, the strangeness of
personality. And how the figure of a young man in white sneakers, seen
at the end of a museum corridor, has in fact no claims on my life or
my person as I best know it but seems for a moment to be my executioner;
yet the executioner mask may conceal a comely face. The day is overcast, the tide and the sea are high. We go fishing and catch
nothing. We drink at twelve sharp and things pick up. We swim in
the surf and things shift quickly from pain to pleasure. The high, the
noisy sea is more like home, more like my coast. We go to the usual
cocktail party; we will have been to seven. A round-faced, small-eyed
man says, "By gum, he's as straight as a piece of string." Mrs. C. tells
me the details of her husband's death. The wheelchair, the hardening
of the arteries—this great, genial athlete; and there might be a scene
of women watching flamingos and discussing in detail the death of
men. After drinking the time passes easily. Wasn't it a pleasant day?
we ask.

•

I bring home from church a green length of palm, not strong in the
conviction that it is blessed and will bless my house but in an impulse
of love. And to write, to get down the church with its yellow, varnished
floor; the homely memorial windows commemorating the dead in tearful

shades of lavender and blue; the stink of hassocks and pew cushions, precisely like the smell of the cushions in the barn cupola; the discreet perfumery, like flowers smelled from a great distance; the sense that this is some reconstruction of the smells of my childhood; and then, to go a step further, that this is the smell of the turn of the century, some fading distillate of the late eighteen-nineties. But then, moving into this gloom, is the measure of the Mass. The language has the sumptuous magnificence of an Elizabethan procession. The penultimate clauses spread out behind their predicates in breadth and glory, and the muttered responses are emblazoned in crimson and gold. On it moves through the Lamb of God, the Gloria, and the Benediction until the last amen shuts like a door on this verbal pomp; and the drunken priest puts out his lights and hurries back to his gin bottle, hidden among the vestments.

•

It is not the facts that we can put our fingers on which concern us but the sum of these facts; it is not the data we want but the essence of the data. It is the momentary and overwhelming sense of pathos we experience when we see the congregation turn away clumsily from the chancel; the encouragement we experience when we hear the noise of a stamping mill carried over water; the disturbance we feel when we see misgiving in a child's face. She is carrying schoolbooks and waiting for the traffic light to change. The carnal and hearty smell of bilge water, the smell of must in the cold pantries of this old house. A continent of feeling lies beyond these. We call them apprehensions, but they have more fact, truth, illumination than the wastebasket, the gunrack, and the cheese knife. Why be afraid of madness? Here is a world to win, to discover.

•

He could separate from his red-faced and drunken wife, he could conceivably make a life without his beloved children, he could get along without the companionship of his friends, but he could not bring himself to leave his lawns and gardens, he could not part from the porch screens and storm windows that he had repaired and painted, he could not divorce himself from the serpentine brick walk he had laid between the side door and the rose beds. So for him the chains of Prometheus were forged from turf and house paint, copper screening, putty and brick, but they shackled him as sternly as iron.

•

So here is the day. What do you make of it? A brilliant morning, the light dealt out over the mountainous banks of the river. Cool. As I eat breakfast on the porch, my coffee smokes, the china cup is cold to touch. Last night I read Katherine Anne. How well she catches the essence of herself, the wit, the didactic style, the attractions of elegance. She fastens her slippers, shakes out the folds of her silvery dress, and fastens the belt as she goes out on a note of asperity and command. It is highly feminine, but a solid style. In some of the emotional scenes she strikes with exceptional accuracy that balance between the ritard of observation and the flow of feeling.

•

Mary *maldisposta* this morning, but then I think how wonderful it is that this marriage should embrace such a multitude of misunderstandings, storms, infidelities, rivers of tears, and still continue on its way, some of the passengers bruised, but nothing serious.

•

To get the difference in degrees of feeling at this time of life. It is Memorial Day. My persistent, my only memory of this in the past was of planting a garden at the farm; a garden that I thought, sentimentally, I would never see mature. I must go away. I spaded up the plot, eyed a sack of potatoes, and planted a patch. In the distance, at the four corners, I could hear the drums of the parade, and now and then a bar of music. My mother would have decorated the family graves with cornflowers and daisies. Now, having served four years in an army and seen many good friends killed in battle, I hear again the music of the parade. I try to remember the names of my dead friends. Kennedy? Kenelly? Kovacs? I can't remember. Up from the river comes the sound of drums, and from time to time a bar of brassy and discordant music. It is very hot. I should scythe the orchard or do other work but I do nothing. It is a holiday, and I seem unable to give the day any other meaning. It is too hot to go fishing, it is too hot to cut the grass. Driving into the village to get a loaf of bread, I see the lines of heavy traffic on the main highway. At four there is a long peal of thunder. It is as though the day had a rigid script, beginning with band music, patriotic speeches, suffocating heat, and idleness, sandwiches and cold drinks, and now the clouds piling up in the northwest and the sound of thunder—all seem a part of some ancient ceremony. I sit on the porch with my sons and watch the storm come down. I have lived through this day a hundred times, it seems, and not a blade of grass has changed. The lightning is yellow. It flashes on the porch like a beam of sunlight. The old dog is frightened and buries her head in my side.

•

Fred comes. He is now a very heavy man, his girth so swollen that his naturally bellicose walk is close to a waddle. "Hi, guy!" he shouts. I wonder if he has come out to borrow money. "Congratulations on the new car," he shouts. I explain that the car is borrowed, but I wonder, later, if he believed me. His manner is broad, hearty; and the heartier it grows the more retiring, narrow, and continent I seem. He has been drinking. "What you ought to do—" he begins, and I squirm at being made a receptacle of unwanted information. The more ruinous his life becomes, the more didactic, informative, and overbearing is his manner. "Now listen to me. . . . Let me tell you. . . . I know all about the Boston Safe Deposit and Trust Company. You want me to tell you all about it. I know all there is to know. Just listen. Stop me if I talk too much. You want me to tell you." But in the end he loses track of the subject, founders, forgets what it was that he was going to explain. There is a rampant force of self-destruction in the man, and I think he has counted so on gin as a painkiller that he has mangled his responsiveness. He has endured many disappointments, indignities, and injustices, and in his determination to rally he has developed a crude mockery of cheerfulness. Everything is wonderful, simply wonderful. Gorgeous. Life is gorgeous, life is wonderful. This is the harshness of despair. "Whatever else I have," he says, "I have four beautiful children. Loving, wonderful children." "I like D. very much," I say, "and he's very loyal to you." He lifts his face, swollen now with years of drink, and says, "They're all loyal to me." I have seen them scorn and disobey him, and they have all run away from home. There is not a grain of truth in this pitiful claim to love. But now he looks like Mother, a painful and bewildering memory, and I remember our conversations—

my struggle for coherence, my desire to put one idea after another, to sort out good from evil, while she skipped, or so it seemed to me, from one wild half-truth to another, from one larcenous prejudice to another. The aim never seemed to be to communicate but to confuse, obstruct, and dismay.

While I am making him some coffee in the kitchen my little son runs in with the news that there is a snake in the yard. I follow him. "There, there!" he cries. I am slow to pick them out, but then I see three lethal pit vipers, writhing in the sun. Two have lost their old skin and are brilliant copper. One is still as dark as a stick. I go to get the shotgun. The gun-shy bitch begins to whimper and bark. The hunting dog begins to bark with joy. My brother, purblind but too vain to wear glasses, stumbles over to the snakes. "I'll tell you what they are. I know all about snakes. Our place is infested with them. I'll tell you whether or not they're dangerous." Mary begins to laugh at me. "He thinks all snakes are venomous," she says. "Garter snakes, milk snakes. Please don't kill them," she says. "They're quite harmless." Before I can clear the yard, the vipers retire into the wall. "Helen Washburn was bitten by a copperhead last year," Fred says, triumphantly. "That's a help," I say bitterly. "Vipers never grow over two feet long," Mary says, "and one of those snakes was more than two feet. And anyhow, people never die of snakebites." The vipers are a clear danger to my beloved sons. Why should she be put into such a contradictory humor? She looks up vipers in the encyclopedia and in the snake book. She is saddened at having to admit they are deadly, deathly. It is a personal defeat.

And in Fred's ungainly walk there is a trace of furtiveness and haste—the hopeful gait of a man who has left a liquor store after having paid for a quart of gin with an unsubstantiated check. Will they call the bank before he gets out the door? Will bells and whistles sound, will somebody shout "Stop that man!"? He enjoys some relief when he gets out the door, but his troubles are not over. He enjoys a further degree of relief when he gets into the car, but his troubles are not over. The car floods, the car won't start. ("I'm calling to check on the bank balance of Mr. Lemuel Estes.") The battery, as he grinds the starter, begins to show signs of weakness. Then the motor catches, he backs out into the street, makes a right turn, and, when he feels safe at last, stops the car, screws the top off the bottle, and takes two or three long pulls. Oh, sweet elixir, killer of pain. Gently, gently the world reforms itself into interesting, intense, and natural arrangements. Thomas Paine drank too much. General Grant. Winston Churchill. He is in the company of the truly great. He stops twice on the way home and, having put away nearly a pint, comes into his house with that air of blustering good cheer, that heartiness that deceives no one.

•

Without the lift of whiskey I wonder if I am not less than intelligent in facing my problems. I am fifty. Can I go on writing stories forever? Why not? I should think of myself in terms not of my age but of my work, which is barely half done. I think that I should move to a hotel, but then I think that I cannot leave my family; my eyes flood with tears, and I empty the whiskey bottle. I should take advantage of my maturity and not be dismayed at the loss of my youth.

•

I dream that my face appears on a postage stamp.

•

It is after dark—just. A summer night, stars and fireflies. The last night in June. My older son stands on the bridge over the brook with a Roman candle. He is a man now. His voice is deep. He is barefoot and wears chinos. It takes two or three matches to light the fuse. There is a splutter of pink fire, a loud hissing, the colored fire is reflected in the water of the brook and lights the voluminous clouds of smoke that roll off the candle. The light changes from pink to green, from green to red. It makes on the trees and in the heavy air an amphitheatre or sphere of unearthly light. In this I see his beloved face, his figure. I cannot say truthfully that I have never felt anything but love for him. We have quarrelled, he has wet his bed, he has waked strangling from nightmares in which I appeared as a hairy werewolf dripping with gore. But all of this is gone. Now there is nothing between us but love and good-natured admiration. The candle ends with a loud coughing noise and voids a spate of golden stars and a smell of brimstone. He drops the embers into the brook. Then the dark takes over, but I think that I have seen something splendid: this young man, the weird and harmless play of colored light, the dark water of the brook.

•

The first page of a new journal, and I hope to report here soon that the middle section of the Wapshots has fallen into shape. I expect that I will continue to report here that I drink too much.

•

The O'Hara book—he is a pro, a gifted man. There is the sense of life being translated, but I think also an extraordinary vein of morbid sexual anxiety. I would like "The Scandal" to be clear of this. I think the difference is between a fascinated horror of life and a vision of life. He is good and rough and not so lacy as me, but I hope to come to better terms.

•

The firemen's bazaar. Seven o'clock. A July night. A rusted and battered backstop stands behind the circle of trucks and booths turned in against the gathering darkness like a circle of covered wagons. Parents and children hasten along the roads that lead to the bazaar as if it might all be over before they got there, although in fact they will get there before it has begun. The sumptuary revolution makes me feel old. Both the boys and the girls are wearing skintight pants, and there are many cases of ungainly and sometimes painful tightness. And in the crowd there are reminders of the fact that there are still some farms outside the village limits. I see a red-faced man, a little drunk, followed by an overworked woman who has cut her own hair as well as the hair of the four shabby children that follow. These are the poor; these are the ones who live upstairs over the shoe store, who live in the cottage down by the dump, who can be seen fanning themselves at their windows in the heat. When you leave at six to catch an early plane, these are the ones that you see at dawn, waiting by the bus stop with their sandwiches in a paper bag. But it is the children I enjoy most, watching them ride in mechanical pony carts and airplanes, suspended by chains from a pylon. Their brilliance, this raw material of human goodness. A very plain woman in the last months of pregnancy, who looks out at the scene calmly and with great pride in this proof of the fact that someone has taken her in his arms. Many of the girls have their hair in rollers half concealed by scarves. Like primitive headdresses and, in the darkness, like crowns.

•

Our relationship remains in suspense. I have neither the boisterousness nor the virility to make the bridge or span between these two
unrelated personalities, and I experience that bewilderment which always overtakes me when some obstruction in my sexual life is felt. I
cannot reach out. I am afraid I may be rebuffed. I cannot transcend
these fears. I glimpse the horrors of incompatibility; the power of lovers
to mutilate each other. At nine-thirty my stomach begins to heave. It
is difficult to breathe. I should be familiar enough with these symptoms
to put them in their place, but they overtake me with such intensity
that they seem to be not a part of life but all of life. I feel racked by
the visible and the invisible world. My guts are drawn with pain.

•

Light and shade, pleasant and discordant noises, the singing of the
cleaning woman and the thumping sound of the washing machine are
dealt like a series of blows. I cannot think of the stories I have to write
without a sharpening of this visceral pain. I cannot invent terms or
images of repose. I grant myself all the privileges of a liar, but there is
no heart in my lies and inventions. There is nothing. There is neither
ecstasy nor repose, there is only the forced illusion of these things. The
span between living and dying is brief and anguished, and the soul of
man is reflected not in snug farmhouses and great monuments but in
fourth-string hotel rooms, malodorous and obscure. This is all there is.
There is nothing. Tired but sleepless, lewd but alone, hopeless, drunk,
sitting at the window on the airshaft in some other country: this is the
image of man. I remember those midtown hotels, the Carlton in Frankfurt, the Eden in Rome, the Palace in San Francisco, hotels in Hollywood, Innsbruck, Toledo, Florence. Here is the soul of man, venereal,
forlorn, and uprooted. All the rest of it—the cheering lights of morning,
sweet music, the towers and the sailboats—are fantastic inventions,
evasions, lies, vulgarities, and politenesses poorly invented to conceal
the truth.

•

A day like autumn, the light fresh, the wind sounding loudly in the
trees. My family off to the mountains, and God bless them. The best I
can do in these three weeks is to work hard and pull the novel into shape.

Perhaps I can go abroad in the fall. I must do something about finding a place to work. I cannot go through another winter like last winter.

•

We rise from sleep all natural men, boisterous, loving, and hopeful, but the dark-faced stranger is waiting at the door, the viper is coiled in the garden, the old man whispers lewdly to the boy, and the woman sits at her table crying.

•

So in the dark hours, awake, I think of the wind and the rain and in my arms a willing love, her dugs hardened against my chest, her hand where it belongs. The night air is fresh. Daybreak spreads along the westbound highways, lighting the legends on the all-night trucks. Daybreak spreads along the westbound highways, and I shall sleep, I shall sleep. I shall conquer death and anger and fear.

•

Rows and misunderstandings, and I put them down with the hope of clearing my head. "I think it's too hot to split wood," say I. "Well, I don't," says Mary. "If it's not too hot for me to rake, it's not too hot for you to split wood." "You do your work," say I, "and I'll do mine." But I am in a bad temper, and I think of the W.s all ordering one another around, working not so much to accomplish anything as to ingratiate themselves with the old king, who was trying, in turn, to ingratiate himself with immortality. At dinner I try to explain my leaving to work on the book. "I feel sorry for you," says Mary, "your life is so miserable. I really feel sorry for you. I won't miss you, of course. If you could only figure out what you want." I cut some edges, but I am angry, and returning to the kitchen I say (at dark), "Can't you figure out after twenty-five years what it is that I want? I want your love, I want to see the children grow and take up their lives, I want to do a piece of decent work." I am shouting. Then she says, "I am going away. I will take a little apartment and live there with the children. You are torturing me to death. You are torturing me to death."

•

Weeding the peony hedge I hear the windfalls in the orchard; hear them strike the ground, hear them strike against branches as they fall to the ground. The immemorial smell of apples, old as the sea. Mary makes jelly. Up from the kitchen, up the stairs and into all the rooms comes the smell of apples.

•

It is my wife's body that I most wish to gentle, it is into her that I most wish to pour myself, but when she is away I seem to have no scruple about spilling it elsewhere. I first see X at the edge of the swimming pool. He is sunbathing, naked, his middle covered by a towel. His voice sounds coarse and unpleasant. He speaks with a slight accent— Italian, perhaps—or perhaps a piece of faulty bridgework. He hogs the best chair, gives out aggressive emanations, says nothing that is not complaining or stupid, and we seem to be natural enemies. But then, a day later, I find him sitting beside me at the table, feel his gaze on me—soft, tender, and pupilless. He touches my shoulder. Suddenly he is all courtesy, kindness, and attention, and I see him in a different light. I see that he is handsome, well knit, but soft enough to do in a pinch. I think that a variety of hints or lures are sent out. He has met me before, he says, with Y, with Z. His soft gaze follows me, settles on me, and I have a deadly itchiness in my crotch. If he should put a hand on my thigh I would not remove it; if I should chance to meet him in the shower I would tackle him. But is this itchiness mutual or is it mine alone: is it only my tassel that is up, down, and sore as a boil? Does he sense this or is he thinking about yesterday's tennis game or a check he hopes to get in the mail? I am determined not to be a supplicant, not to be compromised by my instincts, and so perhaps is he; these are the murderous checks and balances of a flirtation. But then there are the spiritual facts: my high esteem for the world, the knowledge that it is not in me to lead a double life, my love of perseverance, a passionate wish to honor the vows I've made to my wife and children. But my itchy member is unconcerned with all of this, and I am afraid that I may succumb to its itchiness. We are urged to take things as they come, to plunge into life, to race after our instincts, to upset the petty canons of decency and cleanliness, and yet if I made it in the shower I could not meet the smiles of the world. I do not like his voice, his mind; I probably will not like his work. I like only that he seems to present or offer himself as a gentle object of sensual convenience. And yet I have been in this country a hundred times before and it is not, as it might seem to be, the valley of the shadow of death. And, whatever the instinctual facts are, there is the fact that I find a double life loathsome, morbid, and anyhow impossible. So I hear in the night the lightest of rain winds, but it does not draw me out of myself, and when I hear the sound of a fine and covering rain my wish to find some peace in this ancient noise seems childish and unseemly compared to the perverse thrust in my middle. But there is some spiritual element in this drive, some hunger to be taken care of—to put down, for an hour, the intolerable burden of total independence. But I have been here before, and in the end it may be nothing, nothing. Why should I be tempted to throw away the vast delights of love for a chance shot in a shower? And I think I share this trouble with most of mankind.

•

A dark and rainy day, and this rain does not seem to fall calmly from the skies of my childhood. It exacerbates my discontents. At noon I drink the vermouth dregs and lose my temper. Why can't I bring calm and intelligence to this old house, this cozy room, this gentle rain? I am uncontrollably restless. I drive into town and buy a quart of gin. This helps, but not too much, and I must be careful not to succumb to distempers. The rug and the floor are filthy. The clock is out of time. I work on an airplane model with the boy. I clean the rug. Mary helps me. After dinner I sit in the dining room with a glass of gin. I am discouraged. I am close to despair. I watch an educational program on TV in which the fugitive John Milton and his accomplice Andrew Marvell speak eloquently about the ornaments of liberty. Sitting on a pile of cushions in a dirty attic, I think I endure a new degree of discouragement, although I know that I do not. I think that I will be unable to sleep, but I am mistaken. But waking at three or four I think that I have been selling ice cream, the seven flavors of discouragement. Thinking back over my work, I can find nothing to cheer me. But I sleep and wake again full of cheer, opportunity, hope.

•

I take a train up the Hudson Valley on a brilliant autumn afternoon. Read, drink. Strike up a conversation with a heavy woman. Decorous. Educated as a schoolteacher, she has an accent that is prim and enlightened. She mistakes me for an Englishman and I lead her on. She is at first afraid of my intentions. Ultimately, I am afraid of hers. She tells me the story of her life: the fortune lost in the crash, her grandfather the judge; she ran for county supervisor on the Democratic ticket, spent a night in the governor's mansion in Albany. I do not listen carefully, and return to my roomette. I wake at three, bare-arse, my flower stiff as a horn vis-à-vis myself in the long mirror; and I think, Should we bring compassion to the exhibitionist hiding in the bushes of a public park, his pants down around his knees, or lingering in the Y.M.C.A. shower? Is this madness or is it the perversity of mankind? The track joints beat out a jazz bass, versatile, exhilarating, and fleet—some brilliant improvisation on the ardent beating of the heart—and the wind sounds in the brake boxes like the last records Billie Holiday ever made. These blues, these blues. I wake and dress before dawn. Ohio. The country flat. The light, rising in the east, shows the western sky, black as storm clouds.

The old lady sits down. "I will need more butter than that," she says. Then she leans across the aisle and says, "Excuse me for speaking to you without having been introduced, but to see a happily married couple like you and your husband does my heart so much good that I have to say so. We don't see many happily married couples these days, do we? I don't know why it is. My own husband is gone. He went sixteen years ago. It sounds like a long time ago, but for me it seems like a moment. He was a minister. We had a nice congregation in Poughkeepsie. He had never had a sick day in his life. He had never had a toothache, a headache, a cold, he had never had a sick day in his life. Then one morning he woke with this pain in his side. Cancer. I took him to the hospital, but he simply wasted away. I had twelve specialists. When we all knew that the end was near, they let me take him home. He was lying in bed one afternoon and he said, 'Mother, Mother, will you help me? I want to sit in my chair by the window.' Well, I put my arms around him to help him to the window, and he went. He went in my arms. I had seven brothers and sisters, but they're all gone."

Two women come in. The waiter asks if they had a good trip to New York. "Let's write it off," they say gallantly. "Now we're home. The good old Middle West." They look out of the window at the fields, houses, pigsties, the distant groves of oak. The train blows its whistle— a diminished fifth. A mare with a foal, cows, and pigs run away from the track. All the way across Ohio and Indiana the farm animals are frightened by the train.

•

I dream that someone in space says to me: So let us rush, then, to see the world. It is shaped like an egg, covered with seas and continents, warmed and lighted by the sun. It has churches of indescribable beauty, raised to gods that have never been seen; cities whose distant roofs and smokestacks will make your heart leap; ballparks and comfortable auditoriums in which people listen to music of the most serious import; and thousands or perhaps even millions of museums where man's drive to celebrate life is recorded. Here the joy of women's breasts and backsides, the colors of water, the shapes of trees, athletes, dreams, houses, the shapes of ecstasy and dismay, the shape even of an old shoe, are celebrated. Let us rush to see the world. They serve steak there on jet planes, and dance at sea. They have invented musical instruments to express love, peaceableness; to stir the finest memories and aspirations. They have invented games to catch the hearts of young men. They have ceremonies to exalt the love of men and women. They make their vows to music and the sound of bells. They have invented ways to heat their houses in the winter and cool them in the summer. They have even invented engines to cut their grass. They have free schools for the pursuit of knowledge, pools to swim in, zoos, vast manufactories of all kinds. They explore space and the trenches of the seas. Oh, let us rush to see this world.

•

To put down what I know as well as what I hope to know. To describe my alcoholic thirst beginning at nine in the morning and becoming sometimes unmanageable at eleven-thirty. To describe the humiliation of stealing a drink in the pantry and the galling taste of gin; to write about the weight of discouragement and despair; to write about a nameless dread; to write about the gruelling seizures of unfounded anxiety; to write about the horror of failure. The struggle to recoup an acuteness of feeling, the feeling that a margin of hopefulness has been debauched.

•

Hung over after the holiday and feeling painfully worn, I go through the motions of waking, eating, dressing. Go to the train. I think on the platform that I may faint, spin around, and fall down, a searing pain in my side. I breathe deeply of the north wind. A. joins me, and I stay close to him in case of trouble. On the train I tell myself, in a kind of panic, the long story of Donna Orieta, including her cocktail party. I have a drink at the Biltmore, where my hand is shaking so that it is difficult to get the glass to my mouth. A young man down the bar gives me a hound-dog look; when we succumb to alcohol we lose our self-esteem all the way down the line. Lunch at the club, where I am blotto, and go to the Biltmore to dry out. It is, as I have said before, a little like Hell. Fifteen or twenty naked men wander around. None of them is comely. The air smells of pine scent, as unlike the freshness of pine as anything in the world. A fat man in the shower soaps his cock. Does he have an erection? I look away.

•

I skate; I knock a puck around with my son—the pleasures of this simple fleetness, this small prowess. The light on the snowfields, and I see it as I move, all purple and gold. Back here, the library flooded with the last light of day, chrysanthemums, Christmas music on the piano, Ben plays with the manger that we brought from Rome. The setting is nearly perfect, but I seem suspended in it; seem unable either to cast it down or to bring it to a climax. Shall I ask the As, the Bs, the Cs for a drink? Then my narcissism, if that's what it is, will reach a climax. What a beautiful house, they will say, what a perfectly beautiful house. So the sun goes down, the fields turn blue, I turn on lamps and warm myself at the fire. What do I want: a furnished room, a doorway on a windy street?

•

A dark, raw day, me cold and depressed. I might bring it off with a narrator; it means a lot of work. Finish the Nabokov, that violet-flavored nightmare. To construct a novel from footnotes is a brilliant eccentricity, but the homosexual king disconcerts me. Mary takes the boys off to see the Nativity play, and I sit around the dining room drinking and playing records; Schumann and Louis Armstrong. I plan a large cocktail party; I write a letter to the *Social Register*; I give my daughter away in marriage. I should read. I should write. I should translate a page of Italian. But all I do is drink and polish the candlesticks. Oh, to put it down, and to put it down with the known colors of life: the reds of courage, the yellows of love.

•

I dream that I see my mother, leaving the state capitol in Boston, where she has gone to defend some good cause. She wears a long black coat with a fur collar, a tricorne hat. The flight of steps that separates us appears to be the steps of a Spanish church up which the last of a wedding procession is moving. When the procession has gone I go to my mother. "I'm very tired," she says, "I'm terribly tired." Her voice is small, a little cracked. Before I can reach her she falls. Her body begins to roll down the stairs, and I think with horror that she may go all the way, but the fall is stopped; she lies sprawled on the lifts.

•

New Year's Day, and I shall make something illustrious of this year. The entire nation is in the grip of an unprecedented cold wave. Villages and cities isolated. Men, women, and children without heat or food. Etc. J. writes from Iowa; Ohio, rather. He will return. The wind from the river is better. Young Ben, Susie, and I drink and play records. "Shall we open the Upstairs at the Downstairs in the Outdoors?" I ask. Is there something ridiculous about this man of fifty, dancing the Charleston?

During dinner, Susie says, "You have two strings to play. One is the history of the family, the other is your childlike sense of wonder. Both of them are broken." We quarrel. She cries. I feel sick. We make up, but I feel the generation of that bitterness which overwhelmed me on Christmas Eve. I cannot check it. My first resolve is to ask my family to help me with my drinking. Since I seem unable to handle it myself, I must find someone to help me. My second resolve, and this in a spate of bitterness, is that I will learn to disregard their interference. I think, abysmally bitter, that Orpheus knew he would be torn limb from limb; but he had not guessed that the Harpy would be his daughter. I lose at darts to my son and scold Mary about my dilemma. No money, no place to work in, no chair, even, to sit upon. I wake this morning, remorseful, exhausted, to begin a new year. The sky is the dark blue of high altitude.

•

Snow lies under the apple trees. We picked very few of the apples, enough for jelly, and now the remaining fruit, withered and golden, lies on the white snow. It seems to be what I expected to see, what I had hoped for, what I remembered. Sanding the driveway with my son, I see, from the top of the hill, the color of the sky and what a paradise it seems to be this morning—the sky sapphire, a show of clouds, the sense of the world in these, its shortest days, as cornered. Later, much later, clouds rise up all around the sky like the walls of a well, but then, when we are coasting, the sun, very low, breaks through this wall, seems to single out windows from which to flash its chill and yellow light, floods the valley and the house with color. I lay a fire in the library, play backgammon with Ben. Go between games to the window to see the outpouring of color, the waxing moon, the evening star.

•

I struggle with the problems on the last of the book. After lunch I seem in charge of Federico. I read him some rubbish, we walk to the mailbox, at three I make him some lemonade and sneak some gin. Frustrated, I think that I, the novelist, must rock the cradle while Mary, the housewife, corrects, for her pleasure, freshman themes. I read Hannah Arendt on the repulsive moral chaos in Fascist Germany and turn these facts back onto myself. I am the immoralist, and my failure has been the toleration of an intolerable marriage. My fondness for pleasant interiors and the voices of children has destroyed me. I should have breached this contract years ago and run off with some healthy-minded beauty. I must go, I must go, but then I see my son in the orchard and know that I have no freedom from him. Never having known the love of a father has forced me into a love so engulfing and passionate that there is no margin of choice. I cannot resolve the book because I have been irresolute about my own affairs. So these feelings, coming from a variety of directions, center on my slightly intoxicated mind. The immorality of Fascist Germany, Mary's intellectual enthusiasm, Ben's manliness, the neglect I received at the hands of my long-dead father, my guilty love of tranquil interiors, and the itchiness in my crotch come together in a ridiculous collision; and I take the toboggan to the top of the hill. The light is fine, the air pure and cold, the sun is setting, and I think that by going down the hill again and again I will purify my feelings, learn to be compassionate. I partly succeed; but I go on drinking gin.

•

He sat on the edge of his bed, already exhausted before the journey had even begun. What he would have liked, what he dreamed of, was some elixir, some magical, brightly colored pill that would put the spring back into his step, the gleam in his eye, the joy of life in his heart. He took quantities of pills, but they made no difference in the way he felt. It seemed that he had been tired for years. "Before you go, dear," his wife called from downstairs, "would you see if you can do something about the kitchen drain?" This reasonable request reminded him of the variety of his responsibilities. He had taken them all on willingly, but his willingness had not produced, as he somehow had thought it might, corresponding stores of energy. Three children in college, the interest and amortization on a twenty-five-thousand-dollar mortgage, an insecure position in business, a loving and impractical wife, a balky heating plant, a leaky roof, a car that needed repairs, a lawn choked with quack grass, a driveway with weeds, and three dying elms on the front lawn seemed, along with the stopped drain, to excite his discouragement. He had taken care of himself for most of his life. He had supported his old parents and indigent relations, raised his family, greased the sump pump, balanced the checkbook, filed the income tax, assuming that an increase in responsibility would develop an increase in confidence, but what he seemed to have developed instead was some spiritual or emotional curvature, like a hod carrier's back. Sitting on the edge of his bed, he realized that what he wanted was someone who would take care of him. Not for long. He didn't want to flee, he only wanted a respite— a week, perhaps, in which someone else would grease the sump pump, shine his shoes, and travel with him to Cincinnati. Twice in the last year he had waked alone in a hotel room with an acute pain in the vicinity of his heart. Both times he gave the pain ten minutes to abate before calling the desk clerk, and in both cases the pain had subsided; but this was another tax on his strength, another cause for anxiety, and now he wondered, Would he, tonight, in the hotel in Cincinnati, suffer his pain again?

He could not recall a day recently when he had not suffered some kind of pain; and—what was more painful—he could not recall a day recently when he had enjoyed any sort of unself-conscious repose. He had taken a ten-day vacation on a beach, but he had been, stretched out in the sun, as touchy as a triggered rattrap. He had known—in the past—calm, healthy excitement, the pleasures of physical exhaustion, but all of these seemed to have been lost to him long ago. When had he last felt peaceable, cleanly, and strong? He could not remember. But now it was time to clean the drain, time to go, time to summon the crude energies of nerve; he had nothing else. He went downstairs and used the plunger on the drain. The drain showed some improvement, and he experienced a fleeting contentment at this. "You won't forget to buy something for Ella's birthday, will you?" his wife asked as he kissed her goodbye. He walked to the station, step by step. Was this a common condition? Were the pains in his heart, chest, and esophagus, the sense of being harried, the normal terms of his time of life or was he just unlucky? And how would he ever know, since if anyone had asked him how he felt he would have exclaimed, "Fine! Fine? I've never felt better!"

●

Here it is, more or less. There are questions of fact to be clarified and transitions to be improved, and I would like to rewrite the last ten pages, but I don't see much more than a week's revision. The typing was done by a Briarcliff housewife and is execrable.

●

This is not in any way confused in my mind with the New Testament, and I am sincerely interested in criticism. A great many people felt that the "Chronicle" was not a novel, and the same thing is bound to be said about this, perhaps more strongly. I do hope you'll like it, but if you shouldn't I will understand.

●

Waking this morning, I think the book so poor that it should not be published. I think, an hour later, that it can't be so bad. I shall scythe the orchard.

●

And I think about the past—how orderly, clean, and sensible it seems; above all, how light. I sit in a well-lighted yellow room thinking of the past, but I seem, in relation to the past, to be sitting in darkness. I remember my father, rising at six. He takes a cold bath and goes out to play four holes of golf before breakfast. The links are hilly and there is a fine view of the village and the sea. He dresses for business and eats a hearty breakfast—fish hash with poached eggs and popovers, or some chops. I and the dog walk with him to the station, where he hands me his walking stick and the dog's leash, and boards the train among his friends and neighbors. The business he transacts in his office is simple and profitable, and at noon he has a bowl of crackers and milk for lunch at his club. He returns on the train at five, and we all get into the Buick and drive to the beach. We have a bathhouse, a simple building on stilts, weathered by the sea winds. There are lockers for dressing, and a fireplace for rainy days. We change and go for a long swim in that green, dark, and briny sea. Then we dress and, smelling of salt, go up the hill to have supper in the cavernous dining room. When supper is over, my mother goes to the telephone. "Good evening, Althea," she says to the operator. "Would you please ring Mr. Wagner's ice-cream store?" Mr. Wagner recommends his lemon sherbet, and delivers a quart a few minutes later on a bicycle that rattles and rings in the summer dusk as if it were strung with bells. We have our ice cream on the back lawn, read, play whist, wish on the evening star for a gold watch and chain, kiss one another good night, and go to bed. These seemed to be the beginnings of a world, these days all seemed like mornings, and if there was a single incident that could be used as a turning point it was, I suppose, when my father went out to play an early game of golf and found dear friend and business associate on the edge of the third fairway hanging dead from a tree.

•

A fine day in the city—this insular brilliance and freshness. I kill some time in a movie, where I see a fox hunt; lunch with L. There are shells in my eggs Benedict. At Harpers they seem pleased with the book, although I seem paranoiac and keep scrutinizing their remarks for signs of insincerity. I leave the office, have a pleasant drink, take the train home with A., and go to his house. His daughter is having a piano lesson: "Für Elise." The room is full of sunlight. We have a drink. I walk home over the hill; the grass is fragrant and waist high. Mr. H., at sixty, has been discovered to have a pregnant mistress and has got a divorce. I think the sorrow in this house is all my fault. But the voice

I hear sounds one of two notes: anger or weariness. My high spirits are ineffectual. Mary and Susie go off to the movies, and I sit on the terrace with my little son at my side, admiring the lights of evening and waiting for the stars and the fireflies to shine. I tell him to wish on the evening star, and wish myself for the happiness of my wife. We wait until we see seven stars, countless fireflies, and then go in. He falls asleep at once. And it is because of these pleasures that I find so painful the thought of joining the legions of lonely men. But today I seem over-wrought, nervous, and I will go on with the casting out of swine. "Wanna screw?" I ask. It is, unfortunately, my style. She seems terribly tired, her face strained, wasted by what tasks I do not know. How I would love to flip up her nightgown, but I cannot.

•

I wake, feeling myself to be mysteriously at the bottom of the heap, the bottom of something. It is as though a theft had gone on during the night, and I wake to find myself robbed of spirit and vitality. What I seem to feel is that I have lost the hope that love and reason have any persuasiveness in the problems of my marriage; that Mary's struggle with the past is so strenuous and unequal that it would be absurd to expect civility or pleasantness from her. I go into town. My emotional system, no more complicated than the plumbing in this old house and no more prone to breakdowns, seems to be functioning nicely, and I regard the city in the bright lights of a summer day without a trace of anxiety or combativeness. I lunch with L. and his daughter and read Albee's play on the homebound local. The play adds its weight to what appears to be a basic distemper. "He is not," says Mary, "the only person who writes wickedly about women." This makes me cross, and I cut some grass to improve my feelings. But they remain lamentable. We go off to dinner: gentle people in a spacious house; a wood fire burning on this cool summer night; Japanese lanterns in the garden to celebrate the birth of a grandson. My feeling is that it was I who was invited, not she; that it is my charm, good looks, mobility that have got us asked. This is, of course, repulsive. But during the course of the evening she fires a remark across the room that seems to me vindictive. I think the remark should not have been spoken, and I know that my reaction should not be so passionate, and yet I cannot alter either of these facts. I talk with S. and W. when I come home, and, getting into bed, summon the image of someone more magnanimous and adult than myself whose wisdom and compassion I can imitate. I drink with the B.s on Saturday; too much. Swim with the physicist whose hobby is cabinetwork. He is virtually hairless, soft and open in his approach, an object of suspicion. He tells me he was a star of the Princeton water-polo team. What he was doing at Princeton was not clear. The hot-water system backs again into the radiators, a pipe starts leaking, the oil burner defuncts, and I do not seem to have the fortitude to regard these matters with the indifference they deserve. As I am about to climb into my wedding bed for a bounce, I am rebuffed. Then for the next hour, loudly and cruelly, I unburden myself of every resentment I have cherished for the last three months. There may be some justification for this, and yet I am so profoundly ashamed of myself in the morning that I am sick, and repeat that old incantation: Valor, beauty, grace with strength, etc. Mary tells me that she could not sleep; that she lay awake, crying, until three. Anyone so cruel will be punished, and yet these drunken outbreaks seem to have some salutary results. One of the mean things that I said was that I do not like to go anywhere with her, and so she will not go with me to lunch. I beseech her, ask her forgiveness, take her in my arms, and, after drinking three gins, go off to lunch. Whether I appear to be drunken and foolish I do not know and do not much care. I enter the locker room at the pool just as a member of the jeunesse dorée drops his tennis shorts and so we are introduced. I find this disconcerting and am inclined to blame him. He seems uncommitted. So I jaw through a stylish lunch. There is a pretty woman in the company. Home, I sit on the terrace; I feel very tired. My heart pains me and is heavy—alcohol, tobacco, anger, or grief—and the future, when I put my mind to it, eludes me. I hold my younger son against me, and this lightens the pain. Gentle horseplay in the dusk. I sit on the stone steps, still warm from the sun, and wait for the evening star. I drink some bourbon and go to bed, to sleep.

•

So in the morning I say, Leap, my heart, my spirit. Nothing else will do. They must leap.

•

Mr. Y hides in the broom closet, watching his wife through the keyhole to make sure she is not putting DDT in his dinner. The view from a keyhole is quite broad if you are able to move about, but he is not. She goes to and from the pantry, where the poisons are kept, but he can't tell if she's dosing his food with paprika or with something more lethal. She puts the plates on the table and calls, "Supper is ready." She steps out of the kitchen, and he is able to make his escape, retreat to the pantry, and then reënter the kitchen as if he had been in some other part of the forest. "My, that smells good!" he exclaims, of the sauce. "Yes it does, doesn't it?" she says. "I put a little oregano in it." Her smile is wicked, victorious. "What were you doing in the broom closet?" she asks. "Oh, nothing," he says. But the field is hers.

•

Mr. Bierstubbe reached deep into Mrs. Zagreb's dress and lifted out her breasts while she stroked his back and said, "Be good, be a good boy." Her tits were as big as turkeys, they gleamed like marble and tasted to his thirsty lips as soft and various as the night air. But when he woke on Sunday morning Mrs. Zagreb's breasts had turned from a treasure into a torment. They seemed to surround him, to fill the air of the room, to follow him, tempt him, dangle and wobble in front of his nose. They followed him to the train, settled themselves beside him, followed him down Forty-third Street to his club, and when he had a drink before lunch his hunger for Mrs. Zagreb's bosoms nearly overwhelmed him.

•

A. rolls his eyes at his wife and groans, significantly. Well, all right, she says. He strips off his clothes and waits at the side of the bed. She goes down to the kitchen, puts four blankets into the washing machine, blows a fuse, and floods the kitchen. "But why," he asks, standing in the kitchen door, naked and unaccommodated, "why when I ask you for tenderness do you wash blankets?" "Well, I was afraid I'd forget them," she says shyly. "Moths might get into them." She hangs her head. Then he sees something touching and pitiful here, some irresistible wish to be as elusive as a nymph, but she, being much too heavy to sprint through the woods, is reduced to putting blankets in a washing machine. But he would understand that her determination to seem elusive was as strong as the drive in his middle; he would put his arm around her and lead her up the stairs.

•

I open Nabokov and am charmed by this spectrum of ambiguities, this marvellous atmosphere of untruth; and I am interested in his methods and find them very sympathetic, but his imagery—the shadow of a magician against a shimmery curtain, and all those sugared violets—is not mine. The house I was raised in had its charms, but my father hung his underwear from a nail he had driven into the back of the bathroom door, and while I know something about the Riviera I am not a Russian aristocrat polished in Paris. My prose style will always be to a degree matter-of-fact.

•

In the 1890s my father chanced to be in Munich, and, either because it pleased him or because he needed money, worked as a model for an architectural sculptor. He must have been a handsome young man and I know that his trunk must have been well developed since, until close to the end of his life, he worked out for an hour each morning with barbells, dumbbells, and Indian clubs. The sculptor portrayed him as a sort of Atlas or male caryatid and incorporated his figure into the façade of the old Königspalast Hotel, which was destroyed by Allied bombing in the forties. I saw the hotel when I took a walking trip with my brother through Germany in 1935 and saw the unmistakable features of my father, holding on his shoulders the lintel of that massive hotel. Later, in Frankfurt, I found my father's image holding up the balconies and roofs of the Frankfurter Hof. My father was obviously not the model for all these caryatids, but once I had made the association it became obsessive and I had the impression, not unpleasant, that a great many apartment houses, hotels, theatres, and banks were supported by my father's noble shoulders. The war did surprisingly little damage to buildings of this era, and I seemed, only recently, to encounter my father holding up the façade of a hotel in Yalta. I recognized him again in Kiev, supporting the bow windows of a whole block of apartments. He was everywhere in Vienna and Munich, and in Berlin one saw him maimed, disfigured, and lying in a field of weeds near Checkpoint Charlie. Since he had begun his life on the sunny side of the street, having been employed mostly in supporting those lintels under which the rich and the fashionable passed, it became distressing to see how the light passed from these buildings and neighborhoods and that in time the appearance of my father's head and naked shoulders usually implied a fourth-rate hotel, a bankrupt department store, an abandoned theatre, or an incipient slum. It was in the end a relief to get back to my place in Kitzbühel, where the buildings are made of wood.

•

Shea Stadium. A late summer night. In the clubhouse I look around me with arrogance. Who do these people think they are? They think they are who they are. Fathers with sons. Some good-looking women. The sense is that one is having dinner not in a ballpark but in some city on the way to a theatre, which makes the spectacle of the ballpark when one enters it apocalyptic. The sod gleams. This is indeed a park. I think that the task of an American writer is not to describe the misgivings of a woman taken in adultery as she looks out of a window at the rain but to describe four hundred people under the lights reaching for a foul ball. This is ceremony. The umpires in clericals, sifting out the souls of the players; the faint thunder as ten thousand people, at the bottom of the eighth, head for the exits. The sense of moral judgments embodied in a migratory vastness.

•

The battle with booze goes on. I weed the chrysanthemums and hold away from the bottle until half past eleven but not a second longer. To the S.s'. He has been drinking at the club. His tongue is loose; his mind has lost its equilibrium. After dinner he slumps on the sofa and falls into a drunken sleep, his head on his chest, his eyeglasses on the tip of his nose. Thunder and lightning, a sudden rain, a suddenly released fragrance of freshness. "How I love to hear the sound of rain," said the banker.

•

Woolgathering, oh, woolgathering. It is the day of the civil-rights march in Washington. After lunch we drive to a public beach, Croton Point. An abundance of trash cans, turnstiles, ticket windows, men and women in county-park uniforms, worn lawns, pretty willows, water the color of urine, which smells, to my long nose, like an open sewer. A plump lifeguard sits in his tower blowing his whistle, and shouts commands through his electrical megaphone at every infraction of the numerous regulations. It is disconcerting to realize that this gravelly beach, this contaminated bay are all that much of the world knows of these pleasures. I regard the bathhouse with some apprehension. There is a memory here, adolescent, pubescent, of making it with boy chums in the briny chambers; of my friend hanging around the open shower, looking for big ones. Not me, I think. But this seems more an anxiety than a memory, and looking among the few bathers I am struck not with the delights of the flesh but with its mortal boredom, pimply backsides, halitosis, ill tempers.

•

I horse around with the children and a football. Sharpen a carving knife in the kitchen. Mary gives me a shy and passionate kiss, a loving kiss. My memory is full of holes and craters, but I cannot remember when it last was that Mary made an open declaration of love. So we are one another's best once more; and it was not so long ago, two or three weeks, that I glumly ate some hard-boiled eggs and thought of her with bitterness and worse.

•

Ben's dog dumps three loads on the library floor. In the morning I trash her with a rolled-up magazine. An hour later Ben asks, "Did you notice that Flora has difficulty walking? To get to her feet seems to give her much pain." So I conclude that I have broken the spine of my son's beloved pet. I am the sort of man who thinks twice about swatting a fly and when I step on an ant I step on it carefully, to give it no pain. To harm an animal troubles me deeply; to harm an animal loved by my son is crushing. Mary seems to abet my troubles. She reports that my son is in agony; that I might have harmed the bitch, since she has such frail hindquarters. I drink some Scotch, seize a piece of bread and cheese, and stumble out of the house into the woods. I am convinced that I have killed my son's dog. Regard this man of fifty-one, then, lying in a field, gnawing on a piece of bread, his eyes filled with tears. I have killed my son's dog; I have killed my son's affections. It was an accident, but this is no consolation. I walk up the path to the dam, and this simple exercise refreshes my common sense. It may also clear the whiskey in my head. When I return, the dog is better, and when we take her to the veterinary there seems to be nothing wrong with her. So much of one's vitality is spent on false alarms; and I think, perhaps unjustly, that Mary was able to create an atmosphere of morbid anxiety, something like the mysterious powers her father had to extend a feeling of condemnation and doom over his domain. Is this neurotic, is it, as I once thought, some discernible power of darkness? In the afternoon mail there is a letter saying that two pieces have been bought. I am jubilant, but when I speak the good tidings to Mary she asks, oh, so thinly, "I don't suppose they bothered to enclose any checks?" I think this is piss, plain piss, and I shout, "What in hell do you expect? In three weeks I make five thousand, revise a novel, and do the housework, the cooking, and the gardening, and when it all turns out successfully you say, 'I don't suppose they bothered to include any checks.'" Her voice is more in the treble than ever when she says, "I never seem able to say the right thing, do I?" She strays up the driveway. I don't understand these sea changes, although I have been studying them for twenty-five years. For three weeks we have enjoyed transcendent passion, love, and humor. Now this thinness. I cannot control it—a chance telephone call, a dream, can bring it on. So she wanders away not only from me but from us all.

•

I would like not to do the Swimmer as Narcissus. The possibility of a man's becoming infatuated with his own image is there, dramatized by a certain odor of abnormality, but this is like picking out an unsound apple for celebration when the orchard is full of fine specimens. I've done it before; I would like to do better. Swimming is a pleasure, a gulping-in of the summer afternoon, high spirits. It is natural and fitting that a man should in some way love himself. So it is natural and fitting that the roof leaks, but it is hardly universal. So the people who drain their pool are merely a threat. By the time he reaches it, the water will be deep enough for a dive. With Pygmalion there is the need to dignify the situation, to make it urgent.

•

The Swimmer might go through the seasons; I don't know, but I know it is not Narcissus. Might the seasons change? Might the leaves turn and begin to fall? Might it grow cold? Might there be snow? But what is the meaning of this? One does not grow old in the space of an afternoon. Oh, well, kick it around.

•

So the battle against hooch and tobacco goes on. I seem, so far as tobacco goes, slightly ahead; it's tied up with the hooch. When people are sick I think, You might feel a little better if you didn't smoke quite so much, etc. It is impossible to work.

•

In church, on my knees before the chancel, I see, with a crushing force, how dependent I am on alcohol. It is an agony, and one not illustrated by these colored windows, stone walls, the ancient costumes of the acolytes. One needs an alkali desert, dry streambeds, a range of cruel mountains. Pick myself up at half past eleven, paddle the kayak with Ben. Waking, high-hearted and randy, I think with scorn of the book. Why should one turn the powers of the imagination onto the subject of a woman having a tragic love affair? Why should one worry about stink-finger, the wanton glance? Throw it out the window.

•

During the day it seemed to me from time to time that our grief, my own grief, was orgiastic. Walt Whitman being read over the funerary drums. "Hail to the Chief" played to the coffin. The beauty and the sorrow of the widow. I cried like a disappointed child, stuck out my lower lip, screwed up my eyes. He was a splendid man, and the most one can do is take his excellence as an example. What came to me as a surprise was the love he inspired. The perhaps excessive grief, the questions of taste may have expressed the emotional inflexibility, the involuntary hardening of our hearts, the small use we have for tears in our way of life. I was offended at the pride with which the TV announcer described the numerousness of the mourners as if this were competitive, as in a sense I suppose it is. There is something wonderful to be observed here about the goodness of men's hearts and souls. One would never have guessed that the world had such a capacity for genuine grief. The most we can do is exploit our memories of his excellence.

I continue to find it difficult to work here. At eleven I go up to see the services on TV. It is His Eminence Cardinal Cushing, God's advocate, who, God forgive me, sounds the note of mortal boredom. The rites are arcane, the voice is harsh, the Latin sounds neither living nor dead, and over it all an Italian tenor sings the "Ave Maria," a piece of music I dislike intensely. I am most moved by the smallness of the President's coffin. The rush of dignitaries seems comical. Traffic is delayed, as it is everywhere, and it seems that his path to the grave is more tortuous than his way through life. There are the Black Watch pipers, the Air Force pipers, and rifle drill by some Gaels. It might have been simpler, but it is difficult to make choices, I expect, under a burden of grief. I should do this and that, give the hours of my day worth and purpose, but the best I do is stand at the window and watch my sons play football on the grass—Ben favoring Federico, who runs in the wrong direction. M. plays. He seems not effeminate but uncommitted. Knee-high boots, a black leather jacket, a large tail. He is a hat swiper. It is the game he plays. "It's too bad it happened that way," he says of the President's assassination, "but we had to get rid of him." He calls the other boys "niggers."

•

Like many men of fifty, I am obliged to ask for a raise and, like many men of fifty, I am confronted with a blameless, monolithic, and capricious organization, hobbled, it seems, by its own prosperity. The organizations of men, like men themselves, seem subject to deafness, nearsightedness, lameness, and involuntary cruelty. We seem tragically unable to help one another, to understand one another. I am accused of improvidence, and make several long speeches about how I am harassed by indebtedness. *The Saturday Evening Post* has offered me twenty-four thousand, *The New Yorker* has offered me twenty-five hundred, and I will take the latter, I'm not sure why. The important thing is to work and to insist on fair wages for the work I do. Like any man of fifty, I wonder what would become of my children if I should be taken ill, and I think that the miseries of illness have become more mysterious and acute as the world, its cities and populations, outstrips our comprehension.

•

Fred calls. His wife seems to have left him; his daughters are about to leave. "I think I'll sell this place," he says. "It seems a little strange to pull up your stakes at my time of life." What is this, then? A family recollection of ingratitude, loneliness; the cruel denial of every reward. Industrious, unselfish, loving, having fed, clothed, and sent to expensive schools four children, taken his wife to Bermuda each year, he finds himself, at fifty-eight, the beginning of his winter, turned out to a furnished room, cooking his meals on an electric plate over the protests of the landlady.

And yet I think there is some sense that this loneliness is his destiny. Is this my family or is it the family of man? My grandfather is supposed to have died, alone, unknown, a stranger to his wife and his sons, in a furnished room on Charles Street. My own father spent two or three years in his late seventies alone at the farm in Hanover. The only heat was a fireplace; his only companion a half-wit who lived up the road. I lived as a young man in cold, ugly, and forsaken places yearning for a house, a wife, the voices of my sons, and having all of this I find myself, when I am engorged with petulance, thinking that after all, after the Easter-egg hunts and the merry singing at Christmas, after the loving and the surprises and the summer afternoons, after the laughter and the open fires, I will end up cold, alone, dishonored, forgotten by my children, an old man approaching death without a companion. But this must be some part of a man's sense of destiny. We hold, like a trick of mirrors, an image of some fruitful old age—grandchildren bringing in the harvest—and hold as well a conviction that we shall be forgotten, made to suffer cold and hunger, on our last days in the world.

•

I have a drink, go to meet Philip Roth at the station with the two dogs on leads. He is unmistakable, and I give him an Army whoop from the top of the stairs. Young, supple, gifted, intelligent, he has the young man's air of regarding most things as if they generated an intolerable heat. I don't mean fastidiousness, but he holds his head back from his plate of roast beef as if it were a conflagration. He is divorced from a girl I thought delectable. "She won't even give me back my ice skates." The conversation hews to a sexual line—cock and balls, Genet, Rechy—but he speaks, I think, with grace, subtlety, wit.

•

A review of the "Scandal" seemed to me less an attempt to judge it severely and to give it its rightful place among books than to bring to it a determined generosity and enthusiasm that would make the book a financial success and let us live in peace for a year or so. What moved A. to this generosity, this show of power, in fact, remains in the dark. Again, the cover story in its discretion, its cunning, rendered me as a serious and likable person when I could, on the strength of the evidence, be described as a fat slob enjoying an extraordinary run of luck. To use the word "love" to describe the relationships between men is inappropriate. There is, under the most exhaustive scrutiny, no trace of sexuality in these attachments. We are delighted to look into one another's faces, but below the neck there is nothing to be observed. We are happy and content together, but when we are separated we never think of one another. These bonds are as strong as any that we form in life, and yet we can pick them up and put them down with perfect irresponsibility. We do not visit one another in the hospital and when we are apart we seldom write letters, but when we are together we experience at least some of the symptoms of what we call love.

•

The old dog whimpers, cries in pain as she struggles to climb the stairs. She is the first one of us to grow old. In the twenty-five years that Mary and I have lived together we have known very little pain other than the pain of misunderstanding, childbirth, passing indebtedness, and head colds. We have, in fact, known very little in the way of change. We play the same games, walk the same distances, make love with the same frequency. When our parents were sick with age and dying, their care was never our responsibility. So the old bitch, her hindquarters crippled with rheumatism, is my first experience in the care of the infirm. I give her a boost from the rear and her cries of helplessness and misery are the cries of the old. These are the first sounds of real pain that this house, since it became ours, has heard.

•

Reading "The Enormous Radio" I think, One fault is that I have written too much; that my motivations have sometimes been less than passionate. "Goodbye, My Brother" seems too circumspect, seems small. I like "The Cure," but this is a look at madness with a superficial resolution—and yet I don't intend to go any deeper into that storm. What is wrong, where do I fail? I seem neither sane enough nor mad enough. I seem not to have approached a well-defined vision of the world. Can I charge myself with some discoloration, that unclearness I despise in the work of other men? And what should I avoid? Anything contrived, anything less than vital.

•

Mary has the wind up about driving, and me, too. I take three gin drinks and drive my son to the station in Stamford. He needs a shave. The late-winter afternoon, the late-winter night. We shake hands gravely, although I would like to embrace him. Then I turn back. The sun has set. The winter afterglow is white, a glare. Against this are the greenish gas lamps of the parkway. The six-lane highway is crowded at this hour. The shapes of the trucks are monumental. They make a sound like thunder, and smoke pours from chimneys at their stern. They seem massive, deadly, and have for all their tonnage the wistfulness of obsolescence, as if one saw here in the winter twilight the last hours of the brontosaurus and the *Tyrannosaurus rex*. The throughway in this winter dusk looks like the end of an epoch. I can drive no faster than my vision and my reflexes, and the common speeds here outstrip these, and I pretend that Breitburd, a Russian, is with me for company. I point out how numerous and powerful are the cars, how well engineered are the highways, etc. I think of the two-lane roads west of Moscow, the log houses, women drawing water from a well. Turning from an unfamiliar road on to one that leads to my house makes such a profound change in my feeling that I see how provincial and domesticated a man I am. I am coming home; I am coming home.

•

I bucket around the village. Cash a check; buy liquor, a dog collar. The new hardware store is vast and empty and seems to have been empty for months. They will not have the paint you want, the nails you want, the screws you want. "We expect the orders in next week," says the clerk. He used to work at the hardware store on Spring Street, worked there for twenty years. I ask him if he doesn't miss the village. He waves his hand toward the window and the view of the river, but his face is suspiciously red. This empty store, this red-faced man with nothing much to do is a piece of life. I go from there to the greenhouse, where the warm air smells of loam and carnations, and everyone, even the dog and the cat, seems very happy. The Z.s seem to have quarrelled. That's my guess. I buy her a dozen eggs. "That's all I'll need for the rest of the week," she says. But after dark her smallest son comes down the hill with his flashlight to ask for a cup of flour. It is like running up a flag, a call for sympathy, a declaration of the fact that her husband has remained in town for dinner while she bakes biscuits to save the price of bread. The little boy is keenly aware of the importance of this hour, this task. "Did you have a very pleasant Christmas?" he asks as I walk him home in the dark. "Did you receive many gifts?" he asks, thinking himself for a moment a full-grown man. "Thank you very much," he says when we part at the lighted door. "Thank you very much."

•

The old dog; my love. That when we bought her someone pointed out that she was swaybacked and had a rib cage like a barrel. That as a young dog she was disobedient, greedy, and wicked. That she tipped over garbage pails, ripped wash off the clothesline, chewed up shoes of gold and silver, destroyed the baby-sitter's only spectacles, and refused to answer any commands; indeed, she seemed to laugh when she was called. She stole our clothing when we were clamming at Coskata, nearly drowned Mary in New Hampshire, and was a hazard on every beach. That she would retrieve a stick once or twice, but after that she would turn her back and pretend not to hear the command "Fetch." How we left her when we went to Europe, how she nibbled most of the upholstery, how when she heard my voice at the kennel she jumped a fence and hurled herself at me. That the introduction of love in our relationship came that day at Welton Falls. The stream was swollen and knocked her off her feet, and rolled her down a little falls into a pool. Then, when we returned, I hoisted her up in my arms and carried her over while she lapped my face. That with this her feelings toward me seemed to deepen. Her role as a confidante during some quarrelsome months. That my daughter, returning from school, would take her into the woods and pour into her ears her complaints about school, about her father and mother. Then it would be my turn, and then, after the dishes were washed, Mary's.

•

The difficulties with upholstered furniture. How she began in her middle age to dislike long walks. Starting up the beach for Coskata she would seem to enjoy herself, but if you took an eye off her she would swing around and gallop back to the house and her place in front of the fire. That she always got to her feet when I entered a room. That she enjoyed men very much and was conspicuously indifferent to women. That her dislikes were marked and she definitely preferred people from traditional and, if possible, wealthy origins. That she had begun to resemble those imperious and somehow mannish women who devilled my youth: the dancing teacher, the banker's wife, the headmistress of the progressive school I attended. There was a genre of imperious women in the twenties whose hell-for-leather manner made them seem slightly mannish. They were sometimes beautiful, but their airs were predatory and their voices were sometimes quite guttural. The time Susie put her off the jeep and she tried to commit suicide. How when I was alone and heard her wandering through the house my feelings for her were of love and gratitude; that her heavy step put me to sleep. Her difficulties in being photographed. That she barked when I talked loudly to myself. The book-review photograph, her figure arched with greed; the cigarette endorsement in which only her backside could be seen.

•

A white sky at eight, white as the snow, cloudless and so brilliant that it lifts one's eyes, with a faint pain, upward.

•

Lift the weights and look at myself in a mirror, wondering when my muscles will appear. Read Nabokov. The lights of the winter evening shift and now, by chance, the coming of the night seems formidable, some blood memory of the Ice Age. Later, I go out. The temperature is way below zero and the air is unusually dry for this valley. It is that fine cold that seems to frost the hair in your nostrils, and that has some subtle fragrance of its own—faint, keen, and a little like ammonia. I wear only a sweater, but I am not uncomfortable. The timbers of the porch crack in the gathering cold and I am ecstatic. "I want to eat cucumber sandwiches and drink champagne and do it all over again," he said, and she said, "Good night, my dear, you go to sleep, you go to sleep. Good night, my love."

•

After drinking and reading happily for several hours I decide that Federico and I should have a little fresh air. He does not like to coast.

He would rather watch mayhem on TV, or dress and undress a soldier doll. I force him out of the house. The orchard is a sheet of ice. The coasting is not only excellent, it is dangerous, but he hates it. He wants to get back to the house. He lies on his sled, dragging his feet, the prow turned uphill. I rattle down the hill, over the little pond and down the path to the woods. I am fifty-two, not drunk but plainly stimulated. Coasting seems to me a simple means of self-expression, a way of getting a little deeper into that last hour of a winter afternoon. I would like to share this with him, teach him to be unafraid, show him that as well as the world of his cozy room and his mother's box of candy there is the much more beautiful world of the frozen orchard and the late-winter day. But I teach him nothing but dread and boredom, and deepen his distaste for the snow and the cold. He asks a question. I leave it unanswered and go into the house. From the window I see him lying on his sled, thinking wickedly of his father, and I say, "It breaks my heart to see a little boy who takes no pleasure in anything but pushing his head under the sofa cushions. I wish he could learn or be taught some pleasure in running, coasting, etc." Then there is the question of whether or not he should go to see the James Bond movie. I decide against it, but the looks of reproach aimed at me by him and his mother alter my decision and off we go, when the dishes are done. A light snow is falling. The movie is erotic and gory, and I am angry at a seven-year-old boy's being exposed to this. Although I have exposed him to similar movies myself. I am very angry, and think that a mother who takes a seven-year-old boy to such a movie should be censured. I hold my tongue but I expect my feelings are not secret.

●

At the age of seven I conceived an indecent passion for the plaster cast of Venus de Milo that stood on the bookshelf, and, standing on a chair, I tried to look down those draperies that had, for so many centuries, concealed what I desired.

●

I dream that I am walking with Updike. The landscape seems out of my childhood. A familiar dog barks at us. I see friends and neighbors in their lighted windows. Updike juggles a tennis ball that is both my living and my dying. When he drops the ball I cannot move until it is recovered, and yet I feel, painfully, that he is going to murder me with the ball. He seems murderous and self-possessed. I must try to escape. There is a museum with a turnstile, a marble staircase, and statuary. In the end I do escape.

•

Who wants to fall in love, who wants the waiting for a voice, a footstep, a cough, who would choose this?

•

The dentist has just returned from a sixteen-day Caribbean cruise. Grissom is in Gemini orbit. The barber is full of wisdom. In man there is a divine spark. I start a haircut, they start from Florida. Before I am finished with a haircut, they're over Africa. Wonderful. And yet they can't cure arthritis. We can maybe get a man on the moon, but cancer, arthritis, we can't cure. But I have my health, thank God. As the man with the wooden leg says, I can't kick. Get it? Ha, ha, ha, get it? If he kicks he falls down. I can't kick. This is God's country. God picked out this country for his blessing.

•

So I wake thinking that everything will be nifty. In the mail there is a proof of an advertisement that is mostly a picture of me. I drive into town to get liquor for a party. I think of showing the picture to the liquor dealer, but I do not. I do show it to Mary, who says, "What are they going to do with it, pin it up in the post office?" When I object to the sharpness of this she says it was merely a civil question; there were no implications. I object vigorously. Two days later I still object. Should there be some way of seeing this humorously I would be most grateful. Gin seems to be the only way out. But there does seem to be some dreadful incompatibility between the sharpness of her tongue and my oversensitive, not to say childish, nature. The depth of my feeling seems to lie in the fact that I feel threatened and am, like any sensible man, wary of death. I wish I could forget this; and I shall try.

•

So one seems to settle down into this darkness. Time has always mended things. The physical changes are most noticeable: the short step with the toes pointed out, the wounded and musical voice, the dark scowl in the hall or the landing where one passes. Susie feels ill and I am afraid I may be to blame, so I retire to the balcony of the movie theatre where, like Estabrook, I have worked out or waited out so many problems of my life, transmuted into Apaches coming over the crest of the hill, beautiful women drinking wine, the collision of automobiles, airplane views of the Southwest. When I return the air is warm. There are no stars; there is nothing to see but darkness. They sit together and seem happy. Susie feels better; her face is clear. It begins to rain. I open the door to hear the sound. There is a single flash of lightning; a single recessive peal of thunder, and these most commonplace sounds make me absurdly happy. I am what I was—randy, light-boned, happy, all of this on the strength of the sound of water. I take a bath, open the window by my bed to hear the rain, curl up like a resentful child, and step into a panoramic and detailed dream where I turn on a water faucet to fill the ornamental pools of some great estate, hear Tallulah Bankhead complaining about her doctor, see a young woman wearing nothing but a brassiere, and am embarrassed by a flux of young writers who seem to be wearing bathing trunks. I make a lame joke.

•

Good Friday. I neither fast nor make any other observation of this sombre time. I roam from the post office to the church, unsober. The central altar is dark, but on the left the priest has improvised a Mary chapel where there is a blaze of candles and lilies and someone keeps the vigil. I find all this offensive; say my prayers. The day is brilliant for half an hour; clouds come up swiftly from the northwest and now the day is dark.

•

Easter. As I dress for church the iconography seems more than ever threadbare: the maidenly cross, the funereal lily, the lavender bow pulled off a candy box. How poorly this serves the cataclysm of the Resurrection. All the candles burn. Miss F. has worked day and night on the flower arrangements. The organist, truly raised from the dead, improvises a sort of polymorphous fugue. We raise our voices in some tuneless doggerel about life everlasting. These are earnest people, mostly old, making an organized response to the mysteriousness of life. What point would there be in going to church at daybreak to ridicule the

priest? But he does draw a breathtaking parallel between the Resurrection and the invention of television. I hope—I go no further—to
avoid anger, meanness, sloth, to be manly; and, should I be unable to
mend my affairs, to act with common sense.

•

Swept by seizures of vertigo, diarrhea, sexual ups and downs, fits
of laughter and tears, Mr. X entered into his Gethsemane, the 8:32.

A rainy day in town. I slip into a sort of sexual torpor. Anxiety may
be the opening notes of this. On Twenty-third Street I am hailed by a
friend from the Army. We have not met for twenty-three years and we
lunch together, talking about the dead. K. was hit by an artillery shell.
They never found his dog tags. Etc. We walk uptown in the rain. I am
out of sorts. In the window of a store specializing in this sort of thing
I see a photograph of a man wearing a cocksack. He seems to have
shaved his body. For some reason, the picture strikes me as lighthearted
and I think of poor H.

Have mercy upon them; have mercy upon them. The bright and
seemly world they despised must, from time to time, have appeared to
them as a kingdom. Lovers, men with their sons, the sounds of laughter
must have made them desperate. With his hat pulled down over his
eyes, his collar turned up for concealment, he studies the pictures of
undressed men in a Sixth Avenue store window. They seem both muscular and abandoned. He crosses the street to a newsstand that spe-
cializes in this sort of thing, he glimpses the photograph of a naked man
in a sailor hat, a thin-faced youth who appears to be removing his
jockstrap. He goes west now to Broadway, where there is a picture of
a naked youth lying in shallow waves, and another with his legs parted.
His pursuit takes him up to the Fifties, where there are several news-
stands decked with photographs of lewd and naked men. Have mercy
upon him.

•

Board the Century at dusk and ride up the river. One of my reasons
for taking a train is to tie on a can, but I am not too successful. The
bumpy roadbed gives me a hard-on and I climb down from my berth
with the hope that Mary will be awake. She is, it seems, but pretends
to sleep. I join her at dawn, when she is downright disagreeable, and

rub up against her thigh, watching the Indiana landscape. I think of my last trip—the travelling salesman who fell romantically in love with a large white pig, munching acorns in a grove of oaks. Dear Pig, are you willing? Piggy-wiggy, dear. Later in the day he was stung by lust at the sight of a naked plastic mannequin in a Toledo store window. I remember the horses running away from the train, the children waving, marigolds shining like fire around the doorsteps, a woman glancing out of the window at an automobile dump and exclaiming, sincerely, "Home sweet home!" The country is flat and unlovely. There are automobile dumps, sandlot ball fields, graveyards. The home of Alka-Seltzer. The huge industrial sweep of Gary, with pink ore smoke pushing out of its chimneys with an urgency that seems to me sexual. The slums, the federal housing, Chicago. Mary complains about the smell of the hotel, the smell of the train, the smell of the world.

•

When we were in college and used to go up to the river, Aunt Mildred used to urge us to swim without trunks. "Who cares about a little thing like that?" she exclaimed, although in the cases of Howie and Jack it was far from little. She used to sit on the pier where we swam. She had cut eye slits into the pillowcase, which she wore over her head to protect her from the ell-flies. She would sit there looking like an ill-dressed member of the Klan, while we porpoised around naked in that fine clear water. One afternoon she showed up with an old-fashioned box camera and without removing her hood snapped pictures of us diving and swimming. I didn't suppose the pictures would be any good, because of the age of the camera and the difficulty of focussing it through a hole in a pillowcase and I knew that she wouldn't dare have photographs of naked men developed at the drugstore in Howland. I don't know where she had the pictures developed and I didn't see them until thirty years later, when we sold the camp. Mildred was long dead. The pictures had been successful.

•

I think I think of the book not as narrative but as bulk, texture, color, weight, and size. I would like to shake my composure, to howl, to penetrate. I hope, this day next year, to have another book done.

•

At 7 A.M. Mary wakes me and points to a turtle on the lawn. This is a snapping turtle, three and a half feet long, the largest I have ever seen. He moves like a sea turtle, well off the ground. His head is immense; his tail is scaled and spiked. It would be pointless to dwell on this prehistoric anomaly, this vengefulness of time. I get the shotgun and put two Super-X shells into his head. I see the head thrown back and up by the shell, he rises to his feet and falls, and I go upstairs to shave. Mary calls to me that he is moving, and I look out of the window and see him walking towards the mint patch and the pond. I take the gun again, and this time put four shells into his head. I then resume shaving, but he continues to move, and in the end I put ten shells in his head before he is dead. We start down the road to Providence. I have a drink before we leave, and nip along the road, and I think that to catalogue, idly, the vulgarities of our time—the trailer with stained-glass windows, the man who writes jingles for the highway commission—is useless unless we can describe clearly the world that we desire. The turtle seemed to possess the world much better than I—I with a shotgun, my hands shaking from a cocktail party.

•

You have to be patient and you have to like people, says the cabdriver in Washington, shortchanging me two dollars. S. and I walk to the White House. I find the face of the President tragic. He leaves the platform by mistake, and I see his wife lead him back into the music room. Her smile is forced and weary, and it is like looking into the raw material—the exaltations and backaches—of any lengthy marriage.

•

I sleep with my head in T.'s lap, and wake as we are entering Moscow. Oh, how exciting the world is at dark, I think—entering some city and watching the lights go on. The people everywhere carrying yellow leaves. Autumn moving over the broad reach of Europe. London. Autumn roses and forest fires in the Crimea. Red and yellow trees in Georgia. Cold after dark. The roads blocked by sheep. We were the last swimmers in the Caspian. The parks in Kiev were yellow. A bitter fog in Moscow. Today is the arrival of the cosmonauts, the deposition of Khrushchev. As I walk back from the embassy, groups are marching in from every direction carrying flags and posters of Brezhnev. Truck-

loads of men and women. I buy lunch and watch TV. No excitement.
I have a hangover and an unsavory mind. It is that hour when the seemly
world appears useless, worthless. We go to the theatre and see a stunning
performance of Brecht that ends with the Communist salute. I eat caviar
alone in the main dining room and am excited. I sleep.

•

Yevtushenko's recitation in the medical school. Sharp tiers of desks,
the place jammed. Zhenya wears a shirt. The breadth of his bony
shoulders, the length of his arms, the size of his fists. The sharp nose,
the unrelieved intensity of his face, views of his broad forehead, the
impact of this being his role. He has a flat head. He recites for two
hours without a note and is given dead chrysanthemums. I seem to love
him as I love most natural phenomena.

The deluxe train to Leningrad. Rainy midnight. Red plush. On the
radio a soprano sings "Vissi d'arte." So we travel, drinking vodka in
good company. The train whistles, smells of coal gas, the sombre beauty
of Leningrad. Views of the river from the Winter Palace. Back through
the suburbs of Moscow at daybreak. The Ambassador's lunch. A fuse
blows during the cocktail party. Dinner back in the Sovietskaya with
the Updikes. So I get kissed and leave Russia with a tremendous confusion of feeling. All the rest of Europe seems much more successful,
orderly, but I think of Russia as lovable, vast, pathetic. The women in
Amsterdam are beautiful; their heels make a fine click on the floor. The
table linen is white, but in some ways I prefer the Ukraine Hotel—
gloomy, impractical, and smelling of unwashed socks. My Russian memories seem to be fading. I try to recall the brilliance of Zhenya's face,
his airs. I see the Berlin Wall, flowers, graves. H. speaks of the last
days here, the streets on fire, the lions loose, the world that has out-
stripped our nightmares, our subconscious. I found the ruins ghastly
and impressive. So I shall go home on Saturday.

•

When we say "Christ, have mercy upon us," we don't ask for a
literal blessing, I think. We express how merciless we are to ourselves.

•

Waking, one thinks, The rain will come, and after the rain, my
love. First I will hear the sound of water and then the sound of her

footsteps on the stone floor of the corridor, the hall. But what is this hall and why does it have a stone floor? Am I involved in towers, moats, stupidities, and fancies, are these the foolish terms in which I phrase love? Troubadours in fancy dress. There is thunder, lightning, and then rain. I hear first the rain and then her voice from the driveway below the house. She is tired and I leave her unmolested, but see, as I get into bed, through the transparent cloth of her nightgown the darkness of her fuzz: fragrant, delicate, it seems to me a flower.

•

I long so for love that it seems I long for the love of God. But I do not follow Rilke on the prodigal and the love of Him. I go with Ben to the town dump. Two scavengers. One is the stooped cretin who lives with his old parents in the house by the pear tree. The other is a young man who glares at me with a hatred I find mysterious. My son explains that the look of hatred is the look of a scavenger. Scavenging is a most intimate business, and no one wants to be discovered at it. I scythe, wash in the brook, wash in the hose, swim at S.'s with Mary and my son. The lawns are a brilliant green, the sky stormy and clear. A hot night. I fall asleep before I am joined.

•

Oh, to be so much a better man than I happen to be.

•

My difficulties continue, and I can't determine where the blame lies. I sit in a chair under a tree. It is raining. The rain is light. I can hear it fall on the leaves, but the leaves of the tree make a shelter. I think—I have been drinking—that I must speak with Mary, make some stab at candor and perhaps approach love. This may be tactless and stupid. In any case, I speak. "You're just making up one of your little stories," she says. I say that the remark is spinsterish and irrelevant. I speak of those weeks following my return from Russia when I received, for the first time in my marriage, a vocal declaration of love. I ask if she doesn't remember this; if it wasn't true. She replies, "I wish you could have seen your face when you asked that." I cannot settle on any motive for this. Does she think I despise her so deeply that any declaration of love is ridiculous? Or does she mean to say that I am ugly?

She claims not. But how cruel it would be for a woman to call her lover ugly. The children return from the movies and I sit with them in what seems to me a fragrance of reasonableness. Returning to bed, I think I shall suffocate.

•

In the morning there is the familiar anxiety. I fear that I have done and said some irrevocable things; that I have ruined my marriage and exiled myself. I feel both tender and horny. But opening a gin bottle at noon I think that the only declaration of love I have ever received has been rescinded. This is merely at the sight of a gin bottle.

•

The Skidmore girls, some of them are beautiful. One's head swims. Watch for the inch or two of thigh you'll see when they mount their bicycles; watch the bicycle seat press into their backsides. Some of them, much less beautiful, muster a sense of humor and get by on this. Some of them have nothing at all. It is hot, and as in all small towns people complain more bitterly than they would in some larger place. The broad porches are still open, with their straw rugs, wicker furniture, tables with vases full of flowers, copies of the *Reader's Digest*, and, at four, a pitcher of nice lemonade. "It's our outdoors living room," said Mrs. L. A bridge lamp burns at night. Crossing the park where I once saw a woman steal marigolds I think with sudden love of my son Federico; I think with shame of those quarrels he has overheard. How can he grow straight and courageous as he must in a house where there is so much that is bitter and frigid? I am sorry, I am heartily sorry, my son. I love you and will try to stay at your side. Girls pass with shadowy cheeks, with round cheeks, with no cheeks at all. No dogs bark. Have they passed a leash ordinance? I think of what I may do to C.B., but I won't put this down. I am plagued by some circulatory distress, a whiskey thirst, and the bitter mystery of my marriage. They all three go hand in hand.

•

The lollipop clock in front of Edelstein's jewelry store stopped twelve years ago at five minutes to six. A blizzard was raging and the hands of the clock, still at five minutes to six, solidly commemorate the snow-buried streets, the stalled train, the barely visible street lights, the stillness. The clock in front of what used to be Humber's hardware store stopped at 9:10 on an April evening when the store caught fire and was gutted. That was ten years ago. The boredom and the aspirations of a small backwater on an April evening belong to the second clock. They sometimes ask, What kind of a town is it where we have two stopped clocks on the main street? It's that kind of a town.

•

People named John and Mary never divorce. For better or for worser, in madness and in saneness, they seem bound together for eternity by their rudimentary nomenclature. They may loathe and despise one another, quarrel, weep, and commit mayhem, but they are not free to divorce. Tom, Dick, and Harry go to Reno on a whim, but nothing short of death can separate John and Mary.

•

I cut the grass, hoping to improve my spirits, but then I hit the bottle with such vehemence that nothing is gained, much is lost, and this morning I feel sick. I read a biography of Dylan Thomas thinking that I am like Dylan, alcoholic, hopelessly married to a destructive woman, etc. The resemblance stops with alcohol. Once the idea of divorce had occurred to Mr. Halberstrum, he found himself unable to uproot the possibility. It established itself with the tenacity of a thistle. His manifest responsibilities to his children began to seem unreal. He knew how deeply bewildered they would be if he divorced—that this action might be a serious impediment to their growth as men and women—but the ardor with which he dreamed of being free of a way of life that seemed unnaturally debased and crooked made the sufferings of his children distant and powerless. Boarding the 8:23, he thought of divorce. The mountains and the river spoke of divorce. The noise of midtown traffic urged him to divorce. He looked during the business day for associates who had divorced and thought them the happiest of men. He approached his lighted house in the evening with a reluctance that was physical. It was a struggle to climb the stairs. He stooped with despair when he heard her slippers in the upstairs hall. A man with no religious training and no faith at all, he was forced into the emotional and physical attitudes of prayer. "Dear God," he sobbed, "restore to me my patience, my faith, my powers of love; let me forget the bitterness that has passed; set me free from resentment, petulance, and anger. Amen." But she had traduced him lengthily twice in a week and responded to his cozening with a swift kick. Now her voice was soft in the evenings, but it did not reach him. Let us pray.

•

Mrs. Hammer had begun her monologue. Hammer, who had been reading *Time*, took off his glasses and watched her. Her color was high, her style was vivacious, her eyes flashed. He had said or done nothing to commence the scene. "If you think you're going to make me cry," she explained, "you're mistaken. Oh, I know what you're thinking. I can tell by the way you look. You're thinking that I'm sorry for what I said last night. You think I'm going to ask to be forgiven." She laughed. "Well, I wouldn't ask for your forgiveness if my life depended upon it. You hate me, you loathe me, but I couldn't care less. I used to worry, but I won't worry anymore. There's something wrong with you. I think your mother did something to you, and, of course, you never had a father. I think I know what's wrong with you, although I'd hesitate to tell you to your face. It would seem too cruel. I won't give you the satisfaction of a divorce, because it would upset Dora. If I know one thing, it's that Dora loves me. I've protected her from your drunken rages. I've given her the only loving-kindness she's ever known. Oh, I know you're jealous. You'd like to think she loves you, but she doesn't, and she never will. You think you're a great lady-killer, and I suppose some women see something in you, but the trouble is that you don't have any men friends. Men don't like you. When I took the train on Tuesday all the women on the platform asked me how you were, but not a single man mentioned you. Not one. You're always talking about your sexual needs and desires, but if you spent a little more time out-of-doors you'd be more like a normal man and not so sexy. You never go fishing anymore. Well, you almost never go fishing anymore. Well, when you do go fishing you almost never catch anything. Of course, there are exceptions. Well, I may be wrong about this, and if I've said something stupid, how you'll gloat over it! Oh, look at you. If you could only see how smug you look! If you could only see how happy my little mistake has made you! Well, at last I've done something to please you, I've brought a little sunshine into your life. I wonder how long I'll have to wait before you remind me that the last time you went fishing you caught three trout. Oh, well, I've made you happy. It's still in my power to make you happy." Laughing bitterly, she left the room.

•

And in Nailles' happiness, his stubborn insistence upon the abundance of things, his passionate love for MaryEllen, I seem to sense some obtuseness. How could any woman of character live and breathe in so close, unremittent, and airless a love? "I love you, I love you." He said it every day, seizing her buttocks, thrusting his tongue into her mouth. "I love you, I love you," morning, noon, and night. I sense some obtuseness, but I merely sense it; I cannot see it, judge its altitude or nature as one sees the Atlas Mountains from Gibraltar. He is incurable. When MaryEllen—or some earlier girl—said that his love was crushing, he would be bewildered. Envy, sloth, pride, anger—all these things could be crushing, but not love. Standing on his porch on a winter night, naming the few stars that he knew for his son and exclaiming loudly over their brilliance and the beauty of the night, he might appear to her to be a fool, an unredeemable fool. "Oh, it's so beautiful out there!" he would say, his breath still smoking, the sharp perfume of cold coming off his clothing. "Why do you cry?" he would ask. "Why do you choose to cry on such a beautiful night?"

•

Someone had written something in the fresh snow. Who could it have been—the milkman, a boy, some stranger? And what would he have written—an obscenity, a calumny? What the stranger had written was: "Hello World!"

•

He had a concession at the bowling alley. He called it the pro shop, sold equipment, and drilled and plugged bowling balls with some rented machinery. It was dark that afternoon, but you could see him in the darkness, talking into a wall telephone. He had been talking for three-quarters of an hour. He lowered his voice when I came in, but I heard him say, "She's wild, that one, I was into her three times, and she *buzzbuzzbuzz*." He said he'd call back, hung up, and turned on a light. He was a tall, bulky man with a vast belly—proof of the fact that there is little connection between erotic sport and physical beauty. His thin hair was most neatly oiled and combed with the recognizable grooming of the lewd. On his little finger he wore a flashy diamond, flanked by two rubies. His voice was reedy, and when he turned his face into the light you saw the real thing, a prince of barroom and lunch-counter pickups, reigning over a demesne of motels, hotels, and back bedrooms— proud, stupid, and serene. His jaw was smooth, well shaven, and anointed, a piney fragrance came from his armpits, his breath smelled of chewing gum, and he had the eyes of an adder. He was the real thing.

·

Waking, I think that as a social impostor I have gone to some pains to conceal the fact that in the house where I was raised there was an automatic piano. It was called a Pianola and had been won by my father in a raffle. It was not in the living room, where we entertained, but in an obscure room to the right of the hall, yet on Sunday mornings before going to church I would happily pedal away and loudly sing the words of hymns, and on weekday evenings I would play "Dardanella," "Louis- ville Lou," "Lena from Palesteena," or if I felt serious the "Barcarolle," a little Chopin, or my favorite, the "William Tell" Overture, with its storm on a mountain lake. The Pianola was an ugly object, stained the color of mahogany, somewhat scratched and battered by me, but it was a source of great pleasure, which I seem to have veiled as a vulgarity or to have supplanted with a glistening parlor grand, some Schumann on the rack.

·

As I wait for the train, a youth in tight white pants sets off the usual alarm signals, but then I notice that he wears the jacket of a school where I am known, where indeed one of my dogs lives. I ask after my friends on the faculty, ask after my dog, and the air between us is pristine and cheerful. It is facelessness that seems to threaten one, strangeness, a sort of erotic darkness, an ignorance of each other, except for the knowledge of sexual desire; but standing in a public urinal and being solicited by a faceless stranger one senses some definite prom- ise of understanding oneself and of understanding death, as if the natural and sensible strictures of society, raised in the light of day, were too

heavy a burden for our instincts and left them with no immunity to the
infections of anxiety and in particular the fear of death. Run, run, run
ballocksy through the woods, put it in the brushes of nymphs and up
the hairy bums of satyrs and you will know yourself at last and no longer
fear death; but why, then, do the satyrs have an idiotic leer? To have
the good fortune to love what is seemly and what the world counsels
one to love, and to be loved in return, is a lighter destiny than to court
a sailor in Port-au-Prince who will pick your pockets, wring your neck,
and leave you dead in a gutter.

•

I carry a heavy suitcase for a young woman—this simplest vision of
things—but the suitcase is almost too much for my strength, and I am
afraid I will pull my middle out of joint. The shoeshine man's curly
head, between my knees, reminds me of T., whose domesticity was
clearly rooted in an early knowledge of cold and aloneness. Three days
before Easter the city is festive. My shoes are shined, my suit is correct.
There are many youths with long and dirty hair, dirty jeans, and white
teeth. At the corner of Sixty-third Street and Madison a young man
rests on his motorcycle, cleaning his dark glasses. He appears to be out
of things, including the rebellion he has joined. Young women with
skirts above their knees, old women with top-heavy headdresses of cloth
flowers and with wounded feet, a man who has paid his tailor a fortune
but walks like a duck. St. Patrick's, which I enter at the elevation of
the Host, is crowded. At the St. Regis, hair oil seems to be coming
back. Pools of pinkish light stream from holes in the ceiling. I am very
tired. In the old place the bartenders used to hook their wristwatches
(three) around the neck of a liquor bottle. No more. I wonder if the
bartender who serves me served me twenty years ago.

•

On the train home I share a seat with two men I have not seen for
fifteen years. They both now have their white hair, as I shall presently.
They both wear glasses. One of them has an alcoholic and circulatory
ailment that has given his face the colors of an extended bruise. They
discuss their lawnmowers throughout the trip. "I got a double-blade,
three-horsepower Ajax rotary from Warbin's two years ago. I've got my
money back." "Well, I got a single-blade rotary last year, but I'm think-

ing of getting a reel mower this year," etc. The conversation does not shift, for an hour, from the subject of mowers, excepting to go briefly to fertilizer. Warfare, love, money—the natural concerns of men—are barred from their talk. It is sincere, I expect; it is ceremonial: I suppose they dream of leaf mulchers, gasoline mixes. Their aim is probity, and yet it is the mad who, to cure the wildness of their thought, talk in such rudimentary terms.

·

Good Friday, and I do not find the day as sombre as I have in the past. Wood doves. A cloudy sky. Travelling acres of sunlight. I remember the Tenebrae being sung in Rome. This early in the year, the churches were still cold and damp. The poetic force of the sense that this world was given to us and given to us in pain. I will not go to church because B. will insist upon giving a sermon, and I will not have the latitude or the intelligence to overlook its repetitiousness, grammatical errors, and stupidity.

·

I wake. My older son has returned safely from school. The trees are full of birds. I mount my wife, eat my eggs, walk my dogs. It is the day before Easter.

·

I have a letter from an editor at Doubleday who suggests that I title my next book "Cultured Pearls and Other Imitations." How strange and angular that someone unknown to me should go to the trouble of writing such a letter.

·

I watch the young man who drives the drugstore delivery truck come down the street. He has a bellicose and comical heft to his shoulders, as if he were just about to climb into a boxing ring, although his smile is so ingenuous and bright that it seems unlikely that he has ever hit anything. He pushes his neck forward with each step—a little like a drake—and usually, at this time of year, wears a jacket with a hood that lies in a heap on his shoulders. And I think that the writer is, tragically, jockeyed into the position of a bystander. He sees from his window a woman stealing marigolds in the public garden, an old man pissing behind a tree, a game of catch in a vacant lot, but some cruel abyss seems to have opened between himself and these simple and natural sights; you can't, after all, repair a carburetor or play football with a pen in your hand and too sharp and critical an eye in your head.

•

I seem, during the drive, grilled on brute worry. I think I will refuse to make long trips. Time seems Procrustean. My watch says eleven. My stomach aches, my scrotum itches, my heart thumps, my breathing is constricted, and my right eye droops. I look at my watch again and it says three minutes past eleven. I seem racked between the hour and the minute hand. I chain-smoke, and at half past eleven I drink some vodka. This must shock the children, but it is my only way of bringing any sense to the hour. New highways spread in every direction, and Mary observes that the Connecticut landscape with its farmhouses and trees seems, by some seismographic upheaval, to have been transformed into the buttes and canyons of another geologic past. She also observes, in the parish development, that all the native trees—apples and maples—have been cut and uprooted and replaced with flowering cherries, trimmed yews, and a lachrymose shrub that seems to produce showers of white tears; thus, we have a landscape that is both melancholy and gallingly artificial.

•

We meet my son, whom I love. The attachment seems to resist any analysis. I simply love him. His skin is clear, his face is muscular; we mostly joke. He speaks of giving up lacrosse because of the killer mentality of the coach. I do not urge him to keep it up, but I would like to. I want him to be distinguished, but I seem to want him to enjoy an undangerous distinction. I do not want him to burn his draft card and go to prison as a C.O. Do I want him to be pure but innocuous, an anonymous element in the stream of time, good and kind and virtually nameless; to embody that passivity we know to be most dangerous? We lunch poorly among the other parents. There is a lady who went to school in Switzerland with Mary. "We were in school in Switzerland together," she says loudly. There are a few Yankee faces, and I consider myself to belong among them, although I may be mistaken. I consider myself distinguished. One could do worse. We attend a parents' council meeting. The face, hands, and legs of Mrs. X are discolored with hooch, and her hands tremble as she reaches for a cigarette. This most strange, hard-drinking world. The chaplain speaks to us on sex education. A rather pale, clear-faced young man whose most memorable feature is his baldness. His baldness seems both active and plaintive: he seems to be losing his hair as he speaks to us. We are addressed on the urgency of sex education, and the matter of educating students is broken up into the biological facts of reproduction and the subjective and emotional aspects of sex. The fact is mentioned—of which I disapprove—that in their early manhood their powers are greater than they ever will be again. Adultery, masturbation, and homosexuality are brought up sketchily. I flinch at the mention of the last, as I always do. Should we educate our children or should we not? A man who has been picking his teeth urges that we first notify the parents of our intention and then, having received their approval, their opinion, we may proceed.

The process will take two years. One lady wistfully objects to the delay. One lady suggests that we all read an article on sex in *Reader's Digest*. It is moved that we send copies of the magazine to all the parents. "You may not agree with the conclusions," says the lady, "but it is beautifully written." It is Mary who observes, looking into these faces, that no one of us is capable of imagining a useful and candid course on the subject. The exaltations, catastrophes, perversions, and mystifications of erotic love are stamped on all these bewildered faces. And the balding advocate of sexual education: what about him? Why is he not married? Why is he so pale? What games does he play?

•

Murderers, assassins—did you ever know any? I don't mean gangsters or hired gunmen; I mean law-abiding murderers. There's this chap named Marples who keeps saying that he loves me and then tries to kill me. The first time it happened was at a party in New York. I was standing by this long window, and he gave me a push. Right below me was this fence made of iron spears, which I just cleared, landing on my knees on the sidewalk. I tore my trousers, but that was about the only damage—with a little less luck I would have been impaled. That was the first time. A year or so later we went to visit them at the sea. We

walked up the beach one day—great chums—and we came to this tide
rip, where he urged me to go for a swim. I was just about to dive in
when an old man yelled at me and told me the rip was full of sharks.
He said I wouldn't last five minutes. Marples pretended to be surprised
and very emotional about my salvation, although he had practically
pushed me in. Somehow I never resented these attempts on my life; I
never thought that he could bring them off. Sometime later we went to
his house in the country for dinner. There were a lot of people and a
lot of cars, and my car was in somebody's way, and I went out to move
it. He had to move his car. Well, I was crossing the driveway when I
saw this car, his car, bearing down on me at full speed. I sprinted to
safety, and he was very apologetic and emotional about having nearly
run me over. And the last time I saw him he said that he'd heard I was
sick. Excepting for a few head colds, I've never been sick in my life,
but he gave me this very sad look as if I were wasting away. He's a very
quiet man, terribly sensitive, but he's a murderer.

•

The first of June, and the world that was not mine yesterday now
lies spread out at my feet, a splendor. I seem, in the middle of the night,
to have returned to the world of apples, the orchards of Heaven. Perhaps
I should take my problems to a shrink, or perhaps I should enjoy the
apples that I have, streaked with color like the evening sky.

•

Very humid. The air over the Hudson Valley is like a discolored fog.
A baneful sun is reflected in the window of the hardware store. I sit
on the terrace reading about the torments of Scott Fitzgerald. I am, he
was, one of those men who read the grievous accounts of hard-drinking,
self-destructive authors, holding a glass of whiskey in our hands, the
tears pouring down our cheeks. Thunder at three. The old dog trembles,
and is so frightened that she vomits. The wind slams some doors within
the house, and then I smell the rain, minutes before it begins to fall
on my land. What I smell is the smell of damp country churches, the
back hallways of houses where I was contented and happy, privies, wet
bathing suits—an odor, it seems, of joy. When Fitzgerald drops dead,
I burst into tears, as I wept over the account of Dylan Thomas's death.
This morning I cannot remember anything that occurred after dinner.

Thinking of Fitzgerald, I find there is a long list of literary titans who have destroyed themselves: Hart Crane, Virginia Woolf, Hemingway, Lewis, Dylan Thomas, Faulkner. There are those who lived, Eliot and Cummings, but there are few. Shall I dwell on the crucifixion of the diligent novelist? The writer cultivates, extends, raises, and inflates his imagination, sure that this is his destiny, his usefulness, his contribution to the understanding of good and evil. As he inflates his imagination, he inflates his capacity for evil. As he inflates his imagination, he inflates his capacity for anxiety, and inevitably becomes the victim of crushing phobias that can only be allayed by lethal doses of heroin or alcohol.

So I go to the shrink. His waiting room has as wide a collection of magazines as I've seen this year; but the waiting room is empty when I arrive, empty when I leave, and I wonder, Is he an unsuccessful shrink, an unemployed shrink, an unpopular shrink, does he while away his time in the empty office like an idle lawyer, barber, or antique dealer? He has large brown or golden eyes, a neat gray suit, and an office furnished with newly upholstered Victorian relics. I suppose some part of doctors' education concerns the furnishing of the consultation room. Do their wives do it? I wonder. Do they plan it themselves? Is it done by a professional? I feel much better after talking with him. He does seem a little angular, a little inclined to contradict and interrupt. He seems at times to do most of the talking. Mary will go see him, and how wonderful it would be if we could clear this up.

•

Casting around drunkenly for some explanation of my grief, I think that perhaps I sought out and married a woman who would treat me as capriciously as my mother did, but a woman with whom I could quarrel as I could not quarrel with my mother. But I am deeply ashamed of myself for quarrelling. I think I am driven to it, I think I am meant to behave contemptibly, and yet I am deeply ashamed. I am deeply ashamed.

•

On the set I see the uneasy—and I think incurable—paradox with which I must live. Would I sooner nuzzle D.'s bosom or squeeze R.'s enlarged pectorals? At my back I hear the word—"homosexual"—and it seems to split my world in two. R., the stand-in, is a well-constructed young man with a vast expanse of tanned, hairless skin, and I feel for him, or think I feel for him, some sad and illicit stirring, but the moment I talk with him—as soon as I feel his place in the world, the quality of his mind, as soon as I can imagine his wife, or his parents, or the room where he sleeps—these unsavory matters vanish. It is ignorance, our ignorance of one another, that creates this terrifying erotic chaos. Information, a crumb of information, seems to light the world.

•

At the Children's Center, I find my older son holding a little boy in his arms. The boy has been crying all day. His face is contorted and weary. He has no tears left, only dry, racking sobs. "It was his first day," Ben said. "He'll be all right tomorrow." And I think of how painfully alien the world can seem when we first emerge from the rooms, and especially the fragrances, of childhood. Invited—or forced—to spend a weekend with Aunt Cora and Uncle Stephen, you find their bathwater, their sweat, the bacon they eat for breakfast all painfully unfamiliar and you are quite literally sick with longing for the bathwater, sweat, and bacon in your own cozy home, and in this simple cottage at the edge of the sea you taste for the first time the strangeness of those voyages, battlefields, and hotel rooms in which you will, as a grown man, find yourself frightened and alone.

•

But what I want to tell you about is the shrink. I thought our third interview, this one, would be like the end of a musical comedy. We would embrace, kiss on the threshold of his office, and tie on a can after the children had gone to the movies. His office is furnished with those modest antiques you find in small hotels. His desk, or some part of it, may have come into the world as a spinet. There are colored photographs of his children on the table. Why do doctors always impose on us photographs of their children? He wears, I notice, elk-skin walking shoes, quite new, and light socks with clocks, supported by garters. The gaze of his golden eye is vast and steady. His face might be described as soft. The picture, as I saw it, was that I, an innocent and fortunate creature, had married a woman who suffered from deep psychic disturbances. The picture, as it was presented to me, was of a neurotic man, narcissistic, egocentric, friendless, and so deeply involved in my own defensive illusions that I had invented a manic-depressive wife. The troubles of the psyche were described in a specious jargon. In the space of fifty minutes he said "meaningful" fourteen times, "interpersonal" twelve, "longitudinal" nine, and "structured" two. When I asked Mary if the bulk of our relationship hadn't been happy she merely smiled. I am accused of being jealous of her career. The truth here is that because of my mother's business and my claim to having been neglected I have always been oversensitive to a woman who was less than wifely. He speaks with unamicable reverence, I think, of my stormy father-in-law. He hints, I think, at my humble beginnings, and to tell the truth my father was an unemployed shoe salesman and my mother supported the family with a hole-in-the-wall gift shoppe. Soiled underwear hung from a nail on the bathroom door. These are not all the facts, and my parents were people of some quality, I claim. I think he accepts two fixations for truths. One of them is that I am a friendless man. Mary has always claimed this, and I think it not true. She always felt that if I had a party no one would come. The other fixation is that I detest women.

•

I am fifty-four, but I still think myself too young to find my world sutured, to suffer nightmares about throughways and bridges. And I would like to discuss, to ventilate, my homosexual problems. I can vault them or hurdle them, but I would like to stop and give them some examination. And what can I look forward to here? Homosexuality seems to be an important fact in the troubled world I live in, and I mean to cure myself, not the world, and yet I feel, wrongly perhaps, that some of my anxieties can be traced back to this. There may be no solution, but I might be able to study the problem in a less tense and skittish manner.

•

I drink heavily because I claim to be troubled. We talk about the shrink at the table, and I expect I talk with drunken rancor. We go to a third-rate movie and, leaving, I cry, "Why, when I asked if the bulk of our life had not been happy, did you not reply?" "My look," she said, "was my reply." It may have been a sweet smile. I have one drink, no more, and sit on the stone steps. I think myself youthful, even boyish in my misery. I stretch out on the stones, sobbing, until I realize that I am in exactly the position of a doormat.

I sleep in my own bed, although this seems to be an indignity. I wake at dawn, crying, "Give me the river, the river, the river, the river," but the river that appears has willows and is winding and is not the river I want. It looks like a trout stream, so I cast with a fly and take a nice trout. A naked woman with global breasts lies on the grassy banks and I mount her. She is replaced by Adonis, and, while I fondle him briefly, it seems like an unsuitable pastime for a grown man. I keep calling for my broad river, but they seem to have run railroad tracks through the Elysian fields, and I am given a brook with willows. I take a pill this morning, and it seems best for me to take full responsibility for everything that has gone wrong. There is no point in recounting to myself rebuffs, wounding quarrels, etc. One has come through much; one will come through this.

•

In the morning, I am quite shaky and have a flat tire. A garage mechanic who is even shakier than I struggles to change the tire. It takes him an hour, and he mangles the hubcap. When I see him later in the day, he has improved, and I suppose he has a bottle hidden among his tools. I drink Scotch at ten, two Martinis before lunch, and go off to the shrink. His mouth is a little blubbery, and he is not always successful in keeping his hands away from it. When I sit in the patient's chair, still warm from some other breakdown, he turns the beam of his brown eye onto me exactly as the dentist turns on the light above the drill, and for the next fifty minutes I bask in his gaze and return his looks earnestly to prove that I am a truthful man. I don't understand his methods, and, after drinking, I am not sure that this isn't a waste of time and money. He considers me hostile and alienated, and yet, sitting among his reconstructed antiques, he seems more alienated than I. Does he know anything about music, literature, painting, baseball? I think not. When he brought up the subject of my friendlessness and I said that I had just had a very friendly weekend with H., A., and S., I thought he would cry. He explained that I had developed a social veneer—an illusion of friendship—that was meant to conceal my basic hostility and alienation. He seems, like some illusion of drunkenness, to have two faces, and I find it fascinating to watch one swallow up the other. There was a pause in the conversation, and he pursed his lips as if he had just sucked a lemon dry and asked, "What is blocking you now?" He is very sensitive and utterly humorless, and if I dared complain about his use of "meaningful" I'm sure it would wound and anger him. He wants to go over my childhood, and I'll fire this at him tomorrow. The truth is that I am more afraid of bridges than ever, but I wonder if he has the cure. When I asked him he gave me his saddest smile.

•

I go to the shrink, and while we talk about castration and homosexuality there is some circumspection to our dialogue. I have not clearly stated that I have homosexual instincts and that they are a source of painful anxiety. I think I make too much of this. Since he offers me tentatively the opportunity of a confession, I look forward to making one, but something in his manner or the atmosphere keeps me from blurting out the fact that I am sometimes afraid of being queer. I claim to suffer no more than most men, and yet this claim may be at the root of my difficulties. I know the nature of man to be divided, paradoxical, wayward, and perverse, and yet I seem unable to live peaceably with this fact when it is applied to me. My wish to be a simple, natural, and responsive creature seems to be incurable. The shrink seems to have made the conflict obsessive, or pushed it in this direction. Lying in bed, I wonder if I can get it up when the time comes. This is absurd. I cannot evoke the fragrance, the shapeliness, the stirring in my bowels, and yet I torment myself; I charge myself with choosing a girlish boy instead of a lovely and passionate woman. It would be very easy to make out with a girl-boy, but ease is not what one seeks—although I have a sneaking suspicion that it is. All one needs is courage, vitality, and faith, and I very often have all three.

What I need is hopefulness, zeal, vigor, and deep love, and to complain to a shrink about my wife's conduct in bed seems to be the opposite of all this. Complaining seems to be a mode of despair. I cannot bring myself to say what happened, because it would seem to jeopardize the possibility of making out tonight. I want to love and be loved, to be forthright and manly, and I won't accomplish this by snivelling and whining in an air-conditioned consultation room with disinfected antiques. However, I do. But the shrink and I seem to be at cross-purposes. I think he works within a set of rigid and mysterious preconceptions. Who profits by concluding that Mrs. Zagreb is my mother? He accuses me of making a goddess of Mary, and I tell him that of course she is a goddess. Mary and I go to a movie, "Modesty Blaise," which I consider expert, hilarious, and witty. I am happy and excited, and take two bourbons to calm myself; but in bed I go soft, and when I ask for some assistance it is given so halfheartedly that we part. Now perhaps we are coming into the borders of a dark country, but it may be a country of my making. I must avoid getting gin-mean.

•

I want a life of impossible simplicity. I want to make out in the peaceable gray light, either of dawn or of the rain. I want all homosexuals and other disconcerting types to be concealed from me. I want no one to suffer pain or death, to be poor or cold or humiliated.

•

I dream that a lady, looking at my face, says, "I see you've been in the competition, but I can't tell by your face whether or not you've won."

•

I think I return to the doctor today, and I think I have nothing to tell him. But what about the bitter quarrel on Friday night when I proposed a divorce and was accepted? What about our passionate reunion on Saturday afternoon, and what about the fact that I was impotent on Saturday night? What about the fact that I seem to be at sea? This morning, Mary is very brisk and goes off to get the maid before the maid will be ready. But what harm is there in this? I feel, on Monday morning, very sad. If I have been mean, I cannot remember my meanness, because my recollections are damaged by alcohol. I want to love and be loved, and the curtness I imagine myself to receive wounds me deeply. But that I am so easily wounded seems to be where the trouble lies.

•

I would like to come clean on the matter of homosexuality, and I think I can. I think I can see clearly the history and the growth of my anxiety. There was the clash between my instincts and my pleasures, my mother's spectacular ambivalence and my father's fear of having sired a fruit. The climate was anxious. In my determination to become a man, I felt it was my duty to respond to females. My responses were natural and strong, but they were at times short-circuited by this concept of duty. Homosexuality seemed to me a lingering death. If I followed my instincts I would be strangled by some hairy sailor in a public urinal. Every comely man, every bank clerk and delivery boy, was aimed at my life like a loaded pistol. In order to prove my maleness, I resorted to such absurd strategies as not letting my eye rest on the woman's page in the morning *Times*. But now I seem to see it clearly. Homosexuality is not, as I live, an evil. The evil is anxiety, an anxiety that can take on all the shapes and colors of hopeless passion. I trust I will not have to prove this in practice, and at this point some vagueness enters my thinking. But I consider now that if I did bounce L. it would not be the abdication of my character and the destruction of an old friendship.

•

A lonely man is a lonesome thing, a stone, a bone, a stick, a receptacle for Gilbey's gin, a stooped figure sitting at the edge of a hotel bed, heaving copious sighs like the autumn wind. Would Hammer be one of those men who, having made an unhappy marriage, lack the vitality and the intelligence to extricate themselves? His only emotional life is the invention of blondes. His only sexual life is jacking off. He takes his blondes aboard ships and planes; shows them the splendors of Paris, Rome, and Leningrad; orders them four-course meals in restaurants; deliberates over the wine; takes them for walks; writes them checks; buys them jewelry; and falls asleep with their fine, stiff pubic brushes against his naked hip. He is very careful to brush his teeth and shave before making love. Would Mrs. Hammer say, "You're a doormat, you're a henpecked doormat, and don't try to blame me. I'll bet you're the kind of man who thinks that someday, someday, some slender, well-bred, beautiful, wealthy, and intelligent blonde will fall in love with you. Oh, God. I can imagine the whole thing. It's so disgusting. She'll have straight hair and long legs and be about twenty-eight, divorced but without any children. I'll bet she's an actress or a nightclub singer. That's about the level of your imagination. What do you do with her, chump, what do you do with her beside tying on a can? What is a henpecked doormat up to? Do you take her to the theatre? Do you buy her dinner, jewelry maybe? Do you travel? I'll bet you travel. That's your idea of a big thing. Fourteen days on the Cristoforo Colombo, tying on a can morning, noon, and night, and drifting into the first-class bar at seven in a dinner jacket. What a distinguished couple! What shit! But I guess it would be the Flandre, some place where you could show off your lousy French. I suppose you drag her around Paris in her high heels, showing her all your old haunts. I feel sorry for her; I really do. But get this straight, chump, get this one straight. If such a blonde showed up, you wouldn't have the guts to take her to bed. You'd just moon around, mushing her behind the pantry door, and finally deciding not to be unfaithful to me. That's if the blonde showed up, but no blonde is going to. Did you hear me? Hear this! No such blonde is going to show up. There isn't any such blonde. You're an old man with a five-tooth bridge, bad breath, and a hairy belly, and you're going to be lonely for the rest of your life. You're going to be lonely for the rest of your life.

"Well, why don't you say something? Cat get your tongue? Sticks and stones? Why don't you say something? I suppose you think you're saintly to take my abuse quietly. I suppose you're turning the other cheek. Well, if there's anything that can drive a good woman to drink and fornication it's having to live under the same roof with a bloody phony saint. And a big drink is what I'm going to have as soon as I get home."

•

To be stymied sexually, wherever the blame may lie, usually means that I am stymied in my ability or willingness to tell stories. And it seems, this morning, that I have spent half of my married life in such a condition. There are the stories and characters I have invented to relieve myself of some of this—Betsey, Melissa, "The Chimera," "The Music Teacher"—there are hundreds of pages dealing with the lovely woman from whose face the light has gone. H. says that all the fault is mine, and I will willingly take much of the blame, but I would be a fool to take it all.

•

Somewhere in the turnings of sleep I seem to recuperate, seem to bask in the feeling of love again—limber, able, and cleanly. The woman is Barbara, someone I have never seen, and she seems spread out beneath me like a sheet. I seem to hear the voices of my three children, clear and tender. Now when I summon up my girls they arrive willingly. Narcissus has vanished. I think this is a disappearance, not a repression.

•

Mr. Hitchcock, on the other hand, took each morning a massive tranquillizer that gave him the illusion that he floated, like Zeus, in some allegorical painting, upon a cloud. Standing on the platform waiting for the 7:53, he was surrounded by his cloud. When the train came in he picked up his cloud, boarded the no-smoking coach, and settled himself at a window seat, surrounded by the voluminous and benign folds of his tranquillizer. If the day was dark, the landscape wintry, the string of little towns they passed depressing, none of this reached to where he lay in his rosy nimbus. He floated down the tracks into Grand Central, beaming a vast and slightly absentminded smile at poverty, sickness, the beauty of a strange woman, rain and snow.

•

It is early autumn. The leaves are not brilliant, but have enough color to make the wooded hills seem lambent, rising. It is the double meaning of light. On the summits of the hills, doom-crack missile-launching stations bloom like mushrooms. *Aurora gloria*. I count only three fishermen on the banks of the river, abandoned by its sturgeon, shad, shellfish, mallards, and swans. The paper says that raw excrement from the city travels on the tides as far north as Yonkers. The tide is out, revealing, like a fallen sock, the river's shank. I pound around the streets, not quite free from a sense of economic and sexual contest, but hopeful

•

"We used to do things together," he said. "We used to do so many things together. I mean we used to sleep together and skate together and ski together and take walks together and sail together and once we watched the World Series together. Remember? That was when we lived in the house on Pine Street. I came home early in the afternoons, and we drank beer and watched the World Series. That was the year Sal Maglie pitched for the Dodgers. Now we don't do anything together."

•

"You're so unhappy," she said, "that—I suppose—you have to be cruel."

"I'm not cruel," he said. "You really can't call me cruel. I always feed the cats and the dogs. I always put seed in the bird-feeding station."

•

Autumn leaf fires. The cook is drunk. Children make a barricade of leaves. Frost has slaughtered the begonias.

•

To confront, with forgiveness and compassion, the terrifying singularity of my own person.

•

I spend a lot of time these days writing funny letters to the dying. "Charlie only has two more weeks to live. He doesn't know it, and he's still alert, and if you had the time to write him a letter I think it would cheer him up." "When I pushed Hazel's wheelchair onto the terrace this morning she said that she'd love to hear from you. She's failing." "Eleanor has lost her sight but she still likes to be read to, and I'd love to have a letter from you to read to her." Etc.

•

The high polish of these splendid autumn afternoons puts me at a loss. I don't like to return to the office, and I seem to have no chores around this place. Walking alone can be a bore. The Ralph Ellisons stop by, having returned from Oklahoma City. He speaks of the Negro slums, now demolished, in lyrical terms. A source of vitality, music, violence, and sex. He has returned to all his old haunts—drugstores, cousins, friends, and saloons—and found this review of his past a deep kind of discovery. "It was wonderful," she says. Thank you. I am, like Z., obsessed with my unhappiness, and seeing how easy they are with each other deepens my misery.

I read some "Lolita," which seems to me a little putrescent. Here is the inalienable fascination of perversity—known, I think, to all men. At dinner we talk about Horace Gregory, and the conversation seems warm and easy. I should bring more warmth and patience to the table. But something goes blooey, and I am too drunk to recall the collision.

I say, foolishly, that I have done her a favor. Mary says that she hates to have me do anything for her or the children because I gloat over their dependence upon me. She says that I gloated over driving Ben to work this summer and that I reviled Susie for her extravagances. I don't think I really gloat, but it can be observed that she thinks I do. This would explain why she is unwilling to let me get her a cup of tea when she is sick, why she is unwilling to spend my money. Things worsen and grow ugly. I ask what kind of a woman is it who, being approached tenderly, says that she has to put the potatoes in the oven? She says that she can't bear to be gentled by an impotent man. I ask her what made her think I would be impotent, and she says, "You'd better be careful, you'd better be careful." I go upstairs and watch an old movie. We meet in the bathroom, where I ask for some gesture or token of love, some glance, and she makes a face. Then, in a rage, I shout at her in full voice, "You cannot make a grimace when someone asks for love." Just before dark I take her in my arms. I am sick with a need for love. She lets me hold her for a few minutes. I say that I will promise never to shout at her again if she will promise not to make faces at me. She says that she will make faces at me when she is provoked. The worst of it is that my son must hear this abuse, as I heard my parents quarrel when I was a child. I think I and my drunkenness are not completely to blame. Her attitude toward me does not seem to parallel the facts, to shift and change as events shift and change. She seems prejudiced, and her prejudices seem to come from a time of life before we met. I do not often gloat over things done. When she speaks of my impotence I say that I am not impotent with other women. This is a damned lie, since all I've done is neck with other women. I love her; she is really all I've ever known of life, but I think that to be independent would not kill me, although there is the problem of drunkenness. I cannot ask for forgiveness—who is there to forgive me?—but I can make an effort not to shout within my son's hearing. I cannot judge whether or not I'm drunk, but any resolve to drink less would be hypocritical. I am now, at ten o'clock, thinking of a gin bottle. I wish to be loving and simple and loved, and I will remain hopeful.

•

Shaken with liquor, self-doubts dimmed slightly by a Miltown, I board the nine o'clock. I am in misery. Every man on the train seems richer, more virile and intelligent than I, and there are no beautiful women. The man in front of me seems to be a Magyar; an identifiable racial type. The skin is dark; the eyes are brown; he is bald with a thin fringe of gray hair, and he has the kindly smile of an old friend, who is dead. He does not resemble my friend at all, but he seems to have the identical smile, as if this expression—this transparency—were a quality of light and existed independently of one's features. I am shaky and constipated. I get a shoeshine and decide that I am too far gone to sit in a barber chair. Walking and air will help, and I start pounding up Madison Avenue. I notice mostly that the girls are pretty and that the bars I pass are shut. I admire Breuer's new building and go to see P.'s sculpture, which I find less vigorous and exciting than I had hoped. Then down Madison Avenue I pound, and you may have seen me at quarter after eleven, trying the door of each bar I passed and finding them all locked, the night-light burning, the bottles behind bars. I go all the way back to the Biltmore to find an open bar, and then wonder, Will my shaking hands be able to get a glass to my mouth? I manage, and after two drinks am well enough to sit in the barber chair. I am recognized; I speak Italian; I observe that in the forty years I have been coming here half the barbers have died. I discharge my duties at the Century and take a bus downtown. This is the first time I have ridden a bus in many years and I seem, through inexperience, to suffer a form of sexual nakedness. Glancing into the eyes of a strange woman, I am provoked. I jog home on the local, falling asleep over a copy of *Life*. Businessmen sleeping on trains appear, whatever their condition may be, discouraged, helpless, and lost. There is a pretty girl across the aisle, and I seem to inhale her. I can't see enough of her, and she makes me both happy and languorous. I go to bed at half past eight and have a horrendous dream in which Mary is made president of the college. There is a hint of ruthlessness here. I remember watching her father seize a position of power. I retaliate by having a homosexual escapade, unconsummated, with Ronald Reagan. Walking on Madison Avenue, I had been tormented with the thought that my sins would be discovered, although I claim to have committed no sins. My children will vilify and disown me, my loving dogs will bark at me, even the cleaning woman will spit in my direction. Where is mercy, where is forgiveness? It is everywhere.

I have dreams of a density I would like to bring to fiction. We are summering in Nantucket, and I write a letter to some friends in Texas who are planning to visit us. I give them detailed instructions on how to reach the island, using both an atlas and a road map. A woman reminds me that she wore my old clothes during the bombing of Britain. At daybreak, I feel unloving and make no passes and invent a fantasy in which Mary says, "I think I had better tell you that B. and I are in love. I think you ought to know. X has refused to give him a divorce." I am bathed in self-pity, limpid as gin. But how can I gentle a woman who treats me with scorn? Remain hopeful and keep your pecker up.

•

All Hallows' Eve. Some set piece about the community giving a primordial shudder, scattering the mercies of piety, charity, and mental health and exposing, briefly, the realities of evil and the hosts of the vengeful and unquiet dead. I see how frail the pumpkin lanterns are that we light on our doorsteps to protect our houses from the powers of darkness. I see the little boy, dressed as a devil, rattling a can and asking pennies for UNICEF. How thin the voice of reason sounds tonight! Does my mother fly through the air? My father, my fishing companions? Have mercy upon us; grant us thy peace! Although there seemed to be no connection, it was always at this season that, in the less well-heeled neighborhoods of the village, "For Sale" signs would appear, as abundant as chrysanthemums. Most of them seemed to have been printed by children, and they were stuck into car windshields, nailed to trees, and attached to the bows of cabin cruisers and other boats, resting on trailers in the side yard. Everything seemed to be for sale—pianos, vacant lots, Rototillers, and chain saws, as if the coming of winter provoked some psychic upheaval involving the fear of loss. But as the last of the leaves fell, glittering like money, the "For Sale" signs vanished with them. Had everyone got a raise, a mortgage, a loan, or an infusion of hopefulness? It happened every year.

•

I belt down a great deal of bourbon before lunch, futz around. Buy flowers for Mary. The simple pleasure I seemed to take in flowers is vanished. Oh, well. We go—a little rain is falling—to see Pasolini's "St. Matthew." I have been told that Pasolini is homosexual, but he photographs the faces of his people lovingly and beautifully, and his sexual life is no affair of mine. As we leave the theatre, it is raining heavily, and I throw my jacket over Mary's shoulders and feel myself to be seventeen, eighteen, no more. At home I drink some whiskey and brood. I am sad; I am weary; I am weary of being a boy of fifty; I am weary of my capricious dick, but it seems unmanly of me to say so. I say so, and Mary most kindly and gently takes me into her arms. I don't make out, but lie there like a child. Patience, courage, cheerfulness.

So with one word, one word, she mends the wreath of hair. Oh, mend the wreath of hair, make the rain fall, scatter the ghosts. And I seem, most unjustly, to accuse myself.

So I am gentled and gentled and gentled.

•

When D. was a kid he liked to dress up in girls' clothes, and in his sophomore year at college he had a love affair with his roommate. This was gratifying sexually, but it corresponded in no other way to what he expected from love. His roommate was comely and athletic. D. was puny. His roommate claimed that he did what he did only as a convenience or a favor. D. was the lover, his roommate was the beloved, and he was a demanding, cruel, and callous beloved. After his graduation, D. went on to New York and got a job. His homosexual or narcissistic instincts were estimable, but he was unwilling or unable to enter into another love affair as painful as the affair in college. He went to a psychiatrist named Jacks three times a week for five years, trying to understand or cure or alter the clash between his homosexual instincts and the desire to marry and raise a family. At the end of five years, he met a young woman whom he loved. Jacks was doubtful about D.'s ability to marry, but he went ahead in spite of Jacks and seemed very happy—he seemed ecstatic. He loved his wife, he loved his way of life, he loved his children, and yet all of this had not changed his narcissism. In trains, public places—everywhere—he seemed to seek out men younger than he, whose features and tastes corresponded in some way either to his own features and tastes or, perhaps, to those features and tastes that he lacked when he was young. He went to another psychiatrist—Jacks had died—who encouraged him to sublimate his narcissism in various ways. He fell in love with a young neighbor—a married man with two children. He desired the neighbor ardently, dreamed of him, and tried to sublimate this by helping his friend. He got him a job, got him a raise, and advised him on everything including the purchase of

a new oil burner. He did not admire his image in the mirror—he could
see clearly how gaunt and lined his face was—but he loved it more than
any other face that would appear in his lifetime, and boarding a train
he would look around for some young man reading a paperback copy of
Dylan Thomas whom he could help. There always seemed to be some
young man around the house receiving help. D. never touched them,
and if they touched him, as they often did, he would put them away
gently, half faint with desire. I only mention this to point out that
everyone's life is not as simple as yours.

•

Wet lunch at the club. Taking a taxi home I ask the driver to leave
me off at Hawkes Avenue. He thinks I'm crazy. "Let me take you to
where you've paid to go," he says, but I ask him to let me off, and walk
home. It is very cold and the cold air seems as stimulating as gin. I
pound along the road, dragging the heels of my loafers with pleasure.
Why is this? It is the kind of irresolute or sloppy conduct that used to
trouble my father. I think I enjoy dragging the heels of my loafers
because it was something he asked me not to do, thirty-five years ago.

Mary is resting in bed and, fully dressed, I lie down beside her and
take her in my arms. Then I experience a sense—as heady as total
drunkenness—of our being fused, of our indivisibility for better or for
worser, an exalting sense of our oneness. While I hold her she falls
asleep—my child, my goddess, the mother of my children. Her breathing
is a little harsh, and I am supremely at peace. When she wakes, she
asks, "Did I snore?" "Terribly," I say. "It was earsplitting. You sounded
like a chain saw." "It was a nice sleep," she said. "It was very nice to
have you asleep in my arms," I say. "It was very, very nice."

•

Nailles' memories of his marriage were unromantic, even crude. He
seemed not attracted to the conventional beauties. MaryEllen cutting
the autumn roses, MaryEllen in a ball gown, MaryEllen weeping at the
news of a friend's death. Instead of this, he remembered a night when
Tessie had got sick and vomited on the floor beneath the grand piano.
It was about 3 A.M. when he let the old dog out and got a mop and a
pail and started to clean up the mess. The noise woke MaryEllen, and
she came downstairs in her nightgown. Looking up from beneath the

piano, he was deeply moved by her beauty. She got some paper towels and went on her hands and knees to help him. When she was done she stood, striking her head smartly on the piano lid. The blow hurt. Her eyes filled with tears. He, naked, kissed away her tears and led her over to the sofa. He pulled her nightgown up above her breasts and laid her there. Another night, she had asked him to lay her before she took her bath. Then she drew her tub, and he joined her in the bathroom and sat naked on the old toilet while she shaved her legs. "If I don't have a hot lunch," he said, "I get loose bowels. Cheese gives me loose bowels too." "Cheese constipates me," she said. She went on shaving her legs. It was lovely, lovely, lovely. It was what he remembered.

•

Fend, fend, fend off the gin with the *New York Times Magazine* section. My resolve collapses at eleven. I walk the boys to the archery range, set up a target in the orchard. Sneak two bourbons and read some more of the *Times*. An article in defense of the Asiatic war. The timbre of the man's intelligence offends me to the point of desperation. The metaphors are vulgar, the syntax is evasive, the analogies are massive and dishonest, but what I experience most is a sense of alienation and despair: the knowledge that in any conversation it would be impossible to impress—let alone persuade—this stranger with one's own opinions.

•

I take Mrs. Zagreb out to lunch. Oh, what a rascal! I think she's a little crazy, but the effect on me is stimulating, and we both chat excitedly about our terribly interesting lives. We could talk all afternoon. She let the cabdriver (very good-looking in an Italian sort of way) buy her a drink and the bartender (he must have been good-looking; he's very tall but he's pretty old) drove her into New York. I take a nap, and wake with a stupendous feeling of magnanimity and love. Mary is upstairs, correcting papers in bed, but when I feel in her pants she puts me off. I don't care. I sail off to the florist's and buy flowers for Mary and Zagreb, thinking two women are better than one. What a rascal, what a libertine! Z. gives me a French kiss. Swept along on my magnanimity I walk the dog over the hill, noticing how like flowers (pansies) are the dog's tracks. A leaf, some leaves. I do not much lift my eyes to the clouds from whence cometh this, the light of this winter afternoon. My house is brightly lighted, and Mary is in the kitchen making rolled beef, which I like. We are all happy, it seems, until at dinner Freddy begins to bawl. I finesse this, but something has gone wrong. I ask Mary if she has read Merwin's poems. "I've read several of them twice," she says, and goes upstairs to correct papers. But now she seems to me stern, unfeminine, more than I can master, and, at the thought of screwing, my cock begs to be excused. What is this? I think with pleasure and without shame of how feminine and sensual X was; of how, having dressed to make a telephone call, X, on returning, stripped and bounded back into bed. I also remember how sappy X was—the sense of having been disinfected, the bitten lower lip. I read until ten, when I find Mary in bed. I am given a sweet kiss, but she is asleep when I return from my bath. She is wakeful during the night, but when I ask if I can do anything she answers impatiently. Keep your pecker up.

•

It seems—or it seems to me—that it is terribly difficult for Mary to thank me for anything. When I gave her an electric typewriter for Christmas, she refused to open it, look at it, or acknowledge it in any way. She not only did not thank me; she did not speak to me. Exactly eleven months later, she came to me in the dining room, gave me a kiss, and said, "Thank you for the lovely, lovely typewriter."

•

The house was dark, of course. The snow went on falling. The last of the cigarette butts was gone, the gin bottle was empty, even the aspirin supply was exhausted. He went upstairs to the medicine cabinet. The plastic vial that used to contain Miltown still held a few grains, and by wetting his finger he picked these up and ate them. They made no difference. At least we're alive, he kept saying, at least we're alive, but without alcohol, heat, aspirin, barbiturates, coffee, and tobacco it seemed to be a living death. At least I can do something, he thought, at least I can distract myself, at least I can take a walk; but when he went to the door he saw wolves on the lawn.

•

The fact of the passage of time seems, to my great surprise, a source of sadness. One can put a sort of varnish on the facts, but one cannot change them. In the space of a day you find that the barber, bartender, and waiter who have served you for twenty-five years are all suddenly dead. Waking in high spirits is a matter of stepping out of one's dreams into an aura of love and friendship, but to take a roster of one's most vivid friends is crushing. X sits in a wheelchair being read to by a nurse. Y cruises the Mediterranean in his twin-diesel yacht, suffering terribly from boredom. M. is a reformed alcoholic with a damaged brain, trying to sell magazine subscriptions over the telephone. A. is an unregenerate alcoholic, bellicose, absentminded, drunk for three and four months at a time. These were the men and women one rose in the morning to meet, talk, walk, and drink with, and nearly all the brilliant ones are gone. I think of Cummings, who played out his role as a love poet into his late sixties. There was a man.

•

Our conversation goes, by my account, like this. Me: Good morning. She: Good morning (*faintly*). Me: May I have the egg on the stove? She: You know I never eat eggs. "Goodbye," I say, after breakfast. (*Silence.*) "Would you like a drink," I ask at five. "Yes, please." "This book is very interesting," I say. "It must be," she sighs. I chat during dinner, but she remains silent. These are the words we exchange during a day.

•

Bright stars and intense cold when I go to bed; in the morning the bluish darkness of another snowstorm. The usual Friday festivities. I take Mary to see "Zhivago." It would be fun to parody the screenplay. The battlefield scene ends with a closeup of a pair of eyeglasses. Not broken. There are many such cues: fur hats, flowers. Cuts from opulence to poverty. A rich and loving young couple ride their sleigh through the snow. Camera up to a lighted candle in a frost-rimmed window. Dissolve frost, and we see a very poor and loving couple. Terrible music, and all the sets are overdressed. Overdecorated. A ballroom frilled with drifting snow. The passengers crowded into a freight train for days have gleaming linen, lustrous hair, brilliant complexions. Watching the hero and his blonde in bed, I think how long it's been since I've been involved in some volcanic, unseemly, irresistible, and carnal affair. Is this age? Will I never be caught up helplessly in the storms of history and love?

•

Palm Sunday. Ten above zero. I get to church before the doors open, and am badly chilled. This, I suppose, because I've harmed my circulation. Miss F. has arranged the palm fronds in a fan above the purple cloth of Holy Week. She sits at a distance from her father. There is a blond young woman ahead of me who has a nervous habit of shifting her head that I find charming. Her taffy-colored hair conceals her face. I want to see it, but then I am afraid I will be disappointed. What am I doing here on my knees, shaking with alcohol and the cold? I do not pray, but I hope that my children will know much happiness. I believe that there was a Christ, that he spoke the Beatitudes, cured the sick, and died on the Cross, and it seems marvellous to me that men should, for two thousand years, have repeated this story as a means of expressing their deepest feelings and intuitions about life. My only noticeable experience is a pleasant sense of humility. Kneeling at the chancel, I notice how expertly the wooden lamb holds in the crook of his leg the staff of Christ's banner. The acolytes have red dresses and muddy loafers. Leaving the chancel, I see the face of the blonde and I am disappointed. I take home a palm frond, not to cleanse my house of its ills but to demonstrate that I want my house to be blessed.

•

And the sad men, the lonely men, those who are unhappily married, drop to their knees in garages, bathrooms, and motels asking God to help them understand the need for love. Unbelievers, every last one of them. Who is this God with whom they plead? He is an old man with a long white beard like a waterfall. Why do they, adult and intelligent men, behave so ridiculously? They seem forced to their knees by a palpable burden of pain.

•

Not drunk, not very drunk in any case, I decide that we should have our quarterly talk. "Things aren't going well," I say. "I don't know what you're talking about," says she. "Do you think this is the way a man and a woman should live together?" I say. "No," says she. "Well, let's talk." Her face is strained and pale, the eyes not protuberant but brilliant, the brows well up. "You destroy everything you love," says she. "I love my children," say I, "and I haven't destroyed them." "Let's leave the children out of this," says she. "I love my friends," say I. "You don't have any friends," says she. "You simply use people as a convenience." Then we go into the routine where she says she wishes I could see my face. This is followed by the fact that I deceive myself, that I am a creation of self-deception. She's said this before, and once offered to tell me some terrible truth about myself and then said it was too terrible. I don't know what she's aiming at here. Is this homosexuality? Has she determined that I am a homosexual? I have had my homosexual anxieties and experiences, but I find women much more attractive than men, and think it fitting and proper that I make my life with a woman. She then says that she knows herself absolutely, and that I know nothing of myself. This sort of judgment—which is how I think of it—bewilders me. How can any adult claim to know himself much better than another does? There seems to be some impermeability here. It seems to me unnatural. I don't understand it at all. I say that I am a loving person, and she asks how can I be a loving person, since I never see anyone? There is a digression here on the loneliness of the novelist, but I do see people and I do go out to them directly and warmly. I ask—it seems to me one of the few aggressive points I make—if she is afraid of being dependent. "I am," she says, "completely independent of you." I say that as a provider I've given her whatever she wanted. She says I haven't. She then says that I'm very funny about money with the children. I say that I've given the children whatever money they wanted, and that I've never reproached them. What does she mean by "funny"? She doesn't wish to discuss the matter. I say that I'm not much of a banker. She assents, laughing bitterly. There is much more, but I seem unable to recall it this morning. I mention the love I feel for my sons. "That's the only reason I'm sticking around," she says, getting to her feet. "Is that what you're doing?" I ask. "Sticking around?" "You take advantage of everything I say," she says. "I wouldn't have said that," say I, and covering my poor, poor cock with my hands I kiss her good night, take a Nembutal, and check out. Waking in the morning, I summon up my girls, but they do not come. It is she, who has indicted me as venomous, emotionally ignorant, a bad provider, self-deceived, whom I desire. I don't, I won't, admit that this is sexual masochism. There is too little evidence for this in the rest of my life. I sincerely doubt that this is a wishful repetition of my mother's dominance. I think maybe it's just bad luck.

•

On the morning of my daughter's wedding, it is raining. I climb
into Mary's bed, and she climbs out of it and climbs into mine. Later,
naked, I urge her to sit, naked, in my lap, but she makes some excla-
mation of distaste and turns on the television. I find these rebuffs a
serious depressant and, using this as an excuse, I take a little gin with
my orange juice. Mary descends on my eggs, but she is quite welcome
to them. On the street, a north wind is blowing the rain. On Fourteenth
Street, two men, one of them with a peculiar head of yellow hair—it
is dyed or perhaps a wig—slink out of a lunch counter. I think they
are queer and that they are going to spend the day shoplifting. I buy
an umbrella and some aspirin, and step into a dark, pleasant bar where
I drink one and a half Martinis. Another faggot comes along the sidewalk. He wears moccasins, no socks, green velour trousers, and a
sweater; but his means of locomotion is what interests me. He seems
sucked along the street like an object in a wind tunnel, although there
is no wind to speak of and no source of suction. Ben is at the hotel,
and we dress and go off to Lüchow's. There is the desperate scene where
I can't find Susie, and finally we reach the church. She seems frightened, and I am pleased to give her my arm and some support. This is
a scene I have imagined countless times, and now it is being done, is
done. I observe nothing of the reception beyond the fact that it is beautiful. "What a beautiful party it is!" I keep exclaiming. Where is the
keen-eyed observer who could pick out the wrinkled skirt, the time-
ravaged face, the drunken waiter? There is a sharp exchange with Mary.
I have drunk so much that I cannot count on my memory, but I think—
or claim to have suggested—that we must make some plans for ending
the party. "You," says she, "are the spectre at the feast." The best thing
to do is to assume I provoked this. Later, I drink whiskey in our maid's
kitchen and speak broken Italian. I return at dark. It is raining. Ben
is on the porch and I embrace him and repeat the remark about the
spectre. "I'm on your side, Daddy," he says, "I'm on your side." I should
not have done this. I don't really want him on my side.

•

I have a drink at quarter after eleven. Go to the B.s' at noon. I sleep
and wake and drink and sleep again and wake and drink. I suggest that
we discuss a separation or a divorce. We will sell the house, divide the

price, etc. She can go and live with her beloved sister in New Jersey. This is all preposterous and drunken, and, hearing the songbirds in the morning, I realize that I don't have the guts, spine, vitality, whatever, to sell my house and start wandering. I don't know what to do. I must sleep with someone, and I am so hungry for love that I count on touching my younger son at breakfast as a kind of link, a means of staying alive.

•

But Monday morning. Overcast. 9:30. I will go to the dentist in half an hour, and I would like a drink. I write, at breakfast, the biography of a man whose dependence on alcohol was extreme but who, through some constitutional fortitude, was able to ration his drinks, to exploit alcohol rather than have it exploit him. He never drank before noon and, after his lunch drinks, not again until five. It was a struggle, it always would be, and by the time he was fifty he realized that there would be no suspension of the fight. He would never be able to pass the whiskey bottle in the pantry without sweating. On Saturdays and Sundays he would paint screens, split wood, cut the broad lawns of Evenmere, looking at his watch every ten minutes to see if the time hadn't come for a legitimate scoop. At five minutes to five, his hands trembling and his brow soaked with sweat, he would get out the ice, pour the beautiful, golden whiskey into a glass, and begin the better part of his life.

•

Now Thursday morning. Twenty minutes to eleven. I am in the throes of a gruelling booze fight. I think a tranquillizer will retard my circulation. I could cut grass, but I am afraid of pulling my ankle. There is really nothing to do but sit here and sweat it out. I can write myself a letter. Dear Myself, I am having a terrible time with the booze. Ride it out.

•

Waking at dawn. A new dream girl. This one is Chinese and has a magnificent arse, small breasts. She is followed by another, who wears a sweater the color of raspberry jam and a string of very small pearls. Then I am in Rome in the big apartment, attended by A. I am, as I usually am in these reveries, an invalid, eating from a tray. I ask her

for the big blue pill. It is a large capsule, the color of the sky. I take it
with a glass of water, and she retires to the front room to work on her
book about Byron. As I slowly lose consciousness, the sound of her
typing fills me with happiness. How unlike me. I wake in the late
afternoon. The function of the blue pill seems to be to spare me any of
the tedious hours of day or night. It is always a fresh morning, a brief
noon, a massive twilight. I never experience the pitiless tedium of 3
P.M. When I wake, A. asks if I want a drink or a cup of tea. She makes
me a galvanic drink and herself a cup of tea. Then, as I bask in the
effects of alcohol, she draws herself a bath and dresses, very elegantly,
for a reception at the T.s'. When she kisses me goodbye her kiss is dry
and tender. She leaves a blue pill on the table, and as it begins to get
dark I take this, squirm sensually in the sheets, and go back to sleep
again. She wakes me when she returns at ten, orders some supper from
the café on the corner, and tells me about the party. Then she undresses,
climbs into my bed, and after we have fucked I take another blue pill
and will know nothing, not even a dream, until nine in the morning,
when I am waked by the maid who brings me breakfast. Sleep is my
kingdom, my native land, I am the Prince of Sleep. Do we see our age
in the poverty of our dreams? The threadbare dreams of middle age.

•

I think of my brother's ruin—that boy of summer. Whatever happened? Quarterback. Drinking Coca-Cola in the field house. Captain
of the undefeated hockey team. Happy with his friends, nimble with
his girls, he loved his muzzy and dazzy. Oh, whatever happened? Married in the church of Christ, randy in bed, quick at business, a loving
father, lucky at cards and dice—what happened? Did he find his wife
in someone else's bed? As the order vanished from his own affairs, he
sought to order the world. "This is the way you do it." "Listen to me."
He pissed in the umbrella stand, drop-kicked the roast beef, waved his
prick at Mrs. Vanderveer, and called in the morning to ask if everyone
was all right. He spent that year in New York. Went around with an
art director who lisped. Lumbered after the Madison Avenue whores.
"I never drink before lunch," he said, and maybe he didn't, but he
certainly used it after the twelve-o'clock whistle blew. Six Beefeaters
and a beer, and then it was time for the afternoon drinking to begin.
He broke his ankle in a soccer game, locked himself up in the bedroom,

and drank ten quarts of Gilbey's. Oh, whatever happened? He had his first attack of claustrophobia at LaGuardia Airport. He thought he would suffocate, and he always carried a flask after that. He was such a charmer. He was charming at his clubs, charming at his parties, and when he broke down he was charming at Alcoholics Anonymous. And he was terribly misunderstood. In this respect he was practically a nut. Nobody knew the score, and when he told them they wouldn't listen. But where did the self-righteousness come from, the pained and beatific smile, the pose of moral superiority? "If I know one thing, I know that my children love me." You can draw a line easily enough from the summery boy to the club drunk, but where did the priggishness, the homely maxims, the phony hopefulness come from? "I've always done the best I knew how to do. No one can say that I didn't." How could he have come so far from the frisky quarterback, the locker-room horseplay?

•

My ancient Uncle Hamlet, that black-mouthed old monkey, used to say that he had enjoyed the best fifty years in the history of his country and that I could have the rest. Wars, depressions, automobile accidents, droughts, blackouts, municipal corruption, polluted rivers. He let me have it all on a platter.

•

The *cafarde*, and how mysterious it is in its resistance to good fortune, love of all kinds, esteem, work, blue sky. I try to console myself with thinking of all the great men who have suffered similarly; but reason has no effect on the bête noire. It could quite simply be alcohol, since alcohol is the sure cure.

•

Off we go to Ben's commencement. So spread out in folding chairs on a grassy quadrangle on a summer's day—this seems to be a rearguard action of the genteel. A few women cry as the graduating class marches in. The boys are a mixed bag—long hair, short hair, handsome, homely—but the force of good and evil in a hundred lives is felt. When they are seventeen and eighteen, their faces still have the purity of caricature. The vast noses, the wide-set eyes, the big mouths, all these things that time will regulate and diminish are intact. Rising to our feet, we sing loudly, "We gather together to ask the Lord's blessing." Here are the same faces one sees on the Nantucket boat. The tranquillity of the ceremony arises from the fact that we are a community of values. We went to the same schools and colleges and parties, we summer on the sea islands, there is an unusual sameness to our clothing, our incomes, our diets, and our beliefs. Winthrop Rockefeller gives the address. "Would that the famous Greek philosopher Aristotle were in our midst today. Would that Einstein could be with us. You have been given the tools of education. How you apply them is your responsibility in this world of bewildering and accelerated change. By the year two thousand, we will have perfected our technological society, but what about the soul of man?" The prizegiving is interminable, and I go out to the car and have a drink.

•

Hammer puts a dime in the lock of the men's toilet, and enters it, but not for the usual purpose. He gets to his knees in the privacy of the toilet, bows his head, and says, "Almighty God, Father of Our Lord Jesus Christ, Maker of all things, Judge of all men . . ." When he has finished his prayer he stands, dusts off his trousers, and takes a flask from his pocket. He fills the cap with whiskey, making appreciative groans.

•

Lace an uneasy stomach with gin, cut grass in the heat, swim in S.'s pool where the water is stinging cold. Zowie. Dress in the clothes of an eighteen-year-old. One of those old men with white hair you see racing around in two seater convertibles. Mary talks as if she had a cold, and when I ask if she has she says she's breathing through her mouth because I smell so horrible. I seem to suffer from that degree of sensibility that crushes a man's sense of humor. Nothing important has been said, nothing that can't be forgotten in an instant, and yet I seem to see in the remark so much of her character and our relationship. S. is going to Stratford to see some Shakespeare. She is dressed in bright colors. Her friend the widow is in black lace and I think she is not this old. Overdressed women going to the theatre. Rob and Sue come out, and I swim again with them. They stay for dinner, but somewhere along the line a drink too many. Ben, having quarrelled with his girl, is reunited with her, but I spend a lot of time kissing her, and she doesn't mind. What about a man making out with his son's date? What about that? L. sits in his Mustang, vomiting between his knees. The hair is very long, the face too small, undistinguished, the complexion bad. He is too drunk to drive or do anything else, and we put him to bed. I talk with his father on the telephone—a patient, loving man who is not alarmed by his son's drunkenness. My own son is drunk, opinionated, insensitive, and sentimental about the collapse of his friend, roughing his hair and saying, "I'm sorry you're sick." It gets all mixed up, and all I can recall this morning is that: the girls, the vomiting, the London broil, Rob reading Conan Doyle, my empty glass.

•

A round for me, or so I claim at nine. I dream that I wrestle a spry Negress in the library apartment at the Academy in Rome. P. is in the next bed, trying to make out with someone I don't recognize, who keeps saying, "You're just wasting your time." At dusk Ben and I cut the playing field at the Children's Center. Father and Son engaged in charitable acts. I agree to take Mary and Federico to Rome and interview Loren, but Mary does not seem cheered. They go off to the movies, and I wander through the house saying loudly, "How happy I am to be alone, how happy, happy, happy I am to be alone." I drink on the terrace, wish on the evening star, chat with the dogs. The doctor calls. I think of him as a young man with an uncommonly round face, round eyes, and an enthusiasm for medical science that does not include any knowledge or respect for the force of pain. He seems to possess some vision of a rosy future in which there will be pills to cure cholesterol and melancholy, pills for sloth, lust, homosexuality, anger, anxiety, and avarice. "Try this red one for your fear of planes," he says enthusiastically. "Try the yellow one for your fear of heights. Take the white one when you have the blues." Pills, pills, what beautiful pills they have these days. They're working on an elixir of youth, but they haven't quite got the bugs out of it. I'm confident they'll have it next year.

•

The H.s. They live in a modest house on the hill, without servants. They have no children. He is a thin, thin-faced, markedly unattractive man, whose lack of substance or color seems emphasized by a mustache that might have been drawn with a grease pencil. His clothing seems cheap and his shoes have a papery look. She is also thin. They look rather alike except for the mustache. She wears no jewels. No paintings hang in their living room, and the Danish furniture might have been bought in the village. The remarkable thing about them is that their declared income for the year was two hundred and fifty thousand, but the tax collector claims that their return was one million six hundred thousand dollars short. They paid a tax of one hundred and fifty-six thousand. What can they do with this kind of money?

•

Rain in the night, and as it falls straight into the valley it seems to be an undoing, an unloosening sound. I feel as if I were unravelling a snarled fishing line. Happily.

•

The *cafarde* followed Hammer, but followed him without much guile, either because it was lazy or perhaps because it was an assassin so confident of its victim that it had no need to exert itself. On Friday, Hammer flew to Rome and checked in at the Eden. On Saturday morning, he woke feeling cheerful and randy. He was just as cheerful on Sunday, but on Monday he woke in a melancholy so profound that he had to drag himself out of bed and struggle, step by step, to the shower. On Tuesday he caught the train to Fondi and took a cab through the mountains to Sperlonga, where he stayed with his friends, the G.s. He had two good days there, but the bête noire caught up with him on the third, and he took a train for Naples at Formia. He had four good days in Naples. Had the bête noire lost track of its victim or was it simply moving in the leisurely way of a practiced murderer? His fifth day in Naples was crushing, and he took the afternoon train to Rome. Here he had three good days, but he woke on the fourth in danger of his life and made arrangements to take the noon plane to New York. So, by moving from place to place, he could count on two days or sometimes three each week in which he felt himself to be a natural man. The *cafarde* always followed. It was never waiting for him at his destination.

•

Reading old journals, I find that the booze fight and the *cafarde* have been going on for longer than I knew. I guess I'm stuck—a little stuck, at least—with the booze fight. Old journals help, but there is a strain of narcissism here. At the back of my mind there is the possibility of someone's reading them in my absence and after my death, and exclaiming over my honesty, my purity, my valor, etc. What a good man he is!

•

I dream: Enabling legislation was passed by Congress yesterday making it a statutory offense to have wicked thoughts about President Johnson. Suspects will be questioned by the F.B.I. with the aid of a lie detector.

•

I find on the floor of Ben's room an unmailed letter to L. He may have meant me to read it, and I put this down with the hope that I won't mention it to Ben. He is alone, he says. He is crying. He is alone with Mum and Dad, the two most self-centered animals in the creation. Dad wanted him to drive west in an old car, but he's bought a new car that he likes and that has a long guarantee. Dad thinks he's so great to have given me a car, but the only reason I got it is because I know how to handle him. He gave me a long speech on responsibility, but he was so drunk he couldn't remember it in the morning. I told him where he could put his car.

•

Nailles might write a reply to Tony: I found your letter addressed to God in the middle of your floor after you'd left. You must have wanted me to read it. I've never read a letter of yours before. I don't understand why you feel the way you do. I don't think I've ever gloated over what I've been able to give you. If you feel guilty about being on the receiving end of things you might, to lessen your guilt, imagine that I gloat. It's the only explanation I can hit on. My own father was able to give me almost nothing: no affection, love, clothing, or food. He was penniless, friendless, old, and wretched. It is important to me, of course, that I have been able to give you what I lacked. When I see you drive off in a bucket-seat racing car, with matched luggage packed with new clothing, I am very content, but I did not give these things to you. There is not enough self-consciousness in my support of you to let me use a word like "give," or "share," or "contribute." You are welcome to such money as I have, exactly as you are welcome to such love as I have, and that seems boundless. You wrote, in capitals, that the only reason you were able to get anything out of me is because you know how to handle me. This puts my serene love in terms of flattery on your part, stupidity on mine. In what way have you handled me? You answer me. When I've wished you good morning after we've stayed up late a few nights talking about sex while I had my nightcap, I've always made it clear that you were under no obligation to keep me company.

I do not understand why you should say that your mother and I are the people in the world you most hate, unless you feel so deeply guilty about your behavior that you are unable to blame yourself and must blame us. You say that we are the most self-centered people in the world when, in fact, our love for you verges on fatuity. Aside from erotic reveries, you are the first thing on my mind when I wake, and when I sleep I sometimes dream, lovingly, of you. I remember watching you, like a swain, while you fired Roman candles into the brook; watching you ski in the orchard; watching you ski at Stowe. Climbing a mountain with you and your cousin, I had a painful wrench at my heart and thought that it didn't matter, because I was with my son. Night after night in Saratoga, unable to sleep, I imagined that we climbed together over the Dolomites. It is possible, I suppose, that in order to become a man one has to mutilate the carapace of one's father's affections. I pray that this is not so. You mention someone's bullying you, and I wonder if there is some unself-conscious connection between the terrors of your adolescence and your feeling for me. . . .

But if Nailles wrote such a letter he would destroy it.

•

I would not want this to degenerate into the journal of an invalid, but pain, discomfort, and anxiety have dominated these weeks, and I have a feeling that the medicine makes me dopey. I drink at eleven to still an unruly gut, and read about Ben Franklin in Paris in the 1780's. The day is unseasonably warm. Hornets and yellow jackets fall into our soup and our cocktails. Wasps swarm on the upstairs porch. A stupid possum comes up the front steps. I think he is wounded or rabid. He is in no hurry. A small snake, marked with deep red, black, and white, lies on the stairs to the garden. Geese, snakes, wasps, the flowers in the garden all seem apprehensive about the inalienable power of the

coming winter. A. comes, and I lose four straight games of backgammon
and am bored. I think this is the medicine. It is so warm and fair that
we have dinner out-of-doors. Sitting on the terrace, I see an orb of light
appear in the atmosphere, as large and brilliant as a full moon, only
orange and green. It throws a double reflection on the haze. I rush into
the kitchen and urge Mary to come out and see this mystery, but she
is washing a teapot and it is difficult to get a woman away from the
dishpan, even to see the millennium. When she comes out, the orb has
faded, but there is still some luminous vapor in the air. T. asks me for
a drink. After much talk he says that he has lost his job. Thirty-five
years old, with three children. He seems cheerful, and confesses to
having stolen the Help Wanted section from my Sunday *Times*. He goes
on to talk about his father. That man, he says, has an unclean spirit.
He bought his sons train tickets to their colleges and did nothing else.
They worked as grocery clerks, hospital orderlies, waiters, etc. That
man, he repeats, has an unclean spirit. I am superstitious about con-
demning one's male parent. Leaving them, I have a nightcap and think
of how little my father did for me. He did not even give me bus fare;
but he didn't have it, and I think his spirit was pure.

•

For the last time (I pray) this is the journal of an invalid. Feeling
poorly as well as frightened, I go to bed after lunch. I see the golden
leaves outside the window, see a shaft of light reflected on the glass,
and sleep until five, when I dress and go down for a drink and some
supper. Back to bed at eight: I am very happy in my bulwark, my
sanctuary, my firm, clean, warm bed, and I think that my infection
was probably brought on by the gruelling burden of nervous tension.
How unwarranted and mysterious it has seemed. Vertigo on the station
platform. Will the blacktop fly up and strike me between the eyes? I
never know; but it never has. Vertigo in Grand Central. Walking in
the city with my son, I stay close to my club so that in case I collapse
there will be some place where I can be taken. Scrotum-grabbing vertigo
on bridges, tunnels, and freeways. So I think that some organ was
bound to give—and one did—and that the cure is rest. Rest was all I
needed, and I needed an uncommon amount of rest because the burdens
were uncommon. Waking from time to time, I think that I am no longer
sick, that I have been granted some great bounty. I am stirred by an

immense gratitude, but at whom can I aim my thanks? The divine intelligence cannot go from bed to bed like Santa Claus. So I am grateful, humble, convinced that the worst is over.

•

My only brother, after twenty-five years of hard drinking, including three critical alcoholic crises; after having lost his job and all his worldly goods, his wife, and the trust and affection of at least two of his children; after having found everyone who employed him stupid and unresponsive, and after having drifted around furnished rooms on the South Shore, selling advertising time for a small radio station; after having been seriously crippled with arthritis, and after having reached the age of sixty-two, calls at nine while I lie sick in bed. The voice is exclamatory and cheerful. He asks after me solicitously, as he used to when he had been drunk for a week. I am pleased to think that we share a durable constitution. I remember how mysteriously our relationship took on the nature of a contest. He is driving to Colorado on Saturday, while I, so temperate, industrious, etc., can scarcely drive to the next village.

•

Sunday morning, jumpy and megrimish. The President, on the deck of an aircraft carrier, says, "Your weapons and your wings are the swords and the shields of our freedom. The names of your planes—Phantom, Intruder, Hawkeye, Vigilante, Skyhawk—they are the watchwords of our liberty." We will fight for freedom of speech wherever it is threatened, even if we have to sacrifice our own freedom of speech. Day after day the makeup man at the *Times* runs the photographs of dead or wounded soldiers cheek by jowl with the Tiffany advertisements. The war is not going to be won at cocktail parties. Republicans and Southern Democrats have hamstrung the anti-poverty program. Men and women of Jewish descent are blackballed at the country club. Next to armaments, the nation's largest-selling product is whiskey and drugs. Wall Street capitalists are real, militaristic, and avaricious. You can see them on the station platform any morning, the overt and cheerful sponsors of tyranny all over the world. They raise the bonds for Salazar, Franco, Papa Doc.

One knows all of this, and the corruption of the war is inestimable—the dead soldier and the Tiffany bracelet. This is madness. And yet I don't want "Bullet Park" to be an indictment. The admissions committee at the club does not scandalize me. Neither does the fact that D. has sold a bond issue for Franco. But without an indictment I seem to have no moral position—no position, in fact, at all. Hammer was not such a fool as to assume that Bullet Park, because it is affluent, is sinful. I would not be such a fool as to assume that, because Hammer is comfortable, happily married, and has few discernible moral mandates beyond the mandates of mannerliness, he is a villain. What I wanted was an uncomplicated story about a man who loved his son.

•

Half awake, I remember how totally important my brother was to me—the center of my world, my universe. With him at my side, no harm could befall me. He did not begin to destroy himself until after we had, at my insistence, separated, but I think that his drunkenness and madness could have been more of a blow than I have ever admitted.

Ben returns with a beard and a shaven pate. We go to the M.s' party. More old friends. When we return I go downstairs to hang up the stockings. "What right have you to hang up the stockings?" says Mary. "You didn't buy any of the presents." This is the night our Saviour was born. Prince of Peace!

•

There is still snow on the trees; it is that kind of snow. One sees it out of the windows here like some extraordinary garden. It is the kind of snowfall about which girls write verse. "How like a fairyland it seems/a veritable land of dreams/The garbage pail with ermine cap/and all the lawns a pearly nap." There is an uncommon silence when I walk Federico to the school bus. The light is eclipsed and lovely. One wants to see it all so clearly.

•

The second of February, the valley darkened by fog; but I wake with no *cafarde*, no hangover, no aches, no pains, no shakes, no megrims, no racking thirst, no hunger for pills, no strange sensation in my cock, no anxieties, no crushing and nameless sorrows, no tremors; a healthy, well-preserved man in his fifties, at peace with the world.

•

Having nothing better to do—which is a mistaken position to have
got into—I read two old journals. High spirits and weather reports recede
into the background, and what emerges are two astonishing contests,
one with alcohol and one with my wife. With alcohol, I record my
failures, but the number of mornings (over the last ten years) when
I've sneaked drinks in the pantry is appalling. As for the marriage, a
number of things appear. The most useful one is a view of marriage
that is neither larky nor desperate; a sense of how large a continent this
is, and how complex are its burdens. Sentiment and intelligence seem
more important than passion. There are many accounts of sexual and
romantic ecstasy, but they are outnumbered by an incredible number
of rebuffs. It literally pains me to contemplate this. I urge myself a
hundred times to be cheerful and keep my pecker up, and how puerile
this advice seems. Another alarming fact is the number of people, from
my point of view, who appear to feel that I am in the right. Do I appear
to the world to be henpecked? I think not. I think this is a part of the
vastness of this continent. I think my mistake is to consider marriage
vows as something on a valentine, and marriage itself as a simple romance. (Try it for Hammer, painful as it may seem.) And another
disconcerting thing about the old journals is the recurrent mention of
homosexuality. But why do I blame myself for this? Homosexuality
seems to be a commonplace in our time—no less alarming than drunkenness and adultery—but my anxiety on the matter is very deep and
seems incurable. I suffer, from time to time, a painful need for male
tenderness, but I cannot perform with a man without wrecking my self-
esteem. What, then, is my self-esteem? It seems composed of impon-
derables—shifty things. It is, at its worst, I suppose, a deep wish to
placate Muzzy and Dazzy. It is, at its best, a sense of fitness that
approaches ecstasy—the sense of life as a privilege, the earth as something splendid to walk on. Relax, relax.

•

I brood on the lack of universality in our sexual appetites. A loves
his wife and no one but her. B loves young men, and when these are
scarce he makes out with men who impersonate youth. C likes all comely
women between the ages of twelve and fifty, including all races. D likes
himself, and jacks off frequently. He also likes men who resemble him
sufficiently to make the orgasm narcissistic. E likes both men and

women, depending on his moods, and I don't know whether he is the most tragic or the most natural of the group. None of them share, at any discernible level, the desires of the others. They share customs, diets, habits of dress, laws, and governments, but naked and randy they seem to be men from different planets.

•

Easter Sunday. The temperature at 72. No one can remember such a fine day in this part of the world. "I've never seen such a beautiful Easter," we say to one another. "Have you?" Last year it snowed. Flowers in the garden, and the birds in the trees seem to be singing an invitation list: Peabody-Peabody, Tickner-Tickner, Trilling, Ewing, and Swope. A law firm? It is a serene day for me. The empty tomb. Life everlasting. I lie in the morning sun thinking about the mysteriousness of obscenity. All those cocks and balls drawn on toilet walls are not the product of perverse frustrations. Some of them are high-hearted signs of good cheer. We go to the egg hunt, mostly out of respect for P., and the party is ostensibly one of those informal gatherings in which the social rituals seem heightened by the absence of neckties. I remain happy and serene, thinking in the middle of the night of the love I feel for my sons.

•

I read Roth's continued accounts of jacking off in Jersey and else-where, and there is something intensely interesting about the three-finger squeeze, the full-fisted yank, the four-hundred-stroke orgasm, etc. His accounts of his youth are a universe apart from my limpid record of an artistic aunt and a cousin who played Beethoven. My parents were not Jewish, and our house was large and well appointed. In self-defense, and there is much of that in my thinking, I observe how my curiosity leaps, but that my best interest soon lags. F., sitting in the front row of a vaudeville show, noticed that the man beside him was yanking his prick. F. asked politely what he was doing, and the man explained that if you pulled it long enough white stuff squirted out of the end, and you had a wonderful feeling. F. went home and gave it a try and told me about it at school. Lying in bed that night I jacked off while listening to a philosophical radio commentator. The orgasm was racking; my remorse was crushing. I felt that I had betrayed the fatherly voice on the radio. F. and I used to pull one another off in theatres, rub one another off in the golf club shower. One rainy day at camp when the administration had broken down and we had nothing to do we all doubled up in bed. I first got an Irishman named Burke with a big prick and a very fatherly embrace. Then I switched over to F. for the second trip, but when we had come we dressed and, standing in the rain outside the tent, decided to swear off jerking off. I don't remember how long this resolve lasted, but my jacking off was mostly a genuine extension of love. Roth is always alone, and there is never any question in his mind about his maleness, although he does say that he missed being a faggot by luck. So I come back to the bitter mystery, bitter and legitimate. I claim to enjoy some invincible maleness, and if I am mistaken I will stick to my claim. But I am frightened of color-lessness, the thought of being a homosexual terrifies me, and I am frightened and ashamed to recall that G. sucked me off, that P. doesn't want to marry and have sons and a home, and I flatly deny that mine was a guise of sexual cowardice—that I didn't have the courage to pit my homosexual instinct against the censure of the world. I didn't find the world that contemptible.

•

At the edge of the swimming pool—twilight, of course—D. and I sit bare-arse, smoking, undisturbed by each other's nakedness. "I never had an electric train," he says. "My father never took me to a ballgame, never once. He took me to the circus a couple of times, but he never once took me to a ballgame."

•

Updike's cover story and I quite sensibly envy his gifts I defend myself by saying that he has developed an impractical degree of sensi-bility, and that my own stubborn and sometimes idle prose has more usefulness. One does not ask, skating on a pond, how the dark sky carries its burden of starlight. I don't, in any case.

•

Ben comes home with a barefoot friend who has a fan-shaped beard and fuzzy hair. Ben is now a photographer, and my reaction to this is to mention all the famous photographers I have known (one) and to explain a subject of which I know nothing. This is unfortunate. His hair is long, his sideburns protrude, his face is lean and handsome, and he seems no longer to be my son. Who is the father of this young man? I think I remember the night when he was conceived; we had spent a month in the mountains and stopped at my mother's house in Quincy on the way back to New York. We talk about drugs, sex, blacks. Everybody takes hashish, pot; a lot of his classmates have been arrested. His girl is infatuated with him, and in her photographs one sees how full, yielding, and lovely her face has become. "We make out four times on Saturday," he says. "Then I pretend to sleep while she cooks my breakfast. But it's just like getting married, and I don't want to be married yet. She says that I can't leave her, that if I leave her she'll wither up and die, but I've got this other girl in Baltimore. She's been staying with some people who seem bohemian." I remember (egocentrically) what it was like at his age to enter another household.

•

I read the Solzhenitsyn with pleasure and think that I will read until dawn as I did with Tolstoy forty years ago. Fortunately, I have enough common sense to go to bed. It is forty years later. The book is not only an exhaustive indictment of Stalin's tyranny, his hired torturers and murderers, it also seems to be an indictment of the backwardness of the Russian people. This is, I think, because Russian literature, in spite of the fifty-year struggle for change, shows less organic growth and change than any other literature. We do not find characters out of Sterne and Trollope wandering into contemporary English literature, but in this book the cruel and stupid bureaucrats are the same men we met in Pushkin and Gogol. That woman writing with her finger on a steamy window first appeared in Lermontov. It is an intensely national literature, you might say a provincial literature, so that descriptions of drunkenness and stupidity go beyond the individual character into the national character, the Russian people, and the race. Some European sophistication seems to have rubbed off onto the aristocracy, but today's Russians seem not only backward, they seem determinedly so. On the plane from Copenhagen was a Russian family—beautifully dressed in English clothes—all of them quite plump. What worlds and worlds separate them from the babushkas at the hotel, whose surliness is predicated on the fact that this is a classless society? The French and German invasions don't seem to have affected this backwardness. The linen is stained, it takes an hour or longer to get a simple meal, the rooms are ugly, and in some places, like Yalta, there is no escape from the loud-speakers that broadcast deafening and vulgar music. Solzhenitsyn's prisoners are mostly serious, spiritual, and decent men, but they are prisoners. In Russia one comes upon impetuousness, candor, and vision, but one also comes upon suspiciousness, a sort of cultivated stupidity, and that hopeless obtuseness that Gogol railed against.

•

A new journal, and I have only to observe that I seem impelled to write nothing, not even letters. I can't remember what I did when I finished the last novel. I went alone to Rome late in the winter. As I came to the end of "Bullet Park" I felt the need to overhaul my approach to things; that is, to avoid constructing fiction out of the minutiae of upper-middle-class life: She was the kind of woman who gave all automobiles and many other appliances the feminine gender. The Volks-wagen, refrigerator, and washing machine were all "she," and when they broke down they were described as sick. "She is sick," she would say of the refrigerator. She spoke freely to traffic lights and described the car as being thirsty. . . . I would like to stop this sort of thing.

•

In trying to clarify my past, it would be much easier if I could look back with pure bitterness and scorn. If I could damn the sexual ignorance and suspiciousness of my parents, damn the ghastly wreckage of their marriage, damn the house, the neighborhood, and the schools I attended, it would be clear and easy, but their affairs were a mixture of excellence and stupid cruelty. The fact that I was often very happy seems in retrospect to be a massive limitation.

•

Federico carves his pumpkin, and we get it onto the porch and lighted before night falls; but either I am morbidly sensitive or drunk, or Mary is *maldisposta*—things are not cheerful. She seized the galleys and read them straight through. "Of course I cannot judge the book," she says, "because I know in every case the facts on which it is based. Hammer is revolting. . . ." Since there is some correspondence between Hammer and me, I am offended or wounded. "Isn't it better than the 'Scandal'?" I ask, but she doesn't reply. Praise, however foolish, is very important to me now. I invent praise.

•

At eight o'clock, on All Hallows' Eve, in the middle of a TV show of incredible vulgarity, the President of the U.S. announces that we will stop bombing in Southeast Asia. He is tired. The face seems wasted, one might say corrupt. He uses the first person pronoun more often than I think is necessary and seems, through a massive egotism, to have damaged his ability to communicate. There is no jubilation to this announcement, but this may be because I am drunk. I am skeptical, and the possibility of expediency or cynicism is inescapable.

•

Election Day, and I have the brains not to stay up for the returns. Mary's friend arrives quite late, and I do not see her; and why should I take such an uneasy dislike to someone I have not seen? Unable to sleep, I make out with Mia Farrow in Leningrad and wander around Rome again. I have, in my memories, walked around Rome so often that these days I find myself in the slums that ring the old city. Past the Borghese Gardens I run into slums; I see the slums on the Aventine, the slums past Santa Maria. Santa Maria, I say, was constructed to commemorate a miraculous fall of snow. There are some splendid early mosaics, but they are so poorly lighted as to be invisible. Coming into Rome on the train during a thunderstorm on some late afternoon, I saw a naked man in a shed, washing himself from a bucket. He was washing himself very carefully. Why should this figure seem so enviable? He might be going to work in a dirty trattoria and suffer the abuse of a distempered cook. Driving toward the sea from Siena I saw a young man pulling off his bathing trunks at the edge of a stream. On the steps of a boat club in Venice I saw a man taping an oar. Why do I long for these circumstances? It seems that in my coming of age I missed a year—perhaps a day or an hour—so that the consecutiveness of growth was damaged. But how can I go back and find this moment that was lost?

•

I have been on the spiritual, alcoholic, and emotional ropes for six weeks, and I don't know how to get off them. To ration my drinks is one way, but this sometimes amounts to nothing but a struggle. I could go to a shrink, I suppose. I could get more exercise. There is a path through the woods that I can take this rainy morning; but instead I will take the path to the pantry and mix a Martini. Look, look, then, here is a weak man, a man without character. Dishonesty is what one means, purposeless dishonesty. It is the most despicable trait. You take a nap and claim to be tired from work. You hide a whiskey bottle in the closet and claim to be a wiser man than your friends who hide whiskey bottles in the closet. You promise to take a child to the circus and have such a bad hangover that you can't move. You promise to send money to your old mother and do not.

•

The legitimacy of otherness. The dentist. The eyes are, for a man, soft; the mouth pretty; the face a little coarse now with age and fatigue but must, when he was younger, have been appealing. On his hideously elaborate office wall is a photograph of the warship on which he was dentist; also a photograph of him in a scant basketball uniform—a comely youth. I think my suspiciousness is perhaps more prominent than his oddness, and yet there is some otherness here, and if we became friends our friendship would be based not on a shared enthusiasm for professional football but on a shared memory of aloneness, improbable dreams or ambitions, disappointments.

•

Dressy, scented, strung with pearls, and quite alone, they order beef Wellington and leave it half eaten. It troubles me that their dilemma should seem so apparent. The jocular businessmen at the bar—laughing and drinking—offend me deeply because (I think) so little of their nature is hidden. This is the square world and I detest it. Walking on the streets, I am not pleased by the crowds. Looking for a pretty girl, I find none; and even if I found one she would not be my salvation. Because of this, perhaps—this invertedness—the dark hotel room, and my own nature I have, at dusk, a powerful yen for Ganymede. I love him. I want to talk with him, embrace him, debauch him. I call him, and the sound of his voice pleases me. I wonder if this could have something to do with my early life with my brother. He says that he may call me later. Oh, what bliss it will be! But when I come in at eleven the yen has vanished, and if the phone rang I think I would not answer it. It is not the ardor of my desire that astonishes me but the mysterious ease with which it comes and goes. So this is my nature; this and gin.

•

As for holy matrimony, she wrote in August of the same year to her old friend Lady Agatha Simmons, it is not all advantages. He has, of course, a male member. It is an ugly color and has a tip like an enormous radish. He likes to thrust this, rudely, into my privates. Then he makes a pumping movement, and presently there is a discharge of fluid from the radish. When this happens he makes loud animal noises. I do hope he will soon tire of this.

•

We leave for the tropics in a light fall of snow. The traffic on Long Island is hellish, and if the plane had not been delayed we would have missed it. I say that the planes we travel in these days are a little like the buses that used to take the unemployed from city to city in the thirties. The air is bad, some of the seats are broken, there is a general atmosphere of disrepair, nomadism; and this is hyperbole. The fuselage looks like a tenement roof. We come out of the snowstorm into a hot night in Puerto Rico. The mixture of black and white seems to generate some sexual force. The powerful eroticism of travel—one travels with a hard-on. There are some prostitutes in the waiting room, including a youth in yellow trousers, his hands draped limply over his prick. He's not bad-looking. How did a boy like you get into a spot like this? Don't you want to marry, have children, breed dogs? Where would one take him, and what sort of performance would ensue? My curiosity proves my innocence. We fly farther south, and at two in the morning, in the harsh light of the airport, we seem singled out more by some force of judgment than by the wish to travel and see the world. We seem penitents. There is a country-club couple, bound, I guess, for the Hilton. His face is boyish and ravaged. She shakes her yellow mane girlishly. It is nearly three in the morning when we reach the inn.

•

I remember none of it clearly this morning. I cannot seem to summon
or recall the sea and the beach. The Caribbean is the color of the
Caribbean, and the sound of the waves is much less vehement, much
less resonant than the sound of the Atlantic. One walks on the coral
strand. Clink clink. The coral under one's sneakers clinks like hotel
china and small change. Golgotha. Clink clink. Fibula, tibia, brain,
kidney, and the bones of a thousand fingers. I do not snorkle, because
(I claim) I am unable to hold a tube in my mouth, and while this is
partly true, it is also true that I suffer from both claustrophobia and
vertigo. I read Graham Greene and sneak up from the beach at eleven
for a scoop of gin. They travel to the tropics and read Rex Stout. They
travel to the tropics to get a tan. The husband oils the wife. The wife
oils the husband. They stretch out in the sun. Ten minutes on one
side. Ten minutes on the other. They lie with their feet in the air to
get some color under the chin. One man has achieved an exceptional
shade of gold. His body—or what I see of it—is hairless, and comely.
His chest is unmuscular, and when he rounds his shoulders he has
small and fetching breasts, like the statues of Apollo. The face is not
much—darkened, I think, by vanity. Returning to the beach at dusk,
I find him with a towel looped around his neck like a skater's scarf.
Aha! Narcissus. Watching the sunset, I drop my trunks and get my
cock between her legs. We make out. We make out at sunset, make
out after lunch, make out before going to sleep. Once while I score she
holds a glass of ice water in her hand and does not spill a drop. This
is not a source of bitterness. This is to observe the invincibility of a
hard-on.

•

Dear Lord—who else?—keep me away from the bottles in the pantry.
Guide me past the gin and the bourbon. Nine in the morning. I suppose
I will succumb at ten; I hope to hold off until eleven.

•

I revert to the expedient of reading my own work as a sort of tran-
quillizer. It doesn't really hold my attention, but it does pass the time.
The pills do not seem strong enough, and I drink at eleven. However,
I take only one nip after dinner and sleep well. I dream a movie in full

color. It begins on a deceptively decorous note and then moves gradually into a bloody Bedouin war. The audience is rapt until the Bedouins leave the screen and behead all those in the front row. "Why, it's real!" the survivors scream as they run into the street. It was produced in Mexico City and was directed by a young woman named Juliet Morro, with whom I have coffee at a café. It is playing in New York at the Left Bank Cinema, on lower Fifth Avenue. There have been 742 performances.

•

Two scoops for the train, a scoop at the Biltmore, a scoop upstairs, one down—five in all, as well as a bottle of wine with lunch and brandy afterward. We rip off our clothes and spend three or four lovely hours together, moving from the sofa to the floor and back to the sofa again. I don't throw a proper hump, which disconcerts no one; I've always had to count on circumstances and luck; so it's all finger-fucking, sucking, tongue-eating, arse-kissing, bone-cracking embraces and earnest declarations of love, with my cock in her mouth and my tongue up her cunt. She is very beautiful. The figure is slender, but her arse is heavy and her breasts are big. "Oh, let me take your cock back to the Coast," she says. "I love your cock. I can't even think of you on the other side of the world without coming in my pants. I've never felt like this about anybody else."

•

I think fleetingly of the subtle effect computers have on our sense of life. We seldom see the consoles that arrange our taxes, bank deposits, salary checks, and medical prescriptions. They are mysterious, entrenched, and, as we know from experience, very often mistaken. A thousand dollars vanishes from the savings account; mysterious traffic summonses arrive from cities we have never visited; we are overcharged and undercharged; and, while we protest these errors, it is with a sense of helplessness. The computer is invincible, unseen, and antic; at times cretinous. It is a blow to our best sense of reality.

•

The substitution of physical pain and infirmity for melancholy seems not to have worked. I am simply saddled with both.

•

I must convince myself that writing is not, for a man of my disposition, a self-destructive vocation. I hope and think it is not, but I am
not genuinely sure. It has given me money and renown, but I suspect
that it may have something to do with my drinking habits. The excitement of alcohol and the excitement of fantasy are very similar.

•

For the next year, he did almost nothing but answer his mail and
enjoy a life of idleness in his pleasant country house in the hills above
the Hudson River. The only writing he did was to make an account of
his drinking. "First scoop at half past nine," he would write. "Held off
this morning until eleven-twenty-two." Sometimes the accounts were
more extensive. "Sat this morning in the parlor at half past nine," he
wrote, "reading the Sunday *Times*." Riots in California. Nudity on the
stage. Wanting a drink but determined not to mix one until Mary had
left the kitchen. I had decided on a gin-and-tonic. Her comings and
goings took more of my attention than the news in the paper did. Had
she made the beds? I went upstairs to see. She had. There were clothes
in the washing machine. When the machine had finished its cycle she
would probably hang the clothes on the line, giving me a chance to mix
my drink. Now she was arranging flowers in two vases. The vases
belonged in the library, and when the flowers were finished she might
take the vases upstairs, giving me a chance to slip into the pantry.
However, when the flowers were finished she left the vases on a table
and began to crack hard-boiled eggs. What was she doing this for? We
were going to the W.s' for lunch and had no use for hard-boiled eggs.
She went on shelling eggs while my thirst got more intense. By the time
the eggs were shelled, the washing machine had stopped. She took the
clothes out of the machine, and put them in a hamper. I was ready to
streak into the pantry, but she didn't hang the clothes on the line. She
then stepped into the parlor—on her way upstairs, I hoped—but she
then noticed a smear on one of the windowpanes, returned to the kitchen
for a rag and some window-washing stuff, and polished the dirty light.
She then returned to the kitchen and, to my absolute horror, unfolded
the ironing board. She seldom, if ever, irons, and this maneuver seemed
to me unfair. I supposed she was going to iron the wrinkles out of the
dress she would wear to lunch. This oughtn't to take more than five

minutes, but five minutes was more than I could wait, and in full view of my wife, and the world, I went into the pantry and mixed a drink. It was eighteen minutes to eleven.

•

On the screen four naked men appeared to be doing something to one another, although the scene was so badly lit that you couldn't be sure. Then the light increased, and there was no doubt about what was going on. A stranger seated on my right put his hand—accidentally, it seemed—on my knee, and I got up gracefully and moved to another part of the theatre. I wanted to avoid encouragement and scorn. On the screen the four naked men had paired off, and the scene appeared to be shot through the opening of a man's trousers. I thought then, but without nostalgia, of the movie theatres of my youth. In the small town where I grew up there was only one. It was called the Alhambra. It was not palatial, but there was a golden proscenium arch, and some plaster wreaths on the ceiling. My favorite movie was called "The Fourth Alarm." I saw it first one Tuesday after school and stayed on for the evening show. My parents were alarmed when I didn't come home for supper. On Wednesday I played hooky, went to the one-o'clock show, and was able to see the picture twice and get home in time for supper. I went to school on Thursday, but I went to the theatre as soon as school closed, and sat partway through the evening show. My parents must have called the police, because a patrolman came into the theatre and made me go home. I was scolded and I believe I cried. I was forbidden to go to the theatre on Friday, but I spent all day Saturday there, and on Saturday the picture ended its run. The picture was about the substitution of automobiles for horse-drawn fire engines. In some fictitious city there were four fire companies. Three of the teams had been replaced by engines, and the miserable horses had been sold to brutes. One team remained, but its days were numbered, and the men and the horses were very sad. Then suddenly there was a great fire in the city. One saw the first engine, the second, and the third race off to the conflagration. Back at the horse-drawn company things were even sadder. The men sat around the firehouse in an atmosphere of dejection. Then the fourth alarm rang—it was their summons—and they sprang into action, harnessed the team, and galloped across the city. They put out the fire, saved the city, and were given an amnesty by the mayor.

I would open my Lifesavers and wait for it to start all over again. It seemed that I couldn't get enough; but I could get enough of what was going on among the naked men, and I got up and left.

•

Yesterday my older son was married. I rang the church bell.

•

Veterans Day. The paper reports an unusual number of patriotic demonstrations, but the *Times* is noncommittal. I wish I could understand those men and women who feel Communism to be an acute threat to their way of life, their spirit. People who favor the war in Asia drive with their headlights on. Between here and Harmon half the cars have their lights burning. I find something menacing in this mute and anonymous means of communication. One takes a stand—makes a threat—but the face is never seen, and nothing, of course, is said. So we pass one another's dark lights and lights that burn—taking sides in a bloody war.

•

In *Esquire*, a piece on the New Homosexuality. I don't know what to make of it. The claim is that once guilt is overcome the eccentricities of the old-fashioned homosexual will be overcome. Men who love men will be manly and responsible citizens. They claim that an androgynous life can be completely happy, but I have never seen this. Drugs seem very important. The old-fashioned faggot with his dry Martinis is a goner, forgotten. There is something wonderful about being one's own man. This is not the part of a man that was written by one's father; it is a question of essence, self-esteem. The fact that I am fifty-eight years old may have something to do with my attitude, my lack of understanding. There may not be such a thing as a normal man, but there is something very close to it.

•

Into town on the 4:40. Night falls on the river. At Grand Central, crowds of commuters wait at the gates. They do not seem undone by death. They seem to be a reasonable, clean, and useful population, a little urgent and a little tired, but I think it would be a fatuous mistake to compare them to the population of Limbo. I walk the streets. Anxiety and perhaps *The New York Times* have built up in my mind a feeling that the city is sinister and dangerous, but tonight the couples that I see on their way to a restaurant or the theatre seem very happy. On Sixth Avenue there are two stores where you can buy colored photographs of naked men and women, displaying their genitals. One can see as much in many Italian cathedrals. It rains. The sound, the voice of New York for me is the sound of taxi horns reverberating off walls. It is not a sad sound, but it is far from cheerful.

•

What I think of as "the maldispositions" continues. This is the longest stretch I can recall. It began in Majorca early in July, and now, with snow expected, continues. Slammed doors, venomous remarks, a general attitude of revulsion and contempt. I think frequently of S., although this could be just another dream girl. She sleeps. She is beautiful. There is a wide hem to her nightgown. She is fragrant, graceful, intelligent. She wakes. Is it raining? Yes. Your hair is wet. I went out and closed the car windows. I kiss her and laugh. Did you get terribly wet? Not terribly. I dried myself off with a towel. I can't hear the waves. There aren't any. It's calm. It usually is in the rain. I'm going back to sleep. Good night, my love. Good night.

•

My older son seems seriously to have switched his allegiance from me to his father-in-law. This is no cause for feeling, merely something to be observed.

•

I board the 2:20. As we go through the tunnel the lights in the car flicker and go out. We make our way into the daylight, but the train seems to move haltingly. The uptown slums are being demolished—have been in this process for fourteen years. I am the sort of man who would regret the rats, broken toilets, and fire hazards of a cold-water tenement because its cabbalistic lintels were supported by rams' heads, scrolls, platforms, and other inventions. But the rectangular tenements that replace them have not a trace of invention. Their bleakness is absolute. No man has ever dreamed of a city of such monotonous severity, and there must be some bond between our houses and our dreams. The train makes its halting way as far as Hastings, where it seems to die. All the lights go out. The conductor and the engineer not only refuse to explain what has happened, they are rude. The train shows no signs of life at all; the lights, the ticking and kissing sounds are all gone. It is too dark to read, and the woman across the aisle from me shuts her paperback copy of "Grand Hotel." Our situation is mysterious, and our response seems to be complete passivity. I think of striking up a conversation, but there is no likely companion around. Would it be different in another country? I think not. I leave the haunted train and, with some other passengers, take a cab. An old man laments the death of the railroads. The trains break down regularly. How wonderful they were ten years ago: speedy, luxurious. Now the equipment is obsolete, the roadbeds are dangerous, the staff is surly. . . .

•

And look at poor W.B. in his liquor store shaped like a dark hallway, selling what he knows will be, six times out of ten, a means of death. He knows the symptoms as well as any doctor: the deepening flush, then a bleacher sunburn; the shaking hands; the desperate telephone calls—"Hey, Walt, could you have the taxi rush over a quart of gin? I don't happen to have any money in the apartment, but you know I'm always good for it." They were in many cases intelligent, courageous, and gallant, but they were headed straight for the cold-turkey ward of the county hospital.

•

Bill Faversham stepped into the bathroom to brush his teeth and found his wife, Martha, in the tub, but she had closed the shower curtains and was invisible. Bill, in a mood that was much more light-hearted than lewd, opened the curtains for a look at her breasts. They were, in a sense, his breasts; he had worshipped them, kissed them, clothed them, and taken them around the world. He parted the curtain innocently, as one might go to a window to see the sky. She gave him a look of pain that was withering, and sank deeper into the water so that nothing could be seen. He turned back to the washbasin. Cheerfulness was obviously his best target, and he banged away at this, knocking down a few of the travelling ducks; but a blow had been dealt, and dealt at an area of his spirit that was already lacerated. He went down to the living room, not so much wounded or angry as astonished at the traumatic and reverberative nature of his experience. He had no coherent memory for ecstasy or pain, but an acute experience of either was a sudden revelation of the sum of his memory. The present seemed like some modest, lighted table at which four people played Russian bank, but beyond them was some dark and cavernous backstage, hung with sandbags and the scenery for yesterday's garden and tomorrow's forest. The present claimed to be supreme, but the truth seemed to lie somewhere between the lighted card table and the cavernous wilderness.

The only light in the living room was the moon. The night was cold and so was the room. It was, or seemed to him, a cluttered room. Any taste for simplicity that Martha may have had seemed to have vanished as she approached her fifties, and every surface was covered with porcelain lions, sets of luster, pots of china flowers, agate paperweights, etc. It made him feel a stranger there. Then he decided to change his name. He had done this before. He was not Bill Faversham. Bill Faversham was flying over the Urals in an Aeroflot 707, a frightened little man sneaking drinks of vodka from a flask concealed in his jacket. He was Tom Brown, Farmer Brown's oldest son, a natural man, a little stupid perhaps, but a free spirit, genuinely loving. He was not Bill Faversham nor was this his house; it was merely a place he had stepped into to get out of the cold. He had no investment in the porcelain lions; he had no investment in the withering look of pain Martha had given him. I am Tom Brown, and this is a strange place where I have come in to spend the night.

The discovery, it seemed, of something invincible in himself, clean, free, and strong, was so strenuous that he threw out his arms and braced his back. "I do not live here," he said happily, ecstatically. "I do not live here, I do not live here, and my name is Tom Brown." Then he loped up the stairs, parted the shower curtain again, kissed his wife's breasts, and went to bed.

•

The contemptuous silence goes on for another day. We drive to a Chinese restaurant for dinner. Mary says nothing. I joke and talk with my son. Our jokes may be childish and banal, and I may be drunk, but this would hardly account for her formidable silence. The restaurant

is crowded, and I am pleased at the sight of families eating good food.
They are mostly families, large tables of parents, children, and grandchildren. Mary does not speak throughout the meal. Since I observe
the others, I wonder what the others would make of us. My son's face
is cheerful, his color is high. I may seem loud and drunk, but what
would they make of this haughty woman who does not speak during the
four-course dinner? She is thought to be good-looking—sometimes beautiful. Her clothing is fashionable and expensive. Why is it that she will
not speak to her husband, will not answer his questions, will not even
look in his direction? She serves herself and her son. She pointedly does
not serve her husband. He asks to be served, and if he is to be faulted
this is it. She pushes the serving dish in his direction, looking away.
She manages to make this simple gesture contemptuous. Have you ever
seen people like that in a restaurant? I mean, have you ever seen a man
and his wife come into a restaurant and the wife not speak a word during
the whole meal? She doesn't seem dreamy, or angry, or even sad, and
he seems not to mind terribly. He talks and jokes with the children.
But have you ever seen anything like that?

     She is silent on the trip home. I am angry, and I don't understand.
Sometimes I think I am being provoked to physical cruelty. Her father
once beat her cruelly, and I sometimes think she drifts back to this
scene. She does not treat all men with contempt. I saw her kissing D.
in the pantry a week ago. I think these flirtations—whatever—may be
some part of the wish to humiliate and destroy; but I may be wrong.
Anyhow, we return and she settles down to read the bound galleys of
a book sent to me (I claim) by a friend. I think of taking the book out
of her hand and tossing it into the brook. It is, after all, mine. However,
this is not, even drunkenly, my kind of thing. I watch TV with Federico.
When there is something funny I call her attention to it, but there is
no response. Since I think anger despicable, I decide to make a stab at
mending my fences with a kiss. I get neither the lip nor the cheek.
What I get is a feeling of revulsion as shocking as a charge of electricity.

     I may imagine all of this, of course, but I come away from my
attempted kiss with the feeling that I have brushed not against madness
but against obsceneness, wickedness, malice, and evil. I am shaken. I
fall asleep, and wake when she enters the bedroom. "Did you finish the
book?" I ask. "Yes." The reply is nearly inaudible. "Did you like it?"
She replies to this by closing the door and running her bath. These are

small matters, very small, really, and yet I cannot sleep. I go naked to
the dining room and sit in the dark, as I have done a hundred times
before. I cannot take a Seconal. I seem allergic to sleeping drugs. I
drink a little whiskey and think about mountains, streams, the back
streets of Rome. I sit in the dark until two or later and, feeling drowsy,
go back to sleep.

•

Assuming that there is some sort of absolution in recording the most
tedious and mistaken conduct, I will set down that the following took
place. The morning was unpleasant, and the few words spoken were
wounding. "Won't you at least let him finish a sentence?" That kind
of thing. I drink. That is a great help. It seems, in fact, to be the only
way I have of remaining relaxed. I am left alone after lunch, and I
wander through the rooms thinking how happy I am to be free of a
censorious presence. I will go to the B.s' for cocktails. I will play games
with A. But then I think I will do none of this. I am tired; I am tired
of these dreary social occupations. I am a man, a free man: I will drive
into New York, I will take a hotel room, I will screw H., and take S.
to the big dancing party. Pow. This is partly genuine enthusiasm, partly
gin. I sit in the yellow chair with a drink, seeming to be the object of
the attentions of two forces—stamina and inertia—represented by two
presences as subtle as the representation of good and evil in some comic
strip. I will go, I will liberate myself, I will relish life! I have another
drink to steel my nerves for the drive. It is late afternoon, and the snow
on the lawns has begun to turn from gold to blue.

The first thing is to write a note, and I do this. Then I must pack.
This takes, I think, another drink. Shirts, drawers, Seconal and Miltown, a brown suit for the seduction and a dark suit for the party. What
next? Call New York and reserve a room. But why go to all this trouble?
says the voice of Inertia. Why not go to the B.s' and have a drink in
front of their fire? Change, move, enjoy your freedom, says Stamina,
and I call New York and reserve a room. But what about dinner? It is
already too late to make a date, and I don't want to dine alone in a
hotel. Watching the light fail, I think that the traffic will be heaviest
at this hour. I am in no rush to get to the city. I put into the oven a
frozen serving of Salisbury steak with sauce, take the tires and the car
cover from the back of my car, have another pleasant drink, and then

eat my steak. Now night has fallen, and I am a little drowsy. Why not take a nap and leave for New York at around nine? I can walk the streets and go to bed early so that I will be particularly potent for H. after lunch. I lie down and fall into a deep—not to say drunken—sleep for an hour. Then I stir myself once more, carry my bag out to the car, write another note, fill my flask, and drink a little more, because it is a well-known fact that I cannot drive when I am sober. I start the car, find that the speedometer is broken and that I have no gasoline. I head for the nearest gas station—a few miles away—and observe that my vision is bad, my driving dangerous. I think this is because my head cold has weakened my alcoholic tolerance. I turn back at the gas station and drive home. I destroy the note, cancel the hotel reservation, unpack my toothbrush and my pills, undress, and climb into bed. I sleep soundly.

•

It is the morning of the day when I will see H. Mary's contemptuous and weary voice cannot reach me in any way, since I am the beloved of a young, beautiful, and passionate woman. I take three heavy scoops to relax for the train trip, although I'm not quite sure they take hold. On the train I sit beside a good-looking woman who seems appalled and terrified by my presence and perhaps by the fumes of gin that must roll off me. I hope to reassure her by reading the *Times* very carefully—including all the editorials, financial page, and sporting section. This seems to work, and a little past Yonkers we get into a pleasant, sympathetic conversation. I am early, and, like all countrymen who are early in the city, I begin to walk. I walk up to the Sixties, cut over to Fifth, have a drink, walk down to Forty-second Street, loiter in a bookstore, and finally beat my way back to the hotel. I have a head cold and am not sober. I go up to H.'s room.

It is not as good as it was a year ago. I somehow—hooch and a head cold—can't get quite on the beam. She's left her husband, and had, I guess, several affairs with celebrated cocksmen, and her infatuation for my thighs seems to have waned, if not died. She is still terribly pretty, and her figure is astonishingly beautiful, the breasts high and full, the waist very small. She is a year older, and I think I can see this in her face. It is a year during which she worked very hard, and there are new lines around her eyes. Her shine is a little dim. Her hair is a curious shade of pink, some hairdresser's triumph. It cannot be caressed ardently, and I dislike this, but I don't say so. I am very happy in her company but not, as I was last year, ecstatic. She laughs at my jokes and says that I look much better than I did. Stoned and with a runny nose, I don't see how this could be possible. We lunch and return to the room, but the kissing is halfhearted, and when I suggest a fuck she says gently that she somehow doesn't feel like it. The fish she ate for lunch . . . I say it doesn't matter. She is expecting a friend at three, and before that, after a display of drunken foolishness, I kiss her goodbye.

On the train home I sit beside a drunken salesman, who calls everyone by his first name and who is marketing a portable oxygen mask. He urges me to try it, and I do—with no appreciable effects. I think this terribly funny, but when I reach home and start to tell my story Mary says, "I would like to hear your funny story, but I have to go to the bathroom." I don't terribly mind the statement or even the fact, but I do mind that it seems to display a kind of feeling that I don't understand. I talk freely about H. I see no reason—and this may be my stupidity—why I shouldn't.

•

Palm Sunday, and I do not go to church to receive that leaf, or frond, that is meant to bless my house. Last year I was in a plaster cast; this year I am on the ropes. On the evening of our anniversary it seemed as though things might be as they had been, for better and for worse. It was the best hour we've had in months. But things are dim in the morning, and grow dimmer, I think, as the day passes, until by late afternoon Mary has stopped speaking altogether. I wash a Seconal down with whiskey and check out.

•

So New York–Fairbanks–Tokyo–Seoul and off into the country of love. Why should it be so like the seasons—a cruel winter and a clement spring? Loving and being loved, I hear the mourning doves. It has been more than a year since their singing—billing—has meant anything but regret, bitterness, and mystification.

What, then, do I remember vividly? The fishbone pines in Fairbanks. This outpost. The light in the sky is gray, but there has been no diminishment in its brilliance for fifteen hours. The faculty wives from Akron, wearing dead flowers and carrying bottles of hometown water.

What a waste of time to ridicule them. They are out to see the world, and what is wrong with that? They will have some excitement, pleasure, a dossier of colored photographs, and diarrhea, athlete's foot, anti-American riots, and the peril and fear of sudden death in the Bering Sea. The smog in Tokyo obscures the city and its mountain. The cabdriver wears a surgical mask. "Made in Japan" was a watchword of my youth. Almost everything for sale in that paradise—the five-and-ten-cent store—was made in Japan. Goldfish, toys, screwdrivers, can openers, beads were all made in Japan. That city, bombed and firestormed, is long gone, but on street corners you sometimes see an old house with curved eaves that was made in Japan.

•

Whatever happened to Johnny Cheever? Did he leave his typewriter out in the rain? Anyhow, he was never known as Johnny by anyone but his friends C. and L., who changed all names to suit them. Eddie, Neddie, Howie, Robbie, and even Petey. Did he write a very clean story? A story about love? A gray day, rather like dusk at ten. J. appears at the pool. He has a kind of looks or beauty that, this afternoon, seems to set him apart from the rest of us. His teeth—their number, size, and whiteness—seem false, although I've been told that they are not. There is a little gray in his Neapolitan curls, and a small but definite bald spot. The features are splendid, the manner is beautiful but manly. He tries, he has in fact been coached, to conceal his lack of education. A rich woman, no longer young, would dream of such a consort. I know him to be genuinely loving, a good fuck, and good company, but he seems, unlike the rest of us, to have an appearance that can be merchandised.

•

Thunder wakes me at midnight. I go from room to room, closing the doors and windows. A bolt strikes close to the house. I smell cordite. What will we find split in the morning? The birch, the tulip tree, the ash? The dogs are frightened, the lights go out. I mount my beloved, and off we go for the best ride in a long time.

•

I cannot describe the Mass without describing my friend, and I cannot describe him in these pages. He was genuinely volatile, eccentric, capable of great physical and intellectual velocity. He never spoke to me of his conversion to the Church of Rome. I cannot guess at his motives. He is buried outside the gates of that city, and the Mass yesterday was performed without his remains and without his widow, who is in London. The architecture of the church was contemporary and highly decorative along lines that in their conspicuous simplicity seemed Oriental to me. What I mean to say is that the usual threadbare iconography of Christendom—the worn carpets, the tarnished vigil lights, the vestments from Brussels—were all gone. Behind the chancel was a rotunda of pale-yellow marble. All the colors or the lack of color was what one finds in a Shinto shrine. An enormous figure in an attitude of blessing hung behind the altar. The three priests faced the congregation. One wore white robes, one's robes were ornamented with fishes, and the third's with a new moon and a cross. In spite of all this elegance, the architect had miscalculated acoustically, and I couldn't hear the Epistle, the Gospel, or the eulogy. The Mass was in English, but I thought it beautiful—a full choir and organ thundering in with the responses. But what one thinks is what it must have cost—one sees Mr. F. on the telephone talking with the priest. "He was a very brilliant associate and we would like a suitable ceremony." "Organ?" "Yes." "A full choir will come to a thousand." "Money, under the circumstances, is of course no consideration, and we will of course make a substantial contribution to the church." "Would you like one, two, or three priests?" "Three, please."

We were a small congregation—really a handful—but he was never a man with a circle of friends. We seemed outmaneuvered by the richness of the church, and surely we were outnumbered by the choir.

•

Happy, happy, happy. I spend the afternoon boiling lobsters, swim, suffer a mild seizure of gin nastiness, plan to take Federico fishing, but we can find no plugs, and the bait store is closed. I see S. tomorrow, but, since Mary is yielding, I have no wish or need for clipping and kissing behind pantry doors. A brilliant day.

•

So we see once more the serene novelist whose antics have bored us for ten years. He is left alone from noon until dark and goes to pieces.

He reads, misreads, drinks, snoozes, repeats vulgar and stupid anecdotes at great length, and is contemptible. I must do better.

•

E. comes over, and we tell each other the stories of our lives; two men of fifty-eight in an empty house. The talk drifts toward money. This does not annoy me as it did. I remember little of what was said. Beautiful, beautiful D. is now sixty years old and proud of the fact that she has been screwed by at least a thousand men. I think of swimming, but I am lame from pushing the mower—this is unusual—and feel tired. The sulfa drug I take seems soporific. I eat a cheese sandwich and a piece of melon in the twilight, take a bath, and go to bed before the stars are out. I wake—I don't know the hour. I am soaked with sweat and shiver convulsively at any touch of the night air; but there is some serenity to this condition. I am sick and I am calm. I dream that some maid is driving nails into the highboy. I explain to her that it is three hundred years old (a lie). "Well, it's about time you threw it away," she says. I see my family—Susie, Rob, Ben, Linda, Mary, and Federico—and how much I love them, how perfect is my contentment! This seems to be not love but a perfect equation in which light is exchanged. And, half asleep, I think I see some way of getting back into my work. It is the old image of spatial arrangements—not tables and chairs but abstract form. The light is sombre but not dim, not soft, a strong, pure gray light. By moving the forms, by changing the spaces between them, something seems to be accomplished. A voice from somewhere says, This is neither erotic nor spiritual. I see a rock pool in Maine, filled at high tide. I wonder if there is any erotic cause for my excitement. I think not. The pool seems beautiful and serene.

•

Make love in the meadow; me not peerless. I scar my naked hip on a wild rose.

•

Thunderstorms, polished air; the light seems honed, buffed, and, late in the day, strikes from a low angle. I swim at around four, but the poignance of a swimming pool in September seems to have lost its legitimacy for me. The pool is real enough and is the crux, the truth of a humid afternoon. There are leaves in the water these days. I am the last swimmer. The wind in the leaves is highly vocal. The light is pure and very elegiac. I enjoy swimming at this time of year. The water is in the sixties. The stones are warm in the sun and I lie naked on them. Happy, happy.

•

A story by Hemingway, most of which involves a young man's four-hour fight with a thousand-pound broadbill. Just as they try to gaff the catch the line breaks. There is courage, endurance, and blood, and the young man's character is formed in the rigors of the contest. There is the old four-stress cadence—"We lived that year in a house on a hill"— sometimes beautiful and sometimes monotonous. I remain mystified by his suicide.

•

The place where they all went. This could be a dream. Who are they? Old girlfriends; barmen; barbers; the friends you make on beaches, on boats, in the army; maids; gardeners; clerks; salesmen; backgammon, football, softball, and bridge partners; all those for whom you felt intensely, briefly, and who have vanished, who, for all you know, might be dead. They are not. They live, those hundreds, on a key between the inland waterway and the Gulf of Mexico, a place that has to be reached by boat. Why have they, so to speak, given up; why have they retired; why have they stopped mixing drinks, cutting hair, cracking jokes, writing books and poetry, teaching school, meeting lovers, dancing, raking leaves; why have they stepped out of that landscape where they seemed to belong? They don't seem to know, or if they do they seem unwilling to say so. They are not terribly old or infirm. They are mostly in their early fifties. Their smiles are still friendly, a little retiring these days, but they still have the gift of making a most casual exchange—setting a drink on the bar—seem immediate, friendly, and absorbing, the citizens of an easygoing planet. Why did they all go away?

•

Rain in the night. Three A.M. Very fucky but no cigar. At nine we go up the hill to see the night-blooming cereus perform.

•

Today gloomy and humid. I walk the dogs in a heavy rain. Water lilies grow at the edge of the pond. I want to pick some and take them home to Mary. I decide that this is foolish. I am a substantial man of fifty-eight, and I will walk past the lilies in a dignified manner. Having made this decision, I strip off my clothes, dive into the pond, and pick a lily. I will be dignified tomorrow.

•

My routine has been to write a page or so on "Artemis"—no more—and mix a drink at ten. This means, since I cannot write and drink, that my working day is very brief. Now, for the first time in more than a month, I have a desk, a lamp, and a place where I can keep my papers. I'm back in a summery country.

•

There would not be much point in describing these last days. On Tuesday we were lovers and on Wednesday warriors. I am told that I am an insane shit, that even when I am loving I am a shit. She is planning to leave, which will be the second time this week. What I will forget and never mention is what I heard at dinner. "What is worse for a woman: to marry a man with a bad prostate or to marry a homosexual?" But where does this venom originate? I might say that she dislikes men, but I know this isn't so. She hates me much of the time, but naturally I can't understand why anyone should hate me.

•

I spend all of the daylight hours immersed in my morbid and clinical obsession. I seem toward dusk to muster a little reason. Mary goes into town to a party, and Federico and I have a pleasant evening together. Should beautiful women read telephone directories on TV I would watch them. Mary returns and I kiss her good night, which is a step, however small, in the right direction.

•

So I think work, work, work—that will be the solution to all my problems. Work will give meaning to my unhappiness. Work will give reason to my life. Twenty minutes later my mind strays to the gin bottle, and I will presently follow.

•

When I get the mixture right, as I seem to have done last night, my gratitude is immense, my gratitude is spiritual. Work, work, work, I say, love, love, love, and I can rewrite the first of "Artemis" or sketch in the remaining narrative. Thinking of the booze fight, I seem willing to settle for this battlefield rather than go to a dry-out farm. It is a battlefield, and I've been advancing and retreating for fifteen years. The last weeks have seen many losses, but today the enemy seems quiet or occupied on some other front.

•

I am disappointed in "Artemis," disappointed and at times frightened, but I think, later in the day, that I can bring it off. It lacks density and enthusiasm, and my search for another method, a new method, has not been successfully completed. Keep trying.

•

The first word I hear on Christmas day in the morning is "shit." I think perhaps I should have an affair with a man. I will go to X and say, "I'll let you have me," and he will laugh and say, "You're twenty years too late. You might, you just might have passed twenty years ago, but now you're nothing but a potbellied old jerk."

•

And so we celebrate the birth of Christ. Let man receive his King.

THE SEVENTIES AND
THE EARLY EIGHTIES

The first day of the new year. No toothache, and I wake feeling very happily horny. I trust the year will end this way.

We walk to the F.s', where we are shown home movies of the Cairo bazaar and where much that is said seems to have been said before. My little camera is my memory, etc. Later, just before dark, I go to see S., a pleasant woman, with an open fire, who gives me whiskey. A drunken scene, for which I am heartily sorry.

I claim again that the Sunday *Times* derails me. Shovel snow, walk the dogs over the hill. Mary's sister calls and when I say she's in Chappaqua she says, "Oh, I'm terribly sorry. Did they let her come home for Christmas?" "Chappaqua," I say, "is the next village." "Oh," says she, "I thought it was a rest home."

•

Drinking with R. and S. and M., I seem to glimpse—no more—the fact that I can be difficult, ungainly, prone to flare up at trifling misunderstandings. I think of my brother, examine what I remember of his conduct and misconduct, since the end of his marriage resembled in some ways mine. He drank too much, and so do I, although I will not end up in a hospital. He seemed morbidly sensitive to any sort of discrimination. I remember his stamping off the playing field. When I asked him what was wrong he said that P. was cheating. We were playing touch football, bluff was half the game. Sorehead. I trust I don't do this. He would punish his wife by refusing to speak to her for a week or two. He merely punished himself, of course. We have the same blood, the same memories, and make, I suppose, the same mistakes. Who, after all, is that man who puts a dime in the lock of the public toilet and in this privacy drinks from a flask of vodka? It is I. When? Last

month, last year, six years ago. I seem to have changed more than the
airport. The imitation orange drink still geysers in a sort of glass show-
case. The coffee is weak. The cock drawn on the toilet door seems a
size smaller than it did last time. My hair is gray.

Are these the accents of contempt or is this my morbid sensibility?
For example, I mix drinks and ask her to join me. "I have to wash the
spinach," she says. The voice strikes me as unnatural, unwarm. I do
not, of course, check on the truth of this. Once I said, "Let's fuck,"
and she said, "I have to find the baking potatoes." "I'll find the potatoes,"
I said, and I did, but when I returned to the bedroom she had dressed.
Saturday night, I suggested again that she join me. I want someone to
talk with, but I also feel that the sound of conversation might relax my
son. Hours pass when the only voices one hears are electronic. To this
invitation she says, "I have to go to the bathroom." "Well, won't you
join me after you've been to the bathroom?" I say. She does, but she
holds a book in front of her face. I talk about Lorca, whose poetry she
is reading. "I will not be lectured about a book you have not read," says
she, leaving the room. I did not intend to lecture her, but perhaps I
mistook my tone of voice. Later—and I may now be as my brother was,
moved in the stumbling and ungainly way of gin, half deaf, half blind,
responding to some blow that was dealt so far in the past it can't be
remembered—"I won't listen to your shit." The raised voice will be
heard by my son, and my good intentions have come to nothing. I climb
another flight of stairs and watch something asinine on TV.

She is, to say the least, laconic this afternoon. At dusk, she takes
the dog for a walk, the first in months. She returns at dark. She is
excited. "I saw Josephine, I saw Josephine for the first time since
Christmas, and I didn't have an apple or some sugar for her." Josephine
is a lonely and unridden horse, owned by the superintendent in the
next place. Now it is dark and cold, and Josephine's corral is perhaps
a mile away. Mary takes an apple and some sugar and goes off into the
winter night. Can I, having dived into the pond in October to pick some
water lilies, claim that she is eccentric? I am pleased to see that she is
moved and excited, but there is an unpleasant trace of skepticism in
my thinking. Later, on TV, a polar bear is murdered. "They've shot
the mother polar bear!" she cries; and she cries, she sobs. "They've
shot the mother polar bear!" And I think that perhaps I should go on
TV, that if I approached her through the tube on the shelf above the
sink I might win her interest and her affection, but I would have to be

disguised as a mother polar bear, or some other wild, innocent, and
wronged animal.

●

I think of my father, but nothing is accomplished. The image of
him is an invention, not a memory, and an overly gentle invention.
There was his full lower lip, wet with spit; his spit-wet cigarette; his
hacking cough; the ash on his vest; and the shabby clothes he wore,
left to him by dead friends. "Let's give Fred's suits to poor Mr. Cheever."
I find in some old notes that my mother reported that he had, just before
his death, written a long indictment of her—as a wife, a mother, a
housekeeper, and a woman. I never saw the indictment. I suppose,
uncharitably, that the effect on her would have been to fortify her self-
righteousness. She had worked so hard to support a helpless old man,
and her only reward was castigation. Sigh—how deep were her sighs.
I have no idea of what their marriage was like, although I suspect that
he worshipped her as my brother worshipped his choice and as perhaps
I have worshipped mine. In my brother's case there was, I think, that
rich blend of uxoriousness in which praise has a distinct aftertaste of
bitterness, not to say loathing. I think that Mary was wounded years
before I entered her life, and who is this ghost whose clothes I wear,
whose voice I speak with; what were the cruelties of which I am accused?
She may look for another lover; I certainly do. Are we, lying in our
separate beds and our separate rooms, only two of millions or billions
who wake a little before dawn each morning thinking hopefully that
surely there is some man or woman who would be happy to lie at our
sides? Happy for cheerful kissing, fucking, jokes, the day to come. I
suppose we outnumber the felicitous by millions, and I must say that
had I been given a loving and uncomplicated woman I might very well
have run.

●

The terrifying insularity of a married man and woman, standing
figuratively toe to toe, throwing verbal blows at each other's eyes and
genitals. Their environment is decorous, a part of their culture. The
clothes they wear are suitable for this part of the world, this time of
year, this income bracket. There are flowers (hothouse) on the table
(inherited). Children sleep or lie awake in upstairs bedrooms. They
seem as well rooted and native to this environment as the trees on the

lawn, but at the height of their quarrel they seem to stand on some crater of the moon, some arid wilderness, some Sahara. Their insularity is incomprehensible. This is an abandoned place.

•

I read the three stories and don't much like them. Phony modesty, perhaps. I've never much liked my work. The point is not to count my losses but to exploit what remains. I pick up "Crime and Punishment" and exclaim with pleasure over the opening sentence. Halfway down page 3 I close the book and watch TV. So the great books drop from our hands. Skating, I swing my arms, swing back happily into my youth, my childhood. The black ice on Braintree Dam, through which you could see the grasses. The instant the sun went down, the ice made a sound like cannon. And I think of the green valley of the Rorty and the hum of wild bees in the hall of the ruined castle. The sound was so loud you could hear it from the banks of the stream. I was thankful that I had heard nothing so romantic earlier in life. Mary swam in the stream, and the water seemed to magnify the size of her backside. My knees buckled.

•

Palm Sunday. Federico and I go to church. During the years that I've said my prayers here the priest's hair has turned white and his eyeglass prescription has been strengthened. J.L. smells of hair oil and toothpaste, a clash of scents. S. seems not beautiful, not at all, but she seems this morning to remind one powerfully of how beautiful she must have been thirty years ago. I remember, years ago, that she cried during the service. Why? The priest, a pleasant fellow, embraces me. I put the palm frond behind the clock, and my house seems truly blessed. I think of the swan, the gorilla, and other monogamous species. It does seem possible on this splendid afternoon that a man and a woman can love each other passionately until death do them part. A lovely hour in bed. Thank God, thank God, thank God, is what I say on waking. Thank God.

•

That voice in the dark that gives me so much advice says, "You will not be as great as Picasso, because you are an alcoholic."

I have a homosexual dream, which deals muchly with the spirit. I do not know in whose arms I lie; I know only that he will take care of me. He will pay the bills, the taxes, balance the checking account, and drive the car through the storm. "Were you lovers?" she asked him. "I wouldn't use that word," he said. "It was more like an improvised contact sport, scored or punctuated by ejaculations."

It was two or a little later. He was woken by his wife, who was crying in her sleep. A heavy rain was falling. She called a man's name three times: "Matthew, Matthew, Matthew." Was this in love or anger, and who was Matthew? He knew two Matthews, but neither of them seemed threatening. She went on sobbing, and he thought how puerile was his concept of a woman. He had reduced this continent of memory and longing into a pussywussy, a yummy snatch. The loudness of the rain woke her. "You were crying," he said. "Yes," she said, "I had a nightmare." She moved away from him and fell asleep again.

•

I drink gin and read some stories of mine. There is the danger of repetition. Walking in the woods, I heard a man shouting, "Love! Valor! Compassion!" I followed the voice until I saw him. He was standing on a rock shouting the names of virtues to no one. He must have been mad. The difficulty here is that I wrote that scene ten years ago. Oh-ho.

•

The hour between five and six is my best. It is dark. A few birds sing. I feel contented and loving. My discontents begin at seven, when light fills the room. I am unready for the day—unready to face it soberly, that is. Some days I would like to streak down to the pantry and pour a drink. I recite the incantations I recorded three years ago, and it was three years ago that I described the man who thought continuously of bottles. The situation is, among other things, repetitious. The hours between seven and ten, when I begin to drink, are the worst. I could take a Miltown, but I do not. Is this the sort of stupidity in which I used to catch my brother? I would like to pray, but to whom—some God of the Sunday school classroom, some provincial king whose prerogatives and rites remain unclear? I am afraid of cars, planes, boats, snakes, stray dogs, falling leaves, extension ladders, and the sound of the wind in the chimney; Dr. Gespaden, I am afraid of the wind in the chimney. I sleep off my hooch after lunch and very often wake feeling content once more, and loving, although I do not work. Swimming is the apex of the day, its heart, and after this—night is falling—I am stoned but serene. So I sleep and dream until five.

•

It seems to me extraordinary that Mary should have summered here every summer of her life; that here is a place, a hill, a dozen simple cottages, and a mountain view that she can return to and find, at least in spirit, unchanged. The famous gardens are dead and so is the gardener. A few roses bloom, choked with weeds, and the three greenhouses have lost some of their panes from the weight of snow, but who any longer wants catalogues of ruin, who any longer studies the sadness of fallen greenhouses? The mysterious spirit of the place—I think it mysterious—remains. There is here and there Charlie's violin music, Bertha's second year German Grammar, moldy copies of the *Vassarian*, and Grandpa's telescope. Things of the past outnumber the new toaster, the new coffee machine, and the new refrigerator. Walking up from the beach, we are unique as one can only be in the summer. Who are they? They are the W.s, and everybody else is less secure, intelligent, and interesting. The cottages are simple frame buildings. Planks are laid on the rafters, and the shingle nails stick through the ceiling. The electric lines are naked and black and are strung through the rafters with porcelain insulators. I wake at night and hear the rain on the shingles. I have not heard this for years. The roof not only receives the rain—there are leaks here and there—it seems to amplify the sound, and with some erotic or infantile thrill I hear the sound increase and louden. Now the storm passes over, the wind blows, and water showers onto the roof. I am three years old.

Thirty years ago, when we were courting, I used to leave the guesthouse, where everyone seemed asleep, and walk, naked, through the woods to this cottage, where we made love. Thirty years later, I still want to make love, but I am given no encouragement and my drive is not great enough to overwhelm the few bitter things that are said.

•

Is Halloween as a masquerade confined to this part of the world? I don't recall it in Massachusetts. A rainy night. Groups of children wander along the edge of the road, disguised as skeletons, animals, and there is even a fairy princess. A boy wears a cape, and a headdress of oak leaves. He must have an artistic mother. The children's only uniformity is that they all carry large shopping bags for the candy they will be given. At the station I give a ride to a stranded nun. "I will say a special prayer for you," says she. The train seems to be making its last journey.

I think, yesterday morning, that I can bring it off: I mean a book. Try, try.

•

New York, Moscow, Tbilisi, Leningrad, Moscow, New York. I have the jet blues as well as the booze fight. It is not that I have difficulty recalling the trip. It is that I cannot always give my recollection significance. A wicked man, asleep on a 707 halfway across the Atlantic, seems a figure of the purest innocence. The stale sandwiches in the London in-transit lounge. We go to the Bolshoi for one of those old-fashioned vaudeville performances—an orchestra, a recitation, a mezzo-soprano. I nearly fall asleep. Waking before dawn, I have the traveller's blues. If there is a knock on the door shall I jump out of the window? There are no exits, fire escapes, or stairs in the Ukraine, and in case of fire we will roast. I drink vodka for breakfast, and we fly to Tbilisi. The first feast is with a family, and all the toasts stress this. The oldest man is toasted first, then the youngest. I find this very moving. The next feast is in the mountains near the Turkish border. I see two women walking along the road with bunches of autumn leaves. Are they going to make medicinal tea or are they going to put the leaves in a vase on a table? Geese, pigs, cows, and sheep wander over the road. A bus collides with a bull. We come to the center of the province, a place of the most outstanding bleakness. This is what Russian literature and Russian song are about. In the distance are the mountains covered with snow. It is dusk in the corridors of the headquarters of the Central Committee. The clocks are broken. The toilet is smeared with shit and urine. In the main square there is a statue of Lenin and there is a cow. So we drive up into the mountains for our feast. The next feast is at the N.s', where Mrs. N. spills wine on the tablecloth. When we reach Leningrad it is 3 P.M., dusk. The city this time seems shabby and depressing. The Winter Palace badly needs a coat of paint. We have a quarrel on the banks of the Neva, the only quarrel during this trip. I love my son so intensely that it amounts to a capillary disturbance. I also loved his brother, but that was different. We rush around Leningrad, dine at the Europa, where I find the dances depressing. Why is this? I think the tall woman with the short man has on her face a look of implacable sexual discontent. He seems to be giving her a dry fuck. Is this because my bladder is inflamed with vodka? We go to the opera, and hook the midnight train. The Kremlin in the morning. The disinfected atmosphere of most offices, except for the shoeshine machine. Our guide seems thrown into life with a more desirable velocity than I enjoy. He is definitely very engaging; definitely engaged. There is a cast in his right eye that makes him seem irresistible. I think that I may faint. The table seems to swim.

The Winter Palace at six. A dark night on the Neva. Snow. Will I have vertigo on the grand staircase, as I once did in Washington? I want a drink, a cigarette, a friend, a more intimate source of light and heat. I think of myself sitting on the B.s' sofa with a second or third drink, chatting merrily with Mrs. X in French. Now I experience a terrifying sense of nothingness. Would such a life be tolerable? Would I not cut my throat? Is this what my friends in the prison experience? So we drive back through the snow to the hotel, where I drink half a glass of vodka and dress for the opera.

Why is it so difficult for me to bring into focus the image of a young man with thick eyelashes on the plane from Tbilisi? Is this a temperamental infirmity, a national trait, a sort of neurosis? Why, watching some kilted pipers crossing a bridge in Ireland, did I feel that my life was passing by? What is this unhappy mystery?

The flight back from Moscow is painful. A gray day. If I feel well enough tomorrow I must do the eight stories.

•

In town with D. His 65th birthday. The face is strong, his gray hair is long. We do not mention his remarkable wife, who choked to death during lunch a month ago. His mistress has called him in Australia and asked him to marry her, and I suppose he will. The barbershop at the Biltmore has been cut in half, and there are only three barbers on the job. Do people get their hair cut elsewhere or don't they get it cut at all? One used to have to wait, reading copies of *The Tatler*. What is the significance of a dying barbershop? The barbers are all old friends, and we talk in Italian. I spend a dollar in tips for being whisk-broomed and drink a Martini at the bar, where there is a new, and more attractive, painting of a nude. The face seems unusually sensitive. But as I walk up Madison Avenue the city escapes me. What has happened to this place where I used so happily to pound the sidewalks? Where has my city gone, where shall I look for it? In the Playboy Club, the Century Club, the Princeton Club, or the Links? In the steam room at the Biltmore, in L.'s panelled apartment, in the skating rink, in the Park, in the Plaza, on the walks where someone behind me makes tonguing noises with his or her mouth? I don't look. I know the city well, why does it not know me? A pair of well-filled boots, pretty legs, a tossed head. A restaurant where all the lights are pink, and so my hands are pink, and pink is the face of my friend. Everybody is pink. Fifteen or twenty men stand at the urinal in Grand Central. Their looks are solicitous, alert, sometimes wistful. They use the polished marble as a glass for pickups, and most of them are fondling or pulling their various-sized and -colored cocks. Why does the sight of fifteen or twenty men jerking off seem more significant than the string music in the Palm Court? One young and attractive man, the point of contact concealed by a raincoat, is making an accelerated jerking, as if he was approaching juice time. These are the darkest days of the year, and when the 3:40 pulls out of the tunnel into the Bronx it is nearly dark, although very few lights burn in the new housing developments. Perhaps everyone is still at work. By the time we reach the river, it is dark, and the only water traffic is barges and tugs. When I was younger I would wonder about the tug crews, wonder about what they would have for supper. I no longer much care. In the early dark the barges seem like mangrove islands—shoal water—you could wreck your boat. Three men behind me are talking loudly about the collapse of the government, the railroads, the U.N. Is this really the end of a world, as they seem to think it is? The men beside me seem so gored and emasculated by time that I look away. One has no gray in his hair, so I suppose he is rather young. His face is finely lined, rather like a woman's. He opens his briefcase busily, but it contains nothing but a printed brochure. Will such a weary face be welcomed anywhere? The face seems incapable of any sensual provocation or response. But when it is time for him to leave he jauntily slaps on a sealskin hat with a bright feather cockade and braces his shoulders in his raincoat. He's ready for the next round. I wanna go home, I wanna go home. I've lunched and had my hair cut, and now I am exhausted and I wanna go home.

•

My daughter says that our dinner table is like a shark tank. I go into a spin. I am not a shark; I am a dolphin. Mary is the shark. Etc. But what we stumble into is the banality of family situations. As for Susie, she makes the error of daring not to have been invented by me, of laughing at the wrong times and of speaking lines I have not written. Does this prove I am incapable of love, or can love only myself?

•

I read "Bullet Park," which is an extract of my most intimate feelings, and wonder why it should have antagonized Broyard. Is there some discernible falling off, some trace of my struggle with alcohol and age? It is a struggle, but I have come through before, and pray that I will bring it off again.

•

In the middle of Sunday afternoon I think that perhaps my dishevelled and unpunctual muse will return. I seem to stand above the characters at hand as if they were pawns on a chessboard. Chess, however, is a game I never learned to play. My mind approaches some unsavory matters, and I put Serkin on the record player and seem to enter into some community of accomplished men, who are passionately concerned with their deepest intuitions about love and death. The music, especially the Schubert, sounds like a powerful narrative. I see the stream, the Roman bridge, the leaves on the trees, the flaxen-haired woman leaning from her casement window. The dialogues are much more forceful and moving than any dialogue in any of the books on my table. I would like the story to be called "Glad Tidings," but I'm not sure where I go from there.

•

It seems today that all I can write is letters. I am too shaken to take the car to the garage. I think of P. inviting me drunkenly to take a nap in his room. What was intended, and are these fleeting hints at erotic tenderness between men natural? What men have I desired? A stranger in a shower in Guam twenty-five years ago, who seemed so comely and so natural that I felt disenfranchised. What did I desire? Is this some force of self-love?

•

My incantation has changed. I am no longer sitting under an apple tree in clean chinos, reading. I am sitting naked in the yellow chair in the dining room. In my hand there is a large crystal glass filled to the brim with honey-colored whiskey. There are two ice cubes in the whiskey. I am smoking six or seven cigarettes and thinking contentedly about my interesting travels in Egypt and Russia. When the glass is empty I fill it again with ice and whiskey and light another cigarette, although several are burning in the ashtray. I am sitting naked in a yellow chair drinking whiskey and smoking six or seven cigarettes.

•

An interview. A young woman. Her eyes are nice, and her figure is fine, but she was not quite the right flavor. I didn't make a pass; I didn't even kiss her. I nag myself with the usual questions and come up with the usual answers. Early and happily to bed. On with the blue skies.

•

Good Friday. No mourning doves sing; no bells ring.

•

I've put it down before, and I'll put it down again, but when I remember my family I always remember their backs. They were always indignantly leaving places, and I was always the last to go. They were always stamping out of concert halls, sports events, theatres, restaurants, and stores. "If Koussevitzky thinks I'll sit through that . . ."; "That umpire is a crook"; "This play is filthy"; "I didn't like the way that waiter looked at me"; etc. They saw almost nothing to its completion, and that's the way I remember them: heading for an exit. It has occurred to me that they may have suffered terribly from claustrophobia and disguised this madness with moral indignation.

In the summer my father used to play three or four holes of golf before breakfast, before he went to work. I sometimes went along with him. The links were only a short walk from the house. The course was set above the river, and from the first fairway he played you could see down to Travertine and the blue water of the bay. Early one morning, he noticed something hanging from a tree in the woods beside the fairway. He thought it was perhaps some clothing left there by the lovers who used the woods at night. As he walked down the grass, he saw it was the body of a man. The face was swollen and contorted, but he recognized his old friend Harry Dobson. He cut down the body with a pocketknife and called Dr. Henry from the nearest house, although he should have called the police. He gave away his clubs that afternoon and never played golf again.

·

In my dreams or reveries—I'm not sure which—I walk along the carriage drive at Yaddo with a man about whom I know absolutely nothing beyond the fact that he wears a dark-blue cashmere suit. He bumps into me in a suggestive and amorous way, and I do not protest. He puts his arm around my shoulders and says how much he likes me, and I say that I like him. We disappear into the woods. I'm not quite sure what happens, but it's profoundly gratifying. We dine at different tables, keenly and happily aware of each other. There is nothing flamboyant. We observe the force of scandal. We approach his room by different stairways and spend the night together. I also imagine us holding hands in a movie. Since, as I see it, nothing of the sort could possibly take place in fact, what room has it in my sleep? There is no such man. With the exception of Endymion, the only homosexuals I've seen there aroused my vigorous uninterest. X was silly and narcissistic, Y had a dental plate that clacked, and Z spit when he spoke. Their sexual tastes seemed to be the product of vanity, stupidity, and bad luck. But dreaming gives me the license to invent this anonymous and manly spirit in a cashmere suit. Is this narcissism; is this some impediment of my nature, put there by my unhappiness with my father? How the light of day, the fire, bolsters and hones my ego. With my eyes closed in sleep I seem to be a very different man. The moral quality of light.

·

The incantation this morning is that I can cure myself. The problem is, can I? Is this thing bigger than either of us, Mabel?

•

Wake at three in the morning and seem to have in my mouth that single grain of sand, that hair, that means my life. Oh, I will have it all back, once more—the work, the girls, and money to burn. Things are less golden at seven.

•

Sauced, I speculate on a homosexual romance in prison. Sober, it doesn't seem to amount to much. Who would it be? A much younger man. Why would he find him beautiful? That the dynamism between youth and age was as powerful as the dynamism between men and women. That he feels the man shaken with the paroxysm of an orgasm, so like pain. They were both men, and the drama of sexual difference was lost. Stacy was hirsute, Johnny was smooth. He would not mention his infatuation to the psychiatrist. Why should he? Under the circumstances, or perhaps under any circumstances, it seemed most natural. Why should he consider it distorted, and root through his childhood to discover the origins of this distortion? He had hated his father, because his father was cruel, stupid, and dishonest. He had not loved his mother, because she did not allow this. There is the set piece about having been merely furloughed from his adolescence and its disorders. That they developed no expertise. They never kissed each other. They simply embraced, caressed, and fondled one another's genitals. Sodomy and fellatio were impossible for both of them. Stacy wondered if this was inhibition, repression, some bow to the society that had imprisoned him. Why wonder? He was content with this rudimentary horseplay, and by "content" I mean that when he was holding and being held by Johnny, the absorption of his flesh, his memory, and his spirit was complete. And then there is the scene in the visiting room with his wife and perhaps his children.

•

Very sticky. I am given such a harrowing glance at dinner that I am nauseated. Why can't I bring this distemper into focus? Once, as I bent down to kiss her good night, she gave me a look of such revulsion that I felt ill. But I seem unable to bring to my feelings and my conduct as clear and strong a light as I would choose. With a disposition made up of suppurating wounds and miraculous cures, I seem unable to distinguish the force the past plays in my reactions. Am I nauseated because of something Mother did or is my nausea the reaction of a healthy man to a situation dominated by sickness? There is, of course, also the problem of drink. I clip the hedges and feel better. I watch with great interest a vulgar TV show. Waking, I ask if she would like me to meet her at the garage. Tears and hysteria.

I sit on the terrace, watching the clouds pass over, watching the night fall. What is the charm of these vaporous forms, why do they remind me of love and serenity? But look, look. There is no glass in his hand. Is it under the chair? Nope. Is it hidden in the flower bed? No, no. There is, for the moment, no glass within his reach.

•

My cruel addiction begins sometimes at five, sometimes later. Sometimes before daybreak. On waking, I want a drink. I imagine that the water glass on the table beside my bed is filled with whiskey. Sometimes there is ice, sometimes none. To entertain myself, I then take one of my imaginary girls for a trip through some city. These excursions are highly educational. In Tokyo we go both to the National Museum and the Museum of Asiatic Art. We spend several days in Luxor. I've not seen H. in two years, and I find her hard to summon. I've not seen S. for two weeks, but she is usually with me these days. We are lovers; we joke; she bakes corn bread for breakfast. All through this tourism I am aware of the glass beside my bed, filled with imaginary whiskey. Things worsen at around seven. Now I can think of nothing but the taste of whiskey. Orange juice and coffee help a little, and I sit at the table sighing as my mother used to sigh. Also my brother. I can't remember my father sighing. I sigh and sigh. At about half past nine my hands begin to shake so that I can't hold a paper or type correctly. At around ten I am in the pantry making my fix. Then my shaken carcass and my one-track mind are miraculously joined, and another day begins.

•

Yesterday my hands shook so that I could not type. In the morning I drank half a bottle of Courvoisier, there being nothing else in the house. In the afternoon I drank more than half a bottle of Bushmills. Early to bed without another drink, but there wasn't much left. This morning—a brilliant day for the first time in weeks—things are better, but I suffer from a slight psychological double vision: a melancholy at the edge of my consciousness that has no discernible imagery. It is rather like a taste. I claim there is some connection between my need for drink and my need for love of some sort, and I'm determined to put it down, however clumsily.

This may be a neurotic condition, some injury done in my childhood. The situation has gone on for many years. Mary responds periodically, but then, in the twinkling of an eye, and for no discernible reason, we enter the galls and barrens and stay there for months. I am not allowed a kiss; I am barely granted a "good morning." This is acutely painful and is not, I think, the lot of every married man. There is the love I bear my children, but this, of course, has its limitations. The need for love is a discernible form of nausea, an intestinal pain. I cure it by imagining that I am with S., although I have not seen her for six weeks. There are three reasons here—I am older than her father, shaken with drink, and afraid of trains. Perhaps I can see her in the fall. S. is too young and Y. is too old these days. I embrace strangers until their bones crack. Thus I embraced T. in the corridor in Moscow. There is more despair than ardor in these demonstrations. I have gone away, hoping that this would improve when I returned. It sometimes does, but seldom. I have thought of taking a mistress, but they are not easy to come by, and I am timid. I claim that my timidity is exacerbated by the situation. After a particularly bitter quarrel twenty years ago I stood in the garage, sobbing for love. We have no garage here, but otherwise the situation is the same. I don't divorce, because I am afraid to—afraid of aloneness, alcoholism, and suicide. These rooms, these lawns, and the company of my son help to keep me alive. I cannot discuss these matters without provoking a venomous attack on my memory, my intellect, my sexual organs, and my bank account. I mean, I suppose, by all of this to justify my having humped the wrong people, but in some lights—the lights of day—I seem to have had little choice.

•

S. has, I know, a farm in Vermont and so I summon this. There is snow on the ground, but the paths are shovelled. It is dark. I am leaving. This is a heartbreaking separation. She is crying. But since I'm making the whole thing up, why don't I invent an arrival instead of a departure? I do. There is still snow on the ground; it is still dark. I come up the walk, carrying a suitcase. She greets me passionately. A fire is burning. It is I who cut the wood. We go directly upstairs, undress, and bound into bed. Then we dress and go back to the fire and have—this I've been waiting for—several drinks. Whiskey, I think. The conversation is about the progress I've made in my work. My depressions are over. I've come into a new way of life, a new cadence, a new enthusiasm. We go into the kitchen, and I talk about my work while she cooks calves' liver and bacon. What do I look like? My hair is white, my abdomen is flat, my back is straight. I am sixty-five, she is twenty-eight. After dinner we drink a little more whiskey and go to bed. It is snowing. I don't screw again, because once is all I'm up to these days. "Once is enough, darling," says she. In the morning, of course, she makes corn bread. I go to an outbuilding, where I work serenely until past noon. When I return, I find a note saying that she has gone to the village for groceries. I have a drink, a large Martini. When she returns I help bring in the groceries. After lunch we take a loving nap. Then I drive to the village and get the mail. Checks, love letters, honors, and invitations. I shovel the walks until dark, when we have the cocktail hour. Roast beef for dinner.

●

My daughter throws up her job and follows her husband to San Francisco. This pleases me intensely. Mary is in a loving spirit, and all is meadows and groves. B_{12} seems to help, although, as they say, one has to help oneself. After the shot I feel that the craving has diminished, and I run upstairs with the gin bottle to show her how little I have drunk. I seem to have forgotten that there was another bottle. For at least half a day I am convinced that all my problems can be traced back to a vitamin deficiency. Now with B_{12} I will be able to board trains, cross bridges, drive across the country. Mary is tender and loving these days, and why speculate on the fact that this might not go on forever? I do not drink after dinner for two nights and have two mornings of feeling like a man. I do not seek it for long, but how wonderful it is to see at least a vision of wholeness, including some mountains.

●

After planning to visit A.A. for twenty years, I finally make it. The meeting is in the parish house of the Congregational church. This is a

new building—by that I mean that the architecture is mildly uncon-
ventional. The main room is very high-peaked, with rafters, and globe
lights are suspended from long rods—a little like the traffic lights at a
busy intersection. The table where we sit, however, is lighted by candles. We are fifteen or twenty, come to confess the vice of drinking.
One by one we give our first names and confess to being alcoholic. But
the essence of the meeting, and there must be one, escapes me. It seems
neither sad nor heartening. One woman describes the neglect her children endured when she was drinking. One describes a five-day binge
in which she locked herself into a room and did nothing but drink. This
was after her husband, a mischief at the local parties, blew off most of
his head. The man beside her describes his binge—six months. He came
to in the county mental hospital. Three of the confessors have been in
mental hospitals, and one of them is still a patient. I suppose he's
furloughed for the night. The long speech I have prepared seems out
of order and I simply say that I am sometimes presented with situations
for which I am so poorly prepared that I have to drink. I don't mention
my visit to the Kremlin, but this is what I mean. We stand and recite
the Lord's Prayer. I am introduced to the chairman, who responds by
saying that we do not use last names. Perhaps I am imperceptive from
having drunk too much, or perhaps the meeting is as dreary as I find
it.

I'm not cured but I'm definitely better. At ten o'clock I still know
where the bottles in the pantry are, and what they contain.

•

Another morning when I seem to see the mountains, seem at least
prepared to see them. I don't know if this is blessedness, luck, or B_{12}.
Yesterday's fine morning was countered by an equally squalid afternoon.
I don't know why. Bad Scotch, the humidity, some chemical instability
in my lights and vitals that makes the lows equal the highs.

•

I want to sleep. I seem to make the remark with some serenity. I
am tired of worrying about constipation, homosexuality, alcoholism, and
brooding on what a gay bar must be like. Are they filled with scented
hobgoblins, girlish youths, stern beauties? I will never know. I desire
women and sometimes men, but shouldn't I exploit my sensuality rather

than lash myself until I bleed? I will never, of course, be at peace with myself, but some of these border skirmishes seem uncalled-for.

●

Vodka for breakfast. Mary mentions her mother for the third time in thirty-five years. "I wanted a Teddy bear for Christmas, and she said I was too old. She pronounced 'doll' with the same terribly Massachusetts accent you have." So we are people we have never met.

I read "Moll Flanders" with diminishing interest. Mary makes and addresses cards. "I shall now take a little rest," says she, wearily. "After that, I will decide what work to do for the rest of the afternoon." She sacks out for two hours. The afternoon is gone. She walks the dog, feeds the horse, and cooks a good dinner, but the atmosphere, so far as I'm concerned, is lethal. Now and then I lie down with what seems like an emotional fatigue, ready for the next round. I watch TV with Federico to distract myself, to enjoy his company, to stay away from the bottle, and to allay the peculiar stillness of this place.

●

I think of the ruses and maneuvers I have used to stay away from the bottle. I have painted the kitchen. I have painted the porch. I have painted a bedroom. I have raked leaves on a windy day, scythed a field, sat in the balconies of movie theatres watching bad pictures, watched TV, walked, cut grass, cut and split wood, made telephone calls, taken massive shots of vitamins and three kinds of tranquillizers, but the singing of the bottles in the pantry is still seductive.

●

I wake with a bleeding nose and think that the Godhead is continence, common sense, and work. I wish I could harness, channel, and exploit the love I feel for my son into industriousness and temperance. I remember walking the road in Saratoga on a winter night, thrilled by my conviction in the Divinity.

●

The gin bottle, the gin bottle. This is painful to record. The gin bottle is empty. I go to the post office and stay away from the gin shop. "If you drink you'll kill yourself," says my son. His eyes are filled with tears. "Listen," say I. "If I thought it would benefit you I'd jump off a ten-story building." He doesn't want that, and there isn't a ten-story building in the village. I drive up the hill to get the mail and make a detour to the gin store. I hide the bottle under the car seat. We swim, and I wonder how I will get the bottle from the car to the house. I read while brooding on this problem. When I think that my beloved son has gone upstairs, I hide the bottle by the side of the house and lace my iced tea. He practices his driving in a neighborhood I've never seen before. These are the hills above the river. The houses are, without exception, small, and close together, and are, without exception, neatly painted and maintained with conspicuous love. Even the wax tulips in the window boxes, the parched lawns, seem produced, tended, and enjoyed with a deep sense of love. Children play games in the street. There is a shrillness to their voices, which seems to heighten as it grows dark. People sit on their porches watching the end of the day—a much more civilizing performance than the double feature at the drive-in, which costs two dollars anyhow. They call on one another wearing yesterday's clothes, torn slippers—the recognizable costumes for this time of day. "From the way the children scream," says Federico, "you'd think I'd run them down." So we drive back in time to turn on the car lights. I watch a Greta Garbo movie with wonderful dramatic situations, confrontations of greed and lust, and in the end this woman, whose beauty has been cataclysmic, is a streetwalker, her brain addled with Pernod. All this because of a broken heart. Indeed, she sees the man for love of whom she has been destroyed cheered by crowds. He offers to help her but she seems not to recognize him, and when he has left she mistakes a bum in the café for Jesus Christ and gives him her last souvenir of love, a ruby ring. This is the color of blood, the caption reads. You died for love. There is no walkaway shot, no rain at all. We go out on the bum discovering that the ruby is genuine. Here is a grand passion—romantic and erotic love shaping a life—and am I wrong in thinking that such passions are no longer among us?

•

The sun shines, and I feel much better. Yesterday, overcast until five, was a bummer. I am, between the hours of eight and six, the only man on these crowded streets who has short hair. At six or a little later, four or five other shorthairs appear. What do they represent? The young seem to be clerks, tellers. The others are middle-aged and have their hair cut as it has always been cut. In the restaurant there is a man with a shaven head, dressed completely in finished black leather. On the street I glimpse a man in jeans who appears to be cruising. At the table on my right is a family. The woman must have been pretty and is pretty no more, but she carries herself well and has her self-possession. He is perhaps fifty, and there is no trace of what he must have been as a young man. They order a moderately priced meal. They have either agreed or been taught not to ask for the filet mignon. Spaghetti and meatballs; the tuna-fish casserole. They say almost nothing to each other during the meal, but they seem not in the least uncomfortable. The daughter is pretty, but I can't see the fourth member, the son, until they leave the table, and when they do leave I see a cruelly crippled spastic whose smile is broad and maybe convulsive or maybe genuine. Make him twenty. Many of the other customers are women with children. Does Daddy teach a seven-o'clock class? On my walk back, I see that some of the classrooms are lighted. On the steps of the old state capitol a man plays a guitar. Beside him is an empty milk container. Two young men with their arms around each other frisk off to the East. Gay Liberation is electing its officers at the other end of town. Do they have a president, a secretary, and a treasurer? But on this late summer night (hundreds of women walking out to the parking lot, leaving the movies, opening the bedroom windows, will say that it smells like autumn), the rightness of men and women seems invincible, seems affirmed by the neon light over the billiard hall, the music from an open door, the stars, the elms, the moon, the river. There seems on this night, at this hour, no possibility, no excuse for those spatial loves moved by mysterious seismographic shifts from the past. Tonight, no men lie in one another's arms.

•

A. comes, and I like him very much. I find him uncommonly sympathetic, and wonder if this is some form of narcissism: do I invent this sameness in our thinking? But this could be an invention of mirrors. At lunch we talk about débutante parties, which is a wrong turn to take, but later he tells me that after leaving me he had a nightmare about his father; that my claim to our equality is unacceptable to him. In a spasm of paranoia I think he is referring to his youth, his intelligence, his freshness of mind, but it seems that he would like to have me as an object of veneration. I believe him to be telling the truth; I cannot imagine him not being truthful. Or anything else unpleasant. We walk up the river in the sun. He is wearing sailor pants and is inclined to swing his hips, and I think people look at us as if we had been scoring, which is untrue. They are closing up the Ferris wheel and the carrousel for winter. Some camera students are photographing this autumnal commonplace. The chairs and tables are stacked on the terrace where refreshments are served. Trucks are taking the benches out of the pavilions. All that is left in the zoo is two bison and two burros. I see very little beyond the fact that I am easy in A.'s company and that the architecture on the west bank of the river is, without exception, ugly. We part the student and the teacher.

•

S.'s dinner party. Thrift shop and municipal dump. The tuna-fish casserole and, for one of the guests, organic vegetables. No hooch. A. is the most important. He flirts with me. The more he flirts, the more he seems like a woman. He shifts his shoulders, swings his hips, and gives me long, bone-making gazes, but we stay within four feet of each other. Who, in this situation, is the innocent? He will walk at my side, embrace me, watch my cock stiffen, and push me away lightly, claiming that he would sooner keep his sexual exploits to the gay-bar pickups and think of me as a member of society and a father image. I don't want terribly to score with him, but if I did I don't think any great harm would be done to the sometimes shining and legislated world. I would sooner not, would sooner play out my straight role as father and husband, grandfather, but I don't feel that a weekend together would compromise me at all. My claims to innocence might simply be an admission of lechery. I think we do very well at table; I think vainly that he's probably not had so good a foil; and here, perhaps, is the charge of narcissism. If he is simply going to bump into me until I am in a state of acute erotic discomfort and then dismiss me with a tap on the wrist, the only sensible thing to do is to kick it.

•

I call A. because he's the person whose arrival I most look forward to. He wears a pink tweed with a flower in the lapel. He tells me about a woman who, during a lunch party, took off a shoe and caressed his genitals with her foot. He is not only homosexual; it seems a profession that takes up much of his time. He tells me that when he does his gymnastics, naked, a man—married, of course, and a father—watches him through a crack in the window shade. I dislike this tale. He seems to esteem his beauty.

•

A brilliant day after the storm. I lunch, joke with Federico, walk the dogs over the little hill. It is bitterly cold in the wind. The light is going. There have been two phone calls in my absence, one anonymous, and I assume it is A. There seems no way of tempering the absurdity of this train of thought. He is probably being zipped into an evening dress by an unemployed photographer's model. They are both giggling, and what else they are doing I do not choose to describe.

•

The last day of the old year, and I mostly want out; I don't know how to work it geographically or financially. My face is flushed with drink; I have lost either my patience or my understanding and have damaged my self-respect. We're back in the old and, I think, despicable routines. Federico and I watch a detective show with the old dog upstairs. Mary watches an English drama in the kitchen.

•

I don't seem to want to write anything but love letters. S. comes, and we walk over the hill, which lightens my aloneness, but at dark or a little later I feel a need for love that has the force of nausea. Jokes, talk, games, are not enough. I want the sensation of love. Mercifully, we get out of the house and go to a movie, where I feel better. Up at seven to try to get gas. All the stations are unlighted and closed. There is no letter from A., and I wait for the mail.

•

My instability or iridescence rises to new heights. I want to write on a sheet of paper, "I love you, I love you, I love you." A hundred times, a thousand times. This is all aimed at the wrong customer. I will telephone. I refuse to sublimate or repress a passion under the assumption that I am discovering a truth. "The scales fell from her eyes," they say at the end of an infatuation that was socially unacceptable. The idea, of course, is that society is invincible, ordained, the very word of God, and if you pervert your erotic drives you make a substantial contribution to the commonwealth. I will telephone, I will telephone, etc. Scotch calms me down. I read notes for "The Art of Fiction." E. comes over. He is having a happy romance with a fifty-nine-year-old widow who works as a guide at one of the restorations around here. We take a trip to Lyndhurst and stop by Dudley's for a sandwich and a drink. The old cook is cleaning mirrors. He is gay but stripped of all his lures, really ugly. This must be difficult for an erotic cult that counts so on beauty. He does have pretty dishwashers. No word from A.; as I might say, Can't you take his cock out of your mouth long enough to write a postcard? This could be the truth.

•

Snow begins to fall early in the afternoon. Sometime after dusk it seems that the oil burner is gone. My car won't start and is very soon buried. The night is cold, and even under a pile of blankets I feel the chill of the house. My heartbeat is then accelerated. I arrange to have the drive plowed so that the repair truck can reach here. I light a fire in the dining room and close the doors. The room becomes habitable but very smoky. The rooms upstairs are dark and cold. Mary speaks of the nostalgia of old rooms. I am reminded of the farm, but my memories are not pleasant. Those cold, dark rooms where my father lived. Tomorrow I leave for Iowa. My reveries are ribald and cozy. My facts, on this snowy day, are very bleak. I think A. will be in New Orleans, and I rather wish this so.

•

I drink a Martini before the morning star is set. Half asleep, I see Mary's face at its loveliest, and this is a pleasure. The images are like photographs in an album: closeup, long shot. I see her standing below me on the drive. I've loved her very much and I like this recollection. I wake for the first time in a month without a hard-on. I think that what I'm doing I have to do, and I hope I do it with the least injury to Mary and whoever else is involved. I cannot live without sentiment, humor, and carnal love.

•

The day is very warm and beautiful. Crocuses in bloom. Mary suggests that we take a walk together. She has not done this in a long time, I mean ten years. My dearly beloved son comes in the middle of dinner to ask for money. He has not come to the house in two years for any other reason. I can hear his wife say, "Go over and ask your father for some money." I've loved him; I've wanted him to marry and love and be loved as he has. I wanted him to have a son and to leave my domination; but now I feel that he is dominated by his wife. I wish he wouldn't always ask me for money. I wish I didn't know that he was ordered, commanded, to ask for money. One's children grow away from one.

The heating plant is working and my intestinal, sexual, and intellectual tracts are cleared. I must work. I call L. and get a hard-on but I don't say so. I split some wood, very little, but I must do this more often. I find it very pleasant. I think of girls: S. eating a candy bar in the parking lot of a supermarket; P. unpacking her own bed linen. I write an advertisement for *The New York Review of Books*: "Revolting, elderly, alcoholic novelist desires meaningful relationship with 24-year-old aristocratic North Carolinian with supple form and baroque biceps. Little gay experience but ready learner. Etc." I can't remember A. at all, and I rather regret this.

•

Toward dark I decide to call A. No one answers the first time. He is there a half hour later. "Hello, John Cheever," he says. The voice seems less resolute than I remember. The edge, the vigor one listens for in a man's voice is not here. Complacency is its worst quality. "I missed you at Mardi Gras," he says. "You would have loved it. I danced in the streets for eight hours, and then I put on white tie and danced at the Comus Ball until dawn." I have never seen him dance and imagine him to be a little ungainly. His back is too long. I feel estranged and think that to fall in love with such a man would be a guarantee of anguish and pain. He would come home late; he would not come home at all. He would put off my passionate advances with a tap on the wrist. How one would long for a woman, even a shrew.

•

And I think of L. in the morning, the lovely unfreshness of her skin. It was the light scent of a young woman who has made love and slept through one more night of her life. Her breasts are the fields and streams of my paradise. Her skin is warm and fine and young, and I mount her, but in our nearness I am keenly aware of the totality of our alienation. I really know nothing about her. We have told each other the stories of our lives—meals, summer vacations, lovers, trips, clothing, and yet if she stood at a crossroads I would have no idea of the way she would take. It is in loving her that I feel mostly our strangeness.

•

On Valium for two days running, and I do feel very peculiar, but it's better, God knows, than sauce. I do not want to return to a strait-jacket with six padlocks. A.'s letters, full of descriptions of flowers, give me a pain in the ass, perhaps because they are not throbbing with declarations of love. He may be very tactfully and intelligently hinting at the fact that there is no possibility of a relationship between us—a relationship of any sort. I somehow think that we will not meet when he comes East. Sometimes this possibility breaks my heart. Sometimes it doesn't. I have a dozen letters to write, but I seem unable to write anything this morning.

•

I think that Valium has a debilitating effect. Walking in the woods, I am suddenly very tired, very tired.

•

On Tuesday I go to the psychiatrist, an amiable young man, but I think he speaks in Freudian clichés. I think my problems enforce my drinking. He claims I invent my problems to justify my drinking. I spent most of yesterday morning going over last year's journal with the idea of giving it to him as an ultimate confession. A. promised to shower me with cards. No cards arrive. I cannot set this friendship in a pestilential Venetian twilight and conclude, as he walks away from me, that what I have discovered is my time of life. The only acceptable message I can arrive at is that our relationship illuminates his untimely youthfulness. Walking in the woods, I would like to see him; someone like him. In short, I am lascivious. This is inflamed by drink and catnaps. The dogwood petals are falling, and the flowers from the tulip tree. Highly sexual.

•

A. sends on a record (Walton-Sitwell) and a note. "For what it's worth, for all my clumsiness and falterings, I love you." To admit that I love and desire him is extremely painful and difficult for me, but once I have made the admission I seem to find it relaxing. I love him very much, at least I do this morning. I love him very much and am happy to say so.

•

A bummer; not really bad, but not good. The director speaks three times: an exceptional man. At breakfast I am asked not to sit at a particular table. We do not play musical chairs around here, says an authoritative woman of perhaps forty, a little heavy. Her hair is neatly and recently dressed, she wears a small string of pearls, and shoes that look like a man's dancing pumps. She represents the club, that little band that exists by closing its membership. Since there was such a group in a line-riflery company, I shouldn't be surprised to find one in a place like this.

•

I try to find some opening for my work. I don't want the escutcheon and the night of the cats. I don't seem able to exploit my knowledge of aloneness and confinement. I can do the hustler, leaving out anything compromising, and ending with the morgue, but the only perception is the clairvoyance of the hustler; that is, his perfect lawlessness. There is no point in my leaving here until my work is in line.

•

The reform of alcoholics. This will be for a month, and I trust that I can make it. We lunch on meat and rice and Jell-O, and attend a lecture. A personable young lady lectures quite simply on attitudes, but she does mention alcohol as a source of phobias. I could follow this one. Three empty hours lie ahead of us. The magnificent mansions that have outlived their usefulness, their owners, and their incomes have become fortuitous. The bathroom is paved with mirrors, but who really cares? The room is vast, the reliefs of plaster *cherubini* with garlands of fruit and flowers.

•

During group analysis a young man talks about his bisexuality and is declared by everyone in the group but me to be a phony. I perhaps should have said that if it is phony to have anxieties about bisexuality I must declare myself a phony.

•

Fifth day. I think my drinking is of secondary importance. Then I watch a TV show, and the banality of this performance arouses my thirst more keenly than anything else so far. The director, toward whom I have some complicated vibrations, says that a healthy person can adjust to acceptable social norms. The banality of a TV show, certainly acceptable, is what makes me want to drink.

•

The woman in "The Visit" (not Mrs. Loomis) would ask of the others in the visiting room, "How can you get along with this sort of people?" Sixth day. My stomach is unsettled.

My stomach squared away at 3 A.M., and I feel much better. Mary calls to say that if I don't like it here she's found a marvellous place in Connecticut two and a half hours from New York. A new tenant joins us. He's not been detoxed, which is against the rules of the game. He has no bags, nothing but a pair of slippers for the bathroom. He looks like an archetypal loser, a goner, a dead one. It is crowding half past two, and I am uneasy. My insight into incarceration seems to have been bypassed. The balance here was all right—pleasant at times—but it seems broken by the arrival of the stray.

•

Quarter past five. I would drink if I were home. I stand at the window, watching the people on the street. I am confined. They are free to come and go, but they move so casually through this freedom that it seems wasted. Most of them carry something—a carton of cigarettes in a paper bag; enough groceries to make supper for one; a leash, at the end of which is a golden retriever sniffing the gutter. Make kaka. Good doggie. They are free, and yet there is no air of freedom on the streets. I'm confined. At least my situation is enunciated.

At around two I have a crisis about whether or not the curative force and the level of thinking in this place are correctly balanced. I am so uneasy that I nearly fall down the stairs. I come into focus after the lecture, bathe, and sleep soundly in spite of three seizures of the trots. Waking, I feel surrounded by some impenetrable wall of nervous indisposition. There is a way out, I know—a phrase, a memory, an anecdote, a word—but I am at the moment unable to find it. My palms are wet. My thinking is confused. A drink would help. I must wait until I find the way out.

•

The sounds of evening in New York. A baritone practices his scales and sings an aria—Italian, I guess because of the sentiment and the G-sharp. Church bells. The only dog who lives on this block has a barking spell.

•

Waking on Sunday, I realized that I could go out onto the street at ten and be met by a young woman with an extraordinarily volatile and luminous face, the enormous clubby shoes that were worn last year, and when I have kissed her good morning and been kissed she will ask if her slip shows. Knowing that all of this will be mine in two hours, I wonder if I have the courage to leave confinement and seize my natural freedom. This for "Falconer." I put it down poorly. Standing at the window, with my palms sweating, I wonder if I will have the courage to step through this door when it is opened.

The psychologist finds alarming discrepancies in my profile, and when I state a few clear and simple facts she laughs openly and scornfully into my face. "You are mad," she says, a remark that has been made to me by several people, including a total stranger on the plane from Chicago. It is a pleasant and profitable madness. I sleep poorly, with long narrative dreams in black, white, and gray. I seem to have left all my manuscript in Boston, and then I realize that I can't remember the trip from Boston to Ossining or my admission to the hospital. This is a blackout. I must have been quite drunk and mad. I can't remember the hospital at all—not a nurse, not a dish. There was the view of the Hudson, rather flat there; the doctor's red hunting shirt; my wife and children coming in to visit. But I recall all of this with no legitimate clarity. The sweetness of freedom. Freddy the killer had accustomed himself to confinement and had not prepared himself for anything else. How sweet his cell seemed, his erratic toilet, his colored photographs of long-lost children who would not answer his letters or rendezvous with him in Klein's jewelry store or Macy's men's department. The night of the cats. J. tells me about working over Pepto-Bismol pills with a nail file to make them the size of Antabuse. He stayed off whiskey for six months, but his wife was never home. It was he, sober and unrewarded, who did the shopping, cooked the dinner, took care of the children. "You have your own life in whiskey," she said. "Grant me mine." "But I haven't had a drink for six months," he said. He sipped a Martini three and a half days after taking an Annabus and vomited all over the director's table. A nice fellow, with a sharp bark for a laugh; very pleasant to drink with all night long.

·

I wake at around two from the deepest, sweetest sleep I've known in a year. I think I can work, here or some such place, but I am doubtful about the house by the creek. Returning to that small room with yellow walls might mean returning to all my bad habits. Don't I have the strength, can't I find the strength to overcome the weight and power of environment?

I call Mary at dusk. The bank has miscalculated, and we are being charged for a two-thousand-dollar overdraft. This is all my fault. The Boston statements have not been forwarded, the other statements are lost among my manuscripts, the dog has just jumped into a muddy pond, etc. She is very bad-tempered. This sort of thing provokes my drinking. It makes me afraid to return.

As the dark gathers, I see a gang gathering on the corner of Madison Avenue. They swagger in very good imitations of adults. Uncle Giovanni. Joe the King. At a signal they all start running. Later there is a searing light across the sky until I hear thunder. ("It frightens me," says J. at breakfast. It pleases me, I think.) But the room seems badly ventilated and I cannot sleep. My thinking is alarmingly disjointed. I steal a knife from the kitchen to peel an apple. I see the gang again. These could be symptoms of withdrawal.

•

Across the yard, she puts out two plastic dog dishes for her cocker spaniel and her scottie. She is wearing a housecoat and looks hung over. I have never seen her fully dressed, or looking as if she didn't need or have a drink. Then I think I hear some choral music. One hears almost no music from these backyards. Knowing absolutely nothing about music, I conclude, in a scholarly way, that it must be Puccini because of the ascending and melodramatic scale of flats. I once had perfect pitch, but that was long ago. Then I hear some dissonance and decide that it must be Berg or Schönberg. The soprano then hits a very high note and sustains it for an impossible length of time, and I realize that what I've been hearing is the clash of traffic and a police siren amplified by a light rain.

I read Berryman on rehabilitation centers. When I wake this morning my feeling of dislocation is very strong. I am nervous; my vision is poor; I keep singing Dartmouth songs that I can't have heard for forty years. I'm a son of a gun for beer/I like my whiskey clear and if I had a son sir I'll tell you what he'd do/he would yell to hell with Harvard as his daddy used to do.

•

A heavy rain at five. I am a boy again, a child. I hear the rain strike the air conditioners, watch it gleam on the slate shingles in Thursday's last light. I read, sleep, dream, wake myself with the loudness of my voice. I am riding, wearing loafers, and my loafers keep slipping through the stirrups. "Short stirrups," said Lila. "Did you ride much in Italy?" I never went near a horse in Italy. "She still loves you," said the woman with braids.

•

I've got those picking-up-the-pieces blues; I'm feeling blue all the time. I've got those picking-up-the-pieces blues, can't get the pieces on the line. I've got those picking-up-the-pieces blues, but the puzzle ain't mine.

•

I was sprung from the alcoholic-rehabilitation clinic yesterday. To go from continuous drunkenness to total sobriety is a violent wrench. This moment, this hour, is the sum of the not immutable past and the necessity of a future. I don't know where it began, and I might be able to retrace this year eighteen times without mastering it. It began, I suppose, with the pantomime on the other side of the river and continues this morning with a brief salutation, orange juice, and a little cold coffee. Now the house, containing two people, is still. Laughter seems to be my principal salvation. Laughter and work. I seem unable to resurrect the months in Boston. The role alcohol played is inestimable. I seem to have lost some manuscripts. I claim not to be troubled beyond worrying that they might fall into someone else's hands. I cannot face the shame of having lost my moorings through drunkenness. I seem this morning to have lost twenty pounds and perhaps twenty-five years. One thing is the old drag-ass I used to justify by age. Ask me to take off the storm windows, but ask me tomorrow. Eat. Drink seventeen cups of black coffee. Since I claim this to be a means of communication, I must prove it. What do I have? The escutcheon, booze—but after a century as black as unpolished basalt, onyx, or anthracite. The representation of liberty and justice. The night of the cats. The visit, still unclear. I think of O'Hara kicking the shit in his forties and continuing to work. He was about the only one.

I've changed violently, but nothing else seems to have changed. Looking for a good-night kiss, I find the only exposed area to be an elbow. The dogs wake us before dawn, and when I ask if there is anything I can do, the reply is distempered. Recently, she has seldom enjoyed sleeping with me. I'm the king of the mountain, but nobody seems to know it. You can do the set piece about watching the visitors leave.

Day No. 2. I'm still very uptight but I think I won't take Valium. The set piece I'll aim at will be on liberty. There are three points of hazard. One is the euphoria of working at what I think is the best of my ability; one is the euphoria of alcohol, when I seem to walk among the stars; one is the euphoria of total sobriety, when I seem to command time. That bridge of language, metaphor, anecdote, and imagination that I build each morning to cross the incongruities in my life seems very frail indeed.

•

In Russia, in the 1860's or 70's, one would have written, "The tiny village of X, a hundred and twenty-seven versts from Moscow, was mentioned in the encyclopedia as the place where a landowner had successfully bred a dog with a cat." In France, a little earlier, one would have written, "*La peu que nous savons de la petite ville de B——, nous savons parce que là se trouve un homme à deux têtes.*" In my own country, in the fifties and early sixties, one would have written, "The little mill town of Pearl River was one of those small industrial communities that welcome the driver with a sign saying 'Old in Tradition, Youthful in Growth' and that are covered by a single Zip Code." Today we are, thank God, spared these euphemisms and can say succinctly, "The little village of Pearl River was an asshole."

•

Seventh day out of stir. It will be a week at 11 A.M. No meeting last night, but I think I'll need one tonight. Work, sandwiches. My only brother arrives at half past two to scrutinize my sobriety. We both seem rather clumsy about the facts of age. It turns out that he's had a prostate operation, followed by a blood clot that nearly killed him. He pisses ten times a night. My digestive and urinary tracts are crippled by their encounter with institutional food, and my asshole is quite sore. Time sits with us at the table, an unwelcome stray. My brother goes into New York, looks at Grand Central, is frightened, and comes home. The phobic curse of my family, all of whom were afraid of heights, crowds, thunder, wealth, and fame. No, thank you. My daughter comes. She seems a little breezy. I read Carson's biography, and I shall report to A. Half awake, I have a glimpse of my iridescence, or my erotic stratifications. At the lowest, a shade below the subconscious, I embrace Z. This may be the comprehension of death by the love of death. At a stratum approaching consciousness, I embrace Y at that disarmament table where my social and my erotic natures put their signatures on an honorable truce. Fully awake, I embrace X. She stands on the highest step of the stair, stands in the sunlight, calling, "*Ben tornato, caro, carissimo.*" I will draft two letters before I get to work.

•

I miss Big Brother's telephone calls and wonder if he's sauced. He shows in time and we go off to an A.A. meeting in an Episcopal church

behind the Hartsdale canine cemetery and across the street from the
hair-transplanting center. "Southern California," says my companion.
The church, with its mortared fieldstone walls, aimed at being Trini-
tarian and wound up looking like a Neapolitan grotto. "Everything but
the Virgin Mary," says my companion. So, another meeting of no great
moment passes.

•

Mr. Cheever says that his knowledge of confinement has been informed by the two years that he taught at Sing Sing; by being confined,
as a writer, to a typewriter and a small room; and by having spent several
months in various rehabilitation clinics for chronic alcoholics.

•

Twelfth day out, and I shall stop counting.

•

My sixty-third birthday. I feel as well as I've ever felt and thank
God for this. Ben can't come; Susie will be late. Mary says, "Shit, I've
got this big piece of meat," etc. It doesn't matter at all. I am very
fortunate and should go to church. Yesterday I worked, spaded the
peonies, won 20¢ at backgammon, spaded some more, stepped in dog
shit, took off my stinking shoes, and, washing the dogs, punctured my
right foot on a cultivator. Mary bandaged the wound, and I went off to
A.A. I could do a scarifying description of an old man in an ill-fitting
suit, celebrating his 38th year of sobriety. They put out the lights and
bring a cake with lighted candles down the aisle. An unseasonably cold
wind blows out the candles. We sing: "Happy anniversary to you," etc.
One might point out that he could have done as well dying of cirrhosis,
but that would be sinful. Returning here, I have acute pains across my
middle and crawl naked and unwashed into my warm bed, where I fall
asleep almost at once. Now I suffer from excessive loquaciousness, woolgathering, "Muskrat Ramble."

•

Mary goes on one of her protracted shopping trips. One can only
overlook that which is not to be understood. A letter from A., somewhat
looser than his recent correspondence. I am spared a list of the perfumes
that float in his window. He seems to be back on his tease routine,

something I have seen clearly only for a moment. Read Saul. The wonderfully controlled chop of his sentences. I read him lightly, because I don't want to get his cadence mixed up with mine.

•

Work in the garden, which is much untamed, with Federico. Buy cauliflower and bean seeds, and, later, three moribund trees. My regression involves a lively concern with the property. I don't recall doing much. I read, make a stab at hedge clipping, eat a nice dinner, go to A.A. in Croton. The damp and cold church basement. A woman with the blazing makeup and straw-colored hair of the town whore who used to work in Woolworth's when I was a boy. A heavy woman with as much makeup. Our heavyset Irish leader, who twice, for mysterious reasons, speaks of unmanliness. "I mean, now you can feel tenderness for a man without no guilt," he says. I split before the confession, which seems to take place at covered tables. Watch asinine TV with my son, sleep, wake on Sunday with work to do, but I seem, involuntarily, to be obliged to observe the day of rest. The dogs dig holes in the lawn, and I swear at them. Mary swears at the vacuum cleaner. Toward the end of the afternoon, I recall what I have done, in the rectitude of this environment. I could not, yesterday, and in this environment, confess to any of this, and yet I claim to be unashamed.

•

J. calls, T. calls, A. is the last to call. I lunch with T. and meet A. at the train. He smiles as he runs up the stairs, smiles both with his mouth and, it seems, with his hips. As he crosses the waiting room there is less of this. I take his hand with deep ardor but release it to turn the steering wheel of the car. I am profoundly stirred, but there appears to be no intellectual equivalent. A. seems, and no one else does at this point, to magnify the incongruities between my social and my erotic drives to the point of combustion. It is all forgotten in a night's sleep, but I would like a better understanding of myself. Ben calls to say he has been offered a good job. My eyes fill with tears of happiness. I think of my father's sentimentality, aimed more often at the world around him than at me. He could weep over a fading rose. I think I will not write A. until he writes me. I must do "The Cardinal."

•

A letter from A., who refers to my beauty, my boyishness, and my lucidity. I snap at this bait so greedily that I cannot see my foolishness. I try to imagine the cynicism that would have been involved had I, at twenty-four, flattered my elders. We laugh at dinner, and while I am upstairs I hear the little dog singing. Susie arrives, quite high, and I am a little apprehensive about hubris, but I have no advice to give her. We go up to the pool, but I do not swim because my shoulder is still lame. So to bed; and at daybreak this Thursday seems like something placed in my open arms, placed on my lap; a bulk, a richness of light and darkness.

•

I read a short-story anthology from which I have been conspicuously excluded and see how right they were to leave me out. The tone of the stories chosen—most of them excellent—is much more substantial and correct than my flighty, eccentric, and sometimes bitter work, with its social disenchantments, somersaults, and sudden rains. I do see why some people describe my characters as weird; I see this before it gets around the corner.

•

At the A.A. meeting, I try to work myself into a conversation, but with no success. I sit alone, not uncomfortably. The first speaker is an alert, vigorous woman, whose legs have gone. The second is a very fat woman with a long history of arrests, jails, nut wards, suicide attempts. "I used to weigh two hundred and fifty pounds," she says. It looks to me as if she still weighed two hundred and fifty pounds. The next is an elderly runt, the kind of social steerage whose enlistment the Navy used to encourage. One also saw them in the infantry. Great at doing their own washing and ironing; reliable and punctual when sober; and, with or without a record, moving with the dancey, back-to-the-wall airs of a convict. His voice is close to inaudible. He repeats himself. He describes contracting to gold-leaf the dome of the Baptist church. He sold the gold leaf and gilded the dome with paint he bought at the five-and-ten-cent store. After fifteen years the dome, he says, is still shining; but we all know the Baptist church well, and we know it has no dome. The next is a large, young man, not fat but close to it. He wears a cotton pullover that shows his voluminous breasts and belly. His dark hair is long, and a thin lock hangs directly in front of his right eye. He removes this from time to time with a toss of his head. For me this is painful. My own right eye grows lame. Lying on a sidewalk outside a bar, he shouted that all he wanted was a little peace of mind, a minute— or maybe two—of being at peace with himself. All he wanted, after sixteen years of drugs and dope, was a minute of this and he never got it. My eyes are wet. The aggressive woman speaks again. She gave away her washing machine (while drunk) and had to take her washing to the public laundry, where she drank from a pint in the toilet. Shopping at the supermarket, she suddenly abandoned her groceries, drove home, and drank a half-pint of bourbon in the coat closet, exclaiming wow, wow, wow. The confessions are too lengthy, I guess, but in spite of my recognition of these cruelties, and my wet eyes for the fat man, the confessions seem to me to go on for too long, and I entertain the thought of a drink. There is no subject and no predicate for what I feel. This I don't know, but I do know, moving blindly, that the answer is, "Nix."

•

I wake at six. Last week I heard the bells of Trinity while I spaded the garden. This Sunday I will go. Kneeling, I am too deeply moved to shape a coherent prayer. I would like my daughter's happiness, some largeness of my comprehension, but my feeling is inchoate and close to tears. One wouldn't want to cry in the chancel, would one? The candles, the fires, are countless, and much of the force of this ritual is ancient and bold. I believe in God the Father. What a courageous declaration! The movements of the priest, the acolyte, and the communicants are like some vestige of a pavane. It is the tower bell that rings as we approach the mystery of the Eucharist. I am deeply moved. Leaving the church, I greet the priest, who has changed from his very heavy vestments—an inheritance from the haggard chorus boy who used to bless this flock—into the service white. "Good morning, John," he says. He is the same priest—unnamed and uncalled-for—who gave me Communion when I was last thought to be dying. I've not seen him since. There is no mention of God's will. We settle for an ardent handshake and loud laughter. We are both crying. The rain is so heavy that going from the church to the car and from the car to the house I get so wet that I have to hang my clothes to dry in the kitchen. I would like to call him, but I do not.

•

Uncommonly hot and humid. Reading Henry Adams on the Civil War, I find him distastefully enigmatic. I find him highly unsympathetic, in spite of the fact that we breathed the same air. Walker Evans once said that he was queer, and this struck me as an idle remark; but his descriptions of Milnes and Swinburne, and the posthumous gossip of the period that is, alas, known to me, bring the matter up once more. Absolute self-knowledge is, I believe, never a claim of a thoughtful man. The enormous, subjective prejudice that manipulates so broad a field as our memory is only a glimpse of the prejudices and whims that affect our judgments. So here is vastly connected Henry in London, quite androgynous and absolutely incapable of admitting any such condition. Here is the distortive force of society, and here is a most unnatural bloom. He praises a father he would happily murder and anticipates Freud's illuminating the Commandments with Oedipus Rex. Honor thy father, that thy days may be long.

•

So we have The Return from the Mountains. I've been content these three weeks, and one source of my contentment has been the conviction that I can see my limitations from a different altitude and in the light of a different time of day. "Hi," I shout. The response is faint. I lean for a kiss. There is none. If my questions are answered at all they are answered with a sigh. The groceries I bought are worthless, the corn is questionable, and would I mind if it is thrown away? "Not at all!" I exclaim, which means that it will be served. This is perversity and madness. She sweeps the floor, empties the wastebaskets, and spends the next two hours cleaning the refrigerator. Federico and I go for a swim. "She does not do this because she is mean," says Fred. I do not embrace him or shake his hand. I don't know what to say to him. I've lived with his brother through the same scene, and his brother now considers me contemptible. I can say to myself—to no one else—that his brother is full of shit; but I do realize how mysterious and beautiful his person is, and that judicious reproach, or even common sense, are cruelties in this case. I have been told to avoid emotional crises and extremes of heat and cold. This triumvirate will kill me. My heart is racing, from an emotional crisis. The sun is hot. The water is cold. So the scene is set for my assassination, but I must go into the pool to wash off this emotional uncleanliness, and so I do.

•

I am afraid to enter the house. I read on the porch. When I step in to get a drink, Mary asks in a sweet voice if I would like some crackers and cheese. So it is the old routine that her brother used to call Pavlovian, but this, perhaps, is taking it too far into the past. Clearing the table, I must struggle to keep from throwing the serving dishes onto the floor, but this was true—I remember this in detail, even to the figure on the carpet—when I was fourteen and alone with my parents. "Dear heart," she says to Fred at table. Out from under my feet goes another rug.

So through another summer night to the parish house, where I see people I like muchly. And I see how and why and how cleverly I catch the sound of the wind changing its quarter, the loudening clash of night sounds, and the moon's being not quite full. I am troubled by the fact that this eccentricity can be used by me to justify my other eccentricities; to justify sexual engorgements that I will always doubt. And driving home through the summer night—through an uproar of noise (including the great horned owl in rut) and a confusion of odors—I think how contemptible is a woman who accepts her livelihood from a man for whom she has nothing but scorn and loathing. But what are her alternatives; what, then, is she to do? Neither of them can afford to set up separate households.

•

New journal. The right front tire needs air, and the car needs gas. This morning I am sad; quite naturally so, I think. That is, no unease is involved. I seldom wake in a vile humor, but I am often thrust into one. Seeing, in an unspeakably vulgar TV show, a man and wife touch each other lightly and tenderly, I am stricken. I always remember L. saying, "But I deserved better." There is, of course, no such law. I think I know enough about the possible relationships between men and women to name my marriage as obscene and grotesque. I think there is nothing wrong in taking inordinate pleasure in the company of someone who will smile at me over the eggs. I've been breakfasting alone for years while my wife in the kitchen screams obscenities at the refrigerator. But it seems not quite right to put onto the shoulders of someone else the burdens of this miscarriage. I don't think I have anything to worry about other than alcohol.

•

The sad day is followed by an emphatic morning, and all my anxieties about drink and unrequited love and other masks of death are gone, as if my prayers had been answered. So I wander around the dining room restating the fact that any image of the Divinity will involve me in a taxi accident and a delay on my way to the airport where I would have boarded a plane that will crash, killing everyone aboard; that it is His hand that maketh me to stumble and thus avoid the adder; that it is He who led me safely by the hornets' nest before they could swarm and sting me to death. One is dealing with a mystery, and it is the depth of this mystery that accounts for the crudeness of those images that overlook our prayers: those old beavers with golden hats, those sappy angels, those grave and stupid apostles and prophets.

•

Up the river to Yaddo for the first time in many years without the company of alcohol. I remember promising myself that I would not take my flask into the toilet until Hudson. I remember, on the wall of some seminary, a large representation of Christ nailed to the cross. I remember (I was coming south early in the spring) a baggage cart on some platform, heaped with bundles of green palm leaves for the coming Sunday. Those were pleasant times, and so are these. When I was a boy I thought as a boy. The duck blinds, I see, are gone. A ruined house and a ruined castle are appealing, not at all like derelicts but, as the light pours through the gutter windows, like some graceful spinoff of our passion for building. The river is rough, but I can't find evidence of a wind strong enough for this, and I guess it could be a tide rip. I think of bridges I may be too frightened to cross, of my fear of throughways, but all of this is remote. My only unease is over the intensely intellectual nature of my pleasure. Alcohol at least gave me the illusion of being grounded. I count now on cutting and splitting wood, swimming in cool water, orgasms, and perhaps gluttony. I may simply mean a good appetite. In Albany, I lack identity because I have no credit card, but I don't hurl myself into this sort of crisis. At the bus stop I drink iced tea and admire the restoration of a building across the street. On the bus I sit beside a sleepy drunk, but my nose must have lost its keenness because I can't smell alcohol. He has been fucking all day, he says, and is going to rent a building and fill it with pinball machines to fleece the young.

So here. There are flowers from A., and presents. If he loved me as I love him he would always be there; he would have met me in Albany; spent an afternoon hanging around the bus stop. We meet in the back of the house as I go in for dinner. We kiss. I'm getting cheeks these days from everyone. After dinner we walk around the lakes. When I put my arm around him he seems both heavier and taller. I ask if he will be my lover, and he refuses, both kindly and politely. I have no response, certainly no pain. I enjoy his company and would enjoy his skin, but I miss neither. I could be unpleasant. I could call him a bore. Any unpleasantness at all here would be wicked. I shall ask him for little or nothing, but I shall not say so. Someone says that one of the members here is a sex goddess. I am wakeful and think that I can seize this opportunity. In the morning I look forward to seeing A. and the goddess in that order. I will kiss A., most lightheartedly, hold his hand at breakfast; kiss the goddess, and slip my hand around her waist. But how can this man, genuinely male and solid, kiss another man with such tenderness and pleasure, and plan to love the young woman with the long hair? It seems quite possible without any loss. I just don't happen to have been invented by an advertising agency. The message is: Praise be to thee, Oh Lord, of Thine own have we given Thee.

•

Halfway through the meeting I have a deep seizure of melancholy. Looking out of the window, I admire a maple that has begun to turn and think how like a rose it is—some enormous rose tree. I long to be out of the yellow plush chair and the other constraints of the afternoon. I also long, or I might, for A., although I would not cross the street to see him. And then I see that it is not he whom I love but someone in my remote past, in my emotional substructure, whom I loved. My brother, I suppose. I would have destroyed most of my lasting relationships for his sake. I sometimes find his company distasteful, but I remember, in Iowa—sometimes in bed with a lover—enduring the deepest longing for him; perhaps the deepest longing for something unlikely or something of the past. After the meeting I pass a football with J. and P. I go to the cocktail party wearing a sweater. These are all stabs at the past, but why should I worry, since I think them successful? "You are pale," says J., and I am suddenly tired. My toothache and my cold become serious. I am sick. I have wanted the other side of the medal, and now I have it. I have it through most of Sunday, when I have a fever and am slightly delirious. I remember what I want, no more. Pieces I used to play on the piano, friendships of all sorts. I stagger a little when I walk, and this is the darkness that I sought. At its worst it is regressive. My father will come home, not—as I've written—with a new fishing lure, but with a new marionette theatre. That's what I really wanted. And I think of my family—mostly my brother and sometimes my mother. We are in a group photograph—me usually on the far right or in the background, usually holding a glass. We seem printed in some color other than the rest of the group, but we do not have the intelligence to understand this, and thus we will always be a little ungainly, a little foolish, and at times intensely unhappy. So, past my fever, I wake again with nothing to say, really, but a thanksgiving.

•

There is a letter from A. I have been convinced that I love him; I must have written him a hundred love letters; I have anticipated his company, enjoyed his conversation intensely, and have experienced much excitement about his career. He is not my lover, and the fact that I have been rebuffed may have much, much more to do with my feelings than I can comprehend. In short, he does not seem to appreciate my enormous charm, my power, my et cetera. At times, indeed, he seems quite indifferent to my gifts and my management of them. What a dilemma! And I, perhaps, through loving him, have given him character and intelligence, which he does not in any way want to possess. I do not know what his sexual partners are like, but I guess they are quite beautiful and muscular. I cannot imagine any consummation. I find the substance of his letter offensive and the writing rather giddy. He seems determined to present himself at times as an offensive homosexual, and I do not understand why he does this. He may be repeating some scene with his father. I don't think his behavior really deserves this much investigation, though. He may simply be performing his role.

On his first afternoon, he is aboard a beautiful yacht; on his first night, he is at a homosexual movie. My only feeling is one of doubt, knowing when the New York planes hit the Coast. It doesn't really matter, but why should he want to alienate me; why should he want

me to imagine him swinging his ass around, an ass I can't have? And
why should I ever have experienced love for such a silly man? Are all
my loves this unwise? And so I shall not be mean.

•

So we go up the rocky road to where I summered so happily for so
many years. I know the place very well, I know every hummock on the
lawn, I sidestep down the steep, wet hill to the house where I was a
lover, a husband, a father, a mountain climber, a heavy drinker, and
seem to have suffered no losses at all. I am terribly cold. We go down
to the house, which is one of the shabbiest places in which I have ever
spent any time. The washbasin and bath are built for midgets. The
rugs and the furniture have missed their date at the municipal dump.
The shade on the one lamp is smashed and burned and still wound with
cellophane. The cobwebs are thick, and when the rain begins the roof
leaks. It leaks into a tin full of seashells that Josie Herbst gave to my
daughter years ago. She painted a pretty pheasant on the lid and on the
side asked, "*Kennst du das Land, wo die Zitronen blühn?*" The past redeems
much of this shabbiness—my beloved dog Cassiopeia chewed the holes
in the rug—and I am not particularly interested in shabbiness, but the
house seems comical, considering the love it inspires. The front room
is small, dark, useless, and wet from the leaking roof. A wretched light
burns in the small bedroom. The unpainted wallboards (shingle nails
are driven through) have the gleam of silk, the depth of water; the
electric diagram is black with white porcelain insulators where the cords
touch wood; the sound of rain on the roof is amplified; and there will
be the morning.

I light a fire in the kitchen stove and in the dining room—all things
that give me pleasure. S. cooks me a pleasant breakfast. Outside it rains
and rains. B. gives us a few orders, and I split kindling while Federico
cuts small wood with a hacksaw. We joke about having received our
orders. Look, look. I am cutting kindling. My son is cutting wood with
a hacksaw. Look, look. We are good boys. We are not bad boys. We
may get an extra serving of eggs goldenrod at lunch. This is all quite
true, quite ridiculous, and for me, laughing with my son, quite wonderful. I am happy to see a tubful of kindling. I stop at the car and get
a box of crackers. Mary calls from the porch, "If you wish some cheese
with your crackers there is some."

•

On the day we leave, I wake before dawn. The morning star is so bright that, seeing it through the trees, I mistake it for the moon. All the stars are shining. I light the stove, eat a big breakfast, and presently we start. The clouds have lifted, Cardigan Mountain can be seen, and the hills are a phenomenon of light. So we go down the once narrow roads in the first of the light. There is smoke from the chimneys—wood smoke, which is much less direct than the jets of smoke or vapor you get from other heating plants. Wood smoke spreads on the wind, flattens in the rain, and is, of course, fragrant. Here are signs and ruins of the contrition of the past: a beautiful barn, a beautiful church that is now an insurance office. There are more signs of vagrancy than anything else; but you said this before. The spread of the country reminds one of some Biblical promise, although it holds no true promise. But it is beautiful and heartening. "SEE THE DINOSAUR FOOTPRINTS," says a sign. "OPEN WEEKDAYS FROM NINE TO FIVE. CHILDREN HALF-PRICE." And above the sign one sees the Laurentians, clearly scored by the glacier into forms that are a little like waves. There are high, green pastures, bright-blue duck ponds, fire-colored hills, colonies of trailers, and the Housatonic and the Connecticut rivers. "I have to piss," I say, as we enter Hartford. "That's too bad," says Mary. "I will piss in the thermos," say I, lightly. "You will not piss in my thermos," says Mary. "I am about to piss in your thermos," say I, unfastening my trousers and taking out my cock. "Don't you dare piss in my thermos," says Mary. We are in the thick of the Hartford traffic. I empty cold tea out of a jar and piss in the jar. I am very relaxed and happy. I have to piss once more. Back here, I walk the dogs, light a fire, eat heavily, and have briefly the illusion that I've gained height. I watch some TV that I think rather clever and go very early and happily to bed.

•

So, I've come through that much of the darkness. I think, not pretentiously I hope, of the old quotation from Plato, "Let us consider that the soul of man is immortal, able to endure every sort of good and every sort of evil." What else would one say? I come into town too fast for a mooring at A.A. and do not stay for the double feature. It helps, and I am perhaps most uneasy about getting back on the sauce.

So the book falls into place, rather like "The Country Husband,"

and what did that amount to? Some compliments and a three-hundred-dollar prize; not enough to feed the dogs. There are the usual stones in my way. I must move all the manuscripts this afternoon. Neither the vacuum cleaner nor the dishwasher will function, but the splendid thing about working happily is that it leaves me with very little energy for bitterness, anger, impatience, and long indictments. When you are working well everyone will want to clean the floor under the chair where you sit, and long-winded gossips will call on the telephone every ten minutes.

So it goes through the leaves. Then, mercifully, we skip the scene on the water tower. A simple, declarative statement. So through the school, the parting. It is then that we have the examination of his love. Then the cuckold, the dungeon, the night before the cardinal was expected Jody returns. I think I can type it out and be done with it tomorrow.

Even if I don't finish until the end of next week, it doesn't really matter.

•

I think I cannot accept the simplified moral that breaking sexual taboos leaves you open to every other sort of accusation. I am cold. Mary is cleaning the rugs. Oaths rise up the stairwell. I should go to Dom's for the snow tires and the radiator checkup. I must borrow a bicycle pump and steal a valve cap. I could spade the tomatoes and transplant the peonies. Reading old journals, I find a few set pieces and some proof of my own virtue. One would like to act impetuously, but one has been photographed, one has been discussed, and the dross of the looking-glass is part of my craft. I cannot completely escape—Oh, look, look at the horny, tireless, clean man! I can only pray for the right mixture. I think of the cardinal, but with no great urgency. How marvellous it would be to finish this in the spring, by which I mean before the bank account runs out. By which I mean God's willingness. This, it seems, will not be my last book, and so some portentousness has slipped out of the room.

•

So the holiday, the snow, the cold, the brightness. I have a mild stomach unease. I think of the holly tree in Hanover—probably the largest holly in the Northeast and very probably planted by some English settler. I think I can remember its darkness, and I do remember that some florist attacked it with a hacksaw and stripped the lower branches. Did I go around to the neighboring florists to see if I could find signs of our tree? I doubt it. I do remember training horse brier around the tree so it could not easily be found. I do remember imagining a letter from my mother, received by me in the Army, urging me to come home at once and protect the holly tree. This was a crib from "The Late George Apley." It is less adventurous than I would like. There is the height and the darkness of the tree. And I remember a letter from my father: "Do not underestimate the importance of anniversaries—Christmas, birthdays, and so forth. They are of the greatest importance to you and the people you live with." And for Farragut in prison there is the broad and bitter irony of celebrating the equinox; the mysteriousness of the world we live in; the magnanimity of God, who gave us his son, condemned to a cruel and a lingering death for our sins at the instant of his humble birth in a manger; and the healthy and preposterous concept of the family. There are the photographs that were taken in September. The blasphemy of the prison is no greater. The sense of all the world wrapping, unwrapping, decorating; the green tree strung with jewels and burned; the gasping sound of resinous needles exploding in the heat; a memory of the blackbirds in the autumn pulled through space.

·

In reading old journals with Farragut's letters in mind, I come on the fact that, for nearly three years, I wrote A. love letters and received flirtatious letters from A. I think I will destroy these pages of the journal. I cannot arrive at any satisfactory recollection of this passionate love. The recollection of any infatuation is bound to seem mysterious, but I would like to go further than to exclaim about my self-deception. During this time I seldom saw him. He had in his favor the fact that he was outstandingly gifted, and, I thought, comely. He wrote continually about his homosexuality. What troubles me seems to be aesthetic. How did this long-waisted man come to take such a dominating position in my pastoral landscape? Here were the trees, the grass, the dry stone wall, and the stream that might contain trout. What is this curious figure doing here? I was lonely—a fact that I can state easily enough, although

I am absolutely incapable of imagining a loneliness powerful enough to grant him a commanding place in this scene. They say that people born under my constellation are truly halved. Here, again, one comes to aesthetics. No one is half a man. I find this unacceptable. I was cruelly torn when I left my brother, cruelly torn when R. left me. I was torn, but not bisected. I had quite enough steam to go on. Why, then, should I have so needed A.? I need him no more; I rather dislike the thought of seeing him again; but one always says this about a love affair that is unrequited and has been forgotten. And then, thinking of opportunities, I remember that while feeling complete with L., I could at certain hours of the day—dusk, of course—feel, even with her in my arms, a profound longing for A., who would appear long-waisted and quite ridiculous in comparison. Is contempt at the bottom of this longing—must I, for a total erotic gratification, embrace someone who is naked and contemptible? If this is true I find it unacceptable. I find it truly unacceptable.

•

So, the heaviest snowfall in many years. How pleasant to be sober. Mary seems troubled, but then I always counter by saying that I, too, am troubled. She does not speak to me all day, except to ask for the salt. But it doesn't really matter, or it matters that there is someone else in this house. And I wouldn't want a wife who was sitting in my lap all the time, who denied me the considerable privacy I need. So she watches TV in the kitchen. I watch TV in the attic. I think she is deeply troubled, but I am successful in not mentioning this to my daughter, and I think it will pass.

And about that little snow-buried town where I once spent a winter and the men used to get together in the bar and talk about their wives; one of them explained to me that when you're dealing with crazies you have to understand that they don't like it, either. For instance, if you get a crazy who is very contrary and you tell her she is not going to be murdered, well, then she will insist on being murdered. I mean she loves life—the trees and the buildings and the men and the women and the dogs and the birds—but if you tell her that she can't be murdered she will insist on it. You have to understand this. And more about that little bar.

•

On the question of crypto-autobiography and the fact that the greatness of fiction is not this, I am writing not from my experience as a
teacher in prison but from my experience as a man. I have seen confinement in prison, but I have experienced confinement as a corporal
in a line rifle company, as a stockade guard, as a traveller confined for
thirty-six hours in the Leningrad airport during a blizzard, and for as
long again in the Cairo airport during a strike. I have known emotional,
sexual, and financial confinements, and I have actually been confined
to a dryout tank on Ninety-third Street for clinical alcoholics.

•

This, I think, will be my last long narrative, and that is exciting;
but what have I got? The escutcheon—and I might be able to write an
overture around this—the interview with his wife, the cats, the love
affair with Jody and Jody's ascent, the drug addiction, and the three
letters. That's it. And what do I intend? A story about a man of forty-
six who enters prison. He falls in love with Jody, who escapes; he is
visited by his wife; he suffers the agony of drug withdrawal; and he
escapes. You've got to have more narrative in your bag than that. So he
must have some failed escapes. Other attempts and other relationships.
With whom? E. J. Farragut entered the Falconer Jail on the 23rd of
March. All right, I want something beautiful, and it will be done by
June.

•

I must make a stab at the income tax, have my pants dry-cleaned,
prune the grapes, etc., and ride my bicycle. There seems to be such a
thing—for me, at least—as a pledge of sexual allegiance. There are
juicier orifices, more musical laughter, vaster and darker fields of comprehension, but I was born in this country and shall serve under this
flag.

•

I do prune the grapes and will today paint the iron and do the wisteria
and the roses. I suffer an inconsequential interview and after dinner,
lacking TV, read Updike on Borges and Nabokov. I am grateful to John
for having presented the masters so splendidly. I have not liked Borges,
but the quotations John gives leave me feeling that the blind old man

has an extraordinarily beautiful tone, a tone so beautiful that it can, quite gracefully, encompass death. And there is Nabokov, who can be better than one thinks possible. This, then, is the thrill of writing, of playing on this team, the truly thrilling sense of this as an adventure; the hair, the grain of sand in one's mouth; the importance (but not at all a selfish one) of this exploration—the density of the rain forest, the shyness of the venomous serpents, the resounding conviction that one will, tomorrow, find the dugout and the paddle and the river that flows past the delta to the sea.

•

So I think that we, the good writers, are at bottom ungainly. Re-reading, I deeply doubt my judgments. At A.A., a strange parish house, I wonder if this book is not simply a testament of conversion. Conceal this. I do observe how loudly and with what feeling we say the Lord's Prayer in these unordained gatherings. The walls of churches have not for centuries heard prayers said with such feeling. Deep. So I know how it ends. Ransom is in for twenty-five years for hijacking an airplane from Miami to Cuba. Kidnapping. The hijacking law hadn't been passed. And the stranger gives his coat to Farragut. "I want you to have it." So he puts on the stranger's coat and with it a peace that he cannot understand; and in character, prone to misunderstanding, he gets off at the next stop.

•

Ski briefly into a stand of pines. There is in them the sound of the wind, loud and faint, and I will skip the similar sound of traffic from the throughway. That's for another writer on another day. I see the strength and beauty of the copse and think that it reminds me only of a photograph of an old woman who has written, "Standing among my great trees, I think of all my loves."

She was the queen of Romania. I know what she meant, but I have no similar feelings. I do observe that the light in the copse forms four distinct strata. There is first the whiteness of the snow, tracked by my skis. Then there is the color of the pine boles, or trunks; the color of cinnamon, an inward color that seems to need very little light to be drawn out. Above this is the darkness of deadwood, as dense and impalpable as smoke, and above this the stratum of fresh green that depends upon sharing the light of the sky.

•

I think the work is successful and that I may be rich and famous. I claim not to care. I can always scythe my fields and walk in the streets. It is the strangeness of this excitement that I must examine. Why should it seem to be so strange to succeed? I do not mean pride or hubris; I mean only to have solved most of my problems and to have exploited, to the best of my intelligence, my raw materials. Take your rightful place, I say, standing at the bathroom window, free of the fact that I have always been content with second best. I am not better than the next man, but I am better than I was.

•

So, Easter morning. Mary is sick. I wake early, feed the dogs, and drink coffee. That this is Easter morning is very clear to me, as it was when I was a child. Put that in your pipe and smoke it. Driving over the hill past St. Augustine's, I think the experience is absolute. Christ is risen, and it all follows—the eggs for fertility, even the candy rabbit. I am deeply moved. My eyes are filled with tears. I am late for Mass. The altar, dark last Sunday, is filled with light, and during the climax of the ceremony I cry. It is not possible for me to diagnose religious experience. I say my prayers beside a woman dressed in white, a dental technician, or nurse. A man leads a cripple—a spastic, I think—to the altar. I think—sentimentally, perhaps—how glorious to be taken to the fire in defense of this faith. And I also think that the ecumenical church, with no fires at all, is progress.

•

Cutting the field in the middle of the afternoon in order to plant a cherry tree, I feel how profoundly important such work is to me. Then I recall, by chance, my mother's drinking herself to death, and think of her as uncommonly clear and strong. It is at about this time that my brother dies. A. calls later. I cry. He seems, as most people I love have seemed, to be lost, to be suffering a loneliness more painful than anything experienced in life. I read the prayer book, but—other than that God will not be a stranger—the descriptions of life everlasting are not what I have in mind. The next day my sorrow seems visceral. Susie and Ben are here. Ben does seem estranged. Susie and I talk about the family. I am inclined to make a legend of the Cheevers, and this can easily be done, but it seems idle to me. I will write a eulogy, including the fact that my brother wasted half his life. Susie throws some light on our intractability—my swiping a cigarette and Fred's cleaning his fingernails with a fruit knife. We seem to have got the provincial eccentricities of New England, but we seem to have got them wrong. This seems unimportant. I am late for church and am very heavy-spirited until I drink a great deal of coffee.

Coming in late to Communion, I see what someone else—my son, for example—might see: a homely building of common granite, with an archer's parapet and a clock that has lost its hands, built with the wealth of the 1870's when the village was a lively river port. Now impoverished and in debt, barely kept together by the hands of the faithful, it might seem to a young man no more than a husk, lacking even the distinction of ugliness and ruin. Built to accommodate hundreds, the church on this and almost every other morning has perhaps a dozen communicants. The priest, from some African country and trained in an English seminary, is wearing heavily embroidered vestments inherited from his homosexual predecessor; he reads the Epistle and the Gospel in such a distorted accent that almost nothing can be understood. The young man would observe that he could not pump gas, sell appliances, or even weed a garden, and so the young man might observe that the priest's choice of becoming God's advocate was a position of retreat. The carpet is, of course, worn; the colored windows are flashy and vulgar; and the black cleaning woman plays a very modest tune on the organ. The words spoken by the priest and the responses from the rest of us would make no sense at all to the young man. This is a cardhouse, a silly game for children who are much too old for such games, a threadbare display of provincial wealth and absence of taste. But to me this is the climax of the week.

I had not, because it reminded me of a movie in the forties, planned to report this, but this is what happened. Early in the service I hear, in the distance, the sound of trumpets. This sort of thing has never disconcerted me. Then, as the ceremony continues, I hear below the trumpets the commanding beat of drums. It is the fire-department band, practicing for tomorrow's parade. The music is quite distinct—they must be at the crest of the hill when we make the general confession— and as they come down the hill the trumpets and the drums fill the church, and when we exclaim "Holy, holy, holy, Heaven and earth are filled with Thy glory" not a word can be heard. The windows rattle as the band comes by. Then, in the front pew an old spinster, a spare relic of the past of the village and of the church, turns to the rest of the congregation to express her feelings at having the word of God obscured by the fire department. She is laughing. When I wish the priest a good morning, I see the band—men, boys, and girls (one with very fat, white legs, of which she seems proud) dressed in approximations of the uniforms of the Canadian Northwest Mounted Police.

•

The telephone rings at four. "This is C.B.C. John Updike has been in a fatal automobile accident. Do you care to comment?" I am crying. I cannot sleep again. I think of joining Mary in bed, but I am afraid she will send me away. I think I am right. When there is a little light I feed the dogs. "I hope they don't expect to be fed this early every morning," she says. I do not point out that John will not die every morning, and that in any case it is I who feed them. This restraint costs me nothing. When I go into the kitchen for another cup of coffee she empties the pot into my cup and says, "I was just about to have some myself." When I insist on sharing the coffee I am unsuccessful. I do not say that the pain of death is nothing compared to the pain of sharing a coffeepot with a peevish woman. This, again, costs me nothing. And I see that what she seeks, much more than a cup of coffee, is the gratification of a sense of denial and neglect—and that we so often, all of us, put our cranky and emotional demands so far ahead of our hunger and thirst.

As for John, he was a man I so esteemed as a colleague and so loved as a friend that his loss is indescribable. He was a prince. I think it not difficult to kiss him goodbye—I can think of no other way of parting from him, although he would, in my case, have been embarrassed. I think him peerless as a writer of his generation; and his gift of communicating—to millions of strangers—his most exalted and desperate emotions was, in his case, fortified by immense and uncommon intelligence and erudition. John, quite alone in the field of aesthetics, remained shrewd. Mercifully, there is no consolation in thinking that his extraordinary brilliance presaged a cruel, untimely, and unnatural death. His common sense would have dismissed that as repulsive and vulgar. One misses his brightness—one misses it painfully—but one remembers that his life was dedicated to the description of enduring—

and I definitely do not mean immortal—to enduring strains of sensuality and spiritual revelations.

So the call about John's untimely death was a fraud. I have decided, says my daughter, that it was an overambitious stringer, who saw the name on a police blotter and tried to cash in. This is a wish founded on the desirable simplicity of being charitable; one of her best characteristics. I am distempered, forlorn, and idle.

•

So, tomorrow I go to Boston to bury my brother.

•

My most frequent thought, during the funeral of my brother, is that my thinking is superficial. Any tears I shed are facile. The architecture of the early-eighteenth-century church is splendid. The smell in the vestibule of wood, the heat, and some salt from the nearby sea is, I think, unique to this part of the world and unlocks my memory. The high arched windows with their many lights must make it a cruel place to worship in the winter, but on this splendid summer day they make of the building a frame for the trees and the sky. I do not miss my brother at all. I think that he, with my mother, regarded death as no mystery at all. Life had been mysterious and thrilling, I often heard them say, but death was of no consequence. Some clinician would say that, while I part so easily with my brother, I will, for the rest of my life, seek in other men the love he gave to me.

•

So, to and from Massachusetts for Federico's graduation. Mary does the driving, a heavy chore. I think that in another twenty miles, or fifty, or a hundred, we will turn off onto one of the two-lane highways of my youth, with their trees, houses, and wonderful smells ranging from pond water to a newly cut hill or field. Here there is no sight line for the eye, nothing to smell but exhaust, nothing to see at all but dynamite craters and the tracks of gigantic backhoes. Here is a battlefield. The railroads are bankrupt, and subsidized by taxes. They are bankrupt because it is cheaper to truck freight than to send it by rail. The highways are also supported by taxes and represent the clash of two spheres of influence, motivated mostly by avarice. The highways will be the first to feel the diminishing sources of energy. It is difficult at this point, perhaps impossible, for me to imagine someone moved by greed. Here is the evidence. The twenty-wheel, three-axled trucks that can with a trifling misjudgment or some small malfunctioning wipe out three families on their way to the mountains roar down the ten-lane highways with the force of a cyclone. Among these are the nomads travelling with their homes, their boats, their curtains and rugs, and people like us bringing a son home from his commencement. What can one expect from a nomad society? The great trees have been preserved. This takes money. The lawns are splendid and have the intense smell of vegetation you find in a greenhouse. It is a summer's day, and there may be a thunderstorm. So we move, a hundred or more, over the fragrant grass at that particular pace and in that particular spacing one only finds in crowds on a summer's day, moving or even drifting toward some peaceable performance.

•

Approaching the fortieth year of my life, I had published well over a hundred short stories that expressed my feeling of life as intense and profoundly broken encounters. I then had two children and was into the fifteenth year of my marriage and hoped, in my first novel, to celebrate a sustained relationship over a long passage of time. I had not lived in New England for more than a decade, and the past of my family, beginning with the seventeenth century, appeared to me with some perspective. The pattern of my life during the year in which the "Chronicle" was completed was thought, in the Iron Curtain countries and by my daughter's generation, to be a bitter irony, a response I never quite understood.

I worked four days a week on the "Chronicle," with intense happiness. On Mondays, Wednesdays, and Fridays, I had a course in advanced composition at Barnard College. My weekends went roughly like this. On Saturday mornings, I played touch football until the noon whistle blew, when I drank Martinis for an hour or so with friends. On Saturday afternoons, I played Baroque music on the piano or recorder with an ensemble group. On Saturday nights, my wife and I either entertained or were entertained by friends. Eight o'clock Sunday morning found me at the Communion rail, and the Sunday passed pleasantly, according to the season, in skiing, scrub hockey, swimming, football, or backgammon. This sport was occasionally interrupted by the fact that I drove the old Mack engine for the volunteer fire department and also bred black Labrador retrievers. As I approached the close of the novel, there were, in my workroom, eight Labrador puppies, and on my desk the Barnard themes, the fire-department correspondence, "The Wapshot Chronicle," and a correspondence with both the American and the Royal Kennel clubs, since the litter had been sired by an English dog. Any account of the months in Russia is thought to be the hilarious account of a capitalist trying to forget the tragedy of his way of life. Nothing could be further from the truth. My happiness was immense, and I trust that the book will, in some ways, be a reminder of this.

•

The fact that I seem unable to enjoy an erection seems to be associated with my painful sense of estrangement. Painfully estranged, I go to take the train. I watch a man training a dog to lead the blind. The dog is struck when he goes too close to a sign. A bearded young black on the platform bends his knees, runs his hands up his inner thighs to his crotch, and shouts with joy. Having just returned from a Communist country, I regard the advertisements in the light of my memories. Two magazines are advertised not for their content but for their increase in advertising linage, and circulation. A coming generation is promised in terms of its vitality, its beauty, and its spending power. Alcohol and tobacco are praised between celebrations of two broken-down Broadway shows. If I were a Communist I would remark that the east bank of the Hudson River, down which I travel, is an economic, cultural, and human ruin. The roadbed itself is so rough that it is not possible to read a book, and the bankrupt railroad is supported by the government, but I count among my friends people who took substantial fortunes out of the railroads earlier in our history. The large industrial plants are obsolete and abandoned but for the spotty tenancy of sweatshops for the production of cheap clothes and shoes. The cultural sorrow is represented by a travelling, state-supported art show in a tent. Look, for the human ruin, into the faces of the other passengers. The river is broad, and continuing efforts to cleanse the water are effective. I am charmed by a mountain on the western shore. It has the appeal of a woman's breasts, of a friend's shoulder bent in gentleness. I am pleased with the sight of a sail filled with wind. I am depressed. It is God's will that I should not pursue this depression, but Plato observed that the soul can endure every sort of good and every sort of evil.

•

Irving Howe praises a novel for its brilliant exposure of the nettles that lie inevitably at the heart of family life.

I pay the bills and wonder about the costliness of this modest way of life. I bring brioches for S., and she says that the sight of me on a bicycle is beautiful, beautiful, beautiful. I'm very pleased with this— very pleased, in fact, with this relationship, which has got to be quite humorous and innocent. An old lady comes for lunch, and when she touches at the very edge of my egotism, at its most distant periphery, I blaze for a moment with impatience. Bad marks. I read George Eliot and find myself to be so physical a person, so tactile, so crude, that when anything is touched—when Deronda at last puts his hand around an oar—I am thrilled. I see a TV show on India and think about the importance of leadership; the questionable holiness of a free press; and that the paradise, the true paradise in which the stubborn and irreducible goodness of man reigns, is possible. I think of love, most often as a tragedy. And so try "The Island" for science fiction; and thank God that this planet from which I came is not a vulgar, low-budget, unimaginative dictatorship of women in peplums and men in diving gear, travelling in tubes through a civilization that has the sterility of an endless airport without the lunacy, the sweet uprootedness one finds in Heathrow or Leningrad. The strain of waiting for the publication, I mean the reception, of "Falconer," and the lack of interest of Paramount and the Book-of-the-Month Club, is not too difficult to bear, but it is, nonetheless, a strain. So the most you can do is fill in the time.

•

It will be close to three years since I have enjoyed any naked, sexual engorgement. This is a painful handicap. Getting into my car after a shower of rain and feeling the wet seat on the skin of my buttocks reminds me of the ecstasies of the skin. The last, I guess, was an Irish girl whose name I can't recall. She was about twenty, and, dropping her clothes, asked if I had ever seen anything so beautiful. I never had. It would not last, she added; her breasts were not as firm as they had been last year—and there was no true sadness in her observation. There was no sadness at all in our night together. She telephoned, not long ago. Thinking about Bennington and now about Ithaca, I thought, I think, in terms of the appearance of some lover who will undo me, engorge me, and grant me a contentment I have nearly forgotten. But after a month or so the sorrow sets in.

And I think of simple and pointless equations such as the Pefferdons. Pefferdon was born on a Midwestern farm in the 1880's and grew to be a young man of exceptional intelligence, charm, and craft. Owing to his remarkable gifts, he was under-secretary of the Treasury at twenty-four and went on to become one of the world's leading bankers and attempted, with J. P. Morgan, to corner the world's currency. He married a striking young blonde, who was a gymnastics instructor. To be a millionaire in those days was great fun. One had yachts, planes, a private dentist, and the deep conviction that one was a recognized prince. His four children were raised in these princely surroundings, and his youngest daughter, very beautiful and truly innocent—determinedly so, perhaps, considering the artificiality of her environment—fell in love with Herbert Dillon. Dillon had something of her father's giftedness. He was the son of Irish immigrants—domestics. His father was a gardener, and his mother an upstairs maid. He was an extraordinary athlete and had golden hair and that sort of geometric nose that promises great happiness—although there is, in my experience, very little you can do with a nose. Nancy Pefferdon was the lover in this romance. Dillon married her, reinvested her millions to buy partnerships, humiliated and presently destroyed her with his infidelities (highly publicized), and invited his current mistress to her funeral. All the Pefferdons were dead, and the great estate was up for sale. Dillon fastened his trousers long enough to buy the manor and the acreage, sold it to the most unscrupulous developer in the Northeast, who swiftly turned it into a suburban slum. So we have from rags to riches in one generation and from riches to plunder and the proliferation of a vulgarity that the Irish domestics hoped to escape when they fled Galway. But who cares, who really cares?

•

I am depressed for two days—a loss of vitality, perhaps sickness. It is difficult to grasp. It is very cold, and when I am in this humor my memories of cold are vivid. There was the cold of the farm in Hanover where Fred and I gave up hugging the fire and began to drink whiskey. I remember the hired man's toilet, the wooden seat gleaming with frost. I remember the cold of the furnished rooms I lived in in New York. My unease in the cold comes naturally. I buy sand at the lumberyard and sand the driveway. The cold and the movement please me, but as the afternoon wanes the cold intensifies, and I am tired and uneasy. I sleep and wake and feel fine.

•

Alienation seems to be the word. I feel alienated. This is keen but not painful; no more than a premonition of physical pain, which one has experienced and will again. At church this morning I think that the Mass ends not with a prayer or an amen but with the extinguishing of the candles, like the scattering of fire that closed the congregations of savages. This is close to portentous. Lunching with friends, I may miss some opportunities, as I do in playing backgammon. At around two a fine snow begins to fall. This is the snow that I, as a young skier, literally prayed for. It is very light, but copious; it is the sort of snow that fell on a happy afternoon last year when I skied with P. Night falls; the snow goes on and on—"five inches of powder on a packed base," one used to read. I shovel the stairs. The snow is like nothing, like air; and yet it holds the light that comes from the windows of the house. My daughter arrives in the middle of the storm after a dangerous journey. I much love her, pray for her happiness, and go to bed in my old bed, where I dream of a love.

•

After—on this shadowy winter morning—a string of harmless negatives, Mary closes with, "Well, you've never read any of his poetry." "I've read more than you," say I. So silence settles over the house and may not be relieved for a day or two. I feel poorly. Yesterday I skated. There are two rough places on the ice that will trip me up, and I worry about these in the middle of the night. I look into the woods for some signs of vitality, and all I find are the clusters of cones on the hemlock. Soon, I think, it will all be a blaze of color, first the dogwood, then the azalea—unpopular with me—then the greenness. I think of summer in terms of sexual discharges and iced gin. The last is impossible, and erotic playmates are not too easy to come by these days. I think that in a sexual discharge the genes and chromosomes are swiftly replenished, but the spiritual commitment is much more lasting.

•

I am galled at my lack of physical bulk and galled that this should concern me. There is really little evidence of this in all the photographs I have, but I fear being taken for an elderly bosun's mate, that gentle clerk in the hardware store who knows the whereabouts of all the nails, the rifle-company typist, the small museum guard in a worn uniform who says softly, "It is beautiful, isn't it?" I think of myself in West Berlin, toastmaster at Iole's wedding—bang-bang, a dynamic, lambent flame. So, having no bulk, one counts on spirit. I skate, shovel the snow, and think that I see in some unidentified tree a trace of greenness and lightness. This seems to be what I've been looking for. But on the dark or mysterious end of things I imagine, when I lie down for my nap, that I hold in my arms some unsuitable lover.

•

Waiting for another photographer and interviewer, I operate at a thoughtless level. Phil Roth calls to say that he received "Falconer," and would I give him John Updike's address. The rivalry among novelists is quite as intense as that among sopranos.

•

In the long psychoanalytical conversation we have been discussing, it seems to me that we might discuss the importance of our beginnings. To conceive a child, my father told me, is as simple as blowing a feather off your knee. He may have been speaking of my chance conception. Conception also, as we know, can be the consummation of a passionate and ecstatic response to life. A child demands love, which is easily given under most circumstances; rudimentary care, such as food and clothing; and, in a society with few conspicuous traditions, some broad instruction in good and evil. One's opportunities are not boundless, but they are not, I think, bounded by the sticks and stones of our beginnings. The most rudimentary genetic construction gives us a chance to improve on Great-Uncle Ebenezer's career as an inventor, or to continue the career as a concert pianist that was so suddenly ended by Cousin Louisa's influenza. In our countenances we find a diversity, a richness, and a promise that may be impeded but that is surely not crushed by the fact that Grandmother was an exhibitionist. "I think," I tell Susie, "of the richness you and your brothers have brought into this house."

•

Up from the meadows, up from the fields of corn, up from the deepest strata of my consciousness, swims my girl, my left knee in her crotch. In the higher strata, closer to waking, the others loiter, and while they may pick my pockets and do other things, I think no lasting damage to either of us will be done. "I wish you were here," said H. "We could have gone to the Degas show, and I have fresh shad and asparagus." Lying naked on that broad bed, I would have been very happy. But I do remember that the apartment is a sublet—I see, past the theatrical draperies at the window, the walls and windows of another apartment, and I am keenly aware of the fact that I am sixty-five. I do not seem to miss my youth. There is nothing so graceful as that. My youth seems taken from me. Then M. calls and will call again tonight. And I truly feel that there will be no darkness in this friendship. There is a membrane, a caul of darkness, that I think I recognize in homosexuals, and I think this is not our destiny. There will be in my life pain and grief, I know, but I think there will be no waywardness. That there might be a sexual consummation here seems likely, but it seems no more than a stone in our way.

•

So, you wake at half past six with the mounting hots, and by ten o'clock you could, like a riggish cat, mount a stuffed jaguar or fuck a rusty doorknob. This mounts until half past twelve, when company and lunch have a soothing influence. You drive into the village to get some milk, and the sight of the village, the stab at orderliness with which the buildings are grouped, the thoughtful look in a young woman's face as she leads her children across the street seem to be the manifest beauty we hope to achieve. Then one is engorged with melancholy— slightly relieved by a dozen pigeons taking off from the roof of an old building. The day is hostile. The sky is gray, a discouragement, but the gray light is strong. The love music in the supermarket is sad, terribly sad. The woman ahead of me, wearing diamond rings and heavily made up, waits patiently to pay for a small bag of potatoes. In the barbershop a brutish and corrupt policeman wearing a mud mask sleeps. Into the barber's comes a young woman with something to sell in a heavy box. She is very skinny. Her hair, home-dyed and home-waved, is a candy hue that went out of style ten years ago. She has spent the hour after high school on her makeup. "I know that you would be interested in—" "No," says the barber rudely. I want to give her all the money I have. Half an hour later I see her standing by the highway with her box. She seems not to know where to go. I think she has invested her savings, or some borrowed money, in something she believes to be highly desirable. She dyed her hair and improved her features and, imagining success—oh, so lightheartedly—has been met with rebuffs. I think her experience—standing by the side of the road—is a part of all our lives. I cherish this. And so it is nearly dark, one has nothing, nothing at all, and one has everything. I will answer letters, light a fire, and read.

•

I endure, am forced into, and triumph over exhaustive carnal speculations and fantasies. I feel no guilt. When I announce that I have weeded the upper garden, Mary exclaims over the fact that I must have destroyed her bed of herbs. There is nothing very wrong about this, nor is there anything lovable in her frame of mind. The company of my son does strengthen my position. When a woman exclaims bitterly, "And now, I suppose, I must cook dinner," the force of the remark is plaintive. How slender is her sense of usefulness. But this is not one's first response. I seem to be approaching a great crisis in my life, some ampule perhaps of death, and yet I am convinced that a flood of light will save us both. I spend most of the day planting the garden that was destroyed by woodchucks in our absence. This is an occupation I thoroughly enjoy. The only difficulty is that it leaves me with some lameness in my right shoulder, and when I go with my son to see a Woody Allen film I observe that none of the actors seem to have spent the day with a spading fork. The film lacks (I think) the heft and the smell of soil. And I glimpse the inflexibility and the parochialism of my tastes at this time of life. And so as soon as the sun is on the garden today I will return there.

•

The holiday parties we go to might be described as provincial. This would be adequate but not truthful. We go on the night of the Fourth to see the fireworks at the club, something I first did perhaps twenty-five years ago. It is a pleasure to see so much of my life. The vast Palladian façade, built on the bones of murdered workers, and the men and women spread over the lawn are thought to be a show of wealth and privilege (although my friends from prison would say that it ain't got no class) and I remember, unwillingly, the villa of a papal duchess. But here is the grass, the crowd, the twilight, and the terrible dance band playing "When the Red, Red Robin." One has heard the same dreary music for so long that one would expect the players to be infirm, but they are youthful, and so what one encounters is enduring vulgarity. The buffet supper is over. The light is dimming. The band begins to struggle with "The Star-Spangled Banner" and very, very slowly the diners get off their chairs and onto their terribly expensive shoes. A little flag, constructed of fire, is ignited. Its sputtering can be heard, and one section of a crimson stripe falls to the grass. There is some applause, some cowboy hoots, and then, with a half-dozen mortared detonations high in the air, the show begins.

I watch the man, barely visible in the darkness, who ignites the mortars with a flare and then runs like hell. There is some enormous universality and excitement in the way he ignites a fuse and takes off. This is youth, this is the excitement of a summer night, this is mischief, this, in fact, is sin. This is also my partiality to a rudimentary participation. I canoe on the Main and in the canals of Amsterdam and Venice.

I get to know the quality of the water, the distances in terms of strength, and enjoy the privileges of a bystander. The fireworks are mortars and set pieces. They seem quite traditional. There is the French school: pale colors that arc at the zenith and give, for half a second, the illusion of a rotunda. There are the Neapolitan extravagances of red and green, and the phosphorus waterfalls. We sigh like lovers at the fire, applaud the fire, estimate the cost of the fire. We are charmed by the fire. "Mother can't find her largest diamond," says a young woman. Her "a" is improbably broad. It would excite the suspicions of a busboy. "What do you think someone from a place like Russia would think about this?" a young man asks. Oh-ho. I remember my old-fashioned friends who used to call across theatre lobbies remarks such as, "Lisbon was divine, but the King has laryngitis." So the last chain of mortars jars our eardrums, fills heaven with fire, and we go back to the exclusive parking lot.

•

So, I feel lost, and doubly lost because I'm not sure where I am. Climbing the hill to get the paper, I seem to be going down a dirt road to swim in some lake. The feel of dirt under my bare feet and the breadth of the kitchen garden on my left—or the cut hayfields on my right—will diminish my sense of being lost, as will my swim in a cold lake. And so here, rather than venting my candor and my amorousness, I spade the fallow garden and weed the stairs. And today I will clip the hedges and fertilize the tomatoes. I think about my aloneness, about the many things that are meant by this. I claim to be thrilled by the indifference of the young because it gives me a sense of my self—my carcass and my intelligence—that has the robust ring of truth. And I am of that generation that can remember when every cash register had a small, marble shelf. Suspected coins were flung against this to tell by their ring whether or not they were counterfeit. It was to become for some of us a metaphor for good and evil, with a dependence upon the verb "rang."

So I feed the tomatoes as well as the Swiss chard, and, finding no love letter in the mail, I view both my losses and that which is beyond and above them, that which has always been represented by the mountains. The inclination to sadness is plain; so is the robust laughter from the mountains, and, while I am not quite content with this, it is enough to keep me moving. Pedalling up the long, gradual climb, I see both myself and my adversary. I display a kind of hasty optimism that seems comical. Velocity seems to be all that I've ever possessed. I pass a house where the vegetable garden is planted every spring and is always, by July, a thick wilderness of weeds. Is the man always transferred to another job? Do they divorce or simply take a long vacation in Europe? And then I pass the house that stands forever in the darkness of a grove of maples, susceptible to dampness, rot, and human depressions. A homosexual couple once lived there, quarrelling bitterly about hairpieces, etc. I then pass the beautiful garden of the two brothers who used to pump gas at the station. From the open windows of the house I hear two highly cultivated voices discussing the price of fried chicken. These are rich and educated women, and I wonder have the brothers married, do they have successful sisters, what is this foothold in the upper class? A burst of music explains the voices as television, and I shift gears and coast down the long hill with the wind in my face. I remember at Bennington, on an autumn afternoon, drawing a tub of water and turning on the TV. I got into the tub and pretended that the room was full of people. It was full of voices. But I am tired of such loneliness.

I read some stories of mine. Their preciseness galls me; I seem always to be plugging at small targets. I hit them all right, but why don't you get the 12-gauge double-barrel and go after bigger game? And the lack of genuine climax galls me, too. I have been racked by a big orgasm as often as there are stars in heaven, but I don't seem to get this down. However, I think the stories an accomplishment.

•

So my hours of happiest comprehension seem limited. They are roughly from six to eight in the morning, and it is now half past nine. For reasons, perhaps, of decorum, comprehension, or dishonesty I recast my dilemma in the light of those days when my brother left for Germany and I lay on the sofa crying for him. The sofa was a ridged, Victorian piece of furniture constructed for straight-backed callers taking a cup of tea. This I remember vividly. I wept for a love that could only bring me misery and narrowness and denial; and how passionately I wept. And so I weep again (not really), and go out for dinner looking, really, for nothing but company and warm food.

•

A new journal, and since more than half of the last novel was encompassed in the last journal I hope that something will be accomplished when I complete this. Alone, and much less lonely (I claim) than I am with my wife, I eat sketchily and the first thing I think of when I wake is that I must have lost weight. I will weigh myself. By a loss of weight I mean that I will have recouped some of that youthful beauty I never possessed, that I will be kissed and caressed and worshipped. I see how far all of this is from the realm of common sense. Anyone who caressed and worshipped this old carcass would be someone upon whose loneliness, fear, and ignorance I preyed. This would be the exploitation of innocence. This I see as I swim so briefly through that part of the stream that represents common sense. I will get into other, more seductive, waters, but there is always the chance that I will return to this.

•

I go into town to see F., a charmer, an Eastern European with just that margin of irresistibility that is necessary for the world of film. Then I go down to see H.'s show. It is sold out, but I get a seat in the last row of the balcony. She's a very attractive woman, and I feel estranged in my balcony seat, and it would be vulgar of me to review the intimacies we have enjoyed—but none since the snow melted, and this is August. Instead of taking her to supper, I leave before the end, walking to the station. I look, rather wearily, for the prostitutes, but there are none. There are tourists in the city, men and women with children, and young men with their arms around the slender waists of their girls. The beauty of girls seems to have dimmed for me, and the truth is that I no longer have the kind of bone that is needed. This, I trust, will pass since I have a bone in the mornings. But am I growing old, and should I accommodate myself to this? When does one's spirit yield to one's chemistry? The last time I scuffled with a woman the lingering perfume on my skin and my clothes lasted for three marvellous hours, and I remember the skein of L.'s hair across my face. But there is at corners, waiting for traffic lights, the sense that the time has come to part with all of this. Is this supine; is this less than courageous? Will I be content with one-night, one-hour stands, really, when, after I have come, I wonder why they don't get dressed and go away?

•

So, as an unnatural and undeservedly lonely man, I go to the diner for supper. The waitresses are all meant for us, and I love them. Bringing me bread and butter and a glass of ice water, she is like the dove bringing a green branch to the ark. I hear a couple behind me. "All you want to do," says the man, "is to pick a fight. Whatever I say, you'll use it as a springboard for a fight. If I order celery and olives you'll pick a fight over that." He seems to have got all my wife's lines, and, remembering them, I think them perverted and unnatural. They are quite insane. I have never, I think, thought of my wife with more finality. But I have only nine days here before we go to the sea, and so I will wait for the beaches and the Atlantic. Walking around the place that contains so much of myself, I feel that to live here is not truly a compromise, that it does not suffer the lack of light, the malodorousness of a compromise. So I shall cut wood, set some stones. Answer your mail, pay your bills, go to the dry cleaner's and the laundromat.

•

This is truly the worst kind of day the Hudson Valley can produce. Its Precambrian memories are refreshed, and the vines, some of the earliest in botanical history, grow with great rapidity. The light is melancholy, the air is lethal, everything one touches is wet, and I, of course, am lonely. Yesterday, doing what the Boy Scout Handbook forbade, I observed that my imaginary partners are chosen not for reasons of sentiment but for their obscene expertise. Mary calls and seems both friendly and intelligent, and I glimpse the landscape of my marriage as a fertile and well-lighted place, where I can be malicious and untruthful. This does not last for long. The chairs and tables all speak in complaining, embittered, and hateful voices. "How long," the stove asks me, "has it been since you have heard in this room a clear and loving voice?" It was twelve years ago, on the night when I first returned from Russia. "My mother wanted me to be a boy," she cried, and let me hold her passionately.

•

This is a splendid sea. I play backgammon with a young man for most of the afternoon and come out two games behind. Into the village I drive to A.A., which helps immensely, and where I think I see two gays sitting in the corner. I think I am completely mistaken and that the fault is mine. A woman confesses to her sins. She weighed 280 pounds; she couldn't climb a flight of stairs; she couldn't drive; she couldn't do anything but drink, and even that was difficult because she would vomit most of the first bottle. I think of my mother at Christian Science Testimonial meetings, confessing to having been so enchained by the flesh that a cancer was destroying her. And so we say the same; our confessions all deal with self-destruction and love. Look away from the body into truth and light! We find, in these church basements, a universality that cuts like the blade of a guillotine through the customs we have created in order to live peaceably. Here, on our folding chairs, we talk quite nakedly about endings and beginnings. When I leave the church the village has the charm, eclipsed for me, of a restoration or a stage set. The nostalgia is openly false. The beauty of the architecture is striking and splendidly preserved, but the clash of a whale-oil port is nowhere; and how absurd to look for it. This is a place for vacationers, mildly in search of a quaint past and a nice answer.

•

This is the sort of seaside hotel about which people used to write romances; here one met the lady with the dog, here old Aschenbach came in his woolly underpants, watching a youth sport in the sea.

•

I could write to X that when I say I need you what I mean is that I need the swiftness with which you respond to the importunacy of my needs, and that when I am with you I am as close as I have been to another person in some months. I could write this, but I will not, because some of it is bullshit and because it wouldn't get me anywhere. I could write a humorous report on the bicycle situation here, but I really ought to try to be serious. The only urgency I seem to feel is the urgency—and the mysteriousness—of my sentimental and my carnal drives. I seem to be married no more. Mary is charmed by the simples of the Atlantic—its iconography—which is truly the iconography of birth, and she walks up and down the shore and covers the windowsill with shells and stones that have a spectrum of great delicacy and beauty. She comes to the breakfast table with thistles and beach-plum sprays, bayberries and other wild and delicate specimens evolved by the prevailing southwesterlies, and while she is charmed and charming I am moved mostly by a sense of parting.

•

The runt, the vagrant, in the pew ahead of me in church. I notice first the unwashed, uncut, uncombed brown hair partially concealing tipped ears that someone would describe as elfin. The pallor, I think, is Polish, never having been near Poland. From the cowlick one can anticipate every thread of his clothing, either lifted from some bin in a charitable bureaucracy or bought in some back-street, downhill, cut-rate Army & Navy store. The north-woods-lumberman's jacket is colorless and seems made of bad, thin air. There is no point in holding up for scrutiny the sketchy wash trousers and the wet sneakers with their knotted laces. "You are twenty-three? twenty-four?" you might ask.

"I'm thirty-five," he will say. "I know I look young." What he means to say is that he looks undernourished and immature, and when he stands for the Gloria he has the posture of someone waiting in line for a handout. He is waiting in line. He will always seem to be waiting in line. Utterly alone, picked up by your headlights at dusk standing on the road shoulders of Route One Million, possessing nothing but his clothes and maybe three dollars, he will seem to be standing in line. But he is on his feet for the Gloria, drops loudly to his knees at the first hint of prayer. Where did he learn his High-Church ground rules? He is, I conclude, imitating the woman ahead of him until I see him slide into base seconds ahead of her when we switch from the Epistle to the Gospel. So he learned them in line, I conclude, learned them in some church orphanage, where you lined up for the Holy Eucharist before you lined up for the boiled egg and the day-old bread. He leaves the church ahead of me, and the priest asks, "You've been away?" "Yar," he says. Then he turns to me, very brightly, and says "*Hi!*" I can't imagine where we met. I think he cut the ivy off my chimney two years ago. What do I want? I want to fatten him, mature him, dress him, and send him to Yale. Driving my car around the block, I crank down a window, planning to speak and ask him where we met, but he, of course, has vanished. Those are his accomplishments. He can queue up and vanish.

•

I wake from a dream or reverie of last February, or this February, or some February to come. I am working at West House. I wake at six or seven, drink coffee lightheartedly and naked in the kitchen, dress and walk through the snow to the garage, where I kiss beloved B. and am given a plate of scrambled eggs. Back at the house, I work until one, when I eat my sandwiches and take a rest. The days are getting longer, but it starts to get dark at four, and I put on my skis, and pole happily around the widest circle. I come in after dark, take a shower, and am dressing when I hear G. at the door. She is a loving, intelligent, and beautiful woman, and why should this be so remarkable? You will say that is the old chimera, but why should a loving, beautiful, and intelligent woman exist only in the imagination of a lonely man? Her hair is dark. This, I think, is a new note. She is not terribly young, but her face and her skin show no trace, no trace of age that can be seen by these old eyes. I am not sure what we do—we might do any-thing—but whatever it is we are contented with one another. I seem to take her to a restaurant, and we spend the night together. In the morning we have a terrible breakfast in some roadside place, but the coffee is good. This seems to me a poem, or perhaps a song. And I wake happily from another dream in which I think I live and walk in an accomplished, representative government that is efficient, visionary, and victorious. Bureaucracy has vanished, along with smallpox, and we have gone on to better things.

●

I was crowding forty when I stood under an apartment-house canopy and planned to write "Oh, what can you do with a man like that!," and so on, through the end of "Goodbye, My Brother" and those other stories and novels that record my break with irony and dismay. And here is that New York at the close of the Second World War that so few of us remember: one stood in line at Rockefeller Center; the 20th Century to Chicago was on time; almost everybody wore a hat. The singular force of time through which one seems to swim let me describe everyone with gray hair until my own head turned gray when everyone else's hair went brown.

●

Mr. Ross insisted on a degree of decorum. One could not, of course, use a word like "fuck." One complained, of course, and published stories elsewhere, but I, it seems, had my own concept of decorum, and when Mr. Ross used the word "fuck" at the lunch table I would jump. Having noticed this, Mr. Ross would, at lunch, throw a "fuck" in my direction now and then, to watch me jump. He was, himself, not a decorous man, but he taught me that decorum can be a mode of language—born of our need to speak with one another—and a language that, having been learned, was in no way constraining.

●

So, he stands in the forest, making his choice. On his left is the girl, dressed in white, with yellow hair—golden, really. Any gesture or movement she makes—picking a leaf off her skirt—seems to involve an increase of light. The other is dark-haired, dark-eyed; even the luminousness of her skin is dark. She is slender, long-breasted, with very long fingers. The girls represent—quite unoriginally—night and day, gravity and weightlessness, the sun and the moon. The girl with yellow hair represents a boundless chain of lighted rooms; the easy talk and laughter of friends and lovers; healthy pride, and a winning score. The other represents one room, and that quite small and unlighted. She is contentedly friendless and her appetite is for out-of-season grapes. And yet it is the declivity of her back that his fingers seem to want to trace, and by fingers, of course, I mean something very different. So he stands in the forest, asked to choose between the boundless light and a darkness whose only charm is mystery. But what he overlooks is the fact that lightness and darkness have their own opinions. If he has invested in tax-exempt municipal bonds, thinks the girl with yellow hair, are they insured? Can he get a taxi on a rainy night? Will he be cross at the fact that I am always ten minutes early for everything, everything, and that I eat candy bars between meals and leave the wrappers in ashtrays? Does he snore? thinks the representative of darkness. Does he have a morning cough? Does he have no consideration at all, since it is twenty minutes past the time for my blood-pressure pill, and I am allergic to the roses with which this forest is filled? He even overlooks the trees, who have their own thoughts and anxieties. A virulent rust, invisible to the eye, can wither the mightiest of them. A wisteria vine, no more today than a strand of hair on the trunk, can bend and break the spine of an oak. He stands in Arden—a forest whose richness and profundity he can never comprehend, deceived as he is by the importance of his choice.

•

There is a degree of *mensongerie* in some of our loves, but this seems most exaggerated in the love of men. Chucky was a runner-up in some three-round provincial golden-gloves contest eighteen years ago, but he now swaggers around the steam room like the winner he never was; and the lovers he mounts, young or old, seem to feel transported to the manly world of fighters. It is as though some old whore claimed to have been the centerfold in the most golden days of *Playboy*. She wouldn't make any such claim. And so we have an enlarged—and, I think, unsavory—element of delusion and regret. We are all, sooner or later, shadows, but we are not overwhelmed.

Floating around in melancholy, I recall my claim that my life was brightly lighted by the sun until my adolescence. But there is a photograph of me, taken, I think, when I was seven, that would refute this. The face is of a boy whose father regretted his conception and wished that he was not alive. We, the fatherless, sit around trying to top one another's tales, and I think myself lacking the love of a father, and, living with a father who wished me dead, think I've won the game. The truth is impossible to arrive at, but, even when I was in my twenties, he closed and locked the door in my face. So I think I have never used the scene where the doctor comes for dinner, and I will put this down. I remember my father's detestation of me as I feel for the roots of some destructive vine—the vine, of course, being my bewildering love. To be mistaken in love, to—like Capote—take a lover who will strip your apartment of all its valuables, is something that can be parsed in fifty ways; but it seems to me no more than the mysteriousness of love. It has always been dangerous; its other face has always been death.

•

An overcast and foreboding sky—not really dark, because there is light in the woods when I walk the dogs—but a serious sky. It is very cold. Only a little snow falls. See the old man, walking through the woods, pouring into the ears of his dogs the griefs and frustrations of his marriage; and on the hill at the edge of his land are the graves of five former dogs, into whose ears he poured his laments, even as they lay dying. Oh, why does she spit in my face? Why does she knee me in the groin? Why has she not spoken to me now for eighteen days? The dogs pick up the scent of deer these days and find the walks exciting.

•

So, thinking of H., I think of her as a sunlit playing field, into which I have, often enough, jogged out with my football, ready for fun. But then, to be honest, there were the days in which I hid in the bushes at the edge of the field; there was the hockey game I missed because I couldn't find my skate laces; and the football scrimmage I sidestepped because my jockstrap was either stolen or misplaced. In short, I have been a coward. In retrospect, I think myself blameless, but this darkness in my nature seems inexpungible. I have been a coward, and perhaps it is cowardice that we see in this old man, haranguing his dogs with tales of his unhappiness.

•

My son drives me to Mt. Kisco to pick up my new car. He seems happy with his wife and thus estranged from us, and this is as it should be. The new car stalls driving away from the dealer, and there seems to be something wrong with the ignition. I buy groceries at an A. & P. strange to me. There is for some reason no music, and this I miss. The customers seem to me unclean, stupid, and gross, and I see that this level of perception—this seizure of morbid sensitivity—cripples my usefulness as a man. My sympathy for the young women at the checkout counters is outrageous. I want to gather them all in my arms and take them off to Arcadia. I seem tired, and I sleep. Meeting my daughter at the train I observe again how like an enemy I judge the boots, hats, voices, and faces of these men and women who are merely waiting to take a train into the city. I seem to think they plan the destruction of Western civilization. I talk with my daughter, cook supper, and go to a meeting in a smoke-filled parish-house basement where all but two of the audience are shabbily dressed. I remember my happiness with a burlesque company when I was very young.

•

I have no perspective at all. After the interviewers leave, I drive the maid home and walk with the dogs. My sexuality is highly irritable and distorts my view of things. The last of the light has that splendid and indescribable glow that one finds only in winter twilights. Now, for the first time, I see color in the trees. So, there will be spring and summer. And, walking up the hill carrying the garbage pail, I see a holly leaf on the drive. I am as thrilled as Leander was when he saw the green from Advent on the chancel carpet. The nearly black, hard leaf with its thorns means potency and vigor. That it means nothing at all is unimportant. It is important that I am stirred.

I become myself; and so I will try to review what has contributed to my painful sense of loss. My mortality is what I begin with, manifested by my sexual drives. These excitements have always been random, and when I have refused the love of men it has been, I like to think, a choice and not a force of repression. The present problem, if it is that, began a year ago when I found myself alone in a squalid motel with a young man who had none of the attributes of a sexual irregular. We embraced briefly, declared our love, and parted. We have since then met four or five times, but I have thought of him often. The importance of this is impossible to judge. It could be compared to an infection that threatens my well-being, but that is dormant much of the time. Such is my injured heart. He married for the second time in December and left my letters unanswered. What I expected from him was easy companionship, lewdness, and some relaxation of the rigors of living with a wife. On my return from Russia, I suffered a violent spasm of alienation. Darkness, for example, offended me. To read a book, I would turn on six lamps. The only house I have ever owned struck me as dirty, confusing, and costly. In the piles of mail, I found a letter from him, and it was the first that I opened. He hinted at the indifference of his marriage and hinted—no more—at his love for me.

It is impossible for me to describe what followed. I am highly susceptible to romantic love. I remember weeping bitterly over D. and L. I became engulfed in the anticipation of an erotic romance that corroded and destroyed that self-possession that defines a man. Yesterday at lunch I experienced that intoxicating arrogance of the self-declared alien, the sexual expatriate. I am unlike you, unlike any of you eating your wretched lunches in a Greek diner. I am queer, and happy to say so. At the same time, the waitress is so desirable that I could eat her hands, her mouth. This is the cardinal sin of pride. I rest, I sleep. How reluctant I am to admit to taking a nap. Somewhere along the line, my thinking, my chemistry, my genitals, and my spirit are restored; and that makes it possible to continue that voyage or pilgrimage that is one's life. I am not sure of the hour of day. The taste of that given bread and salt that is my life is in my mouth. This would seem to be God's will. I walk the dogs. I skate and tire very quickly. I cook dinner, drive to church, watch a thrilling movie on TV, and sleep happily in my skin for the first time in what seems to be a year. My most despicable moment, I think, is in the post office. There is a woman there in a very cheap fur coat, with two children. The coat has been sprayed with something that promised to make it gleam like mink, but the skin is the skin of a mongrel. The woman's eyes are protuberant. So are the eyes of her two small children, and I regard all three with loathing and regard myself as contemptible for scorning these innocents. I experience the arrogance of a man committed to a wayward cock. This morning, eating bacon and toast, my galling otherness has been conquered. I am not at the Connaught, or the Cairo Hilton, or the Bucharest Minerva. I am in my own house. That I will suffer all these agonies again is likely, but, having come through them so many times, I know that they are not a destination. Even now, writing this, I feel the painful threat of confusion and loss behind the bookshelf and outside the window, but I am happily a man sitting on a chair.

•

It is a week since I waited in this drafty kitchen for my lover. It all seems to have worked out wonderfully, although the composure I enjoy on waking seems not to last deep into the morning. What the hell is a man who made half a million dollars last year doing in an art colony where he sits alone in a room that is obviously furnished in the aftermath of a disaster? The chair he sits in comes from some kitchen. The narrow, threadbare rug belonged in some hall. The bed or cot is one of those expedient surfaces on which we fuck those people whose last names escape us. But what about the white bureau with a keyhole for every drawer, delicate hand pulls, a mirror held up with such narcissistic chasteness that it seems to ask, Who is the fairest of them all? How in hell did this bastion of middle-class chasteness—this repository for sachets, laces, old dance cards, fans, dried flowers, preserved rose leaves, broken beads, and perhaps a pearl-handled revolver—how did this find its way into this bleakest of rooms? There must, of course, have been a flood. Only a natural disaster of unprecedented sweep and violence could account for this feat of dislocation. There must be a chamber pot in the closet, and that half-burned candle in its wretched glass holder is left over from yesterday's thunderstorms, when all the lights always went out.

¹

I seem to have some vision of the waywardness of man and the blessings of velocity. I remember C., driving me to dinner with his wife and sons, blindly stopping the car on the road shoulder, making a wild grab for my cock, and kissing me on the ear. I was polite—no more—and so we continued on to the dinner. And I think of an article in yesterday's *Times* in which Ada Huxtable discusses the architecture of roadside restaurants, meant to catch our sympathies at any speed above fifty miles an hour. There was, long ago, the practical decade, followed by the restorations and the progressive architects, working in their own idiom. What she does not observe is that this nomadic, roadside civilization is the creation of the loneliest travellers the world has ever seen. Quick-food stands that resemble the House of the Seven Gables, Colonial Williamsburg, and the Parson Capon house are not picked for their charm or their claim to a past; they are picked because we are a homeless people looking at nightfall for a window in which a lamp burns, and an interior warmed by an open fire, where we will be fed and understood and loved. The rash of utterly false mansards, false, small-paned windows, and electric candlesticks is the heart's cry of a lonely, lonely people. And after opening a thousand rough-hewn doors, with their false, wrought-iron hardware; after warming ourselves at electric fires and reading a menu that is a reproduction of something from the century before last; we feel that the past will not feed and warm and understand and love us; and so we go on to the future; to the space between the stars where our love is waiting; we eat our wretched food in rocket ships, flying saucers, and pieces of Mars and the moon. Surely we will be understood there. And so one sees this great, nomadic nation on roads built by blackmailing unions and the lobbies of contractors, manufacturers, truck-fleet owners, and politicians of all sorts. We see a great people turned nomadic in their passionate search for love.

•

Absolute candor does not suit me, but I will come as close as possible in describing this chain of events. Lonely, and with my loneliness exacerbated by travel, motel rooms, bad food, public readings, and the superficiality of standing in reception lines, I fell in love with M. in a motel room of unusual squalor. His air of seriousness and responsibility, the bridged glasses he wore for his nearsightedness, and his composed manner excited my deepest love, and I called him the next night from California to say how much he meant to me. We wrote love letters for three months, and when we met again we tore at each other's clothes and sucked each other's tongues. We were to meet twice again, once to spend some hours in a motel and once to spend twenty minutes naked before a directors' lunch I had to attend. I was to think of him for a year, continually and with the most painful confusion. I believed that my homosexuality had been revealed to me and that I must spend the rest of my life unhappily with a man. I clearly saw my life displayed as a sexual imposture. When we met here, not long ago, we sped into the nearest bedroom, unbuckled each other's trousers, groped for our cocks in each other's underwear, and drank each other's spit. I came twice, once down his throat, and I think this is the best orgasm I have had in a year. We slept together, at his insistence, and there was some true pleasure here in discovering, I believe, that neither of us was destined to exhaust the roles we were playing. I remember the acute lack of interest with which I regarded his nakedness in the morning when he returned to bed after having taken a piss. He was merely a man with a small cock, a pair of balls, and a small ass suitable for cushioning a chair or a toilet seat and for nothing else. The remembered exactions of women played some role in this for me. There was no anxiety on my part about whether he had a climax. I took a shit with the door open, snored, and farted with ease and humor, as did he. I was delighted to be free of the censure and responsibility I have known with some women. I could spar with him if I felt like it, feed my cock into his mouth, and complain about how smelly his socks were. And I was determined not to have this love crushed by the stupid prejudices of a procreative society. Lunching with friends who talked about their tedious careers in lechery, I thought: I am gay, I am gay, I am at last free of all this. This did not last for long.

•

To interrogate oneself tirelessly on one's sexual drives seems to me self-destructive. One can be aroused, for example, by the sight of a holly leaf, an apple tree, or a male cardinal bird on a spring morning. As deeply rooted as they are in our sentimental and erotic lives, we must consider that our genitals can be quite thoughtless. They count on us for discretion, cleanliness, and gratification. Without our considered judgment they wouldn't have the life span of a butterfly.

•

A bright day—cold, "fresh," as we say in other languages; me, horny. In the evening paper—in this provincial, small-town newspaper—one reads that a Cuban couple, solitary, hardworking people, who had no friends, lost their son in a drowning accident in the municipal swimming pool and committed double suicide. They closed the garage door, connected a garden hose to the exhaust pipe of the car, and suffocated in each other's arms. "They were so unhappy after they lost their son," said the neighbors. "She cried and cried. She used to embroider a lot and knit and crochet, but after they lost the boy she didn't do anything but cry." Mr. Nils Jugstrom, returning from his job at the Townsend wire factory, noticed a cedar chest on the road shoulder of Route 23. It was a good-looking chest, nearly new, and he pulled over to the side of the road. Opening the chest, he found the mutilated body of a man with dark hair and a full mustache. It was some time before he could get a car to stop, and call the police. He sat alone by the corpse while hundreds of cars, hastening home, passed him with an indifference that he took personally. Deaths, this afternoon, are confined to the local nursing homes. Mrs. Cherryweather found a burglar in her shower stall, carrying her TV. While she called the police he escaped out a window. The high-school lacrosse team made four scores in the last eight minutes of play and defeated Haverstraw seven to six. I like small-town papers.

To have been expelled from Thayer Academy for smoking and then to have been given an honorary degree from Harvard seems to me a crowning example of the inestimable opportunities of the world in which I live and in which I pray generations will continue to live.

•

None of us can clearly remember those years at the turn of the century when the exalted arts of painting, sculpture, and music became so chaotic, so lost in an area of metaphysics that they had neither the vision nor the intelligence to exploit, that they surrendered their spiritual responsibilities and left to literature, and to literature alone, the responsibility of continuing that dialogue—vital to the life of the planet—that we and our kind carry on with one another, with our landscapes, with our oceans, and with our gods.

•

When I was a young man, I woke one morning in the unclean bedsheets of squalid furnished rooms, poor and hungry and lonely, and thought that some morning I would wake in my own house, holding in my arms a fragrant bride and hearing from the broad lawn beyond my window the voices of my beloved children. And so I did. But there was in the air some deep, continuous sound that I had not imagined, and, going to the window to see if it was raining, I saw that the day was brilliant and that the sound I heard was the brook—a reward that my most desperate imaginings had overlooked. The bounty of things, as it so often is, had been richer than my imagination of it. And so I wake this morning. I hear again the roar of the brook. I sleep alone these days, having been exiled from my own bed, closet, and washbasin by a troubled wife. All I hold in my arms these days is a memory of the girl on the Murad cigar box. But my children are comely and loving and self-possessed and walking over those parts of the world that interest them; and my daughter once kissed me and said, "You can't win them all, Daddy." And so I can't.

•

I recall coming into Rome on the train at dusk. I can't remember from where I was returning, but I was returning to a wife or a mistress and a circle of singing children. It was a hot dusk. The train was passing through that shantytown at the edge of the city, where the houses are no more than sheds, redeemed by the wild fertility of their small gardens. In one of these small gardens a naked young man was bathing himself from a pail. I expect he was getting ready to wait on table at some trattoria on the Gianicolo. I saw nothing of him other than his youthfulness, the whiteness of his skin, and the thickness of hair at his armpits and crotch. I loved him. Oh, how I loved him! That he might be a cretin with bad breath and a grating voice would never occur to me. So I entered the city and the circle of friends, deeply saddened to think that I had left my heart in the slums, deeply saddened and walking with the stoop of a guilty impostor. Now that I'm an old, old man, such waywardness seems only some part of life's richness.

•

M. calls and will likely arrive tomorrow. I could have told him not to come, but the alternatives are sinister. Reading old journals, I convince myself that the constants in my nature are healthy; as a man with a vegetable garden, I simply mean healthy as a plant that answers to its description on the package, that has a practical response to the soil and the climate and produces a surprisingly abundant and nutritious crop. The aberrations in my nature seem to me merely shadows, aberrant and passing storms. That I have homosexual instincts seems to me a commonplace. What is extraordinary, I think, is the force that was brought to crush these instincts and that exacerbated them beyond their natural importance. Whether or not we spend the night together seems of no great importance. I enjoy his company. I am lonely.

•

So the grail, the grail; and anyone who thinks of this in terms of genitalia is a contemptible noncombatant. The grail, the grail! It fills one's mind in the early morning as one's skin is filled with ardor. There is no question of compromise or defeat. One wants only to make an exemplary contribution, and if this is accomplished one's ending is inconsequential!

•

And there is the face, which is the most important experience for me and which seems to escape me. I am waiting for someone to arrive on the train. It is toward the end of the afternoon. The train is late. The taxi driver leaves his cab. He is youngish. There is really nothing very specific about him. He is, I think, ugly. If he ever went to a dance—which I doubt he would—he would have trouble getting a date. So, to this stranger, whom I very likely will never see again, I bring a bulky and extended burden of anxieties like the baggage train of some early army. Does he live with his wife, his girl, his mother, his drunken father? Does he live alone? Does he have a small bank account, a big cock, is his underwear clean? Does he throw low dice, has he paid his dentist's bills—or has he ever been to the dentist's? We see the light of the approaching train in the distance, burning gratuitously in the full light of day. At this sight, he takes a comb out of his pocket and runs it through his hair. Is the comb broken? Is his hair dirty? That is not for me to observe. What I do see in this gesture is the man—his essence, his independence; see in his homely face the beauty of a velocity that does not apprehend the angle of repose. Here in this gesture of combing his hair is a marvel of self-possession, and the thrill is mutual and is, it seems, the key to this time of life.

•

One wouldn't want to love oneself. That damages our usefulness. One wouldn't want to pursue the past. That is bad for the posture. And one wouldn't want to be one of those old men who take out their cocks and clear their throats as if they were about to write, with their seminal discharge, one of those lengthy postwar treaties that will crush the national spirit, surrender the critical isthmus, and yield the mountain passes to the enemy.

•

My son and his beloved are down when I return to the house. That I should see him enjoy the love of a loving, comely, and intelligent young woman is an enormous contribution to my sense of things. But I have forgotten to mention the light of this day. It is emphatic, terribly clear, and seems in its force and in the force with which it throws shadows to declare the year's end. "I will not go swimming," I say to Mary, "because I will cry." "I understand," says she. I do not swim (for other reasons) but the pool, dark so early in the afternoon, with its few fallen leaves, would be a powerful experience. Spreading fertilizer on the upper terrace, I think that my son will go and I will never see him again. This is not the worst of my thinking for the day, but it is contemptible; as it will seem contemptible later to think that I should have been born in an earlier period when I would have been better understood. Today is where I live; today gives me my gravel, my essence, the bulk of my usefulness. So I begin by thinking that all I possess is a belief in life's purposefulness. I have not seen my wife so happy as she has been during these few days with our son. And since I see her happy, can't I help her to continue to be? Perhaps I fail. I will invite her to go with me tonight. She will refuse. That I could insist is a possibility. If the clash that may lie ahead of me seems merely a misunderstanding of our times, wouldn't this mean that I must take the posture of one of those stooped trees that stand traditionally beside the water, mournful and a good example of what some young tree would not want to be?

•

Loneliness I taste. The chair I sit in, the room, the house, none of this has substance. I think of Hemingway, what we remember of his work is not so much the color of the sky as it is the absolute taste of loneliness. Loneliness is not, I think, an absolute, but its taste is more powerful than any other. I think that endeavoring to be a serious writer is quite a dangerous career.

•

I have experienced the force of the past in my own life; the profound love of my brother. That I would turn away from this and take lovers and delight in them and marry and raise splendid children would, it seems, in no way diminish the fact that my own true love was my brother. That it was a sterile and a perverse love does not in any way diminish its profundity. So it sounds like the drone pass on the old-fashioned organ, and no matter how many green meadows I sport in, it seems that I will always regret having left my dear old brother.

•

Reading old journals I find Mary railing at me for my lack of virility, and perhaps her disappointments were serious. I find myself enormously happy in her arms. My random bones are listed with candor, and this is some part of the richness of my life. When I am given love I seem quite contented. Such merit as my work possesses is rooted in the fact that I have been unsuccessful in my search for love.

•

So I shift my skating, late in the day, to S.'s pond, where the ice is pristine, but where the reaches are limited. On the big pond you can skate straightaway until you're tired. Here you skate in a circle. The days are longer now. At four I will tire, before the sun sets. The sky is mixed, but there is some blue, and the motion of skating, and the lightness and coldness of the air involve quite clearly for me a beauty— a moral beauty. By this I mean that it corrects the measure and the nature of my thinking. Space, perhaps, is what I mean, but there is the moral beauty of light, velocity, and environment, which seems profoundly sympathetic. I drink tea and jaw and skate until dark.

•

So Sexagesima with Ben. Humor quite bridges any complications about taking Holy Communion with my son. In my prayers, however, I cannot include a second wife for him, or even a third. Another wife, another family, other children—all things that may happen—are absolutely unimaginable. So is my own separation. I wish I could be given some perspective on this old man on his knees in an obsolete church building, quite incapable of imagining that his son, kneeling on his left, whose intense marital unhappiness he has seen at first hand, will ever marry again.

Look at him, look at him. A second marriage is not in his aesthetics.

•

On leaving church, he goes off to run twenty miles, and I go off to skate. There are only a few people on the ice. A due-north wind blows. I enjoy myself and return later in the day. It is Sunday. There are perhaps fifty people scattered over the miles of ice. The voices seem to me to have the lightness of voices heard on a Mediterranean beach before this coast was lost to us through the savagery of pollution. And so these bright and scattered voices remind me of something not lost but vanished. Here is the extraordinariness of people who occupy themselves on a beach. Some of the charm of the scene may be that falls— pratfalls, graceful declines, ball breakers—are some part of the scene, and we will all likely fall before the skating ends at dark. And so up and down we go, around and around, with a degree of self-centeredness that seems to have nothing to do with pride. We seem to approach a state of innocence. Up and down we go, completely absorbed in the illusion that fleetness and grace and speed are our possessions and had only to be revealed. We fall, but so does everyone else.

•

In my small town the dogs are without exception high-spirited and without exception mongrels—but mongrels with marked characteristics of their parentage. You see a smooth-haired poodle, an Airedale with short legs, or a dog that begins as a collie and ends as a Dane. These mixtures of blood—this newness of blood, you might say—has made them a spirited breed and they hurry through the empty streets, late, it seems, for some important meal, assignation, or meeting, quite unfamiliar with that loneliness from which the rest of the population suffers.

•

So, let us assume that you have been given something to say. Something to do is quite simple. You can take your bicycle to Mt. Kisco and ski to the dam. At dinner, B. mentions watching two couples taking the train into the city for some sort of celebration. "Twelve dollars is really a good price for a dinner these days—but don't eat too many of the hors d'oeuvres. They serve these great hot hors d'oeuvres, but if you eat too many of them you can't eat the dinner." He describes their clothing, their accents, and persuasively imagines what the dinner in the restaurant will be like. This reminds me of a scene—Gide, Nabokov, Woolf, or Cheever—where one's insight into the lives of strangers becomes uncontrollable, and one becomes some part of the tragedy. This seems to have been a story I wrote many years ago, and seems to be the image of infinity I have recently been obsessed with. This is the image of the young man in an art gallery looking at a drawing of a citadel besieged by barbarians. He does not yet know that he is being besieged by barbarians himself. I think it is in Nabokov that we try to intercede in the assassination of a character and find ourselves powerless. So what one has is the observer travelling on a train. The traveller's discernment enables him to describe two couples who are going into the city to celebrate a wedding anniversary. The traveller will guess the source of their clothing and its cost, the rooms where they live, the food they eat, their occupations and incomes but then we will come to that point where the observer is tragically involved, simply through having committed himself to observation without restraint. This is a story I seem to have written, and I believe it's been written by others. "Stop, stop, stop—don't look any further," may be spoken by one of the objects being observed. You could use Venga, the sorceress in Bulgaria—or change that to Romania. That is, looking into a crystal ball, or dealing a pack of cards, she finds herself tragically involved in what she sees. To put it simply, she says, "This cave will fall onto us, and we will suffocate."

•

The most extraordinary thing about these mornings is *le cafard*. There seems no reason for this, other than the fact that I sleep in a poorly ventilated room, because both I and the old dog with whom I sleep are inclined to get chills. On waking, I find myself in a lethargy for which I have no words. This would be lessened were I with a lover, and that is a long tale that I will tell later. The first sound I hear may be Mary going to the kitchen to make coffee. Then I hear my dear old dog wagging his tail as my beloved son goes to the bathroom to shave for the day's work, having just run eight or ten miles. Much is expected of me during the day. There is writing to be accomplished, a rich and various correspondence to be maintained, vast sums of money to be banked if that is my inclination, landscapes spread out for skating, skiing, and bicycling, all of which I greatly enjoy; and yet I suffer a lethargy which cannot be distinguished by a name or a description. This is not despair; this is not even the Eastern Carpathian Monday Morning Blues; this enjoys a dreadful force that escapes language.

•

So, Federico leaves. This seems so deep in the skein of things that I have no perspective. On a rainy Saturday afternoon we go together to the movies. We see Dustin in "Kramer vs. Kramer." When we leave the theatre it is growing dark. We walk together across a parking lot. I seem to hear my voice. I am jawing on about film techniques, about the new spectrum that eliminates the light of day. I mean only to say that here is a tall young man with his old father, walking across a parking lot on a rainy dusk on one of the last days of March. I remember—fleetingly—driving him home from school as a boy. We sometimes stopped for a hot pizza and sometimes for fried chicken. None of this is very vivid, although it was at the time. He has, for me, completed cutting an apple tree with the chain saw. I remember, not vividly, his saving my life when a birch fell onto me. So I say that what I love is the world that lies spread out before him. It is nothing so simple as this. It is nothing so simple as this.

•

A book comes, of which I am the subject, and Mary says, "People write those books for practically nothing." This is my reading of the line, but only self-destruction would be accomplished by giving the line seven—or ten—readings. I seem to be up against a clinical situation and to be giving this a clinical response, which is less than excellent. I have come to feel that my failing in every way is imperative to her sense of being alive. I don't know whether I should say this to the children. On that very snowy night before I left for South America I slammed around the streets here in my front-wheel-drive, not at all anxious about having to walk if the car was stuck. S. was having his autograph party. I went to his and had him inscribe a book to Mary. The drive home was great fun. The car gave an exceptional performance. Mary was in the kitchen watching TV. I gave her the book. She looked at me with utter confusion and said, "You really are a nice person, aren't you?" This seems to reveal the fact that only as a perverted brute, scorned by the world, can I be accepted. Should I mention at lunch that I have been asked to make the commencement address at her college she will say, "Think of all the people who must have refused. They're scraping the bottom of the barrel. I hate that college, anyhow." I do feel that it is important to her that I be loathsome, and I think this perception will be, may be of some help.

•

So, I wake a little before dawn—at dawn, in fact. There is light in the air, light in the room; and I can see my clothes on the floor where I left them. The sound of birdsong has begun to be heard, and in the distance—somewhere in the southwest—there is the rumble of thunder. The old dog is asleep or is pretending to be asleep, and I think the thunder might frighten her. There is a flash of lightning, and I count to nearly twenty before the noise of this explosion reaches us. The storm, then, is twenty miles away, I think, and may take another course, sparing the old dog an attack of misery. There is another flash of light, the explosion seems more immediate, and the old dog wakes and whimpers. Then I think that H. is in the East, and how much I love her. I seem to fill with light, a curious radiance rather like the fire of gunpowder. How simple and powerful it all seems. We were meant to love each other. My fear of dogs, her allergy to artichokes, her nearsightedness, and my deafness have nothing to do with the case. We love each other, and so I lie in bed and worry that the thunderstorm will frighten the old dog, but I worry about little else. The light and the discordant racket that birds make increase, and the thunderstorm sulks off toward New Rochelle. This all seems to me a most natural course of events. I have known this marvellous feeling before—known it with other girls, known it with men, known it with that wife who refuses these days to let me enter her bedroom. It seems to me quite as natural as walking.

•

And I think that my wife has cooked for me for forty years. This seems to me one of the great labors of history. She has often served me with bitterness; she has often refused to speak to me when she summoned me to the table; but night after night for a decade less than half a century she has brought food to the table. And I think, lying naked in the early light, that this is an enormous task. And I also think that I have found the will to leave and that I will take none of my quaint souvenirs, since this is firstly the home of my children.

•

So sitting on the porch, reading an uninteresting book, I suffer a loss of memory. I do not know who I am or where I am. This is easily corrected with movement—I efficiently plant a row of broccoli—but I think it must be observed should it worsen. I think I mentioned it to the doctor and got no response. It is the sense of a level of consciousness that I do not comprehend: some firmament beyond mind, very like the structures in space—this is the imagery—but, for a moment, over-whelming. I am not in this world; I am merely falling, falling. Examining this, thinking (because of our psychoanalytical habits) of some form of guilt, I think I may, as a young man, have tasted some ultimate in futility—getting off a trolley car in Boston on a winter night—and fled from this with a velocity that now claims me as its victim. It could be, of course, that my old heart is not pumping blood into my old brain.

•

I weed the peonies, pretending to be some old Irish gardener, long dead. I do recall Mary's line when I asked sentimentally of the flowers, "Oh, where did you find them?" "I picked them," was what she snapped. I truly think she is unpleasant today. I sing loudly to the old dog, "I picked a lemon in the garden of love, where only peaches grow."

•

Tomorrow is my 68th birthday and I am uneasy, although not pain-fully so.

•

In the evening paper one reads that an estimable woman of sixty has, upon her return from a party at the boat club, been strangled. Robbery could not have been the motive, since the corpse wore diamond earrings. The names of ten men have been published. They have been charged with public lewdness in the urinal of the railroad station. But how were these convictions arrived at, and what sort of life can one lead after having been publicized as a public lewd? Turn the page and see how disturbed Sissie and Brozzie are. Muzzy blew the shit out of Dazzy with a 20-gauge shotgun. She then wrote notes to the kiddies, telling them about their dentist appointments, an expected oil delivery, and the plants to be watered. How can these people move about in the world, how can they know love and the pleasures of friendship? Deep

in an embrace, she will say, "You must know that my mother killed my
father and herself." "You must know that I was arrested for public
lewdness twenty-three years ago." "You must know that my mother was
wearing these diamond earrings when she was strangled." Can love
surmount these confessions? I see them on that island, my favorite
island, my favorite island where all those friends and lovers you thought
had been overtaken by infirmity or death are going happily from the
restaurant to the beach or from the beach to the bowling alley.

Oh, give me a world of soothsayers and chimney sweeps!

•

And so, what is the fear, the nameless dread? It is, quite simply,
the loss of one's powers. One's intelligence, one's memory, one's gifts
as a lover. One has seen the grossness of madness. Dismounting from
my bicycle at the head of the hill here to speak with the Z.s, I do not
know where I am. This, I expect, is a fleeting seizure of amnesia.

•

Yesterday I drive to the village to cash a check I have forgotten to
bring with me. Going down the hill toward the bank, I see how the
mountains of the west shore reach down to the Hudson. The foliage is
full grown now, and the day is sunny with clouds that now and then
throw a passing shadow. The mountains and the water seem quite
beautiful, and it is a deeply emotional beauty; it seems to me a memory
of some happiness I have known and lost, and that I am happily in
pursuit of. But the memory is strong, powerful. I can smell the flooring
of the porch on which I sit while I wait for my beloved to finish whatever
she is doing (combing her hair, or boning the fish) and serenely watch
the shadows and the light move over the wooded mountains and the
river. I have been here.

•

In the thirties and forties men seemed to fear homosexuality as the
early mariners feared sailing off the end of the ocean in a world supported
on a turtle's back.

•

A single sentence has been spoken on this lovely summer morning—
an overt contradiction—and now she has gone into her room and closed

her door. And it seems that I must remember—that it is my responsibility to remember—how happy I was as a lover, a husband, a father, a friend, and a neighbor. But now I have no wife, and Mrs. Z. has completely departed from my consciousness. R. enjoys no urgency. I have friends and neighbors and children, and it is not that I lack a wife; I am possessed, but by an exhaustive opposite of what is meant by a wife. This is quite a militant performance, involving castration, public humiliation, and disgrace, and, I suppose, crucifixion if the equipment were available. And is it any wonder that from time to time we encounter a sexually bewildered male?

•

And in my memories of happiness there are, God knows, some thorns, and there is the fact that I was a younger man. I insist that I still possess a capacity for happiness. I think of F. calling from Wilmington to ask, "Weren't we happy, Johnny? Weren't we really happy?"

•

The brute force of loneliness would account for our most spectacular carnal escapades, those erotic collisions in underpasses on rainy midnights. You'll never know whose teeth marks were left on your ass and your forearm, come the morning.

Reading about old age, I am pleased to know that chemicals can account for the depression that seems to overtake me these mornings. Lying in bed with a wish to die, I am happy to know that this is an excess of tryflexon and a tax on my valvular plimbits.

•

This is a story to be read in bed on a rainy night in an old house near a winding and seldom travelled road, with perhaps a view of some mountains, and within walking distance of a stream where one can fish and swim.

•

Old age seems to have presented me with two discernible changes. I think these constitutional. One is an increase in fear. In reading of a Vermont winter I think not of the skiing or the mountains in a morning light; I think only of the cold as some premonition of death. I think only of pain. And watching on TV a film of some waves breaking on a shore in the early morning, I think how far I have gone from this light, this freshness, this sense of being a happy participant. The last time we went to the sea my wife was intensely unhappy. But I think that I must honestly assess both my fear of winter—of death—and this loss of facility in imagining happiness on long beaches.

•

What I would like—to speak very generally—is a celebration; I say from time to time that I would like to write a story about a success, although that may not be in my range. There is the old man who seems to be taking shape—although as I walked yesterday in the woods, pursued by deerflies, it seemed that the old man could be a great bore. Could you write a success story about a man whose determination, whose inspiration, whose giftedness enabled him to dissuade or conquer some force of thoughtlessness? Is there any hero in the literature that I have loved?

•

I do the shopping. "OPEN TWENTY-FOUR HOURS" says the sign, but the store seems caught up in some vortex of decay. The shopping-cart situation is chaotic. Abandoned carts make parking difficult, the carts for use are stuck together, and the boy employed to organize carts is smoking pot and looking at pornographic magazines in the stationery store. Within the supermarket itself the music is ended. I am speaking literally. Here and there one sees a face on a checkout clerk or a boy pushing a broom, which seems so fresh and well intentioned that one knows the human race will outlive the ceremonies of marketing.

•

What the priest says is, "If you are one of those who has waited patiently for the summer I most sincerely hope you are enjoying what we have now. For my part, I have had enough. The church has been very hot, and the fan in the sacristy window makes very little difference. I am hoping and praying that someday we may have a more effective ventilating system. Be assured that you will be in my prayers and thoughts, especially at the Passion play in Oberammergau."

•

The night is hot and airless, and I have a recurrence of that chest pain that seeps into my jaw and that, as I recall, has entertained some doctor. A little freshness comes into the valley, but it is soon gone. The two conversational exchanges with my wife are hideously unpleasant, and then when I enter the kitchen to get a cup of coffee she seizes her lemon juice and flees. It is precisely as though I had encountered a witch. I do remember that as a child she was accused of burning her mother's house to the ground. It may be that her negativism is too deep to be described as iconoclasm. I mean simple matters such as leaving the tap running all night during a water crisis, or unplugging the deep freeze and spoiling a large investment in frozen food. This is the same thing one saw in Heathrow Airport when she was pounding on a door—and weeping. The door said "ENTRANCE IS FORBIDDEN" in four languages, but her action seemed nothing so small as an endeavor to inconvenience her husband. She seemed to be playing out a role in some world other than this, which she has experienced or is preparing to experience. When he first saw her pounding on the airport door at three in the morning he felt that some insight was being revealed to him. It was some years later that he felt merely impatience and then boredom.

•

Dinner is a vast fish, and by lighting a fire of applewood I am able to give the house, for me, some usefulness. It would otherwise be a string of cold and senseless rooms in which an old couple calumniated each other. Fire, we are told, is a chemical process and not an element, but it is for me an element, it is what I mean by an elemental force, and while the night is far from cold, windy, or hostile in any way, it is a night, and the light and warmth of the fire give this place and its sticks of furniture their heft and meaning.

•

I wake with a lack of enthusiasm that seems intestinal. The taste in my mouth and the unease in my intestinal tract seem completely to dominate my sentimental and my spiritual lives. Reading some journals of the year before last I come up against the problem of continence. It seems this morning that I have never successfully mastered this; that the most I have done is to delay my discharges for a week or so, no more. And yet I did, however fleetingly, possess a sense of dignity that seems now to be quite lost to me. The most lasting advantage has been to accomplish some work.

•

I sleep uneasily and wake on a morning of such freshness and lightness feeling such a despair that I can only conclude its cause is intestinal,
although I enjoy exceptional health. It is obtuseness that keeps me from
realizing that I have lived with such contradictions for many years.
"What seems to be bothering you?" says the doctor. Spread out on the
examination table, stark naked, one says, "I feel terribly sad."

•

M. arrives as the clock strikes five and we watch a ballgame, screw,
have dinner, watch another game, and part, at my wish. In the morning
he is late, and my inexperience in such affairs leaves me no traditional
conclusions or anxieties. I am at a loss. When he arrives a light rain is
falling, but we circle the Club Circle Motor Court route. Some villages
in the Carpathians enjoy a forlornness that we find in this country only
in a failing trailer settlement on a rainy Saturday morning. Even some
of the television antennae are broken, and this one universal link is
gone. The clotheslines are empty but for a single bed sheet that holds
autumn leaves in its folds and must have hung there for weeks. There
is a rank of mailboxes, but who would ever write these people a letter?
One quite new car seems to have been abandoned, and while the paint
shines and the license tag is current, goldenrod and daisies grow up
between the wheels. The difference is that this forlornness in the Carpathians seems to have been carried over from Pleistocene days, while
here in this country we seem to have cultivated it.
"Shut up," says M., "you'll turn on the sprinklers." I howl and so
does he. We start north and hit a strip on Route 20. Here are the cut-
rate furniture store; the doughnut factory; the countless outlets for
public-execution food, many of them designed to resemble the mansions
and mushroomy houses of dream landscapes; the Realtors'; shopping
malls; and gallerias; and a drive-in theatre showing "The Night of the
Great Massage-Parlor Bust." But this clustering diminishes and vanishes and we are in what was once farming country, with acre and half-
acre fields divided by light stands of timber. We see churches and houses
that are quite unpretentious but whose façades show a charm and invention that seems patrician. How far we have come from talking dough-
nuts and "The Night of the Great Massage-Parlor Bust"! These houses
enjoy views of this broad and fertile valley that leads from Albany to

Buffalo and lies on the Laurentian plain between the Catskills and the Adirondacks, with an allegiance not to the Hudson estuary but to the Great Lakes. The valley is fertile; the views are vast; the sense for me is of a paradise, since everything I see represents intelligent and peaceful cultivation; avaricious nomadism, which has produced the strip, seems to have no place here. We visit my old friends the T.s and I lose four dollars at backgammon. I have lost my loneliness briefly in a vast, erotic engorgement, but I am still so lonely that, passing a remote farmhouse on whose lawn stands a little statue of a fisherman, bought perhaps from a mail-order catalogue, makes me wonder if the farmer's wife, or the farmer himself, bought this ornament with the hope that the winter would be less lonely. I am with a lover who, whenever I have touched him, has always been responsive, but I think of the pioneers who settled the west and their travels through this valley and my loneliness comes to seem insignificant. We return down the valley as night falls along the lights of the strip, and we go into the terrain of vast highways that link Boston, New York, Buffalo, and Albany, and our progress brings me a sense of dissipated energies. The force one found in the valley with its farms and their views is scattered here, and the sweep of light on the six-lane interstates is nomadic and impuissant. I think of the patrician farms on the hill and that the new houses there are uniform and uniformly vulgar. But I also recall a tract of uniform houses being slowly altered to resemble their owners and eventually triumphing over the sameness and monotony of their beginnings. One cannot intelligently long to reconstruct the circumstances of building a farmhouse two hundred years ago.

●

Fatigue is something I sought, and seem to have enjoyed on my return. I spoke with G.—a truly old and dear friend. Then in my studio I wrote a letter to Mary. I ate dinner with the company and went to an A.A. meeting. This is one of those gatherings where the sense of an encounter is forceful. I return to my studio and watch the ballgame. In the seventh inning I suffer a convulsion called a grand mal seizure. I completely lose consciousness and come to in the emergency room of the Saratoga hospital in the company of a man who claims to be having an epileptic seizure. They are slapping him in the face and assuring him that his seizure is a transparent fraud. I am put in a room with an old man who rails loudly about his bowels. His bowels rack him pitilessly. I would find more serenity almost anywhere, and I am brooding on my escape when a male nurse kindly moves me to another room. In the morning my determination to avoid hazardous investigations of my brain lands me in an ambulance, speeding south. I move into the hospital at home and am given tests for two days. Nothing is concluded; nothing is discovered. Mary is loving, patient, and I can really not recall a time when she has so unselfishly given herself to me. This is not carnal, and I am unable to feel, now, that my carnal sport with M. involves an infidelity. As men who love women we know our acrobatics to be second-rate, and our parting this morning seemed mandatory. We have work to accomplish, and we have appointments to keep. I shall endeavor to write Mary.

•

The fear of insanity, I was told by Cummings, who spoke for much of New England, is an unfortunate display of self-importance. Anyone who makes such an unnatural claim should be taken to an insane asylum and shown how the truly mad suffer gruelling and unremittent pain. I think I remember that B. in her madness suffered an unhappiness unlike anything that I have ever known. But I am uncomfortable (not intensely so) and would like to address Mary, H., and M., although the clarity I would seem to enjoy in this address would so lack warmth and lovingness that it would be frightening. I wake thinking of scrambled eggs, and it is revealed to me that any sustained sentimental life with a man who is not my brother or my son is highly taxing and quite impossible. But the wind blows the leaves off the trees, and the shadows change, and I think that I am an old man and should become more retiring and settle for a male companion and an uneventful life on a bicycle in some very flat country like the Netherlands, moving to the tropics when the cold winds of winter blow. This seems to be a delusion, and one associated with the resumption of my drinking life and consequently a prolonged and obscene performance of self-destructiveness beginning with obesity, a cirrhotic liver, a mistaken memory—and presently—irreversible brain damage. Nothing is asked of me at this hour, nothing at all. I will take the lunch pails to the garage and perhaps bicycle around the block, leaving my manuscript in a cottage where a fire is burning. I could have the manuscript duplicated before I take my bicycle trip, but I will take the trip now, leaving my papers here so I can write letters when I return.

•

I miss drinking. That's the simplest way of putting it. When it grows dark I would like a drink. The Hemingway story, or stories, about Nada—the utter nothingness that is revealed to an old man—seem to correspond to what I've experienced these last months. I do believe in God's will and the ordination of events, and it is perhaps stupid of me to question the ordination of my lying unconscious on the floor, convulsed and senseless. It did bring my wife back to me, and have I ever asked for anything more? I feel that perhaps the sorrow of these days will be revealed to me as having had their usefulness. The nature of this sorrow is bewildering. I seek some familiarity that eludes me; I want to go home and I have no home. I think that I have been ill, and one problem is that I lack vitality.

•

My biggest problem seems to be that I'm not working on my novel and won't be until I return to Saratoga. In reading my journal I see how, in Saratoga, I was available to seizures of lostness. Indeed, I have lost consciousness and my memory. I seem unable to comprehend that experience is consecutive. I was a young man here, then a mature man, and now I am an old man. Here I have been rich and poor, sick and ecstatically well, I have committed fornication with several women and now with a man. It is a struggle to comprehend this. Now I am writing a story about an old man who loves to skate. He becomes erotically involved with a young woman who reminds him of the national anthem at ballgames, and when she rebuffs him he becomes the lover of the elevator operator in her building. The only resolution I can imagine is that he could salvage the body of water on which he skates. I regret that I do not understand why it would seem mistaken to work on the story here, since Saratoga seems to be disputed territory. I trust I will be able to comprehend the passage of time. I am one of those old men; I am like a voyager who cannot remember the streams he has travelled. He cannot remember their swiftness or their depths, he cannot, at times, even correctly remember their names. I like to think that I am prepared

to return to Saratoga and sit in that small house in the woods, quite
uncertain about who I am and what my purpose in life is.

•

So, M. comes, and thinking that my malaise might have something
to do with being crouched over a bicycle we walk up the dam path. We
meet some people—virtual strangers—whom I once assailed on Cedar
Lane and urged to take this walk. They are out to see the autumn
foliage, so why do they all wear dark glasses? They have with them a
fat dog. I am thoroughly happy with M., and I believe he feels the same
way with me, and it is a happiness that I have never known before. I
look, quite naturally, for its limitations, and when my great, dear friend
gestures toward a field of golden leaves I admire the lightness but I
have no wish to write a poem, as I would with a girl. This is not a lack
but it is a difference, and I do feel strongly that we both have work to
do. Parting with M. is truly sweet, but in the morning I wake in the
arms of an imaginary girl.

•

M. and I go to the Pyramid Mall, a shopping center that is four or
five years old but that I have never seen enjoy a sense of prosperity.
Urban renewal is struggling to refresh the old center of the village with
an axial sense of merchandizing which goes back to the horse-and-buggy
days. The automotive strip and the rudimentary village compete with
each other, a competition that is heightened by the price of gasoline but
made unequal by the use of tax money. I have never seen this mall
thronged, festive, or even modestly prosperous. There are many ornamental fountains meant to contribute to the gaiety of the place, but
these have been dry for years. The interior of the bank is a replica of
some cabin in a space vehicle on TV. Galaxies can be seen through
portholes in the walls; the walls are luminous; and the ceiling is concave.
In the line at the teller's window there is a clinically obese woman in
pants and a dwarf with large ears, and in this scene with its suggestion
of space one feels that travel in the darkness beyond the stars is ret-
rogressive and that we are hurtling away from that civilized force of
selection that has taken aeons to develop. And, judging the scene along
moderately conservative lines, what do we find? Vistas, acres of mer-
chandise without the imponderable allure of style and without a trace

of quality. The lack of custom has left the clerks either embarrassingly overanxious or bored and rude. There are three theatres. In one, an old comic is playing the role of God in an amiable farce about life everlasting. The second film is a charming, low-budget account of high-school mores. When we open the door on the third film, called "Caligula," we see someone sucking a cock, and lest we should doubt the authenticity of this we are shown the ejaculation splashing into an antique ewer. None of these three theatres has any audience to speak of. Back in the mall again we notice that the music, the universal music, is "Somewhere Over the Rainbow." We pass a short, elderly woman in tennis shorts who is carrying a battery-operated flashlight that is at least two feet long. This, along with so much else that we see, will never be explained. If we are hungry there are a dozen places to eat and the food is, without exception, that barbarous holiday fare that has been fried and enjoyed at ceremonies and festivals since the beginnings of civilization. This is the food one ate at the execution of the first of the kings, the quartering of the traitor, the hanging of the witch, and the crucifixion of the Saviour. It is not all fried, but much of it is, and you can eat it with your fingers, picking it out of a cornucopia of leaves or a cone of paper while you ride a horse, or paddle a canoe; while you drive a car, or walk up a mall or rialto with your arm around the waist of your beloved. And on TV last night I saw a man speak emotionally about the new beginnings he felt with the Reagan victory. He said with great sincerity that the voters had chosen Reagan for his economic and his foreign policies. One would not want to be supercilious, but I can discern neither. I would describe Reagan's partisan as being slightly ill-favored. His hair was a little thin, his eyeglasses were a little thick, and he wore a heavy, V-necked sweater under his jacket. This seemed to give him some discomfort. He moved his shoulders a good deal and stretched now and then. His symbol for the Carter Administration was a tattered flag, and he spoke with such deep emotion of Carter's failure to control the currency and the oil crises that his account began to sound autobiographical, as if the Carter Administration had been responsible for his personal sorrows, his rained-out picnics and sexual hang-ups, his acquaintance with melancholy and loneliness. I thought that I had never seen this before and that it helped to explain the vote. Someone said that if gasoline cost more than a dollar a gallon and we had two-digit inflation the incumbent would be defeated. This seemed to make sense.

•

I turn on the TV, but George C. Scott is about to defend, with his life, a bridge in the last war with Germany. Actors impersonating combat—the agonies of death and the glory of victory—have been made ridiculous by documentaries. We are all too familiar with the facts to take seriously the spectacle of an actor pretending to die in an artificial trench. I read about Nancy Mitford and remember being in the next cabaña to her on the Lido. Just think of that! She was with Victor Cunard and they were guests of an Italian princess whose name I cannot remember. I never met her, but I'm inclined to suggest that I knew her well. Mussolini gave her father his title, and I once went swimming in her pool with Lord Somebody. Nancy Mitford's brother-in-law—a somewhat broken-down felon—once paid me a compliment. I sleep well and wake to think of a young woman. I shave, build my fire in the hutch, and go to the village, where I buy a paper and a container of coffee. I am one of the few men you can see coming into McDonald's with a container of coffee so that they won't suffer any delay in getting their caffeine. There is a couple—a mother and son, I think. She is one of those women of such exhaustive plainness that you wonder about the moment of conception. What could have compelled anyone to penetrate her? But perhaps she is an aunt. She seems quite happy. The boy is adolescent—twelve or thirteen—and dressed in a yellow costume with a yellow cap with a visor. This seems to be one of those mornings of his life when his strength, beauty, and agility have only just been revealed to him, and while he waits for his scrambled eggs and bacon he poses, absolutely without grace, catches a happy glimpse of himself in some reflecting surface, and pretends, for a minute or two, to fly. They take away four breakfasts, and I expect them to get into a car and drive to the home where Daddy and Sissie are waiting, but not at all. They sit down at a table and attack the four breakfasts with an efficient and experienced air, as if they did this regularly.

•

So, I aim at a longer working day and get unhappily overexcited. I don't find the serenity that I seem to remember while working on "Falconer." It could be a simple question of health, or how many cups of coffee I drink. I cycle the new route, and toward dark and with this room at long last quite warm, I seem to enjoy some repose.

•

I am at loose ends. I go to A.A., this in the parish-house kitchen, an interior that is of first importance to no one. Rummage sales, festivals, and door-to-door fund-raising resurrected the place ten years ago, but now half the fluorescent lighting blinks erratically and half the cabinet doors hang askew. So people talk with absolute candor about the bewilderments of life. "Yesterday was a memory, tomorrow is a dream," says a man who is dressed like a gas pumper and has only three front teeth. From what text, greeting card, or book he took the message doesn't matter to me at this hour.

•

So, I wake this morning and think, What but a truly great country could freely elect for its Chief Executive a faded and elderly cowboy actor whose veins are so calcified and whose memory is so depleted that he can seldom remember the armchair opinions he expressed at yesterday's lunch?

•

And walking and bicycling and wandering I think myself a bad father, and I think that this decision is to be made not by me but by my sons, and I think that by commenting on my loves and my deepest anxieties I jockey myself into the position of a bystander, a traveller, even a tourist, for by claiming to enjoy a degree of perspective I seem to be planning to move on to some other country. I like to think that this is a passing depression, and that I will live the role of a father with the authority of true love and truly be a man of my time and my place.

•

So on my knees in church I am grateful for the present turn of events in my marriage, and I pray it will continue, although I do see that some of the difficulties seem to be part of my immortal soul and that these difficulties were at times made tolerable by my drunkenness. The complexity of my nature seems represented by the morning after the birth of a son. This was what I most wanted in life; it was to be for the rest of my natural life a source of boundless pleasure. He was to be not only an enthusiasm but a salvation. Experiencing and anticipating this great fortune on the balcony of our apartment in Rome I saw a sports car loaded with drunken bucks racing down the street—for Ostia, I guessed—and I deeply longed to be with them. So, this longing beyond the perimeter of what I ardently desire seems often to be with me. But I have been to Ostia with the bucks, and with them my longing for the permanence I have left is much more painful. So on my knees the first Sunday in Advent I pray for courage.

•

The drug I take for epilepsy seems to leave me rather sleepy and unresponsive. That seems to be my message for the day.

•

This is my eighth or ninth day on Dilantin, and I feel poorly. I am expected to pick up my medical records, take the dog to the veterinarian, and find someone to drive me to the hospital for my chat with a leading neurologist. I don't seem able to do much else, although I will try to answer the mail.

•

We dine with M.'s teacher, and I will observe that I find myself less than brilliant. When orthodoxy is discussed, I recall that perhaps twenty years ago I discussed this on a porch in Providence, Rhode Island, where a couple whose names I can't remember gave a large dinner party in our honor. Mary wore a becoming dress that I recall as being vaguely Japanese. What I said was that one cannot, in the space of a lifetime, improvise a code of good and evil, and thus one must resort to tradition. In the morning I am constipated and do not go to church. I go early to Shop-rite to buy cat food. One might describe the few shoppers as ambassadors of a new world. They seem quite strange to me. The air is filled with music. "It came upon a midnight clear," sing a hundred angels, "that glorious song of old. With angels bending near the earth to touch their harps of gold." I think of that mural in Moscow, at the Hotel Ukraine, which depicts the peaccablc kingdom of thc Communist world. Poets read their verse to masked steelworkers, and farmers sing as they reap the harvest that will enrich them and their friends. The irony in both cases seems mostly poignant. I thank a stranger for holding a door open for me. "You are very welcome," he says with charming enthusiasm. We wish each other a good day.

•

There is a story in the *Times* about toxic waste being buried across the river. I might be able to use this. One novel begins with the Fourth of July, one with Christmas Eve, one with the introduction of a man from the upper classes into a penitentiary, and I would like this to open with nothing less urgent. There is the old man and his skating and the news that the pond is poisoned. This is a possibility, but I don't feel it deeply. In *The New York Review of Books* I read a piece on the fact that the American people, in choosing Reagan, chose to vote for an irrecapturable past, a character who is no longer found among us, a landscape and a set of circumstances that vanished long ago.

•

Monday morning at the S.s'. The hostages are being released but the TV commercials have not been suspended, so we have fond wives and mothers interrupted by exhortations to buy shorts and underwear. The inauguration will be upstaged, to some degree, by the release of the hostages, but I suppose they can exploit this. A speaker this morning said that the new Administration would be strong and powerful. No hostages will be taken while Reagan is President.

•

It is that time of year when small colleges with American Indian names and low-digit R.F.D. addresses write to say that the faculty and the student body have enthusiastically chosen me to receive an honorary doctorate in humane letters. Yesterday I regretted two. As I tell it I will claim three.

•

So, at the mortal risk of narcissism, I am that old man going around and around the frozen duck pond in my hockey skates, stopping now and then to exclaim over the beauty of the winter sunset. And I am he who can be seen in the early summer morning, pedalling my bicycle to Holy Communion in a High church where they genuflect and use the Cranmer prayer book. I am also he whose loud cries of erotic ecstasy can be heard through the walls of the Millstream Motel. "You can't go on living like this," says my lover. I'm not quite sure what is meant.

•

So, the old man says, "None of you are old enough to remember the thrill of a consummate civilization. It was a passing phenomenon, rather like the pleasures of light, although we have come to know that light can move worlds. The dates are quite loose, but it would have been sometime between the two wars with Germany. It would be most obvious if you were a young man or woman from Oklahoma, or Salt Lake City, travelling to Paris, or Vienna, or even London. You would be leaving a painful condition of provincial loneliness for some capital city where men and women were all burgeoning in their relationship to one another, in their inventiveness in industry, the arts, and other forms of understanding, as if our lives might be something much more various than a paradise. It was a fact, happily remembered by other old men and women and authenticated by the legislation, the wealth, and the music and painting of that past. But it seems now that we have only our memories, and the provincial loneliness of Oklahoma has become universal."

•

I do have trouble with the dead hours of the afternoon without skating, skiing, bicycling, swimming, or sexual discharges or drink. I read some Graham Greene, whose mastery I admire, but at about twenty minutes to seven I suffer a loss of memory. I know, perhaps, who I am, but I am not very sure of my whereabouts. It may be of some significance that this always happens as I am called to the table. This time I find the seizure uncommonly depressing.

•

I wake terribly blue, and try to remember how often this has been the case; how often I have written about the man who cries at ballgames and Fourth of July parades. I think of how substantial is the gift of prayer; and I am on my knees. And I think of the susceptibility and loneliness of youth, of how this contributes to youth's drive and youth's beauty.

•

The last Sunday before Lent, and this is in haste. The light is brilliant, and my spirits are high, and since this is the first of the month I know these high spirits will be lasting. Remembering my letter to O'Hara, I think, on my knees in church, that I believe in narrative as invention. What I mean to say, of course, is that I believe in narrative as revelation. And in writing to Federico I would like to say something about our closeness having some of the elements of chance and that we are rather like travellers taking the same road, gifted or equipped with remarkable instruments of divination, since the road is seldom travelled, or that at least gives that impression.

And it is with a marketplace that we confound those anthropologists who consider society to be largely a creation of anxiety, theft, and cowardice. We do not gather at that pass in the river to increase our numbers so we can defend ourselves from the tribes in the north. We gather here to exchange our potatoes for meat, our fish for baskets, and our greens for new breads. We are also gathered here to meet our wives, compete in contests of strength and skill, listen to the storyteller recount the night the wolves appeared, watch the thief's right hand be chopped off, and get fairly drunk. The fragrance of our social origins is what gives Buy Brite some of its excitement.

•

At the bank I see D.C., a slender black who does carpentry. "Nails have gone from ten cents a pound to a dollar thirty. You can't keep your head above water." An Irishman behind me, who excites my dislike, goes on about how terrible these times are. "Oh, they are terrible," says D. "All the governor wants to do is build prisons. And they sent that woman to prison for killing her lover, but I know a man who shot his friend right in the face and didn't get six months. He just paid off the right judge. You get three raps for stealing now, you get life. Life! Buddy's brother got three raps for stealing, and they locked him up for eighteen years. He had to serve twelve. But one of my girl friends went to this Arab country for her vacation where if you steal anything they cut your hand off. I mean, you see a pocketbook lying in the street, you try to find out who it belongs to. You go into a store and you want to buy something and the owner isn't there you go out in the street and find him. If you don't they'll cut your hand off." "I suppose," the

Irishman says, "that the judges are corrupt, the lawyers are crooked, even the weather is worse than it used to be because of pollution, but if you buy one of them Japanese cars you'll throw ten Americans out of work. It's just terrible, everything is just terrible."

And only a few hours later an attempt is made to assassinate the President. That he rallies seems to me splendid. That the Chief Executive of a very great nation is felled by an assassin and upon rising says "I forgot to duck" proves the inspired closeness of language and spirit. We seem perhaps closer to the light than we were in St. Petersburg and Sarajevo.

I have a traction bed installed and invest a hundred thousand dollars in an energy-saving transportation-improvement bond issue. M. arrives and it is a great pleasure to meet him. This friendship—with its great potential for confrontations, scandal, blackmail, arrests, suicides, and other tragic ends—seems to me intrinsically easygoing and quite natural. When we embrace briefly at the station before he leaves the car to take a train we both enjoy a mastery over some territories of loneliness that seemed endless. Holding him in my arms and being held in his, feeling his cheek against my cheek, I seem to understand the Copenhagen airport in a snowstorm, or Istanbul, or Cleveland.

This cannot go on forever, this could not possibly be solemnized— it lasts for only a few hours, and I think, sentimentally, that one never asked for more.

So I sit at the kitchen table, drinking black coffee and thinking of Verdi. Through government aid I heard, in the last week, the last scene from "Il Trovatore" and the Requiem Mass. And so I think of the enormous contribution Verdi made to the life of the planet and the enormous coöperation he was given by orchestras and singers and the enthusiasm of audiences. And I think what an enormous opportunity it is to be alive on this planet. Having myself been cold and hungry and terribly alone, I think I still feel the excitement of an opportunity. The sense of being with some sleeping person—one's child or one's lover— and seeming to taste the privilege of living, or being alive. This sense of privilege or opportunity seems to hint, and no more than hint, at other worlds around us. This seems a singular experience.

My neck is lame; and last night I read at the church and lost the last page. What is there to say of the evening? My wife seems to be quite simply the air I breathe. It is a spring night, a lovely spring night.

We walk from the church to the club and at the foot of the street one can see the full sky, a wall of light.

•

So, awakened first by a cat and then by an old dog, I find myself drinking coffee at quarter to six. I am prone to complain, but prone is what I am. It is the old litany. I have no closet, no shirt drawer, and because I invested a hundred thousand in mortgages, I have no ready cash. If the governor can unsnarl an ecclesiastical battle between the Roman and the Greek churches he will be united in holy matrimony on Saturday to a twice-married Greek opportunist whose affairs are, at the moment, under congressional investigation while his gubernatorial affairs are even more chaotic. For the lack of a budget, a million state employees will go hungry over the weekend and more than a million men and women will die for lack of the medicine bought by Medicare. And the old man on Tuesday night who said, "You'll have to speak louder. I may not be able to hear anything you say. My wife threw my hearing aid into the washing machine last night. $400. Of course I don't have to listen to her anymore, do I? Ho-ho-ho. Everything evens up. The rich have ice in the summer, and the poor have ice in the winter."

So, at six I write that all I know is the importance of love, the smell of fried food, and the music of the rain.

•

So, this is upon my return from a week or so in the hospital. There was an early morning when I suffered intense pain. Then there was that part of my consciousness that declared that I was not alone. When I asked who was with me I was told that it was God. It made the pain much easier to bear. When there was another seizure, an hour later, the knowledge that I was not alone was a powerful support.

So, on waking I think of completing the book, but now I feel an invalid. Reading Calvino, who is very close to Pirandello—a master— I find him unsympathetically cute. I am in the wrong country, but I shall return.

So, since sickness seems to be no part of the story I hope to tell, I have almost nothing to say this morning. I finish the Calvino book, which I think one should read although I find it terribly arch. I play a recording of myself reading "The Swimmer" and think it quite good. I watch the Yankees play in Detroit before an empty stadium because everybody in Detroit is broke. Waking, I hear first the three-axle, eighteen-wheel trucks of dawn and then the first birds to sing at day-break. I seem to hold Mrs. Z. in my arms; and all it seems that one ever wanted was a blonde whose breasts were a little larger than one remembered them. That my claim to simplicity can be challenged is well known. However, this seems to be the destiny I seek—or the past I instinctively recall—as I lie in bed in the first of the daylight admiring the songbirds.

·

I go to the doctor, who does something I see no reason to describe; but I feel much better. Indeed, I feel myself this morning. Mary seems bewildered, and when I think that I am not alone in this dilemma I may be sentimental, but it does give me some latitude or—you might say—generosity. So there is a great deal to do.

A Turkish murderer, escaped from an Istanbul prison, attempts to assassinate the Pope. "God have mercy on his soul" is what I say, and had I been asked for a reaction I would have said that I would pray. Many of the celebrities questioned speak of the chaos of the modern world. It seems to me that this is something one accepted years ago. It is a point of departure and not an observation. I will pray; I shall pray; I am praying.

·

I have talked with both Mrs. Z. and R. Her voice has its familiar harshness; she is the pretty girl who loves her jackknife and it seems that what she has is something I must have in the women I enjoy. Her voice summons none of the profound music that stirs me when I talk with R. on the telephone, although I have never found any-thing to say to R. over the lunch table. "Compromise" is not the word to describe my affairs, I think, because my engagement is, I think, very deep, although it appears highly diverse. Mrs. Z. seems, quite unbeknownst to her, to have at times the pathos of a foundling. R. will support me when I am tired. Mary has shared most of her life with me. Last night when I was losing at backgammon there was a hint, or perhaps a memory, of her crying to my opponent, "Beat him, beat him, beat him!" This was long ago and these recollections accomplish nothing.

•

Iole, who has worked for us for so many years, who first came to us one rainy evening in Rome, is now troubled by the sickness of her oldest brother in Rome, her thankless job, and the search for a new apartment. She is not a southern Italian—she claims to be a Roman—but when she is troubled her nose seems to take on another dimension, her eyes sink, and her voice is sorrowful and loud. Mary goes to solace her; not I. I am not guilty, and I have nothing but admiration for Mary's kindness. They will talk mostly about the children, whom Iole has helped to rear. Later, I come into the kitchen and find Mary mending a Roman lamp G. brought me from Jerusalem. It has a relief of a naked man and the flame sprang from his genitals. A cat knocked it to the floor and Mary mends it. She also mends a Japanese bowl that she bought, I think, at Altman's and a decorated china seashell that might, during the years when people smoked, have been used as an ashtray. She has mended the afternoon for Iole, and now I see her mending with dexterity and cleverness these broken things. Unworthiness is not what I feel, but in watching her mending, in knowing how, these days, mending is of the first importance to her, I know that some part of me is wayward and clings to its sense of brokenness.

•

So I think that "Oh What a Paradise It Seems" is completed. I will rewrite the supermarket story and whatever else seems mistaken, photocopy these, and try to find someone to drive me into the city. I do not want to take the train.

•

I take the dogs into the rainy woods and fertilize the rhododendrons, and, feeling poorly, I return to the house. The dogs are wet and muddy, and while they dry on the porch I put on the headphones of my tape player and listen to the Bach Concerto for Two Violins. I think the circumstances striking: an old man with two old and muddy dogs. He listens while two violin virtuosi perform one of the great masterpieces of Western civilization. He listens to this with headphones—he is quite alone in his enjoyment, and his aloneness on the rainy landscape is increased when the concerto ends and he hears the hearty applause of thousands, the noise as they get to their feet, and their shouting. He seems to laugh or cry. The dogs, who can hear nothing but the dripping of the rain gutters, look at me with concern. They are afraid, perhaps, that I have gone mad and will forget to feed them. Ben comes. We are both mistaken in thinking that this is Father's Day.

•

This is upon my return from two weeks in the hospital, and I feel as though I had returned from the grave. That the kidney that was removed was cancerous is something, it seems, given the opportunities I possess, that I could pass over lightly, but I am regrettably morose and self-indulgent about the possibility of my death. I pray that this will pass. On my last night in the hospital I slept without medicine. Waking a little before dawn, I went to the window. The room was air-conditioned and the window was sealed. There had been a thunderstorm, and there was some rainwater on the screen. There was light in the sky and there were lights as well as a few lighted boats along the western shore. When I returned to bed it seemed that these were lamps, maintained by some woman of a very gentle and beautiful disposition. Judging from her voluminous dark hair, lightly confined by tortoiseshell pins, I take it she was of my mother's generation, although she was quite plainly not my mother. I will always remember my mother climbing, fully dressed, into that barrel in which she conquered Niagara Falls. I dwelt on the sweetness of this woman with her lamps, and I prayed for some degree of sexual continence, although the very nature of sexuality is incontinence.

•

The doctor removes the stitches. M. is late. One of the disadvantages of homosexual love is waiting for a man. Waiting for a woman seems to be destiny, but waiting for one's male lover is quite painful. He is twenty minutes late, but when he arrives he packs my things, oversees my departure from the hospital with tenderness and dispatch, points out interesting changes on the drive home while gently caressing my leg, and upon our return removes my clothes, washes and changes my bloody dressing, and delights and engorges my sexuality. The seriousness of this is something I have failed to assess. I hope and pray that the decisions I should make will be revealed. I do feel, this morning, that our being together for two weeks might make our parting intolerable. There are letters to write and bills to pay.

So the day passes on which I seem to have risen from the dead, but toward the end of the afternoon—well past its apex—I conclude that these are the last weeks or months of my life. There seems to be some genuine fatigue and sadness here, as well as some contemptible narcissism. Self-love, one reads, is characteristic of our time; and here is self-love at its most intense. I will not live to see my dearly beloved son marry in February because I would be more successfully conspicuous if I died. This is, of course, loathsome, but I seem to lack the vitality at 11 A.M. to say so.

•

I lunch with my old friend R., who helps to lighten my depression. Perhaps a year ago he spoke openly of his homosexual liaisons, but now the subject is avoided. Sitting on the porch reading in the late afternoon—perhaps at that mysterious hour when one is given an unwanted insight into the tedium of life—I clearly remember being an unwanted child on a hot afternoon when I seemed to find the world more detestable than the world found me. The contempt *was* mutual. I go to A.A. and I am astonished to realize that this is not a social gathering. Why else should men and women meet with one another but to make friends or find lovers? But we are gathered together to save one another from alcoholic suicide. "I have been in mental institutions four times," says a woman with a peaked head. Had T. been there she might have said, competitively, that she had been in mental institutions six times, but dear T. was not with us. She is very likely in a mental institution for the seventh time. One might say that these people are failures, and they are indeed—I seek out evidence of their having failed—but these are my most important companions. We do not meet as travellers, as people buying and selling, or as a group galvanized by some profession, or some condition such as poverty or wealth. We do not meet as people would in a museum, or a ruin, we are not thrust together by some natural disaster such as an earthquake, or a flood. We are gathered here together because we are drunkards.

•

With M. in the city I write some letters and pay most of the bills. He returns quite late, as I had expected, and we are joined by Ben and go to the Highland diner. The impact of this is something I meant to put down yesterday and seem to have lost. It is an old man going to a Greek diner. In their beginnings these places actually resembled dining cars on the tracks of railroads. A conscientious and exhaustive attempt seems to have been made to correct this impression, and now there are pictures on the walls, curtains at the windows, and the light falls from cut-glass chandeliers with cut-glass prisms. What the old man seems to feel is the loss of some comprehension of the ceremony of having dinner, or breaking bread. These people are not travellers, and a sense of wandering cannot explain the diversity in their appearances. They have driven perhaps no more than ten miles to arrive here, and some of them have very likely not been out of a ten-mile radius in years. There are four examples of clinical obesity. There are three women who have to be eased into their booths by helpful relations and wait-resses. A very fat man occupies one stool at the counter and preëmpts two others. He orders two entrées. Then there is the man whose face seems to be a painful representation of the power of loneliness. He is a white-haired, good-looking man, with perhaps a forty-inch waistline— a fact that seems to concern him. He eats no bread or butter, orders no potatoes, and has no dessert. One feels his diet to be a losing contest with his waist. But it is the absolute humorlessness of his face that is so striking. His wife must have been killed in an automobile accident twenty-eight years ago, and he has never recovered from the blow of her loss. It is not the pain of loneliness one sees in his face, but a statement of how implacable and vast a force loneliness can be. What I mean by a failure here to understand the ceremoniousness of dinner is something he could not explain. Picnics struck him as perfectly ac-ceptable, frankfurters cooked on sticks, dry sandwiches eaten on moun-tain summits did not distress him as he was distressed by this Greek diner. These places happened to be run by Greek families, and could it be that their long history as voyagers had brought some incongruity inland? He was happy and willing to meet these strangers as customers, or merchandisers of clothing or groceries, as travellers; or even to share a pew with them in church, but at this hour he joined them for dinner with painful unwillingness.

•

I have done the wash, had the oil changed in my car, bought a loaf of French bread, taken the garbage up the hill, and last night I had a dream that a brilliant reviewer pointed out that there was an excess of lamentation in my work. I had, fleetingly, this morning, a sense of the world, of one's life, one's friends, and one's lovers as givens. Here it all is—comprehensible, lovely, a sort of paradise. That this will be taken quite as swiftly as it has been given is difficult to remember.

•

For dinner, we go to the B.s' where we have lobster that leaves us both a little ill. Ill or not, I wake with the full taste of a depression in my mouth. These are good friends, old friends, and I find our host delightful, but we talk mostly, as old people will, about the decline in services—in this case, medical care—during our lifetime, and I am more of an observer than a participant in this, the only world of its kind that I will ever know. In talking I forget what it is that I was talking about. I am very reluctant to say that I have forgotten what I was talking about, but that is the case. The stratifications of memory that are revealed at this time of life can be bewildering. I presently find my way back into my own conversation, but I am embarrassed to have admitted for, I think, the first time that cliché of old age: "And now I have forgotten what I meant to say."

•

Waking around six I think that the damage to my memory—and there has been some—is a matter of fatigue, and that when I am rested I am given the illusion of being in command and feel self-possessed. But then I feel like one of those old men one reads about in the family-interest columns in afternoon papers. Grampa is having a struggle with age. Gramp doesn't want to grow old. Gramp doesn't understand that even the stars in heaven have their time of brilliance and then grow old. Oh-ho.

And, quite differently, one would not want to be the kind of old man who, upon coming down into the kitchen in the morning and finding a few ants on the floor, would notice how, as he stepped on them, their passion for life on any terms was demonstrated. He had read—perhaps in Fabre—or had been told that their civilizations were hermetic, but there were these adventurers who went out to explore the kitchen sink and the vastness of the floor and to hazard death by poison or being crushed by an old man's slipper. As they fled to the baseboards, hid cleverly under edges of tables, exploited shadows, displaying some considerable knowledge of the visual capacity of a human adult, the old man was astonished at the intelligence they brought to the means of survival. He might better have cooked himself some breakfast and stepped out to see what the weather amounted to.

•

My thinking continues to lack resilience, and I guess it could be my blood count. But when I wake this morning and feel the old dog pushing against this bed I feel some deep and simple love for the animal, and that reminds me of the love one feels for other women and men. The word "dear" is what I use: "How dear you are." It is the sense of moving the best of oneself toward another person. I think this was done most happily within my marriage, although I do remember being expelled to sofas in the living room, although not before the years had passed. I do recall the feeling of moving, rather like an avalanche, toward Mary.

•

Susie and Tad arrive, and we lunch out. I am very pleased with their company. The day is overcast. Now and then it rains. This is officially summer's end, and have I had a summer's day? Of course. I have scythed the woods and picked peas. That I can't, this morning, remember a summer's day is unimportant. I buy fruit for S., lose my gas cap, and look for it along the road shoulders thinking that I am Johnny Cheever, lucky Johnny Cheever, to whom no harm will ever come. I am tailed by a black who is drinking whiskey out of a bottle in a paper bag. I do not find the gas cap, but I have the luck to be able to purchase one. I bring S. her fruit, and walk the dogs in what seems now to be an early darkness. There are hurricanes in Bermuda and the wind here in the trees seems autumnal. The ballgame is rained out and I, with the old dog, go to bed at nine.

•

So the fragrance of Concord grapes at the turning of the stairs here— a strong perfume, and very like the foxy smell of wild grape—reminds me of my youth in southern Massachusetts when this fragrance and the deepening odor of smoke from the leaf fires that were so much a part of our lives in the past established the weeks of autumn and led us into the excitement of an early snow.

•

It is a splendid autumn day in the Northeast, and I would like to describe it to my dearly beloved son in California. It is one of those days when the massiveness of the clouds, travelling in what appears to be a northerly direction, gives one the feeling of a military evacuation, a hastening, a change in campaign maneuvers; and the clarity of the light gives the mountains—and later in the day the walls of the city— such an air of revelation that one sees how susceptible we are to the powers of light. We drive to the city. How long has it been since driving was my manifest responsibility? How unnatural it seems for me to be my wife's passenger! In the city where I have lived for so many years I feel myself a stranger. I remember hearing, when I was a young man, the voice of someone as old and provincial as I saying, "Hurry, hurry, hurry, that's all they can think of."

•

So my wife seems more depressed this morning than she has seemed since my first epileptic seizure. What a sentence with which to begin a story! One would want to bring to this situation only largeness. I prepare her breakfast tray, as has been the custom for these last months. She stumbles into the kitchen and prepares a second breakfast tray. When I point out that a tray is already prepared she replies in a voice that rises close to a scream, "I'm sorry! I'm sorry! I'm sorry!" But I can recall her father stumbling through his wife's bridge party in a bathrobe, and her sister's hysterics. And I remember our younger son saying, "She is not like this."

•

So my wife, unable to speak to me, can now be heard. She opens her window and exclaims, "Oh, beautiful mockingbird! Oh, beautiful mockingbird outside my window!" How very important women are.

•

The day is brilliant, and so is the foliage, although much of the color has fallen to the ground. We think of the autumn foliage as a

beauty limited to the northeastern United States, but surely those countries that introduced brilliantly colored and patterned carpets must have
had an autumn with brightly colored fallen leaves. How else could the
Persians have hit on the idea of gold and crimson underfoot? On the
hill above the old 1840 dam are tall trees, still filled with golden leaves.
These are the colors of victory. Victorious armies, emperors, governments, and football teams have raised these colors. Winning is what
these colors seem to signify. These conquerors' colors are carried across
the landscape as far as I can see. The redness of the marshes makes
the blueness of the water seem to be a thrusting force, and the splendor
of the landscape is emphatic; but I am an old, old man—and it was so
different in my youth—who finds that the bounty and splendor of the
world fail to cleanse the thoughts of his heart. My heart is in some
motel room, howling at a consummate lewdness. However, having tried
seems to be an accomplishment in itself.

•

On waking I think that what has tired me in the last forty-eight
hours is the absence of anything that strikes me as truly genuine. The
people who interview me are sincere, sympathetic, and interesting, but
there is something intrinsically artificial in our meeting. In any case, I
find myself greatly fatigued, and I do remember feeling this weary before
under the same circumstances. So I am pleased to make coffee in the
kitchen and chat with the old dog. I am Bette Davis and the old dog is
Geraldine Fitzgerald in the last scene of "Dark Victory." "Now we have
to learn to live again," says the old dog, and I say, "If I can laugh I can
live." I then begin to laugh, quite tirelessly, while the crawlcredits—
which are, in this case, exhaustive—commence.

•

The first day of the new year in New York Memorial Hospital. I
am confronted with the fact that I cannot type very well. There is some
damage to my dexterity. The confusion of the experiences that I have
travelled through in the last month has led me to ask if such truths,
mostly dealing with the ardor with which we pursue life at a medical
level, are not in some way dim. Now that I know a little more about a
life of quiet desperation, lived hourly in fear of death by suffocation, I
seem to have learned nothing. What I mean to say is that I associate

rapture with truth. Truth has, I think, the sense of revelation and light, and I seem to find no lightness in sitting for hours—hours—in what seem to be basements, dressed in those rags that are mandatory hospital dress, listening to everlasting vulgar and banal music, and waiting my turn at having a bolt of cobalt fired through my diseased bones.

•

Long before dawn I hear a voice whisper, "Oh, my love." It is very faint, that whispered love we give mostly, I think, to children. But I find this morning that it is the woman next door. She wears the sort of high heels Roman prostitutes struggled with ten years ago and her hair is a completely improbable mound of honey-colored glory, but this whisper of love is the closest I will come to reality all night.

•

The day seems unilluminated and quite humorless. The cardiac echo is given to me by a couple I will describe as a self-important young black and a homosexual. I have encountered nothing in the force of nature that would explain the homosexual's pristine boyishness. I can imagine no chain of events that would produce a voice that seemed so caressing. This examination takes close to an hour, and I am told that it was a success. Later, I have a bowel movement, which seems to me of the first importance. R. comes to pay me a call. I then go down to the second floor to have an injection that will make it possible to photograph my bones. In the waiting room we joke about how our hair falls out in clumps. M. pays me a call. I then return to have my bones photographed. It is the end of the day, and I feel deeply depressed. Men and women are going home from work. I see them in the hallway, including an intelligent and charming acquaintance. Those word combinations and tunes that threaten to dislocate my memory begin to appear. I suffer a collapse of vision and humor. I walk alone to the elevator and return alone to my room.

This aloneness usually pleases me, but not at this hour. I say that there is too much *je ne sais quoi* in my affairs and that I will return to drink. That this is a great immoral madness I well know. I see an Alexander Calder on the wall and think that Sandy drank all his life, but I forget that he was not a drunkard as I am. I suffer a gruelling loss of perspective. My beloved daughter comes and she is a sort of paradise. I bask in the many kinds of radiance she seems to bring into the room. But when she leaves I am again tired and humorless. I watch a new TV show and find myself very nearly close to intellectually incompetent. I go to bed unwashed and am forced to settle for an incantatory way of thinking. "I lie naked and warm in a dark room," I repeat to myself until I fall asleep. When I wake at one I continue this incantation. I seem not to enjoy the intellectual latitude that would allow me anything broader than this chant. Toward dawn I have a clean and boisterous dream about being stranded with some very friendly people in the village of Oristano. So carry on. My dearly beloved wife is coming to visit.

•

Rather late on Tuesday night Y. announces that I will go home in the morning and return on Monday for X-rays. M. cheerfully agrees to drive into the city. My feelings are highly confused. At seven in the morning a nurse summons me for a heart scan. I insist on shaving, and after going down to the labyrinthine second floor I find that no one is ready. However, more and more patients are brought in to wait. The sense of waiting, the equilibrium given by the lonely woman behind her desk when she tells some suffering character to sit down and wait, could be investigated by my friend L. When the test is done and I have returned to my room there is another journey to be made. I must have further chest X-rays. Here, again, there are delays, delays that might seem to have been generated by the nature of mass medical examination. I return alone to my room on foot. M. arrives at around eleven and packs up my clean and dirty clothing, my leftover food, my shaving things. It is hard for me to remember anyone's having done this for me before. It may have been done by one of my sons. As I sit in the lobby waiting for M., a woman, quite badly crippled by illness, says to her husband, "You know, sitting here waiting, I'm having strange thoughts. Just sitting here gives me strange thoughts." We drive out of the city. I find the return quite overwhelming and look for an old vial of Valium. It is not where I remembered leaving it on the windowsill, and I think then that perhaps I hid it in some clothing. While my beloved wife and my good friend set the table for lunch I conclude that I will simply spend the rest of my life under the happy power of drugs. That this is obscenely self-destructive seems a possibility. The pain in my chest is, at this hour, my main occupation.

•

This, my guess, is three days later. I take a chill at around five and go downhill much of the night. I dream that I buy a racing car and date a girl much younger than my daughter. We plan to meet in a disco-bargello called All You Can Eat for $300. There is a crowd outside. Waking, I see the heavy snow and think first, that while I was never a great skier, the slopes at Stowe were the most professional I ever attacked and that I managed them poorly. There is no inch of maneuverable snow I have ever skied that I don't cherish. There is no inch of maneuverable snow that I have ever run that I don't remember with fondness. Then I think that this is the very first snowfall of my long life in which I have not been able to participate in some way. Skiing, or coasting, or shovelling the walks. I say this to the dogs while I drink my coffee and it is perhaps their imperturbability that leads me to ask, Whatever made me think that I would live forever?

•

Some lawyers come to talk about my will and my taxes, and I don't find them tiring. I eat a bowl of chicken soup and sleep, and, when I wake, my chemistry seems, for the first time in months, to have arrived at harmonious proportions. I am given the gift of feeling myself. I tell my wife that at twenty minutes to three on January 21st it was decided that I would not die. I am contented and deeply grateful for this. The sensible thing seems not to exploit the sense of contentment. I stay warm and listen to a "Brandenburg" Concerto. I have a good dinner and then hear the Stern-Perlman-Zuckerman virtuoso piece, which along with my fortunate chemistry genuinely delights me. I sleep well enough, but my chemistry in the morning is a little less than limpid. I am expecting a lover and I think continually of his various organs. It is interesting to observe that a man who is very near to death will lose none of his sexual ardor. If I said to you, "I know an old man who keeps in the crook of some tree photographs of naked young men with stiff pricks," what would you say? You would not say anything, of course; you would walk away. But I think I do have something to say, and I will say it on yellow paper.

•

But on the voyage of this maimed ship I seem to have nothing to enter in the log. I have done my obscenities, which seem to me of some importance, but which this morning bore me. The voyage has, from time to time, been serenely free from the unconscionable boredom of unwanted lewdness. I truly think my health has improved.

•

We take a nap after lunch. I accelerate mine with a sleeping pill and enjoy a well-constructed siesta. We climb the treacherous hill together, and I drive Mary to her garage. It will be the second time in a month that I have seen the mountains. Here and there barbershops that call themselves "hair stylists" have opened and Mary asks at one of these if they will cut my hair. The price is fourteen dollars. I find another who asks twelve, and I am agreeable. "I used to be a barber," he said, "before I became a hair stylist." In any case, he cuts my hair. On leaving him I drive to find a garage that will repair the Volkswagen windshield wiper. It is a substantial exertion to get my game leg in and out of the car. At the second garage, after earnest research, they conclude that I need a new part. How admirable they are, I think, how dedicated to the maintenance of cars, and I do glimpse a tasteful buttock and wonder, alas, if this may have something to do with my sickness.

•

In the morning my whole person is quite precarious. I do drink some coffee and boil M. two eggs. Chance fantasies of sudden death—a truck will wipe out my side of the car, sparing M. and somehow leaving him with the cash in my wallet—cross my mind; they are characterized by vulgarity and by the sentimentality usually arrived at just before the drunkard loses consciousness. We start off. I think that I have written so many stories about men whose very reason depended upon the shadow of a falling leaf that I can't complain about finding myself here. We do joke about a BMW, and I find that laughter can carry almost any burden. My daughter is at the hospital and I will not approach a description of her helpfulness. Both she and M. support me through rather a difficult interview. The medicine I have been taking for the last month has done nothing to block the cancerous tumors, and on Tuesday I will take up another course of medicine. So we drive home.

•

There is very bad news from the doctor, and Mary and I embrace and weep. I seem perhaps unable to type, but if I tried I might be able to master the engine; I guess it would be some other morning of my life.

•

This is two weeks and three cobalt treatments later. These landscapes don't, I think, lie particularly in my terrain. One could write about an old man or an old woman with a stick waiting out the later afternoons in those outpatient rooms where the music is tireless and vulgar, where the woman whose taste chose the pictures on the walls and subscribed to the dog-eared magazines has long since gone to other pursuits, and where one waits for ever and ever to hear one's name or number. There is that laundry basket full of toys in that room where tiny children are given curing applications of electricity that would illuminate a large city. If this were all some part of a journey one of my characters was obliged to make I would be fairly well informed.

•

The day of the wedding. Federico first calls about the receipt of a telegram, and I am, of course, happy to talk with him. I then wait for the family to call when the ceremony is completed. It is not my best self that reports this. They call. Mary, to my delight, has been crying. Now they are drinking wine, and there will be a large dinner. I consider my son's judgment in his choice of a wife to be highly mature. M. and I have a dinner of steak, bright-orange fried onion rings, and a salad with a commercial dressing. I go to bed almost at once and sleep soundly. Of our friendship I can say mostly that we are like travellers who help each other along the way. This is a journey, not a domicile. He helps me much to correct my handicaps and overcome the obstacles in my journey.

•

I eat liver for dinner and wake this morning well before dawn with nausea. I plan to rise before Mary, make the coffee, and take the garbage pail up the hill. However, I find that the garbage has already been taken up the hill. I will be obliged to return to the hospital on Monday. This hastening of my schedule is so the doctor can go to Florida for a week. There seems to be no point in complaining.

•

This morning I would like to write about victory. It was in the big hospital, and in one of those rooms where we waited, twenty or thirty of us, either to see if our various organs were strong enough to withstand the rigorous medicines that would be prescribed or to get applications of the medicines themselves. The reproductions on the walls had been chosen with that anxious and sensitive care that I had found in all the rooms. There was a Hopper, a Redon, a Grandma Moses, and an Andrew Wyeth; there was something for almost everyone. On the tables were the usual litter of magazines reminding one of the fact that the weekly periodical seems to have a less natural place in things—seems to enjoy less endurance—than the leaves that fall to the ground in autumn. Here on the covers were yesterday's faces, some of them already forgotten, some of them assassinated, and a few of them crowned.

We were a mixed company of about twenty—some of us in street clothes but most of us in those ragged hospital overalls. We held the large key rings and crude wooden tags that would make it impossible for us to lose or purloin our locker keys. The music tape being played was simply banal. A woman came in from the street, a well-dressed, good-looking woman. It has seemed to me, in my long life, that all well-dressed, good-looking women share certain fundamentals. There is to such a woman's carriage, to the cut and hang of her clothing, an inimitable naturalness that is close to classical. The stranger enjoyed this. She gave the congregation a light and general smile and took off her coat and her hat. She was as bald as an egg. So were at least a third of us, but her beauty dramatized her loss. It was not the baldness of this stranger that was most striking, however; it was the look of absolute victory on her face. She had been infected by cancer; she had scourged the infection; and she had simply returned for a checkup. The look on her face, her air of having bested the tumors and carnage of the disease were beautiful. She was called in before the rest of us and politely explained that she was here for a checkup. It was very brief. "Thank you for waiting," she said when she put on her coat and then her hat, resuming her beauty and her ordinariness. It may have been a turning point in my own cure that I saw this victorious woman.

•

And it was Mrs. T. who always spoke enthusiastically of platinum. "In ten days now," she said, "I go back to the hospital for my platinum."

I don't know, but my guess is that she would be enthusiastic about almost everything: the local train service, the local vegetables, the local flora. "Of course I'm enthusiastic about platinum," she exclaimed. "After all, platinum saves my life. It is platinum that can separate, disintegrate, and destroy those tumors that once threatened my life. Platinum in this case is a force of goodness; platinum is a force of life, platinum is quite simply for me the difference between life and death, and I love it."

●

This is the fifth day on which I feel like myself. I imagine that the feeling will continue and that the doctor will conclude that small doses of platinum are what is needed. Once every six weeks.

●

I have the news of shrinkage, and this is the best news I've put down here in months. My various aches and pains seem not cancerous and thus unimportant. M. is expected on the morning train, and I will be pleased to see him.

●

I come here without having seen the *Times*, which is very sensible of me. I don't seem able to anticipate the limits on my strength, but it is limited. The doctor says that he thinks he can keep the cancer at the point of remission where it stands today. M. comes out, and to hold his hand is to lighten the pain of my disease. In the literature there is a good deal about the healing powers of love and openness. We are not so much loving as savage together, but the consequence, when he goes off to buy chemical fertilizer, is that I lie in the afternoon sun quite contented and happy. He has a healing power for me. I find nothing mysterious about this, and I like to think that no dependence is involved.

●

I might be described as *un homme du siècle* since I live a short distance from a nuclear reactor that has twice been closed down (for hazardous emissions) by a federal commission; the drinking water from the well that was dug twenty-five years ago by a dear friend has lost its savor and sweetness and taken on the flavor of those pollutants and corrosive chemicals that infect the earth; and I myself am so badly crippled with bone cancer that I walk with crutches. But to blame this on our time would seem to me an example of destructive and passive pessimism.

•

In writing Saul I might say that perhaps you and A. already know—and I might have known myself—but it was only yesterday that I received the news that the man who can cure my cancer is in Bucharest. How stupid I've been. He has gray hair *en brosse*; a vast, unclean stomach; and he lives in a four-story building, the top of which is supported by caryatids. This is owned by his mother, a former policewoman. Entrée is difficult, of course, but I have a friend who has a cousin who was tortured by his mother, and he knows someone who can arrange an appointment. This all has to be kept secret since he is scorned and persecuted by the national medical societies, in spite of the fact that he cured Margaret Thatcher and President Mitterrand of their cancers.

•

I choose to see the doctor's suspension of platinum not as the blessing it is but as an admission of the fact that platinum is not working. This puts me into a profound depression, in which I remain this Saturday morning. I think of the courage of my associates, of my closest associates, but the most I seem able to do is to admire their resources. I shall stay warm and read about maps.

•

A very heavy snow begins to fall at a little before midnight. This is the fifth of April. By the next morning, it is a foot or two of powder snow. Legally, it is a legal blizzard. To remember the pleasures of a storm when I was younger, I shovel the stairs and clean the snow off the cars. The snow falls so swiftly that I do this three times in the afternoon. The fall of snow stops about as night falls.

•

In the morning I wake feeling that my illness is a thing of the past. I have not felt so well in weeks. This seems not only well-being but an intelligent grasp of the fact that when I am in the best of health I often suffer profound depressions, random and unsuitable erections, and losses of memory. In any case, I feel that the cancer has been defeated;

and perhaps it has. So, feeling that I have conquered cancer, I stroll happily around the house. A loaf of bread is needed, and I will search for one. What more simple and universal pursuit could there be than a man looking for a new loaf of bread? The last of the unseasonable snow has melted and there is a curious greenness of fragrance in the air that represents what—death! I have not conquered cancer, I have merely worsened. So off I go to the supermarket, which is closed. The sight of this place without lights, without delivery trucks, and without a full parking lot is like some apocalyptic vision. In this society, in this world, at this time of day, finding the supermarket closed is an upheaval. I go to the lesser, and the losing, market and hope deeply that it will not have been forced to stay open in competition; but it too, happily, is closed. Christ the Lord is risen. It is at the bakery that I find the new bread. And how for me a bakery is the heart—and sometimes the soul— of a village! I remember the bakery in the little town north of Rome. I remember stopping at a restaurant in Romania with C. and being told that we could not yet have lunch; the bread hadn't been baked. One smiles at the girls in the bakery and wishes them a happy Easter.

•

What I am going to write is the last of what I have to say, and Exodus, I think, is what I have in mind. In the speech on the 27th I will say that literature is the only consciousness we possess, and that its role as a consciousness must inform us of our inability to comprehend the hideous danger of nuclear power. Literature has been the salvation of the damned; literature, literature has inspired and guided lovers, routed despair, and can perhaps, in this case, save the world.

•

The second Sunday after Easter, I attend church for the first time since the doctor declared me dead of cancer. I kneel, hoping to enter a larger realm of humility and gratitude than I might find alone. The altar is a blaze of light. How golden is the light of the candles! G. is bossy and stands determinedly during the collection, although this is not one of the rituals of our church.

•

I claim that illness has kept me from writing here for several weeks. On Monday M. takes his telephone receiver off the hook. He calls, shortly before I employ someone else. He drives us to town in a heavy rain and this is a pleasure. There is a reception at the Locust Club, which is of no particular consequence; and we have dinner at a French restaurant into which the customers seem to have strayed. That is charming. Driving home in the rain is lovely. M. spends the night at the house, and I am pleased to think of him sleeping under my roof. Off we go again in the middle of the afternoon, when I receive a medal and the family is together. M. drives us back, and while I miss the rain we had last time, I deeply enjoy having him as a driver. We part tenderly on Wednesday, and I think it is on Friday that I ask R. to come for a visit. He is a pleasant young man about whose way of life, whose friends, I know nothing and can imagine nothing. Carnally the drive is very ardent, and we end up in a heap of brush before lunch. I find my orgasm very gratifying and very important. We lunch together, chat, and I put him on a train, but I seem in my ardor to have pulled my chest out of line. This is quite painful. On Monday I go to the doctor, who finds nothing serious; but this morning I find my breathing constricted, and I will now take a little rest.

•

For the first time in forty years I have failed to keep this journal with any care. I am sick. That seems to be my only message. I must, this morning, call the broker, order stationery, and have my watch fixed. I will now lie down.

•

I have climbed from a bed on the second floor to reach this typewriter. This was an achievement. I do not understand what has happened to the discipline, or character, that has brought me here for so many years. I think of an early dusk, the day before yesterday. My wife is in the upper garden planting something. "I want to get these in before dark," she will have said. A light rain, a drizzle, is falling. I can remember planting at this hour and in this weather, although I can't remember what it was I planted. Rhubarb or tomatoes. Now I am undressing to go to bed, and my fatigue is so overwhelming that I am undressing with the haste of a lover. I have never known anything like this fatigue. I feel it in the middle of dinner. We have a guest to be driven to the train, and I begin to count the number of times it takes him to empty his dessert plate with a spoon. There is his coffee to finish, but happily he has taken a small cup. Even before this is empty I have him on his feet for the train. It will be for me, I know, twenty-eight steps from the table to the car, and, after he has been abandoned at the station, another twenty-eight steps from the car to my room, where I tear off my clothes, leave them in a heap on the floor, turn out the light, and fall into bed.

EDITOR'S NOTE

THE EXTENDED PORTIONS of John Cheever's journals that ran in *The New Yorker* and that now, with additions, make up this book were taken from what I estimate to be between three and four million words. That is, perhaps a twentieth of the entire journal appears here. My basic editorial impulse in choosing what to print was, naturally, to represent this vast body of material fairly—to follow the line of Cheever's inner life as he wrote it down day after day, year after year; to reflect, in proportion, the conflicts and the satisfactions of the thirty-five or so years that these journals represent; and to reveal something of how he worked. Repetitions were kept to a minimum, except where they seemed to reflect obsessions that had to be acknowledged. Passages were omitted that required explanation or annotation, or that did not seem complete in themselves. Earlier journals—from the forties, and some scanty passages from before the Second World War—seemed considerably less consistent in their intensity and quality than what was to follow, and I excluded them completely, just as, with Cheever's fervent agreement, I had omitted the fiction of this period from the large "Stories of John Cheever" that appeared in 1978. And there were, of course, scores of entries in each year's journal of little compelling interest, and other entries too fragmentary or obscure to convey much to the reader. (On the other hand, there were many passages of such beauty and force that they demanded automatic inclusion.)

Journals, even if written with an eye toward eventual publication, have no deliberate shape—they simply accrete—and any editor making a selection from such an immense body of work is imposing a shape on the material. Undoubtedly a different editor, making other choices, would have produced a book of considerably different particulars, and perhaps with a somewhat different emphasis. Yet Cheever's journals in any given period are so consistent in theme and tone that I comfort myself with the assumption that *any* extensive selection from them, despite variations in shape and emphasis, would end by revealing the same life and the same talent; in fact, the same man. In other words, I believe that although I had to make rigorous and, I suppose, personal choices in order to provide the journals with a workable structure, their essential truth has resisted my intervention.

The actual editing of the text was made easier by the fact that I had worked with Cheever on his last five books, three of them novels, and so knew exactly the kind of help he expected from an editor, from copy editors, and from fact checkers. In matters of spelling, punctuation, and grammar, he was less than reliable, and he depended on both *The New Yorker* and Knopf to assist him in these areas. Probably my colleagues and I interfered less on the text of the journals than we would have if he had been alive to supervise their publication, since if we were in any doubt as to how he might have reacted to a suggested change, we didn't make it. The individual entries run as written—that is, there are no cuts within given passages (except in less than half a dozen places, where an indecipherable phrase, or a short mundane remark— "Had lunch with D., S., and X at the Oyster Bar"—was too obtrusive). The space breaks between passages may represent a cut inside a long entry or the passage of days, even weeks, between entries, but each passage within the space breaks is complete. The sequence of the entries is Cheever's, with one exception: the opening pages have been moved forward several years because they seemed an appropriate introduction to the journals as a whole. The journals as written are inconsistent in their use of names; people are referred to indiscriminately by both their full names and their initials. I made the decision to use full names for family members and public figures, and initials for everyone else.

The original journals are small, looseleaf notebooks, approximately one to a year, into which Cheever typed his entries (badly), although there are also some passages written in longhand. He did not date most of the entries, which is why we didn't. In this volume there are running heads on every page spread to indicate the year of the entries; these dates come from the covers of the original notebooks, and occasionally from deduction. The final entry in the book is the final entry in the journals themselves—made only days before Cheever's death, on June 18, 1982.

Although John Cheever's three children—Susan, Benjamin, and Federico—gave *The New Yorker* selection their generous support and approval, the responsibility for it was completely mine: they very remarkably refrained from commenting even on passages in which their father spoke of them in momentary anger or disappointment. They then proposed additional entries for this book, most of which I agreed with entirely, and many of which I would have added to the magazine excerpts had there been room. This book, then, has been a happy collaboration, and I thank my collaborators for their acumen, their enthusiasm, and their forbearance.

ROBERT GOTTLIEB

THE TEXT of this book was set in Fairfield, a typeface
designed by the distinguished American artist
and engraver Rudolph Ruzicka. This type displays
the sober and sane qualities of a master craftsman
whose talent has long been dedicated to clarity.
Rudolph Ruzicka was born in Bohemia in 1883 and
came to America in 1894. He has designed and
illustrated many books and has created a
considerable list of individual prints
in a variety of techniques.

Composed by PennSet, Inc.,
Bloomsburg, Pennsylvania
Printed and bound by Courier Companies, Inc.,
Westford, Massachusetts
Designed by Dorothy Schmiderer Baker